The other day, I participated in my first ever book signing event in Taiwan. Honestly, I was nervous because it was my first time meeting fans in real life, but I was very moved by their enthusiasm. It gave me new motivation.

Naoshi Komi

NAOSHI KOMI was born in Kochi Prefecture, Japan, on March 28, 1986. His first serialized work in *Weekly Shonen Jump* was the series *Double Arts*. His current series, *Nisekoi*, is serialized in *Weekly Shonen Jump*.

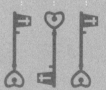

NISEKOI:
False Love
VOLUME 14
SHONEN JUMP Manga Edition

Story and Art by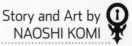
NAOSHI KOMI

Translation ✐ Camellia Nieh
Touch-Up Art & Lettering ✐ Stephen Dutro
Design ✐ Fawn Lau
Shonen Jump Series Editor ✐ John Bae
Graphic Novel Editor ✐ Amy Yu

NISEKOI © 2011 by Naoshi Komi
All rights reserved.
First published in Japan in 2011
by SHUEISHA Inc., Tokyo.
English translation rights arranged
by SHUEISHA Inc.

The stories, characters and incidents mentioned
in this publication are entirely fictional.

Printed in the U.S.A.

Published by VIZ Media, LLC
P.O. Box 77010
San Francisco, CA 94107

10 9 8 7 6 5 4 3 2 1
First printing, March 2016

www.shonenjump.com

www.viz.com

NISEKOI

False Love

vol. 14: Big Sister

Story and Art by
NAOSHI KOMI

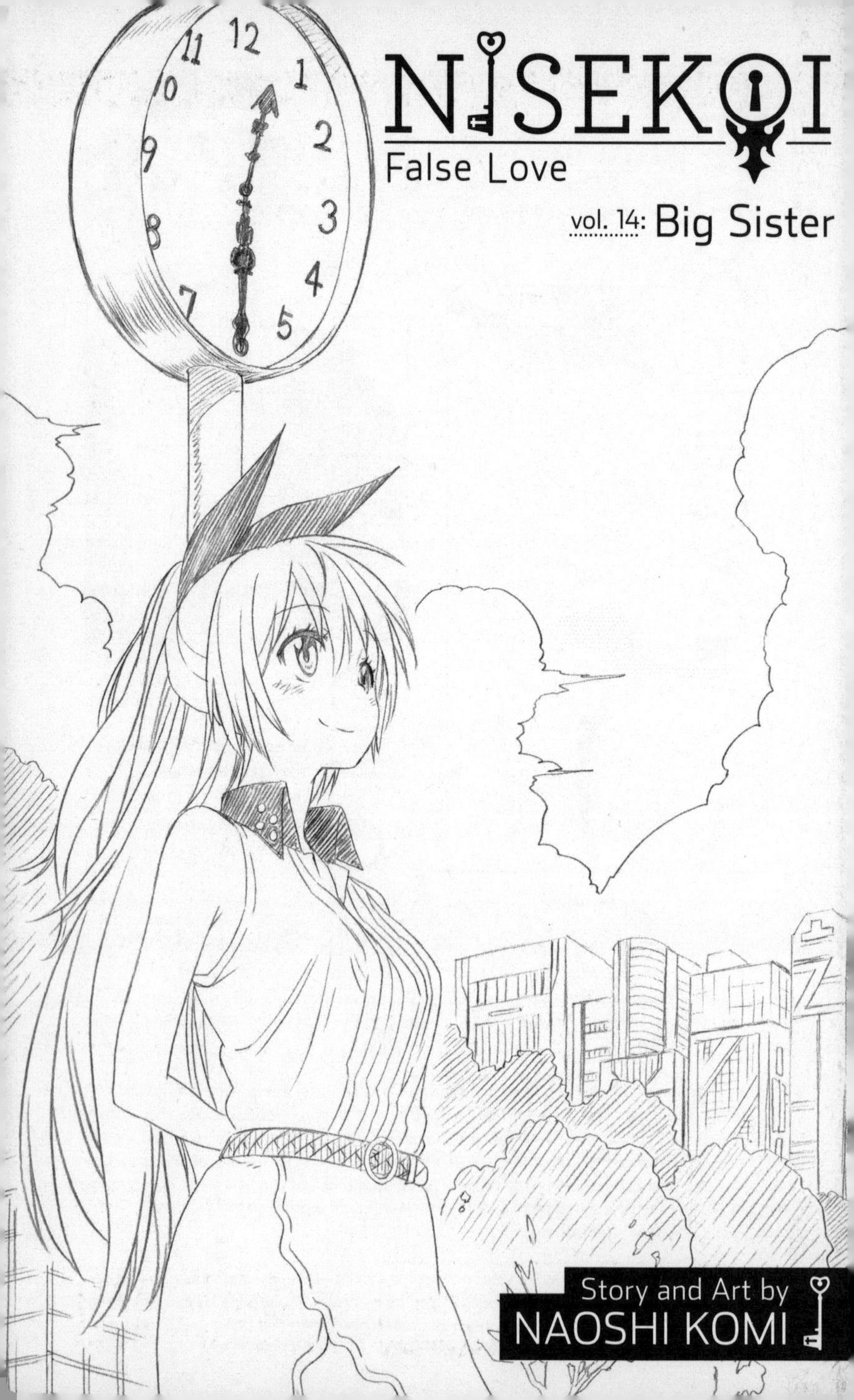

CHITOGE KIRISAKI

A half-Japanese bombshell with stellar athletic abilities. Short-tempered and violent. Comes from a family of gangsters.

RAKU ICHIJO

A normal teen whose family happens to be yakuza. Cherishes a pendant given to him by a girl he met ten years ago. Has a crush on Kosaki.

CHARACTERS & STORY

Raku Ichijo is an ordinary teen...who just happens to come from a family of yakuza! His most treasured item is a pendant he was given ten years ago by a girl whom he promised to meet again one day and marry.

Thanks to family circumstances, Raku is forced into a false relationship with Chitoge, the daughter of a rival gangster, to keep their families from shedding blood. Despite their constant spats, Raku and Chitoge manage to fool everyone. One day, Chitoge discovers an old key, jogging memories of her own first love ten years earlier. Meanwhile, Raku's crush, Kosaki, confesses that she also has a key and made a promise with a boy ten years ago. To complicate matters, Marika Tachibana has a key as well and remembers a promise ten years ago. The mystery keeps getting more complex!

Raku and friends get together to tackle their summer homework. To Raku's delight, Marika packs an ultra tasty lunch for him. Not wanting to be bested, Chitoge tries to make lunch for Raku too, but her efforts keep failing... In the end, she makes him rice balls, and Raku sings their praises. But what effect will Raku's praise have on Chitoge's heart?!

KOSAKI ONODERA

A girl Raku has a crush on. Beautiful and sweet, Kosaki has no shortage of admirers. She's a terrible cook but makes food that *looks* amazing.

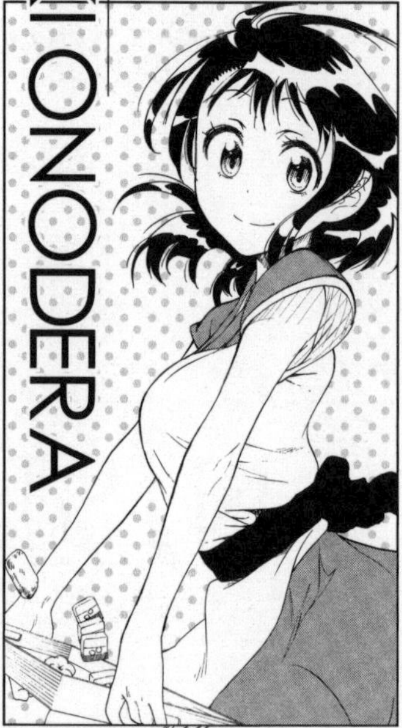

MARIKA TACHIBANA

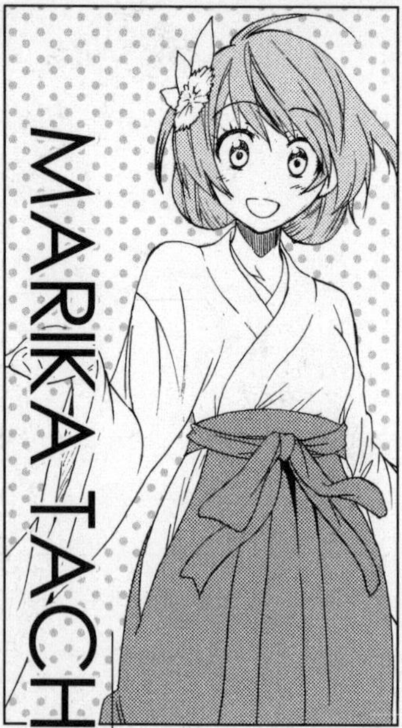

Daughter of the chief of police, Marika is Raku's fiancée, according to an agreement made by their fathers—an agreement Marika takes very seriously! Also has a key and remembers making a promise with Raku ten years ago.

SHU MAIKO

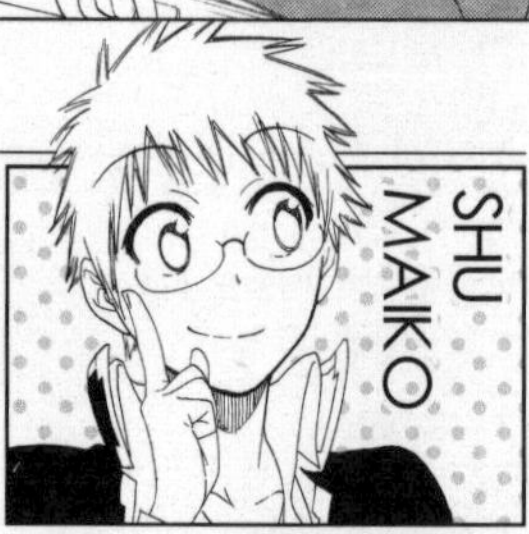

Raku's best friend is outgoing and girl-crazy.

SEISHIRO TSUGUMI

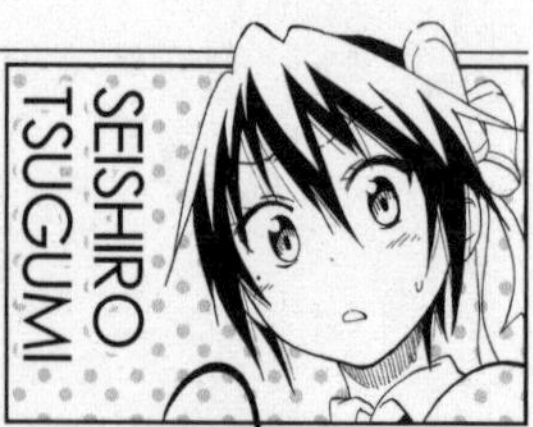

Trained as an assassin in order to protect Chitoge, Tsugumi is often mistaken for a boy.

RURI MIYAMOTO

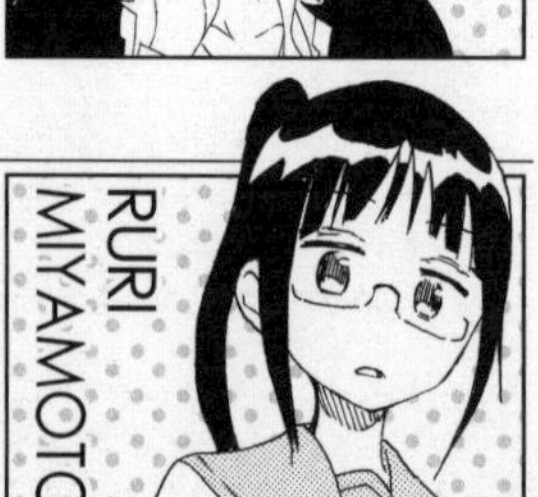

Kosaki's best gal pal. Comes off as aloof, but is actually a devoted and highly intuitive friend.

HARU ONODERA

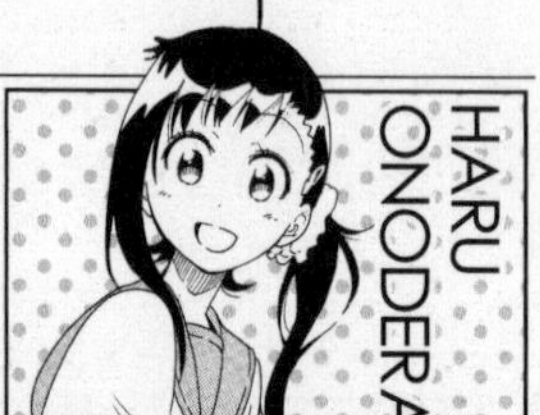

Kosaki's adoring younger sister. Has a low opinion of Raku.

NISEKOI
False Love

vol. 14: Big Sister

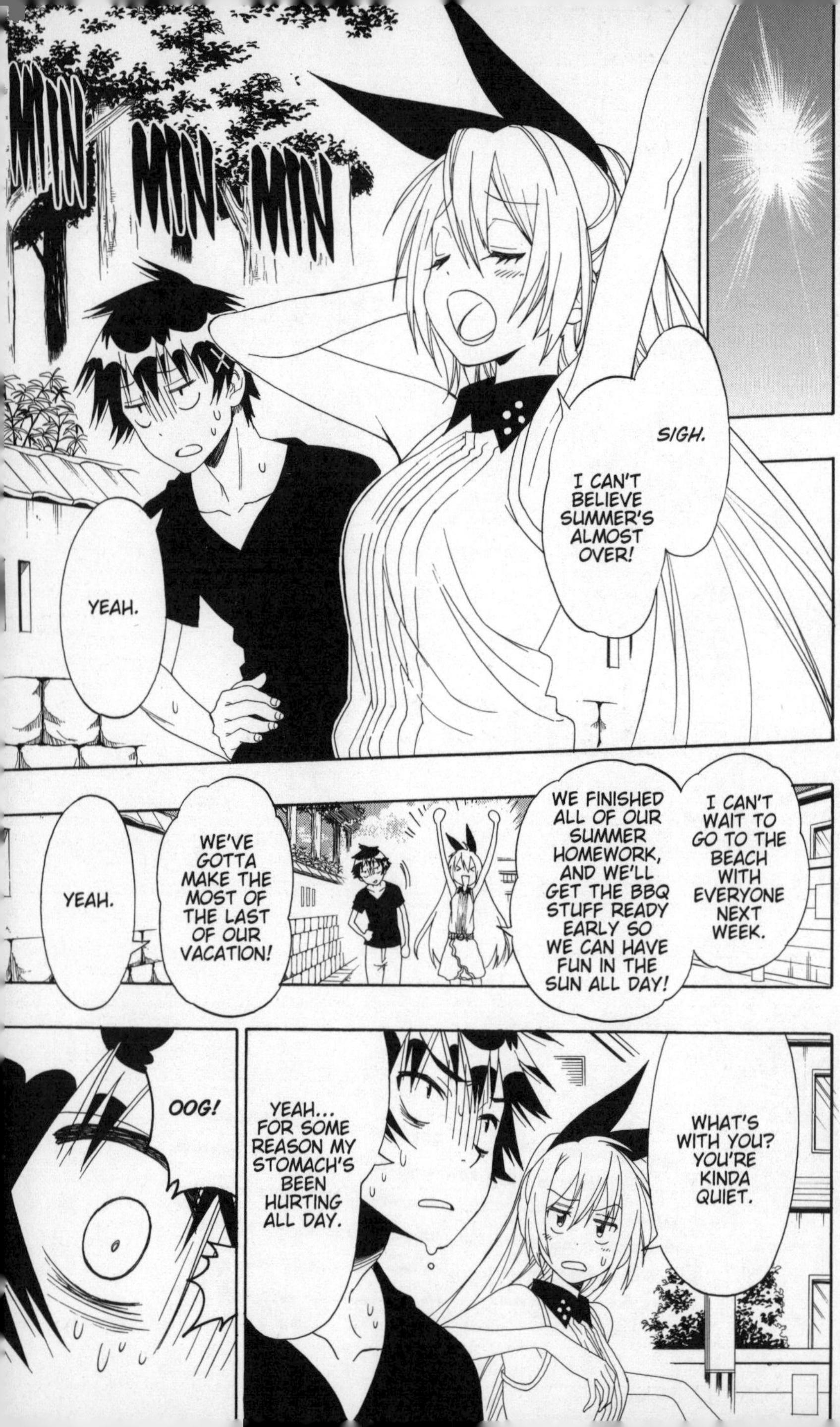
MIN MIN MIN MIN
SIGH.
I CAN'T BELIEVE SUMMER'S ALMOST OVER!
YEAH.
I CAN'T WAIT TO GO TO THE BEACH WITH EVERYONE NEXT WEEK.
WE FINISHED ALL OF OUR SUMMER HOMEWORK, AND WE'LL GET THE BBQ STUFF READY EARLY SO WE CAN HAVE FUN IN THE SUN ALL DAY!
WE'VE GOTTA MAKE THE MOST OF THE LAST OF OUR VACATION!
YEAH.
WHAT'S WITH YOU? YOU'RE KINDA QUIET.
YEAH... FOR SOME REASON MY STOMACH'S BEEN HURTING ALL DAY.
OOG!

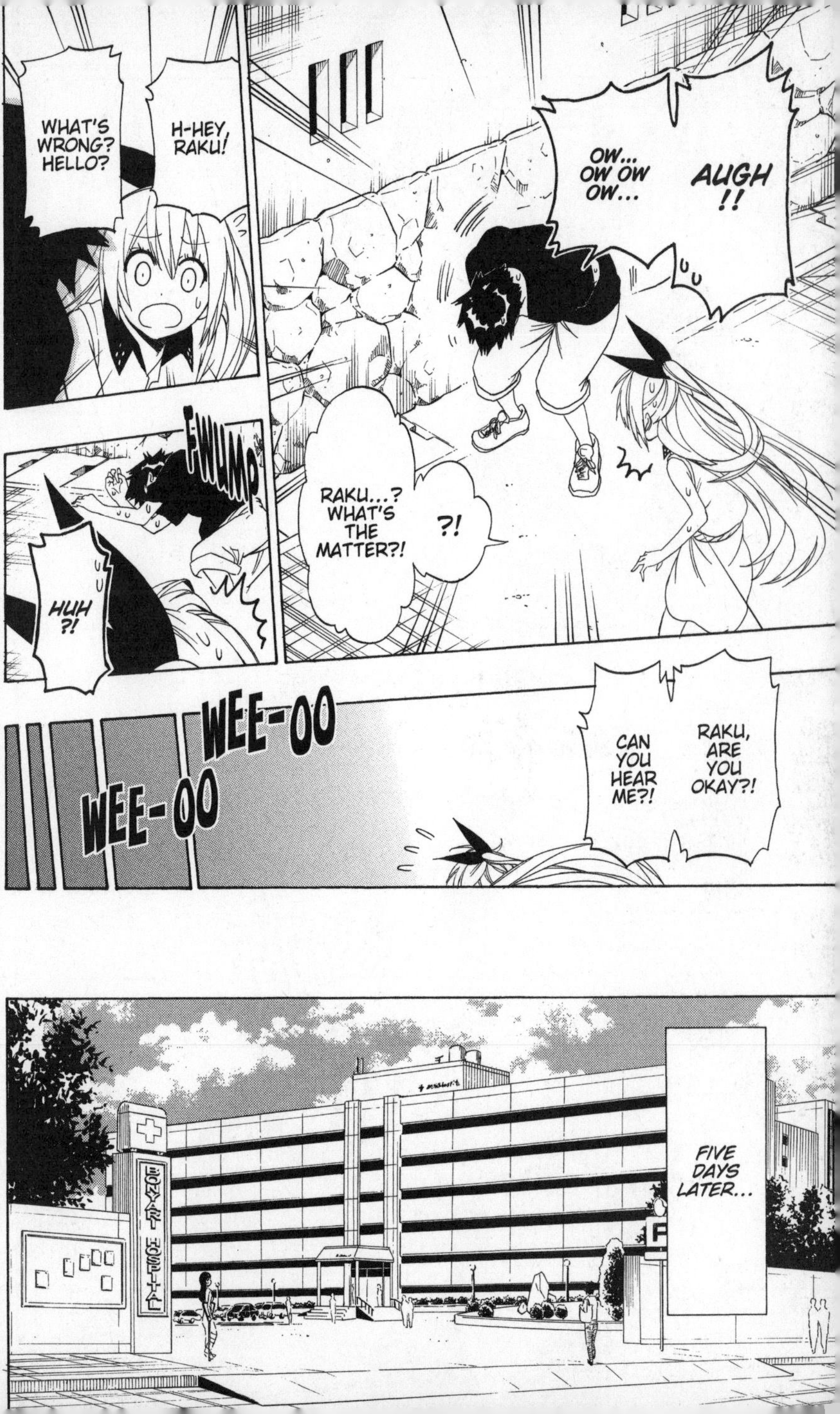
AUGH!!
OW... OW OW OW...
?!
RAKU...? WHAT'S THE MATTER?!
H-HEY, RAKU!
WHAT'S WRONG? HELLO?
FWUMP
HUH?!
RAKU, ARE YOU OKAY?!
CAN YOU HEAR ME?!
WEE-OO
WEE-OO
FIVE DAYS LATER...
BONYARI HOSPITAL

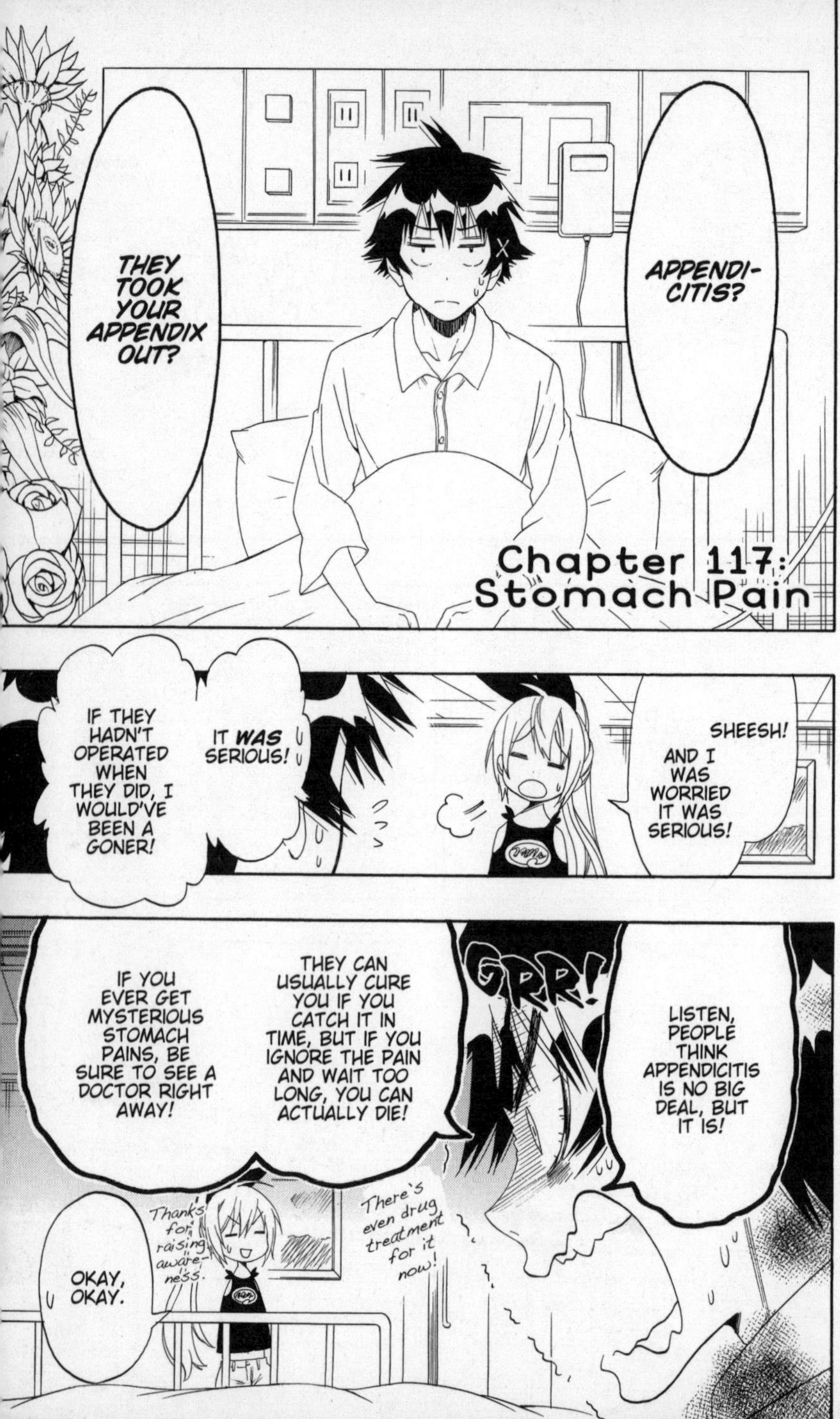
APPENDICITIS?
THEY TOOK YOUR APPENDIX OUT?
Chapter 117: Stomach Pain
SHEESH! AND I WAS WORRIED IT WAS SERIOUS!
IT WAS SERIOUS!
IF THEY HADN'T OPERATED WHEN THEY DID, I WOULD'VE BEEN A GONER!
GRR!
LISTEN, PEOPLE THINK APPENDICITIS IS NO BIG DEAL, BUT IT IS!
THEY CAN USUALLY CURE YOU IF YOU CATCH IT IN TIME, BUT IF YOU IGNORE THE PAIN AND WAIT TOO LONG, YOU CAN ACTUALLY DIE!
IF YOU EVER GET MYSTERIOUS STOMACH PAINS, BE SURE TO SEE A DOCTOR RIGHT AWAY!
There's even drug treatment for it now!
Thanks for raising awareness.
OKAY, OKAY.

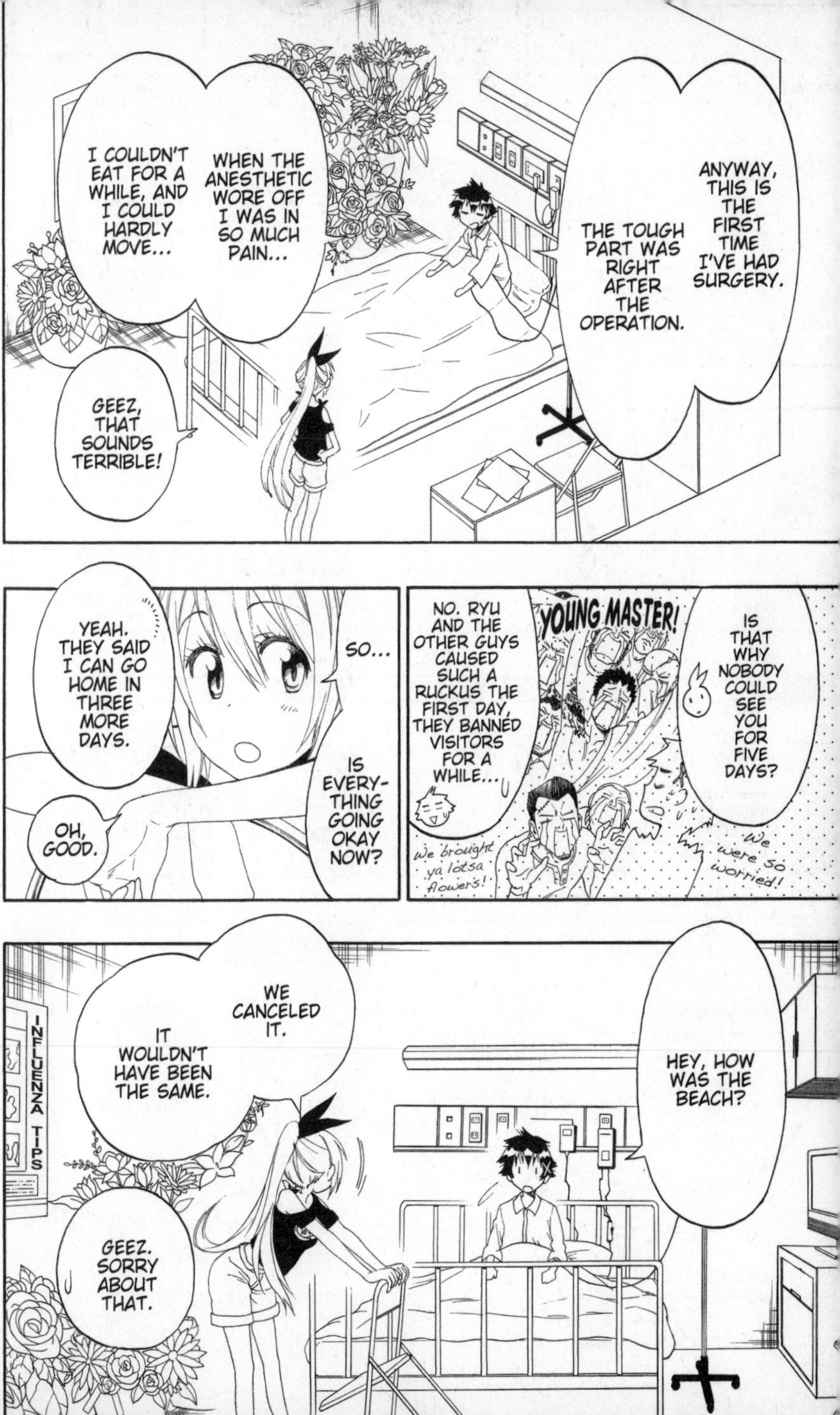
ANYWAY, THIS IS THE FIRST TIME I'VE HAD SURGERY.
THE TOUGH PART WAS RIGHT AFTER THE OPERATION.
WHEN THE ANESTHETIC WORE OFF I WAS IN SO MUCH PAIN...
I COULDN'T EAT FOR A WHILE, AND I COULD HARDLY MOVE...
GEEZ, THAT SOUNDS TERRIBLE!
IS THAT WHY NOBODY COULD SEE YOU FOR FIVE DAYS?
YOUNG MASTER!
NO. RYU AND THE OTHER GUYS CAUSED SUCH A RUCKUS THE FIRST DAY, THEY BANNED VISITORS FOR A WHILE...
We were so worried!
We brought ya lotsa flowers!
SO...
IS EVERYTHING GOING OKAY NOW?
YEAH. THEY SAID I CAN GO HOME IN THREE MORE DAYS.
OH, GOOD.
HEY, HOW WAS THE BEACH?
WE CANCELED IT.
IT WOULDN'T HAVE BEEN THE SAME.
INFLUENZA TIPS
GEEZ. SORRY ABOUT THAT.

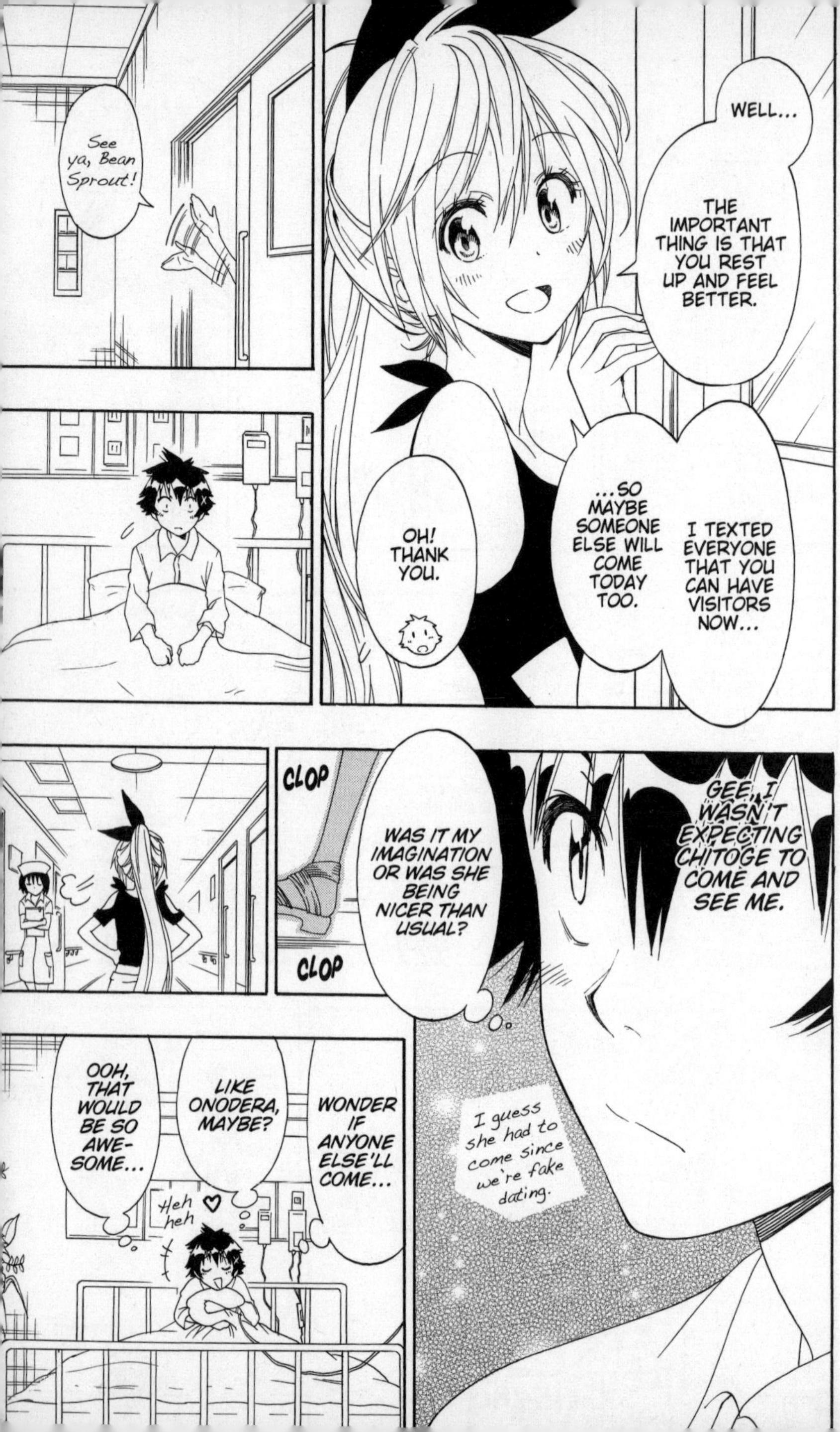
WELL...
THE IMPORTANT THING IS THAT YOU REST UP AND FEEL BETTER.
I TEXTED EVERYONE THAT YOU CAN HAVE VISITORS NOW...
...SO MAYBE SOMEONE ELSE WILL COME TODAY TOO.
OH! THANK YOU.
See ya, Bean Sprout!
GEE, I WASN'T EXPECTING CHITOGE TO COME AND SEE ME.
WAS IT MY IMAGINATION OR WAS SHE BEING NICER THAN USUAL?
I guess she had to come since we're fake dating.
CLOP
CLOP
WONDER IF ANYONE ELSE'LL COME...
LIKE ONODERA, MAYBE?
OOH, THAT WOULD BE SO AWE-SOME...
Heh heh ♡

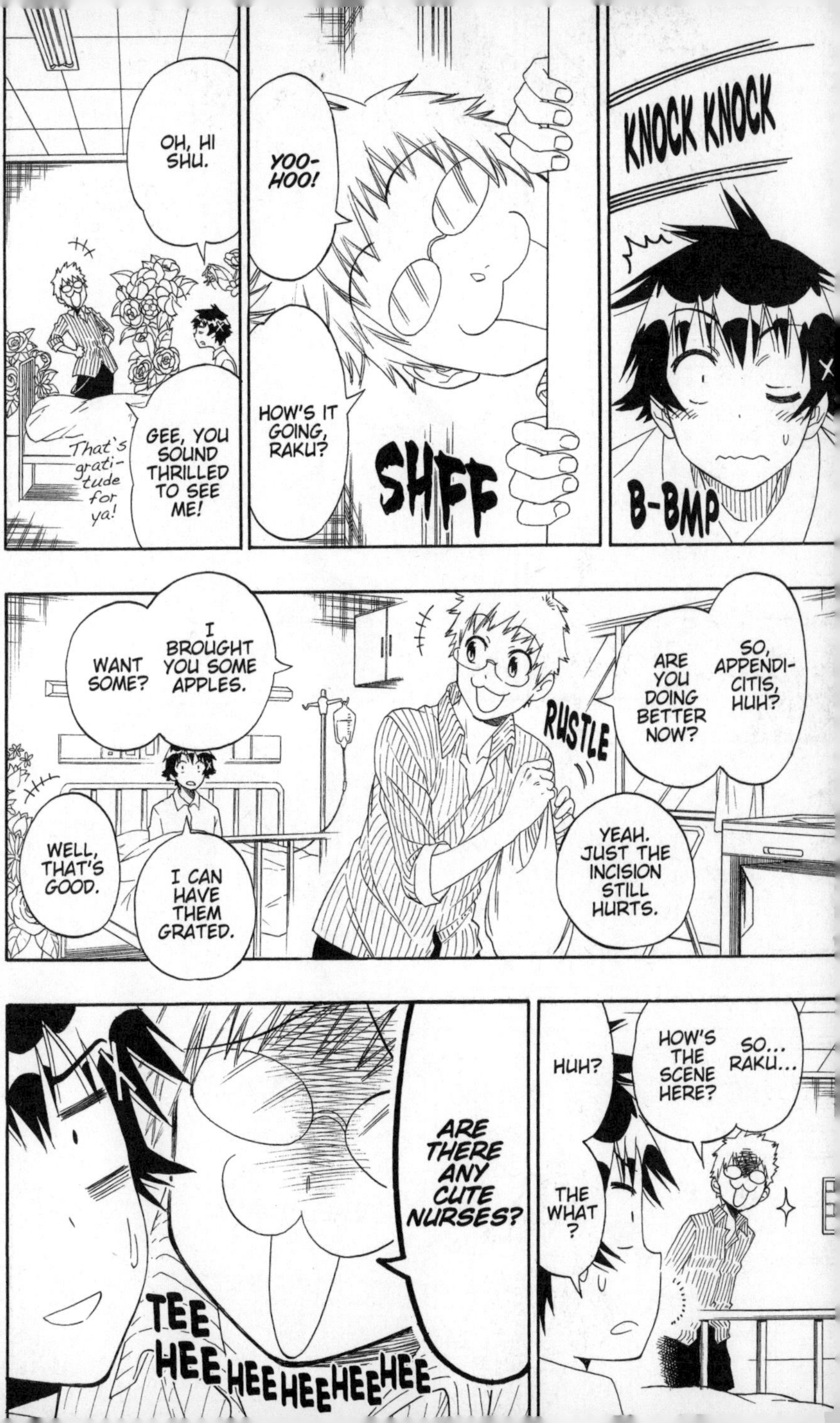
KNOCK KNOCK
B-BMP
YOO-HOO!
HOW'S IT GOING, RAKU?
SHFF
OH, HI SHU.
GEE, YOU SOUND THRILLED TO SEE ME!
That's gratitude for ya!
SO, APPENDICITIS, HUH?
ARE YOU DOING BETTER NOW?
RUSTLE
YEAH. JUST THE INCISION STILL HURTS.
I BROUGHT YOU SOME APPLES.
WANT SOME?
I CAN HAVE THEM GRATED.
WELL, THAT'S GOOD.
SO... RAKU...
HOW'S THE SCENE HERE?
HUH?
THE WHAT?
ARE THERE ANY CUTE NURSES?
TEE HEE HEEHEEHEEHEE

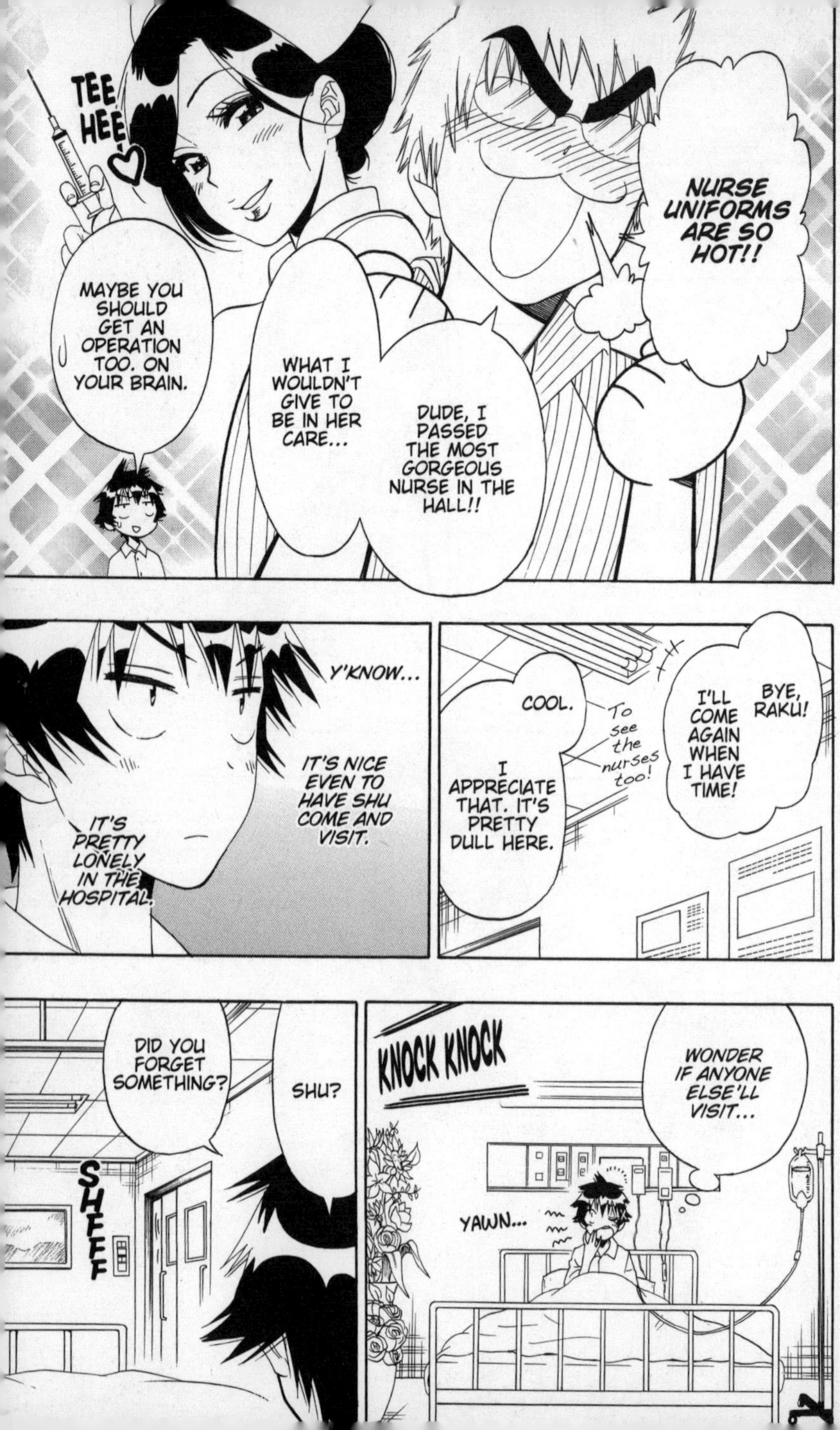
NURSE UNIFORMS ARE SO HOT!!
DUDE, I PASSED THE MOST GORGEOUS NURSE IN THE HALL!!
WHAT I WOULDN'T GIVE TO BE IN HER CARE...
TEE HEE
MAYBE YOU SHOULD GET AN OPERATION TOO. ON YOUR BRAIN.
BYE, RAKU!
I'LL COME AGAIN WHEN I HAVE TIME!
To see the nurses too!
COOL.
I APPRECIATE THAT. IT'S PRETTY DULL HERE.
Y'KNOW...
IT'S NICE EVEN TO HAVE SHU COME AND VISIT.
IT'S PRETTY LONELY IN THE HOSPITAL.
WONDER IF ANYONE ELSE'LL VISIT...
KNOCK KNOCK
YAWN...
SHU?
DID YOU FORGET SOMETHING?
SHFFF

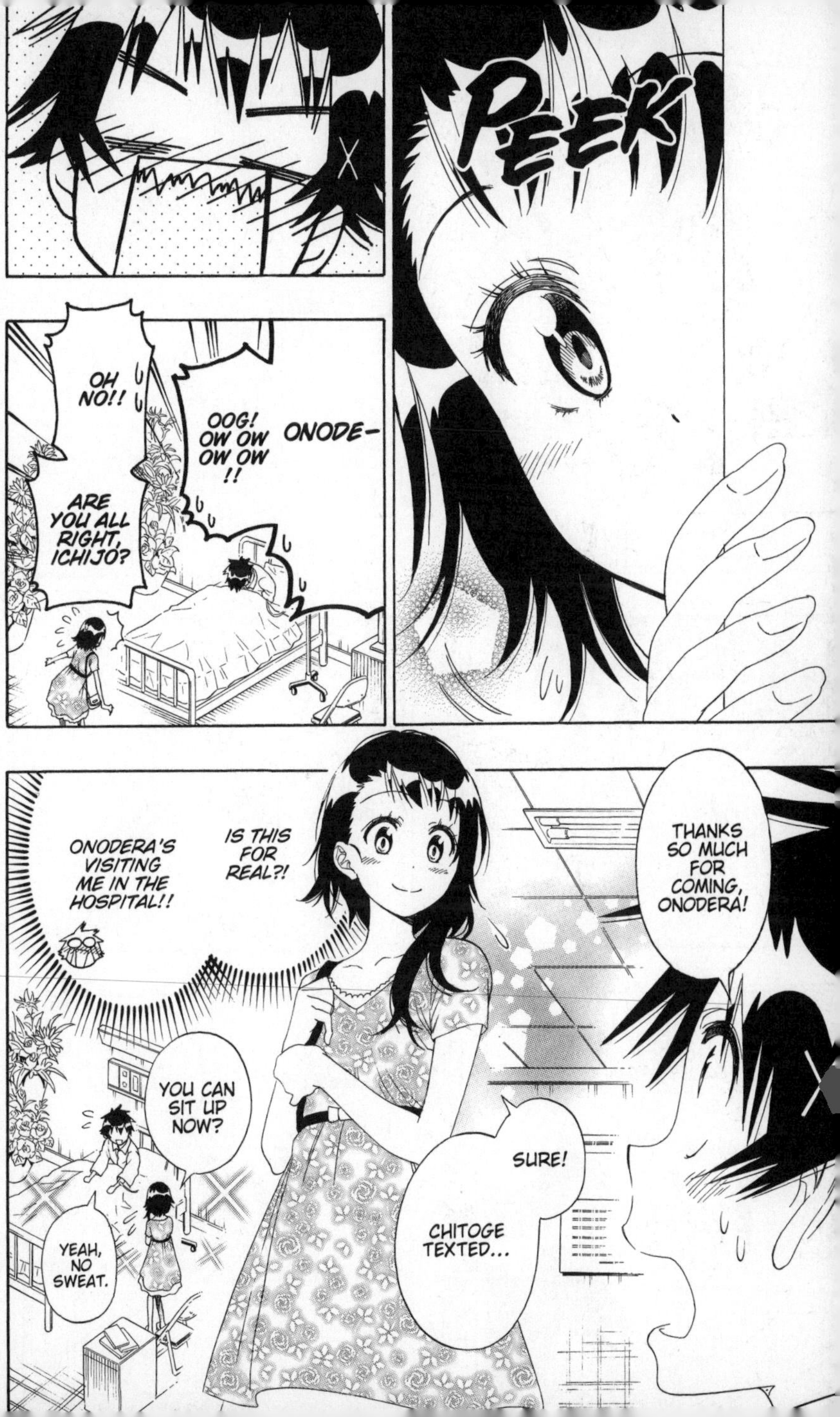
PEEK
ONODE-
OOG! OW OW OW OW !!
OH NO!!
ARE YOU ALL RIGHT, ICHIJO?
THANKS SO MUCH FOR COMING, ONODERA!
IS THIS FOR REAL?!
ONODERA'S VISITING ME IN THE HOSPITAL!!
SURE!
CHITOGE TEXTED...
YOU CAN SIT UP NOW?
YEAH, NO SWEAT.

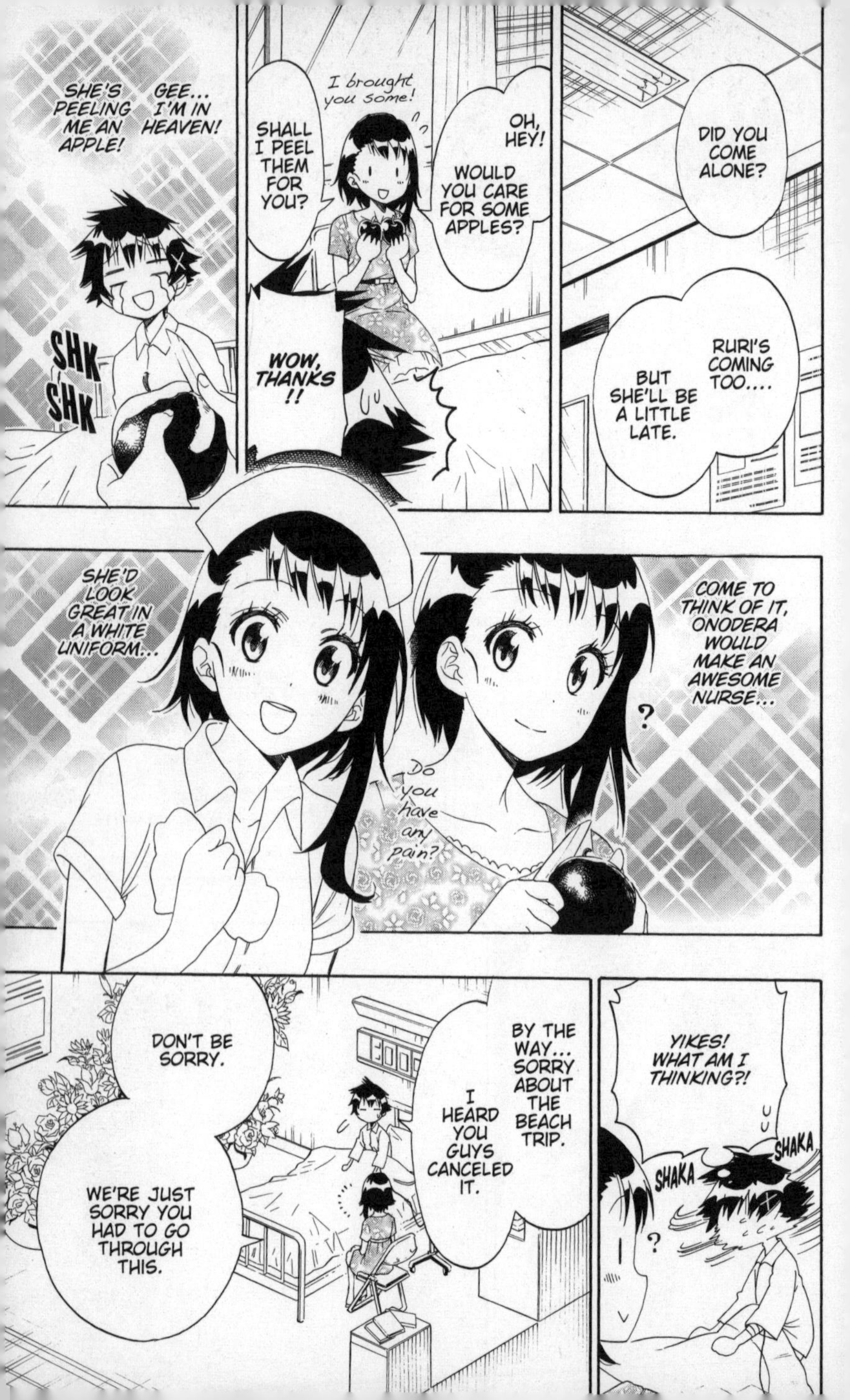
DID YOU COME ALONE?
RURI'S COMING TOO....
BUT SHE'LL BE A LITTLE LATE.
OH, HEY!
WOULD YOU CARE FOR SOME APPLES?
I brought you some!
SHALL I PEEL THEM FOR YOU?
WOW, THANKS!!
GEE... I'M IN HEAVEN!
SHE'S PEELING ME AN APPLE!
SHK SHK
COME TO THINK OF IT, ONODERA WOULD MAKE AN AWESOME NURSE...
?
Do you have any pain?
SHE'D LOOK GREAT IN A WHITE UNIFORM...
YIKES! WHAT AM I THINKING?!
SHAKA
SHAKA
?
BY THE WAY... SORRY ABOUT THE BEACH TRIP.
I HEARD YOU GUYS CANCELED IT.
DON'T BE SORRY.
WE'RE JUST SORRY YOU HAD TO GO THROUGH THIS.

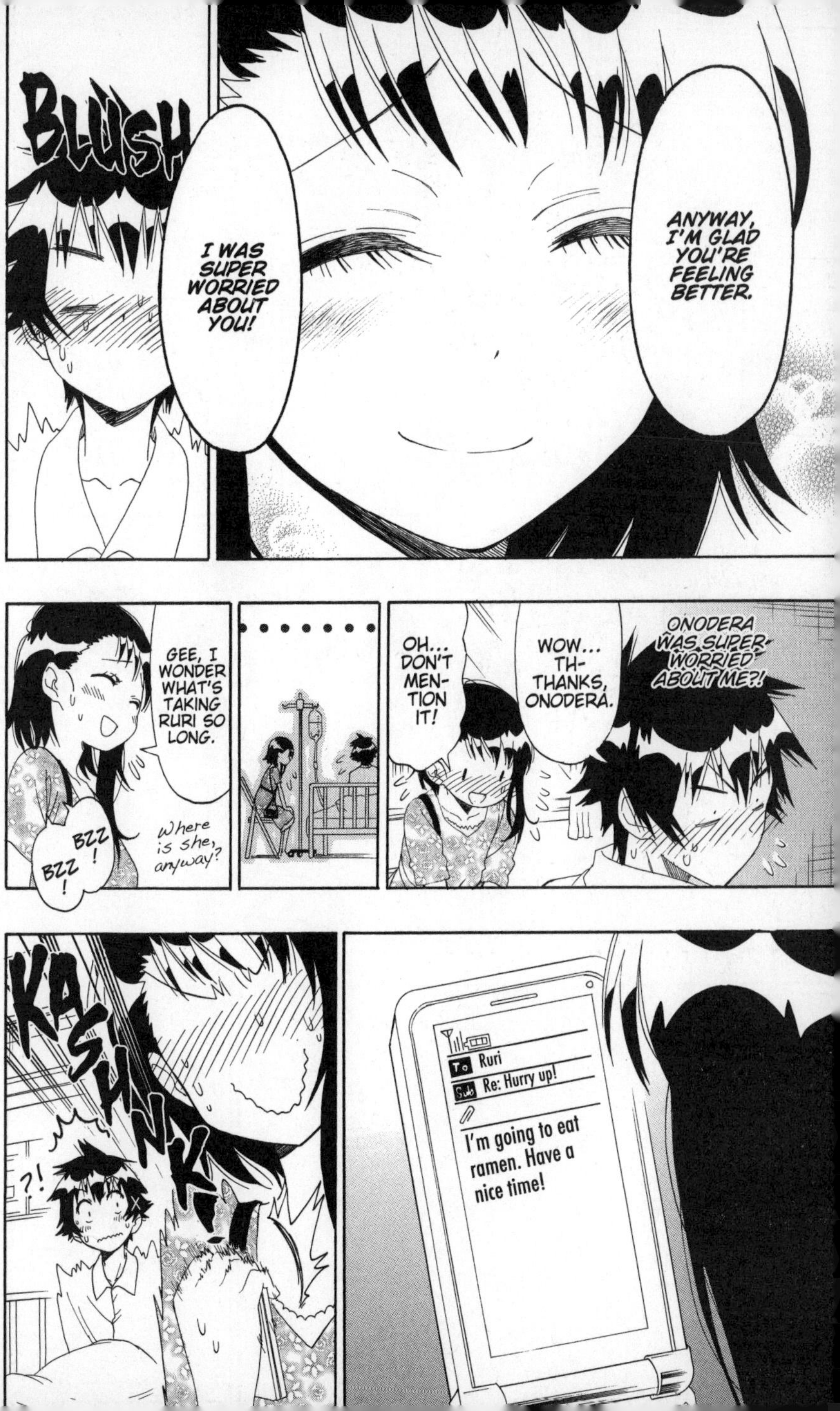
ANYWAY, I'M GLAD YOU'RE FEELING BETTER.
I WAS SUPER WORRIED ABOUT YOU!
BLUSH
ONODERA WAS SUPER-WORRIED ABOUT ME?!
WOW... TH-THANKS, ONODERA.
OH... DON'T MENTION IT!
GEE, I WONDER WHAT'S TAKING RURI SO LONG.
Where is she, anyway?
BZZ! BZZ!
To Ruri
Sub Re: Hurry up!
I'm going to eat ramen. Have a nice time!
KASHUNK!
?!

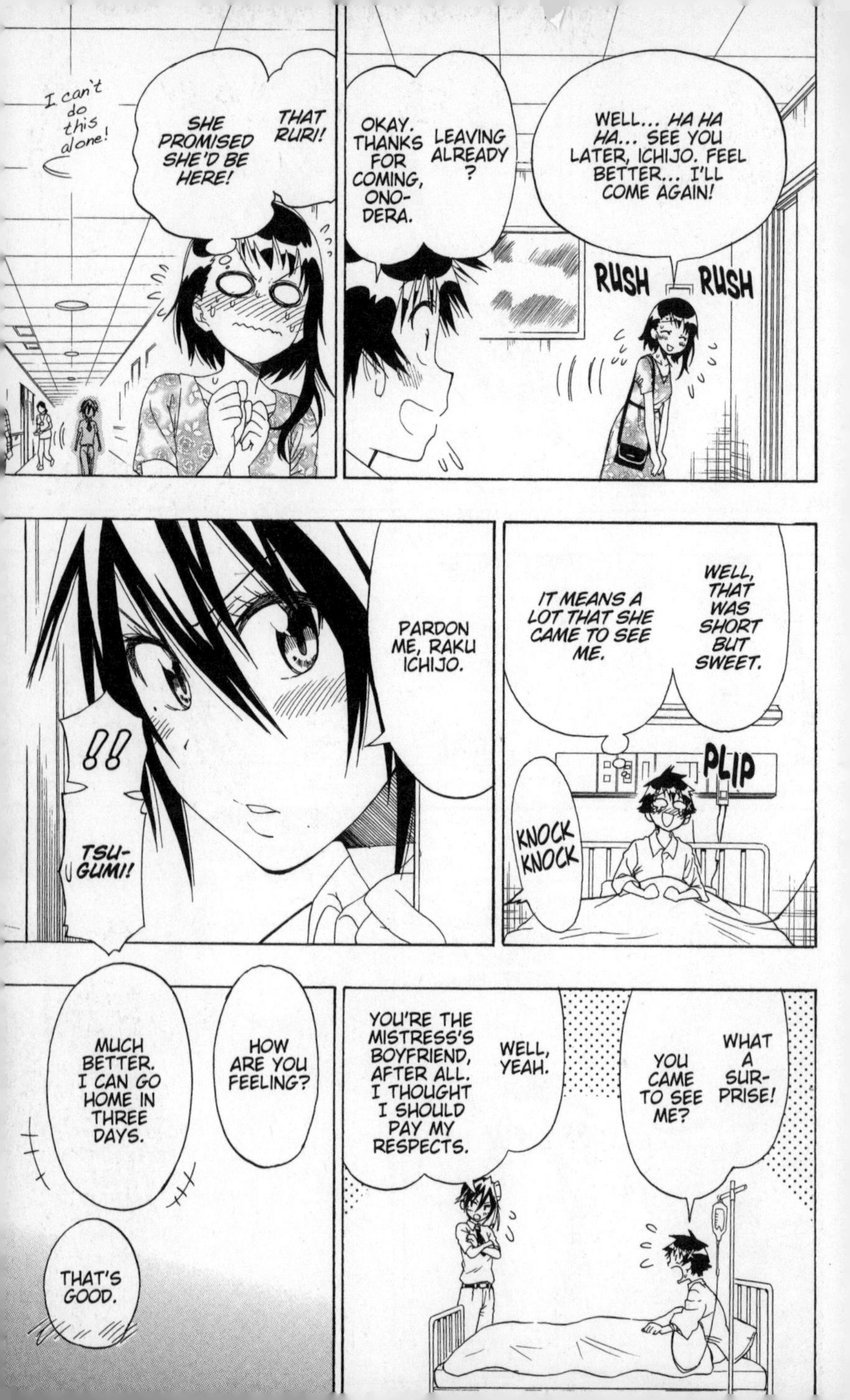
WELL... HA HA HA... SEE YOU LATER, ICHIJO. FEEL BETTER... I'LL COME AGAIN!
RUSH RUSH
LEAVING ALREADY?
OKAY. THANKS FOR COMING, ONO-DERA.
THAT RURI!
SHE PROMISED SHE'D BE HERE!
I can't do this alone!
WELL, THAT WAS SHORT BUT SWEET.
IT MEANS A LOT THAT SHE CAME TO SEE ME.
PLIP
KNOCK KNOCK
PARDON ME, RAKU ICHIJO.
!!
TSU-GUMI!
WHAT A SUR-PRISE!
YOU CAME TO SEE ME?
WELL, YEAH.
YOU'RE THE MISTRESS'S BOYFRIEND, AFTER ALL. I THOUGHT I SHOULD PAY MY RESPECTS.
HOW ARE YOU FEELING?
MUCH BETTER. I CAN GO HOME IN THREE DAYS.
THAT'S GOOD.

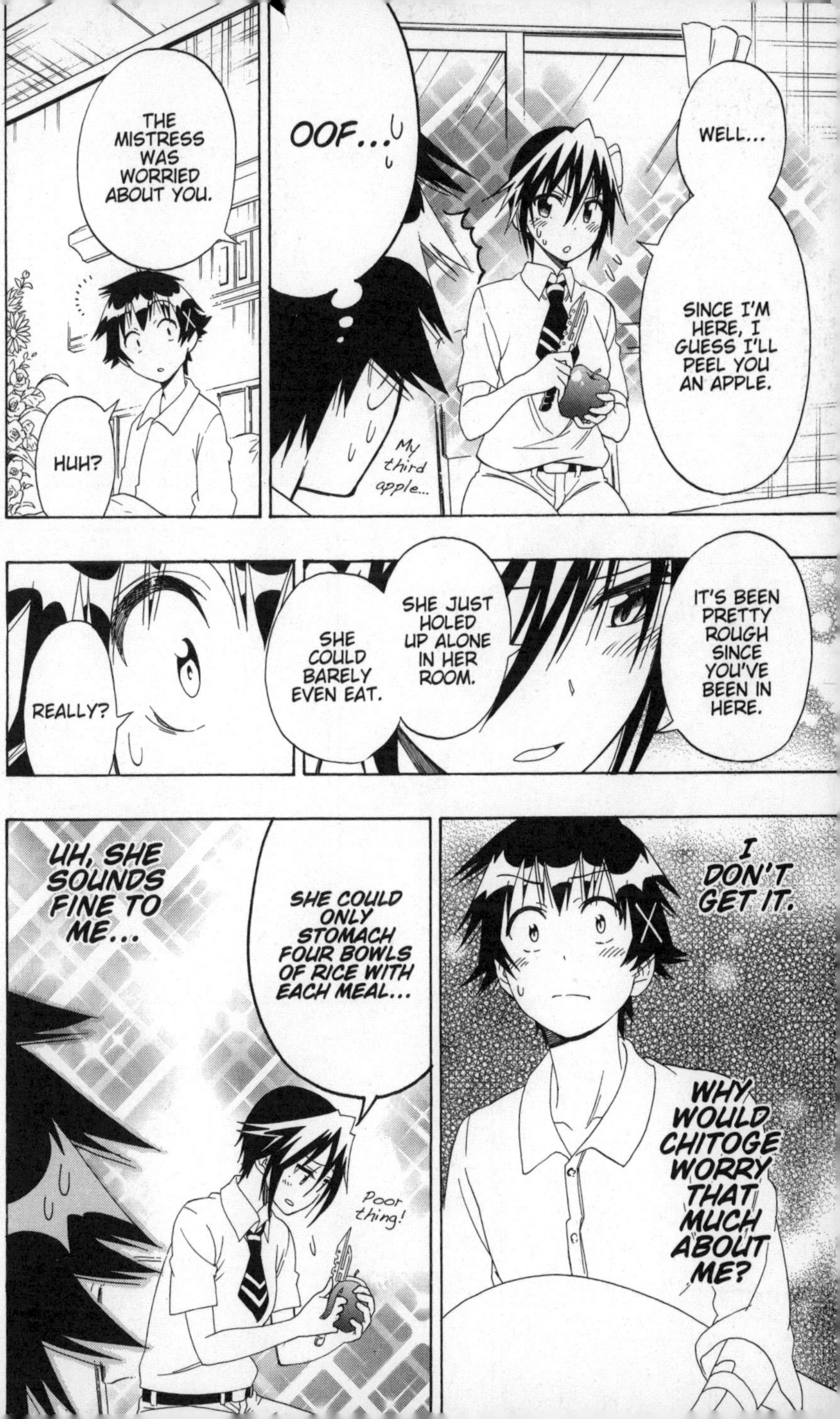
WELL...
SINCE I'M HERE, I GUESS I'LL PEEL YOU AN APPLE.
OOF...
My third apple...
THE MISTRESS WAS WORRIED ABOUT YOU.
HUH?
IT'S BEEN PRETTY ROUGH SINCE YOU'VE BEEN IN HERE.
SHE JUST HOLED UP ALONE IN HER ROOM.
SHE COULD BARELY EVEN EAT.
REALLY?
I DON'T GET IT.
WHY WOULD CHITOGE WORRY THAT MUCH ABOUT ME?
SHE COULD ONLY STOMACH FOUR BOWLS OF RICE WITH EACH MEAL...
Poor thing!
UH, SHE SOUNDS FINE TO ME...

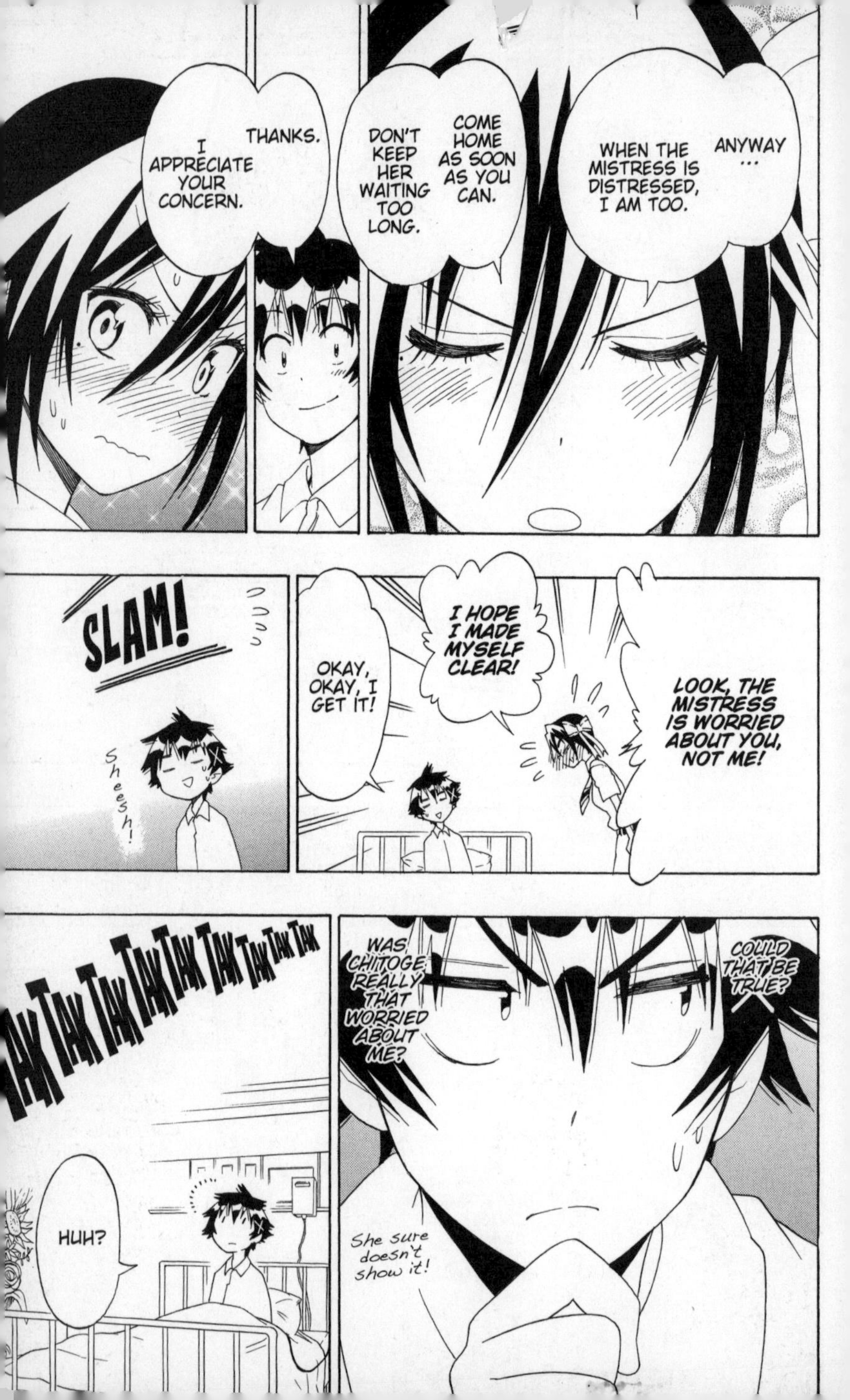
ANYWAY ...
WHEN THE MISTRESS IS DISTRESSED, I AM TOO.
COME HOME AS SOON AS YOU CAN.
DON'T KEEP HER WAITING TOO LONG.
THANKS.
I APPRECIATE YOUR CONCERN.
LOOK, THE MISTRESS IS WORRIED ABOUT YOU, NOT ME!
I HOPE I MADE MYSELF CLEAR!
OKAY, OKAY, I GET IT!
SLAM!
Sheesh!
COULD THAT BE TRUE?
WAS CHITOGE REALLY THAT WORRIED ABOUT ME?
She sure doesn't show it!
TAK TAK TAK TAK TAK TAK TAK TAK TAK TAK
HUH?

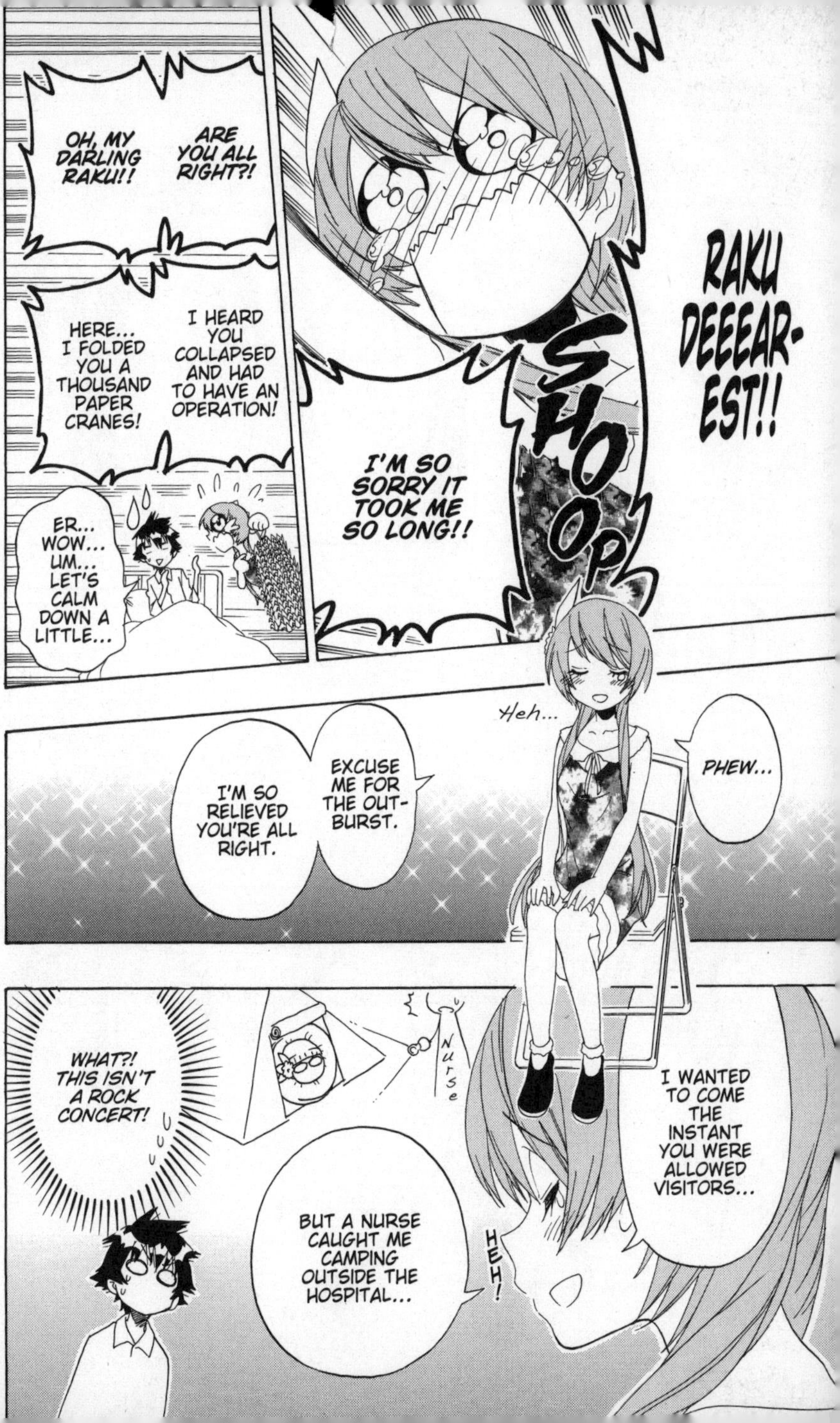
RAKU DEEEAR-EST!!
SHOOP
I'M SO SORRY IT TOOK ME SO LONG!!
ARE YOU ALL RIGHT?!
OH, MY DARLING RAKU!!
I HEARD YOU COLLAPSED AND HAD TO HAVE AN OPERATION!
HERE... I FOLDED YOU A THOUSAND PAPER CRANES!
ER... WOW... UM... LET'S CALM DOWN A LITTLE...
Heh...
PHEW...
EXCUSE ME FOR THE OUT-BURST.
I'M SO RELIEVED YOU'RE ALL RIGHT.
I WANTED TO COME THE INSTANT YOU WERE ALLOWED VISITORS...
HEH!
BUT A NURSE CAUGHT ME CAMPING OUTSIDE THE HOSPITAL...
Nurse
WHAT?! THIS ISN'T A ROCK CONCERT!

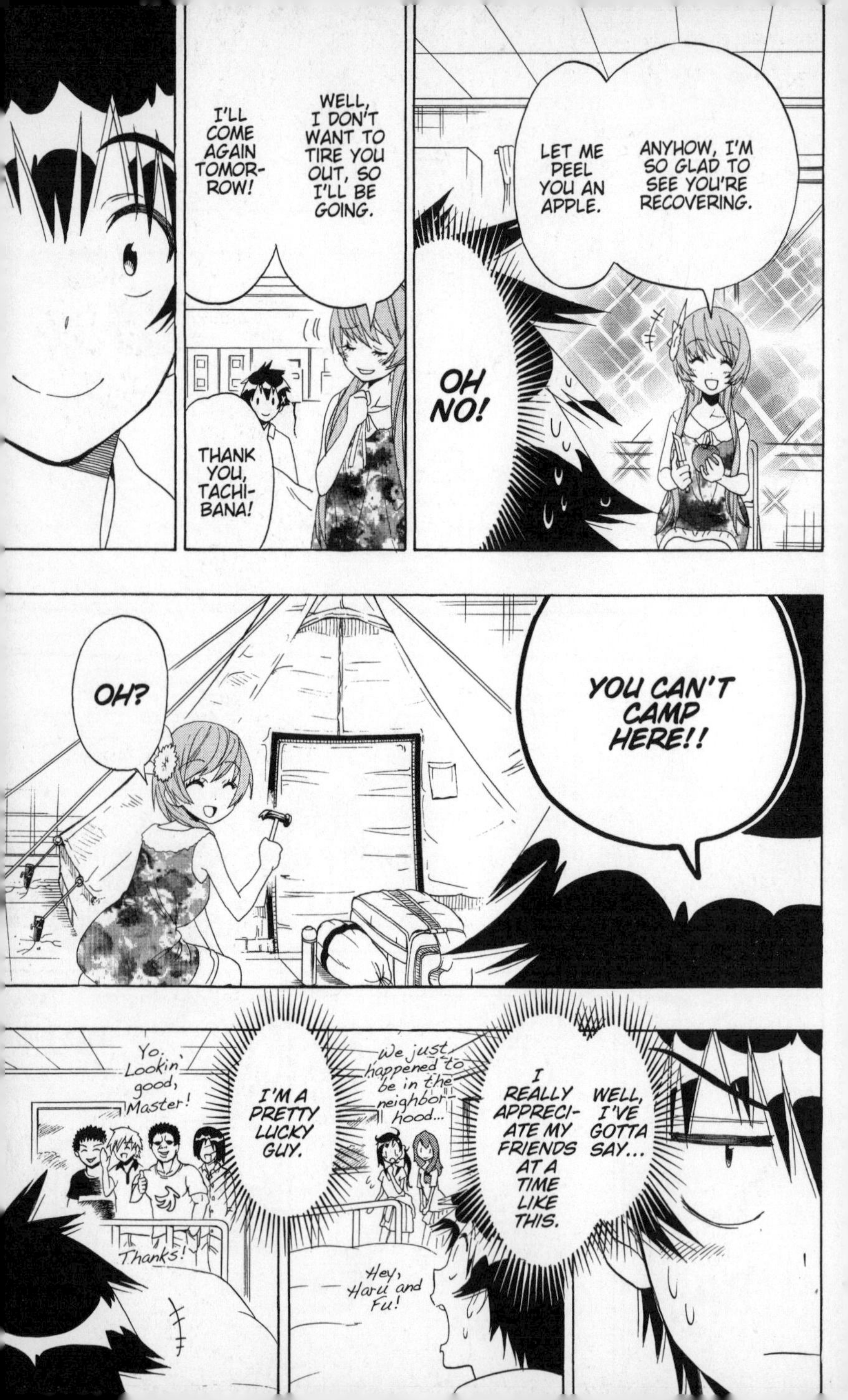
ANYHOW, I'M SO GLAD TO SEE YOU'RE RECOVERING.
LET ME PEEL YOU AN APPLE.
OH NO!
WELL, I DON'T WANT TO TIRE YOU OUT, SO I'LL BE GOING.
I'LL COME AGAIN TOMORROW!
THANK YOU, TACHIBANA!
YOU CAN'T CAMP HERE!!
OH?
WELL, I'VE GOTTA SAY...
I REALLY APPRECIATE MY FRIENDS AT A TIME LIKE THIS.
Hey, Haru and Fu!
We just happened to be in the neighborhood...
I'M A PRETTY LUCKY GUY.
Yo. Lookin' good, Master!
Thanks!

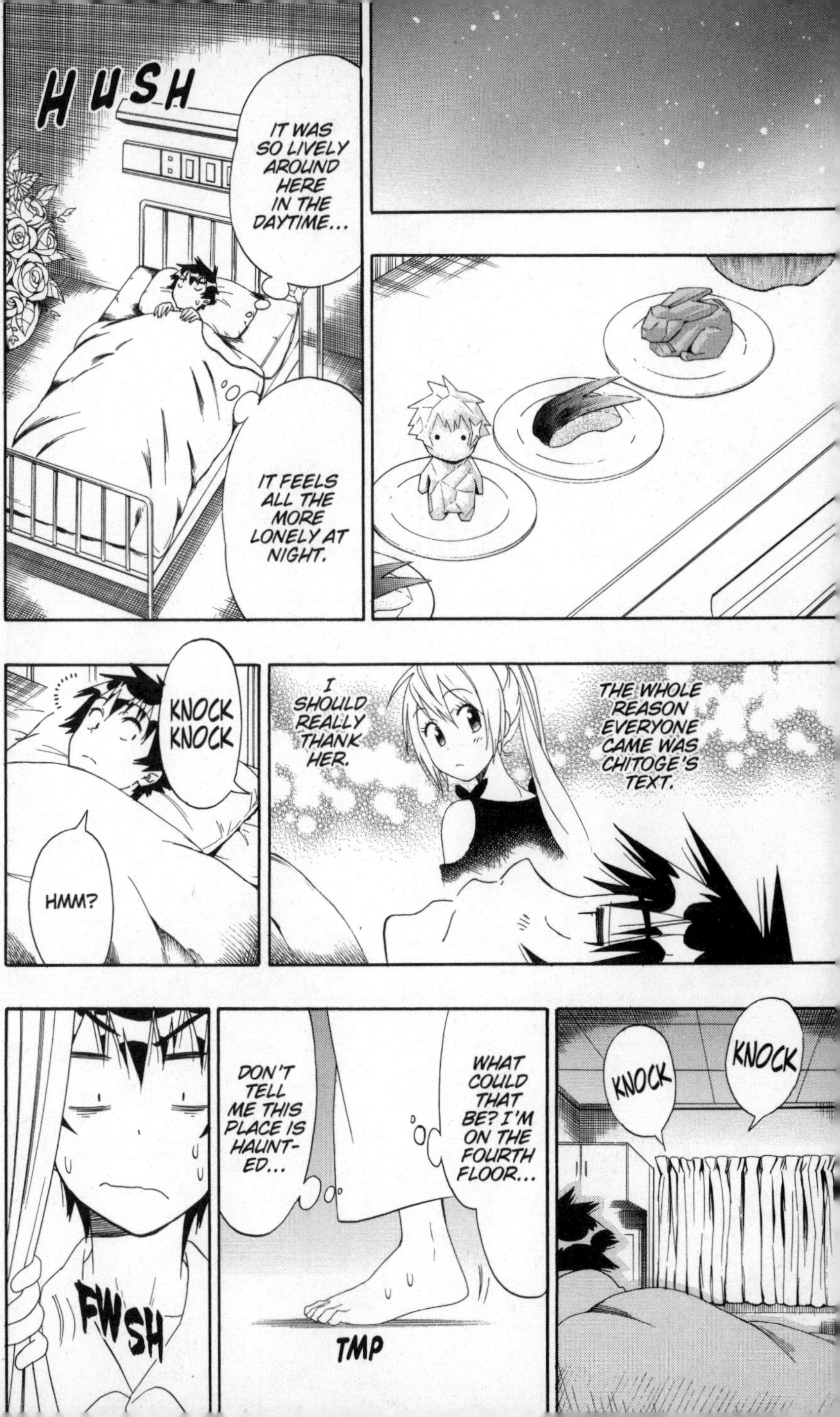
HUSH
IT WAS SO LIVELY AROUND HERE IN THE DAYTIME...
IT FEELS ALL THE MORE LONELY AT NIGHT.
THE WHOLE REASON EVERYONE CAME WAS CHITOGE'S TEXT.
I SHOULD REALLY THANK HER.
KNOCK KNOCK
HMM?
KNOCK
KNOCK
WHAT COULD THAT BE? I'M ON THE FOURTH FLOOR...
DON'T TELL ME THIS PLACE IS HAUNT-ED...
TMP
FWSH

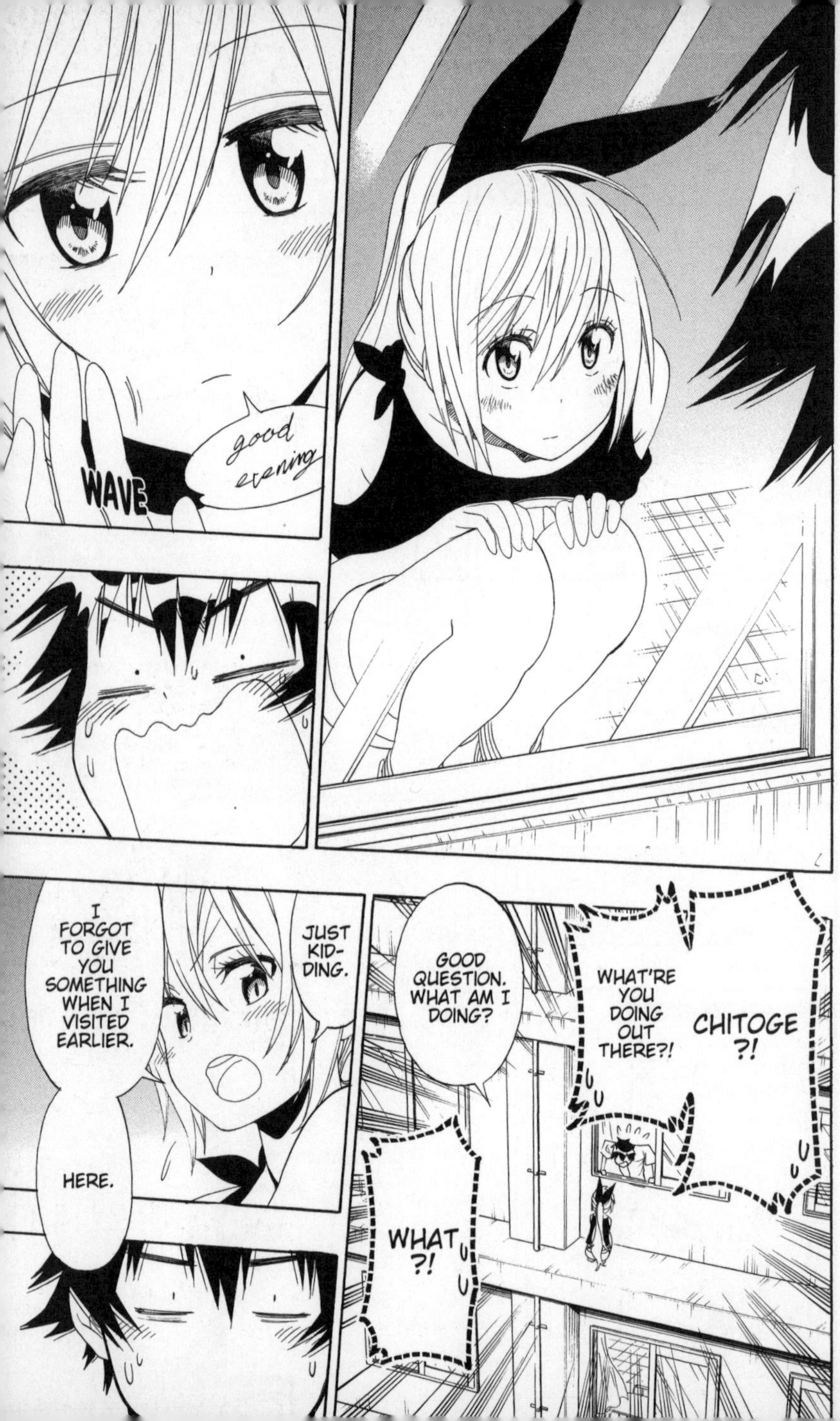
good evening
WAVE
CHITOGE ?!
WHAT'RE YOU DOING OUT THERE?!
GOOD QUESTION. WHAT AM I DOING?
WHAT ?!
JUST KID-DING.
I FORGOT TO GIVE YOU SOMETHING WHEN I VISITED EARLIER.
HERE.

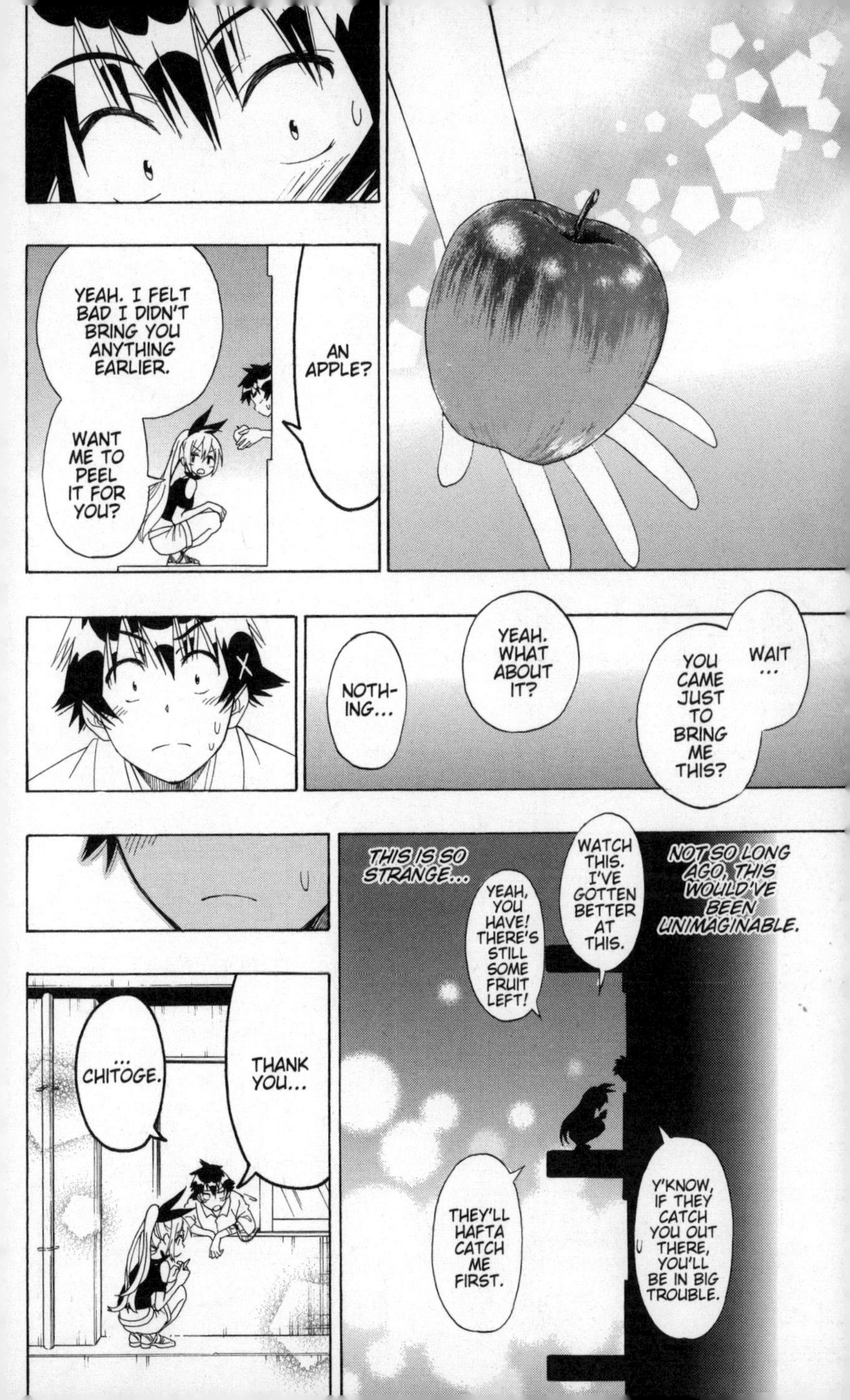
AN APPLE?
YEAH. I FELT BAD I DIDN'T BRING YOU ANYTHING EARLIER.
WANT ME TO PEEL IT FOR YOU?
WAIT...
YOU CAME JUST TO BRING ME THIS?
YEAH. WHAT ABOUT IT?
NOTH-ING...
NOT SO LONG AGO, THIS WOULD'VE BEEN UNIMAGINABLE.
WATCH THIS. I'VE GOTTEN BETTER AT THIS.
YEAH, YOU HAVE! THERE'S STILL SOME FRUIT LEFT!
THIS IS SO STRANGE...
Y'KNOW, IF THEY CATCH YOU OUT THERE, YOU'LL BE IN BIG TROUBLE.
THEY'LL HAFTA CATCH ME FIRST.
THANK YOU...
...CHITOGE.

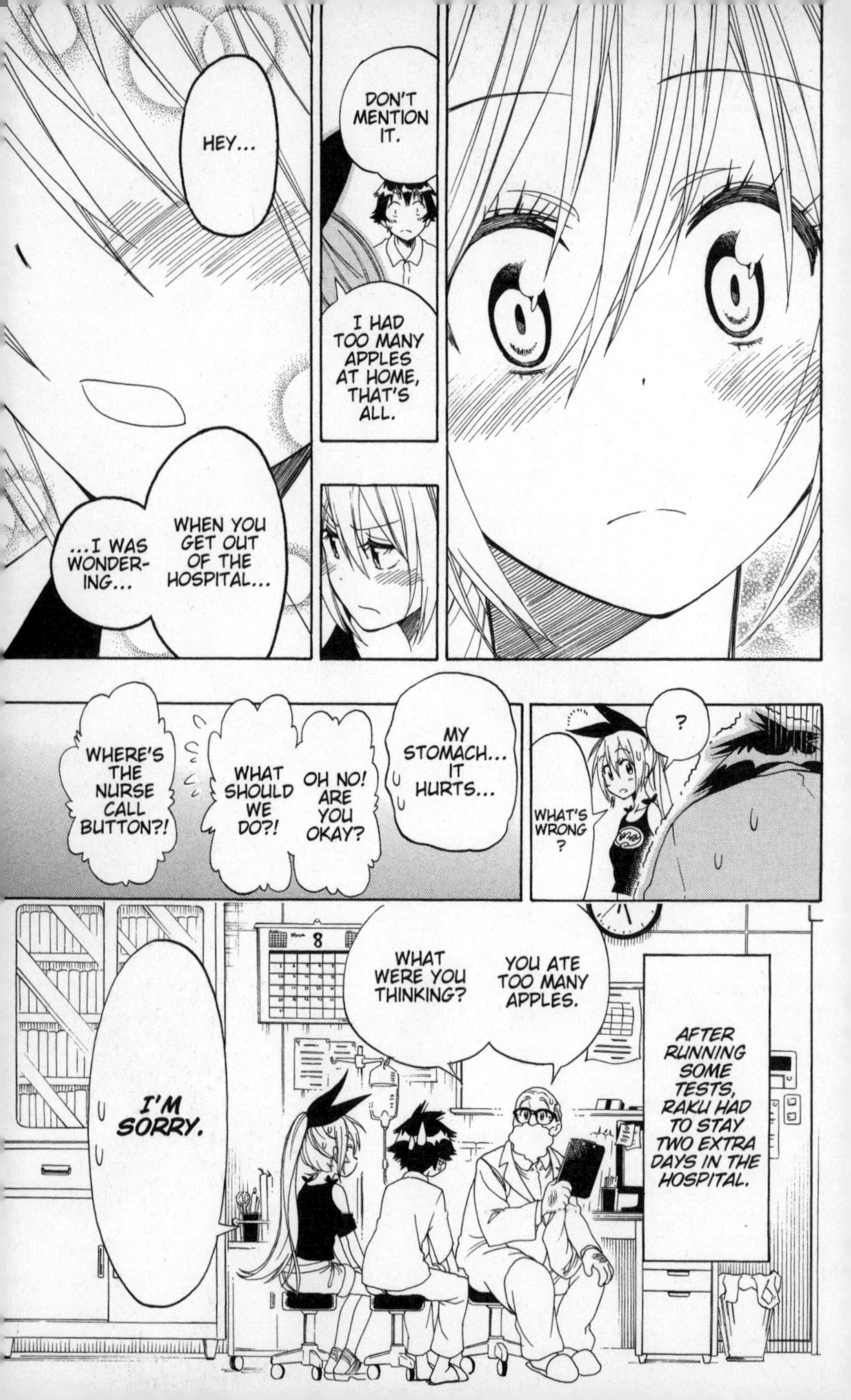
DON'T MENTION IT.
I HAD TOO MANY APPLES AT HOME, THAT'S ALL.
HEY...
WHEN YOU GET OUT OF THE HOSPITAL...
...I WAS WONDERING...
?
WHAT'S WRONG?
MY STOMACH... IT HURTS...
OH NO! ARE YOU OKAY?
WHAT SHOULD WE DO?!
WHERE'S THE NURSE CALL BUTTON?!
AFTER RUNNING SOME TESTS, RAKU HAD TO STAY TWO EXTRA DAYS IN THE HOSPITAL.
YOU ATE TOO MANY APPLES.
WHAT WERE YOU THINKING?
I'M SORRY.

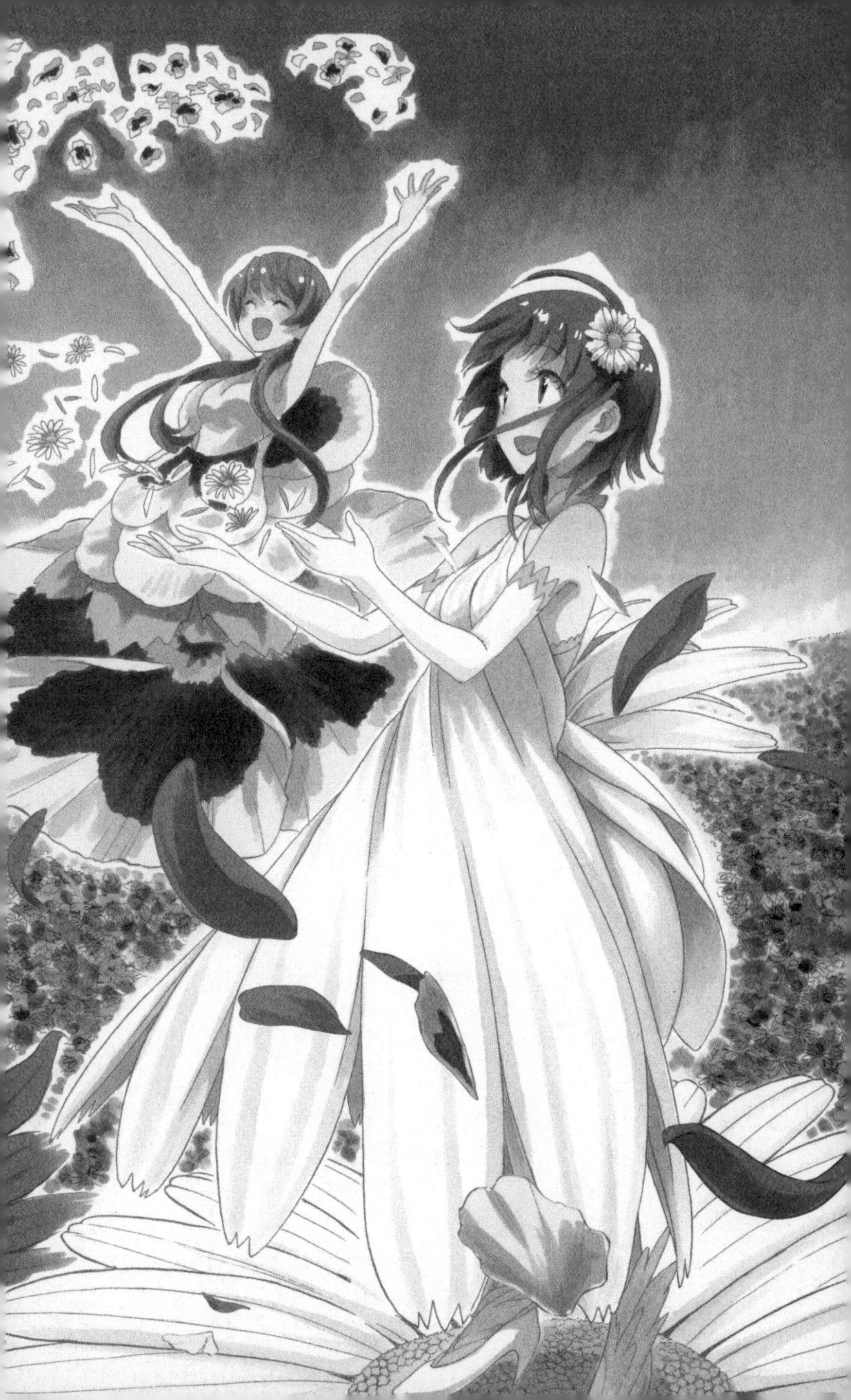

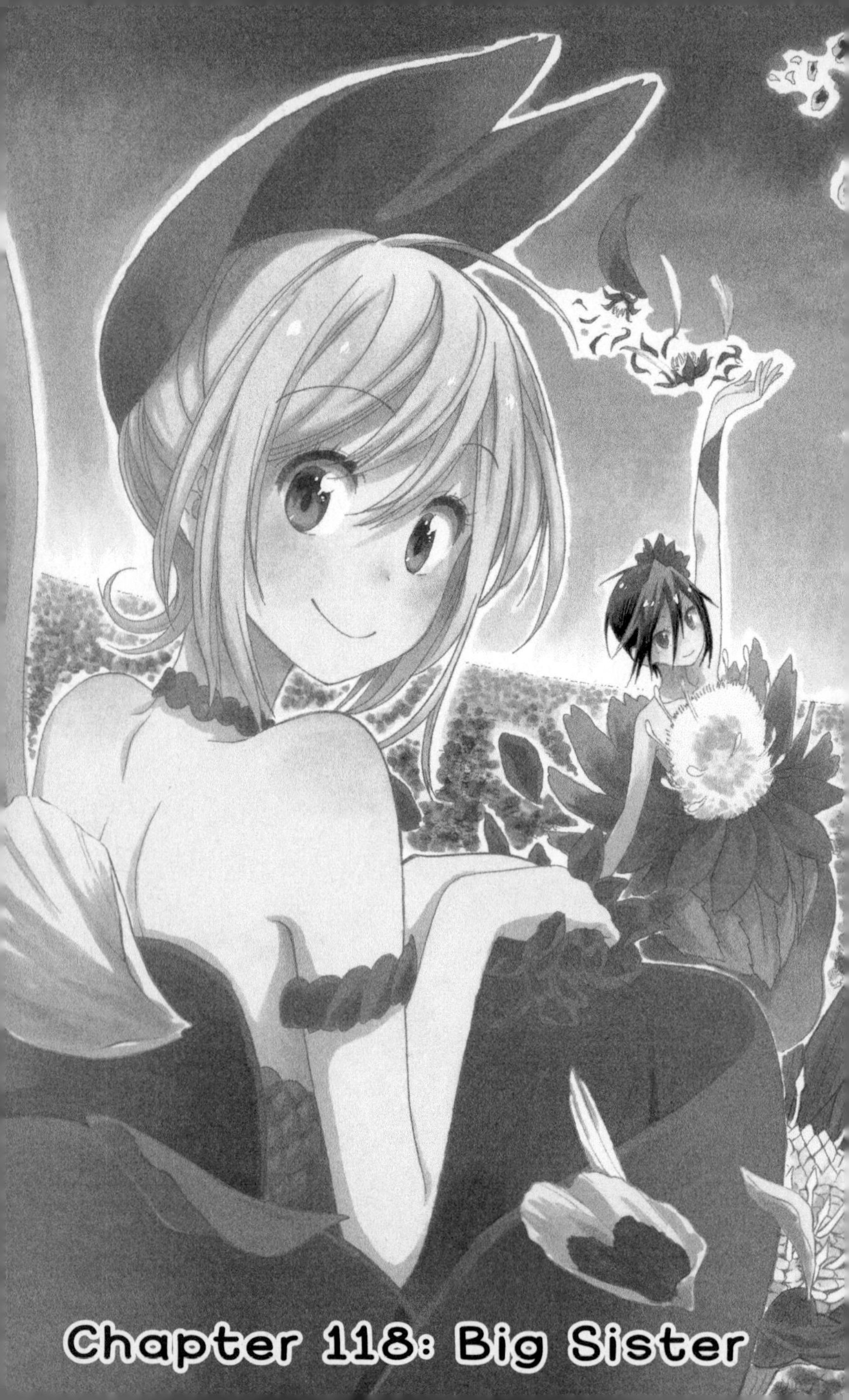

Chapter 118: Big Sister

NISEKOI
False Love

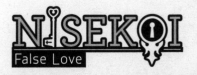

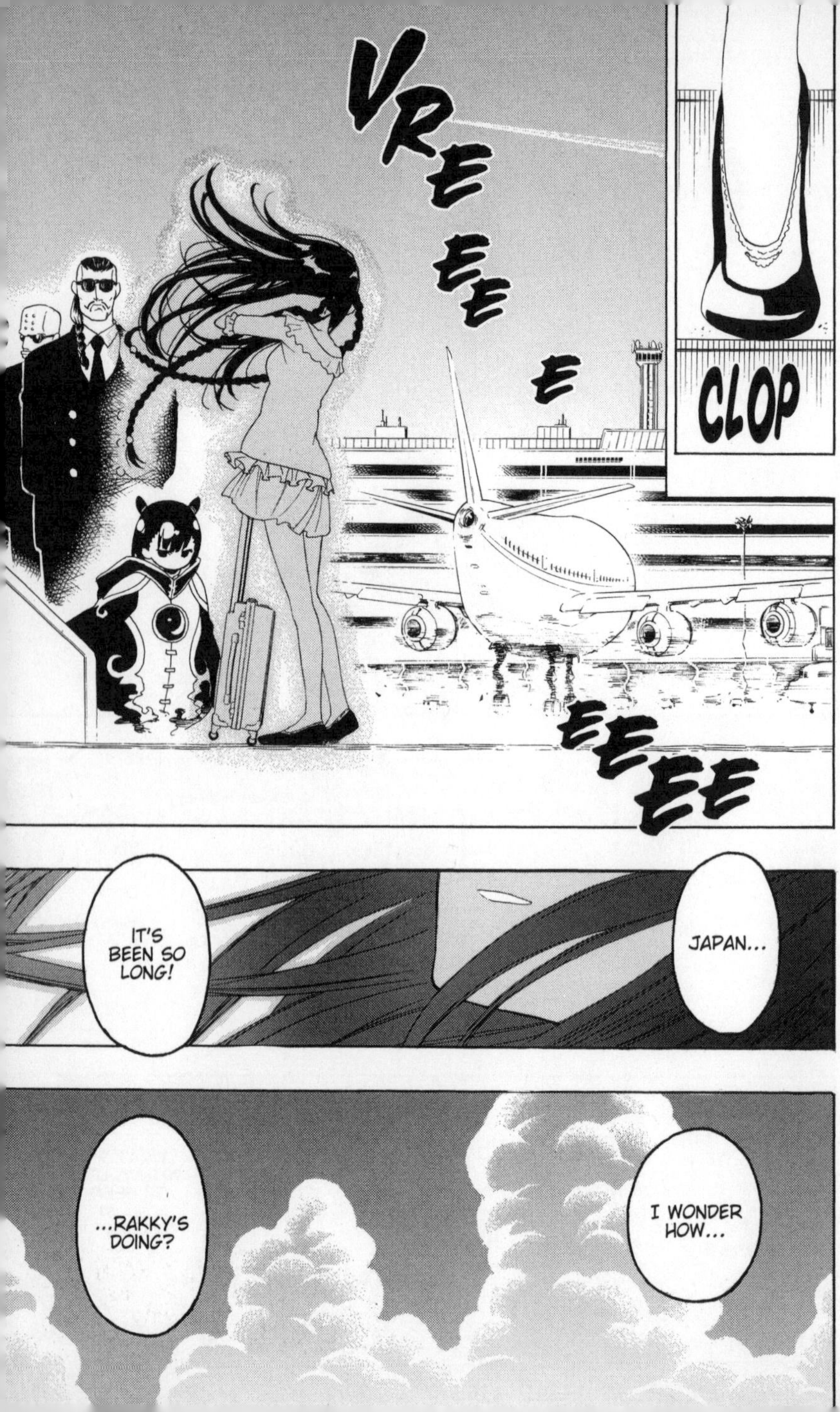
CLOP
VREEEE
E
EEEE
JAPAN...
IT'S BEEN SO LONG!
I WONDER HOW...
...RAKKY'S DOING?

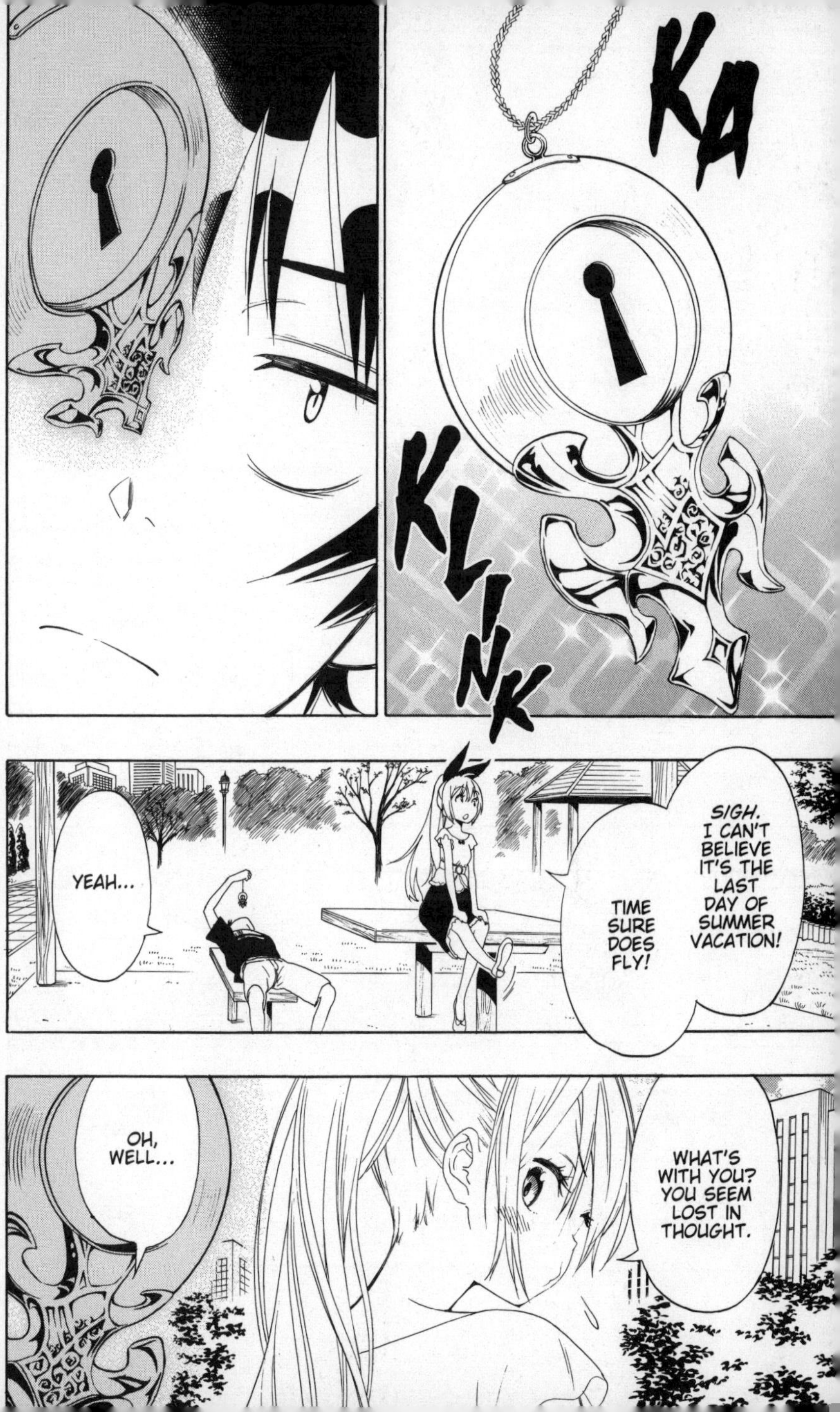
KA
KLINK
SIGH. I CAN'T BELIEVE IT'S THE LAST DAY OF SUMMER VACATION!
TIME SURE DOES FLY!
YEAH...
WHAT'S WITH YOU? YOU SEEM LOST IN THOUGHT.
OH, WELL...

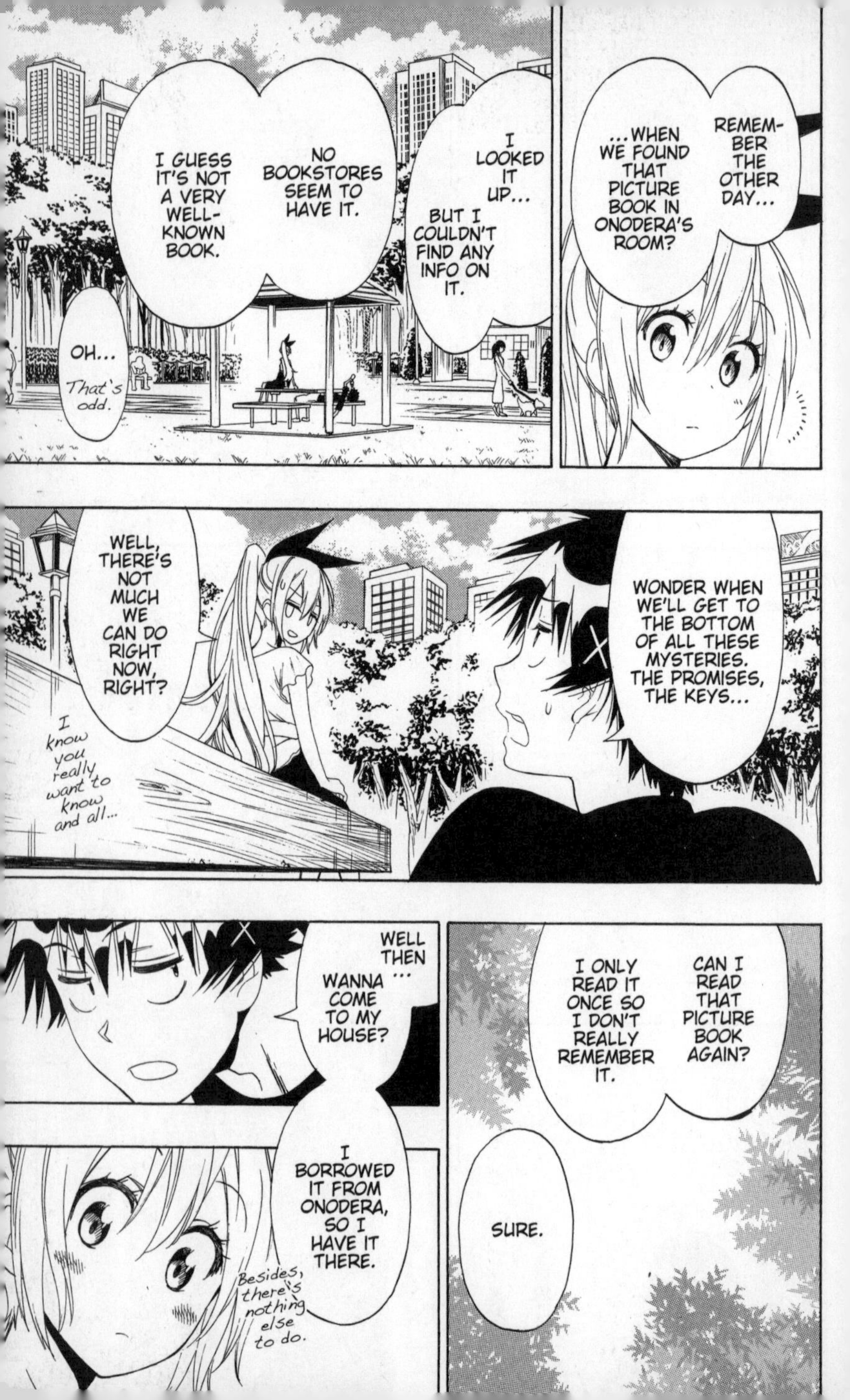
REMEMBER THE OTHER DAY...
...WHEN WE FOUND THAT PICTURE BOOK IN ONODERA'S ROOM?
I LOOKED IT UP... BUT I COULDN'T FIND ANY INFO ON IT.
NO BOOKSTORES SEEM TO HAVE IT.
I GUESS IT'S NOT A VERY WELL-KNOWN BOOK.
OH... That's odd.
WONDER WHEN WE'LL GET TO THE BOTTOM OF ALL THESE MYSTERIES. THE PROMISES, THE KEYS...
WELL, THERE'S NOT MUCH WE CAN DO RIGHT NOW, RIGHT?
I know you really want to know and all...
CAN I READ THAT PICTURE BOOK AGAIN?
I ONLY READ IT ONCE SO I DON'T REALLY REMEMBER IT.
SURE.
WELL THEN... WANNA COME TO MY HOUSE?
I BORROWED IT FROM ONODERA, SO I HAVE IT THERE.
Besides, there's nothing else to do.

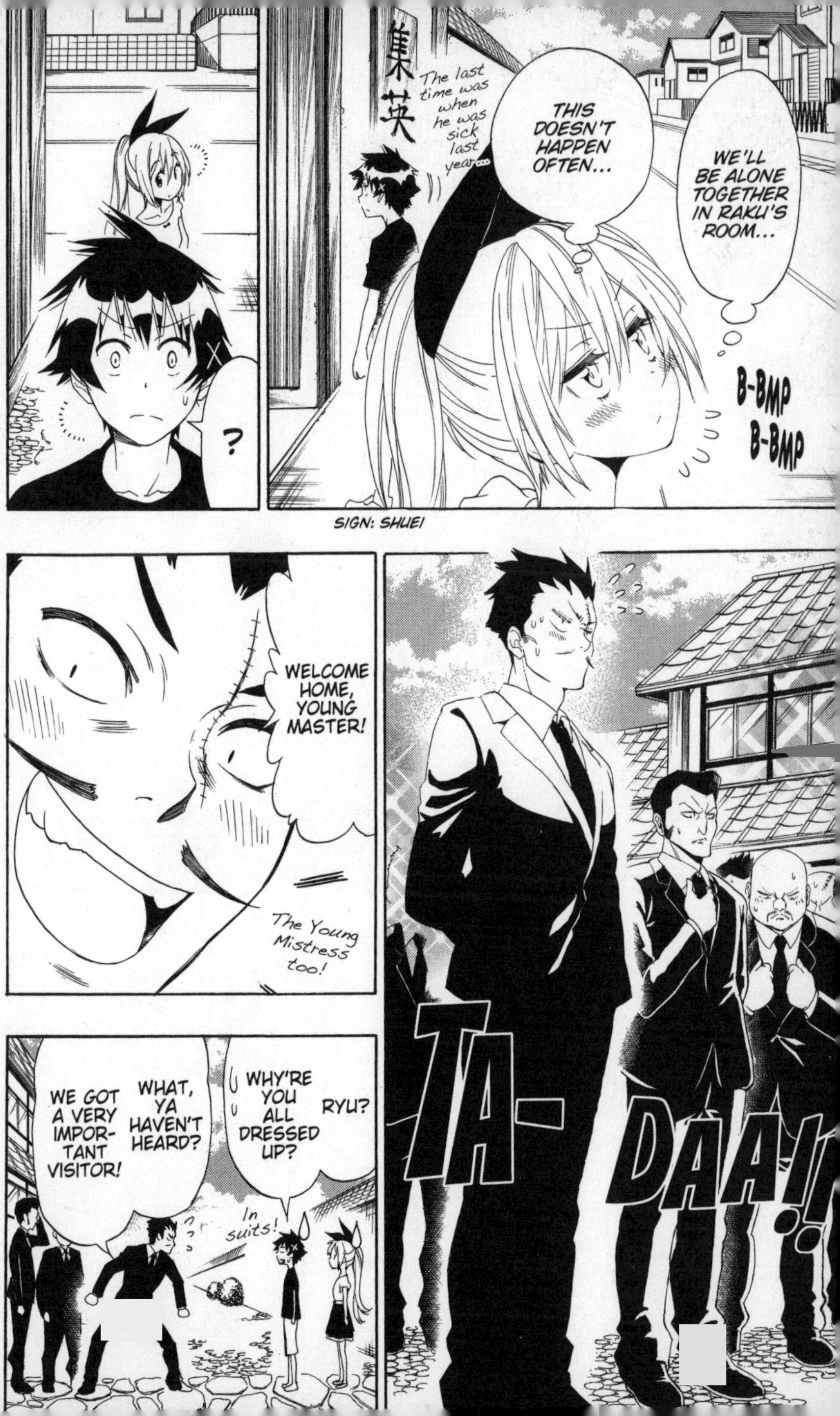
WE'LL BE ALONE TOGETHER IN RAKU'S ROOM...
THIS DOESN'T HAPPEN OFTEN...
The last time was when he was sick last year...
B-BMP B-BMP
?
SIGN: SHUEI
TA-DAA!!
WELCOME HOME, YOUNG MASTER!
The Young Mistress too!
RYU?
WHY'RE YOU ALL DRESSED UP?
In suits!
WHAT, YA HAVEN'T HEARD?
WE GOT A VERY IMPORTANT VISITOR!

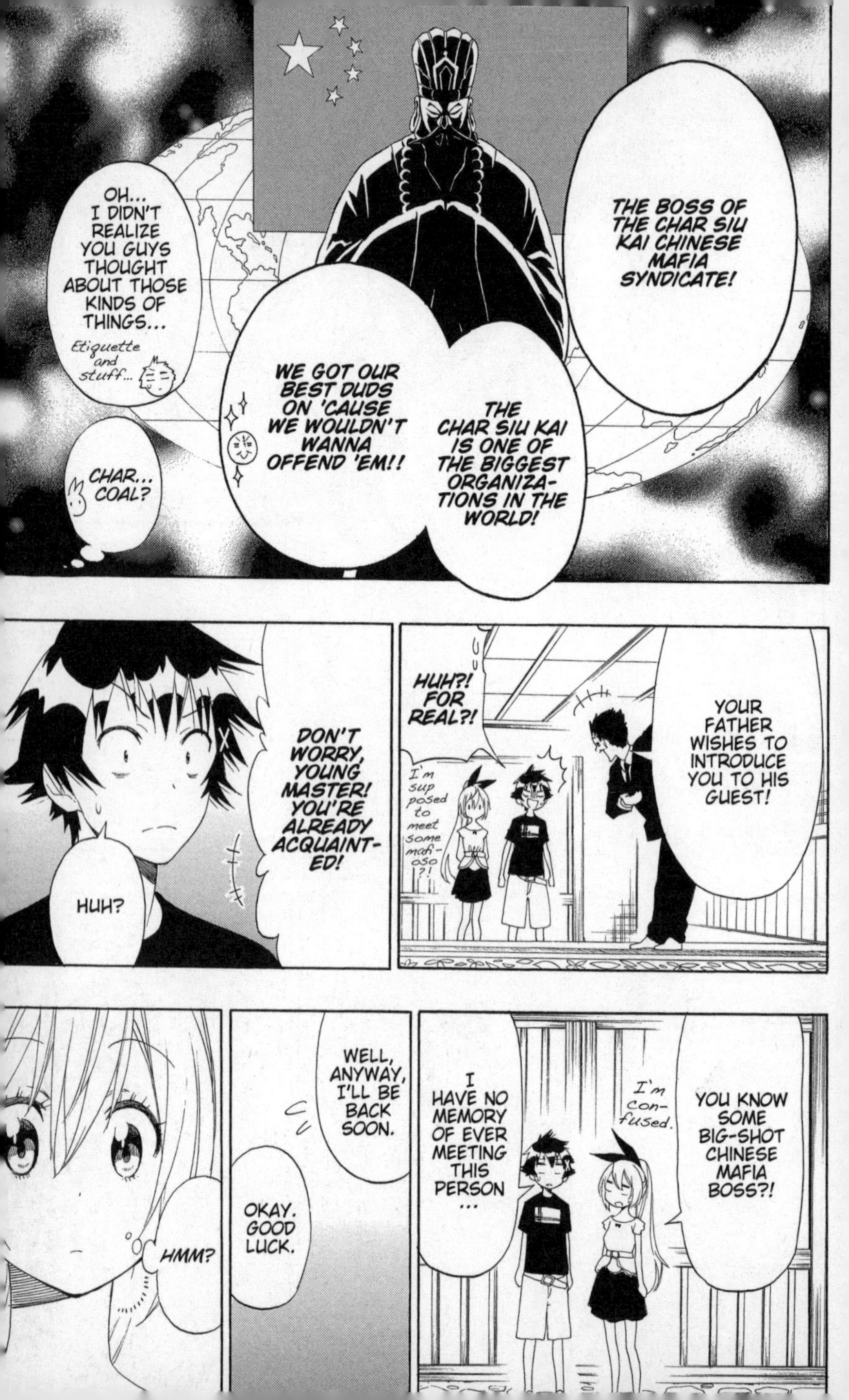
THE BOSS OF THE CHAR SIU KAI CHINESE MAFIA SYNDICATE!
THE CHAR SIU KAI IS ONE OF THE BIGGEST ORGANIZA-TIONS IN THE WORLD!
WE GOT OUR BEST DUDS ON 'CAUSE WE WOULDN'T WANNA OFFEND 'EM!!
OH... I DIDN'T REALIZE YOU GUYS THOUGHT ABOUT THOSE KINDS OF THINGS...
Etiquette and stuff...
CHAR... COAL?
YOUR FATHER WISHES TO INTRODUCE YOU TO HIS GUEST!
HUH?! FOR REAL?!
I'm sup posed to meet some mafi-oso?!
DON'T WORRY, YOUNG MASTER! YOU'RE ALREADY ACQUAINT-ED!
HUH?
YOU KNOW SOME BIG-SHOT CHINESE MAFIA BOSS?!
I'm con-fused.
I HAVE NO MEMORY OF EVER MEETING THIS PERSON...
WELL, ANYWAY, I'LL BE BACK SOON.
OKAY. GOOD LUCK.
HMM?

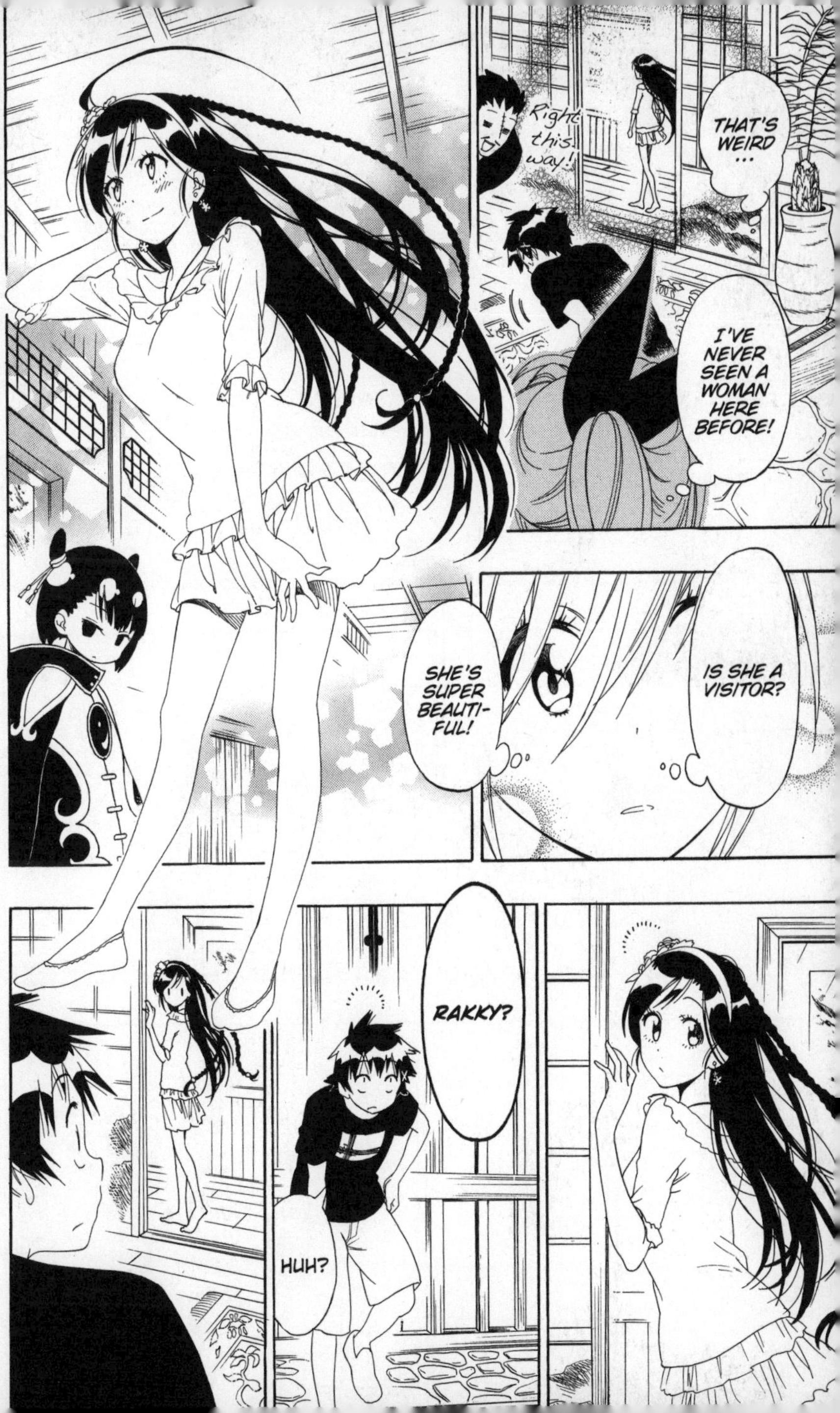
THAT'S WEIRD...
I'VE NEVER SEEN A WOMAN HERE BEFORE!
Right this way!
IS SHE A VISITOR?
SHE'S SUPER BEAUTI-FUL!
RAKKY?
HUH?

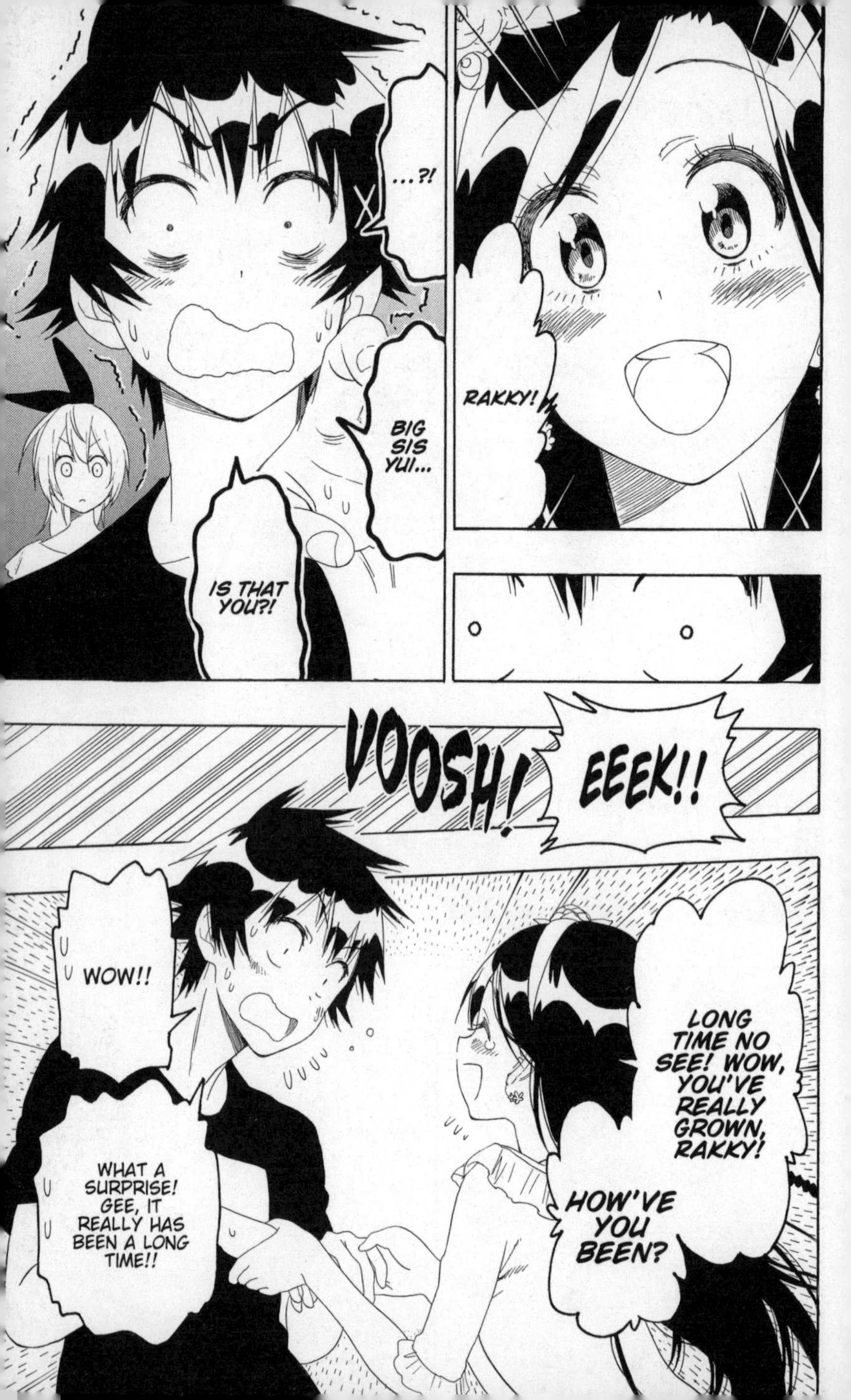
RAKKY!
...?!
BIG SIS YUI...
IS THAT YOU?!
EEEK!!
VOOSH!
LONG TIME NO SEE! WOW, YOU'VE REALLY GROWN, RAKKY!
HOW'VE YOU BEEN?
WOW!!
WHAT A SURPRISE! GEE, IT REALLY HAS BEEN A LONG TIME!!

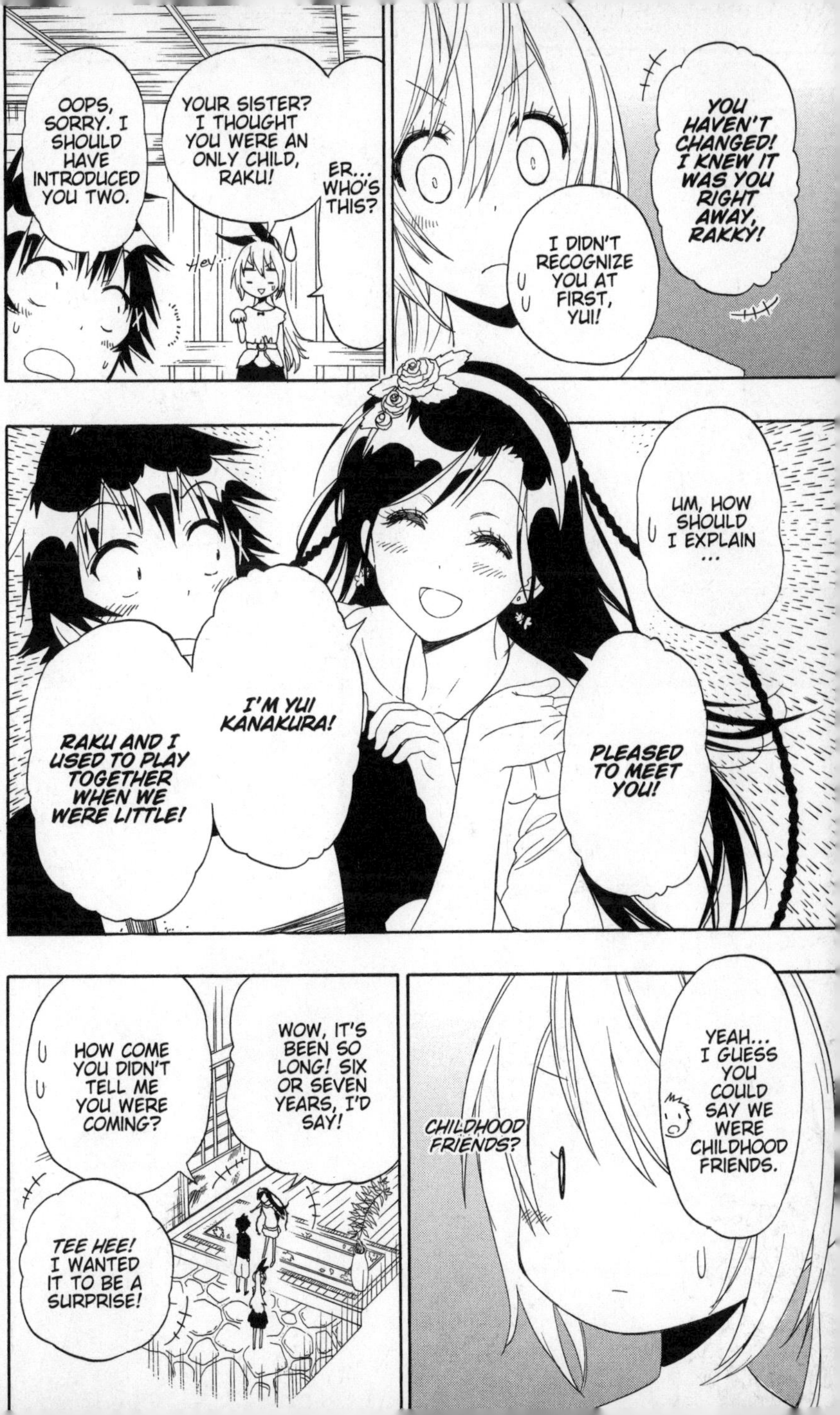
YOU HAVEN'T CHANGED! I KNEW IT WAS YOU RIGHT AWAY, RAKKY!
I DIDN'T RECOGNIZE YOU AT FIRST, YUI!
ER... WHO'S THIS?
YOUR SISTER? I THOUGHT YOU WERE AN ONLY CHILD, RAKU!
OOPS, SORRY. I SHOULD HAVE INTRODUCED YOU TWO.
Hey...
UM, HOW SHOULD I EXPLAIN ...
PLEASED TO MEET YOU!
I'M YUI KANAKURA!
RAKU AND I USED TO PLAY TOGETHER WHEN WE WERE LITTLE!
YEAH... I GUESS YOU COULD SAY WE WERE CHILDHOOD FRIENDS.
CHILDHOOD FRIENDS?
WOW, IT'S BEEN SO LONG! SIX OR SEVEN YEARS, I'D SAY!
HOW COME YOU DIDN'T TELL ME YOU WERE COMING?
TEE HEE! I WANTED IT TO BE A SURPRISE!

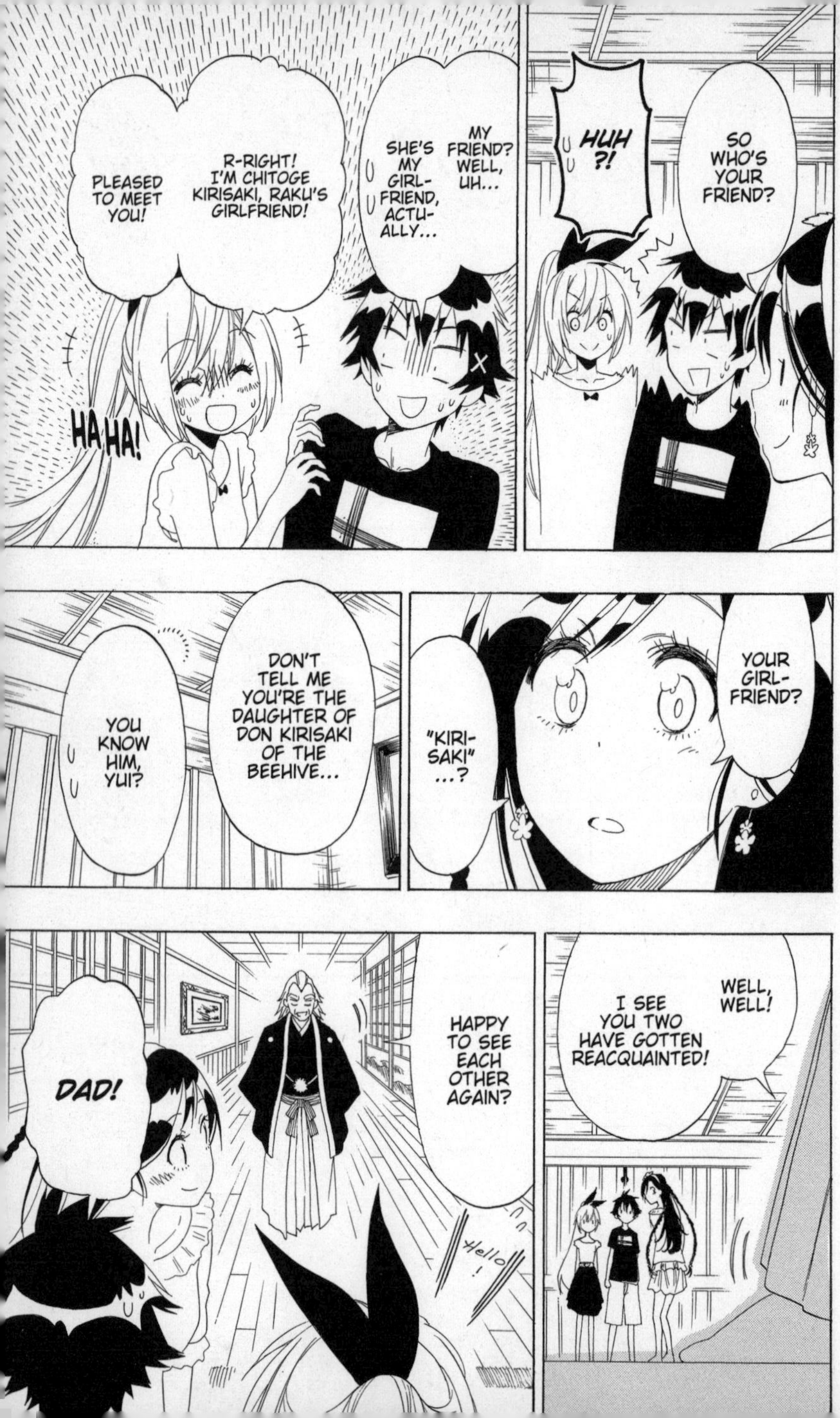
SO WHO'S YOUR FRIEND?
HUH ?!
MY FRIEND? WELL, UH...
SHE'S MY GIRL-FRIEND, ACTU-ALLY...
R-RIGHT! I'M CHITOGE KIRISAKI, RAKU'S GIRLFRIEND!
PLEASED TO MEET YOU!
HA HA!
YOUR GIRL-FRIEND?
"KIRI-SAKI" ...?
DON'T TELL ME YOU'RE THE DAUGHTER OF DON KIRISAKI OF THE BEEHIVE...
YOU KNOW HIM, YUI?
WELL, WELL!
I SEE YOU TWO HAVE GOTTEN REACQUAINTED!
HAPPY TO SEE EACH OTHER AGAIN?
Hello!
DAD!

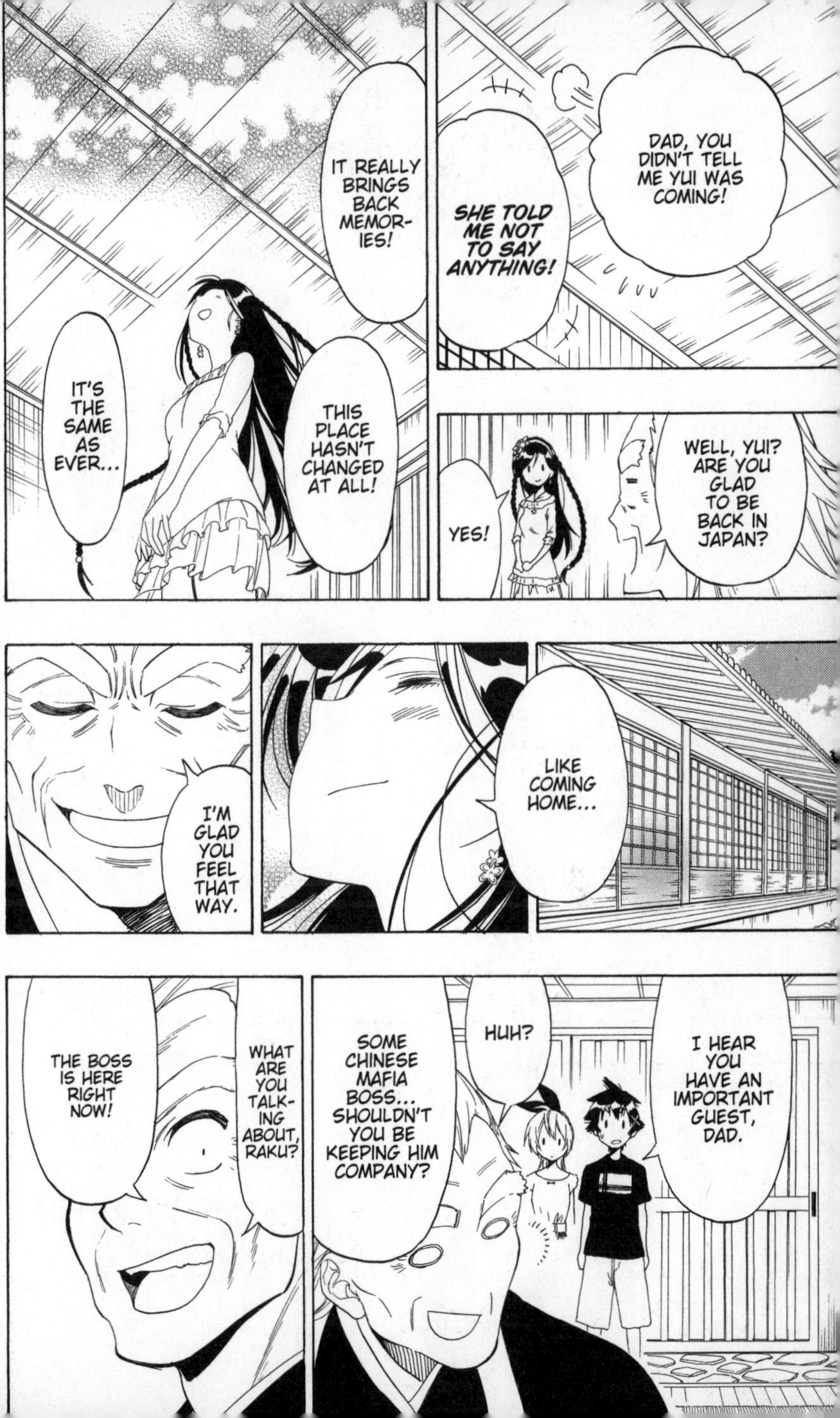
DAD, YOU DIDN'T TELL ME YUI WAS COMING!
SHE TOLD ME NOT TO SAY ANYTHING!
WELL, YUI? ARE YOU GLAD TO BE BACK IN JAPAN?
YES!
IT REALLY BRINGS BACK MEMOR-IES!
THIS PLACE HASN'T CHANGED AT ALL!
IT'S THE SAME AS EVER...
LIKE COMING HOME...
I'M GLAD YOU FEEL THAT WAY.
I HEAR YOU HAVE AN IMPORTANT GUEST, DAD.
HUH?
SOME CHINESE MAFIA BOSS... SHOULDN'T YOU BE KEEPING HIM COMPANY?
WHAT ARE YOU TALK-ING ABOUT, RAKU?
THE BOSS IS HERE RIGHT NOW!

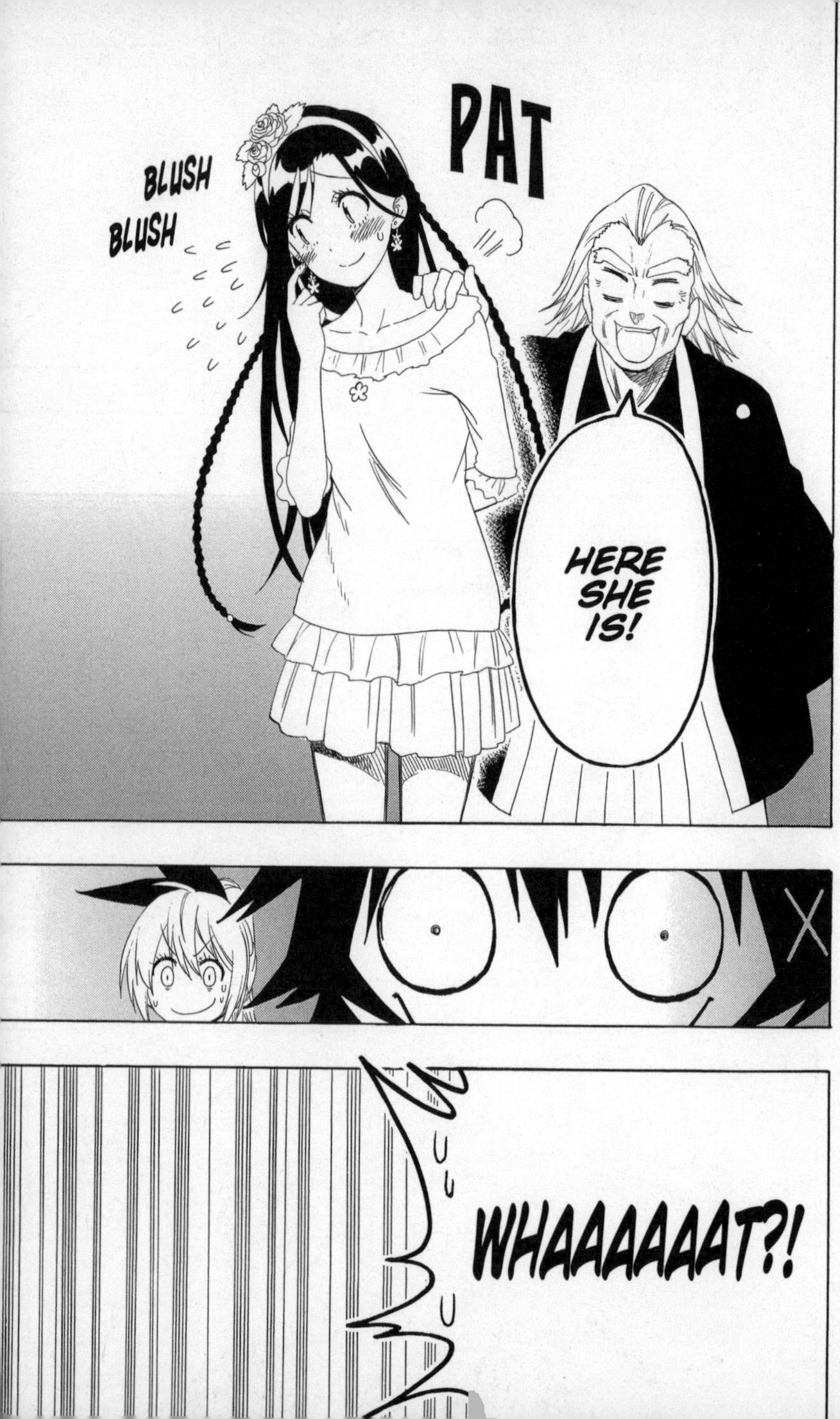
PAT
BLUSH BLUSH
HERE SHE IS!
WHAAAAAAT?!

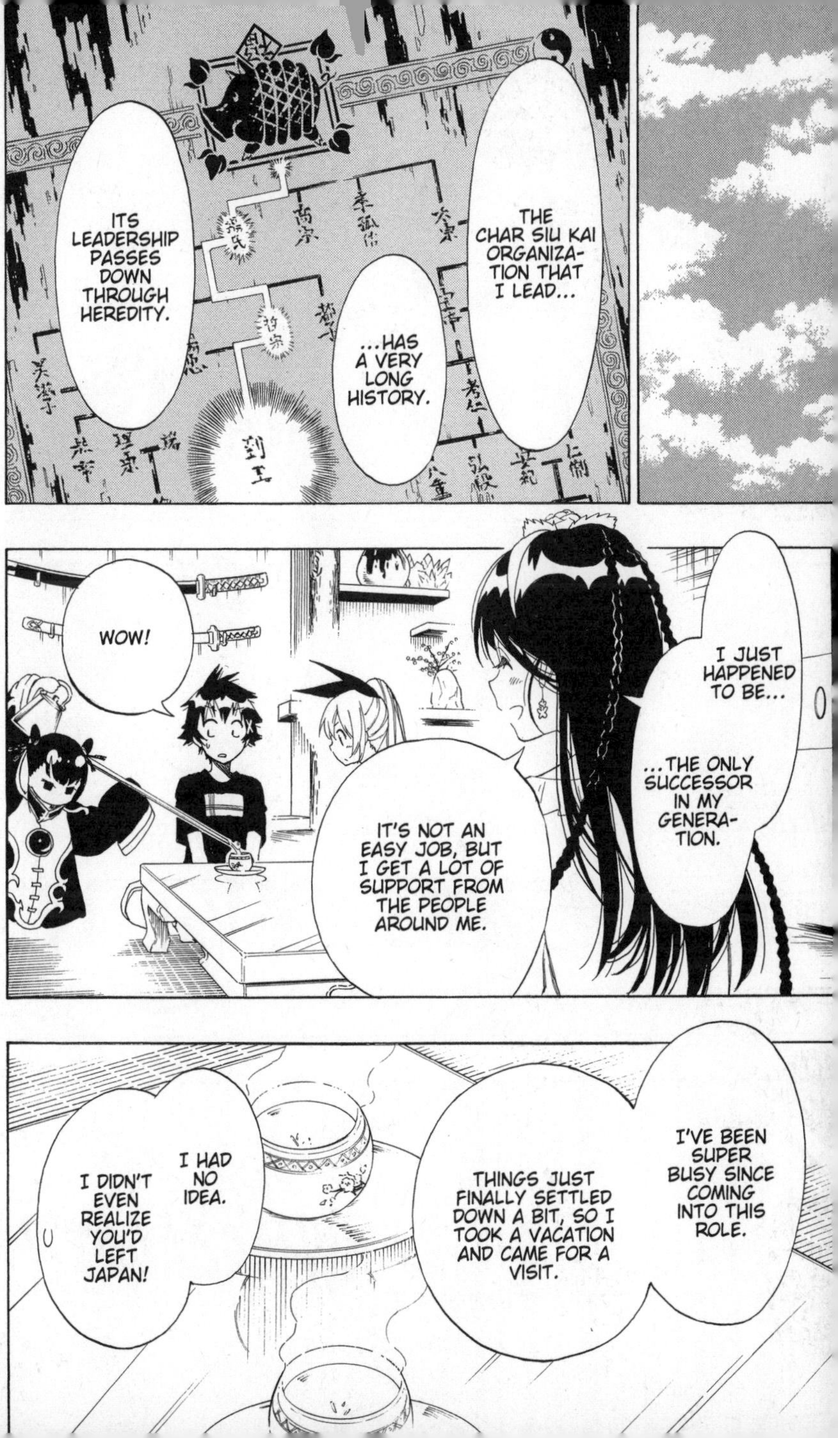
THE CHAR SIU KAI ORGANIZATION THAT I LEAD...
...HAS A VERY LONG HISTORY.
ITS LEADERSHIP PASSES DOWN THROUGH HEREDITY.
I JUST HAPPENED TO BE...
...THE ONLY SUCCESSOR IN MY GENERATION.
IT'S NOT AN EASY JOB, BUT I GET A LOT OF SUPPORT FROM THE PEOPLE AROUND ME.
WOW!
I'VE BEEN SUPER BUSY SINCE COMING INTO THIS ROLE.
THINGS JUST FINALLY SETTLED DOWN A BIT, SO I TOOK A VACATION AND CAME FOR A VISIT.
I HAD NO IDEA.
I DIDN'T EVEN REALIZE YOU'D LEFT JAPAN!

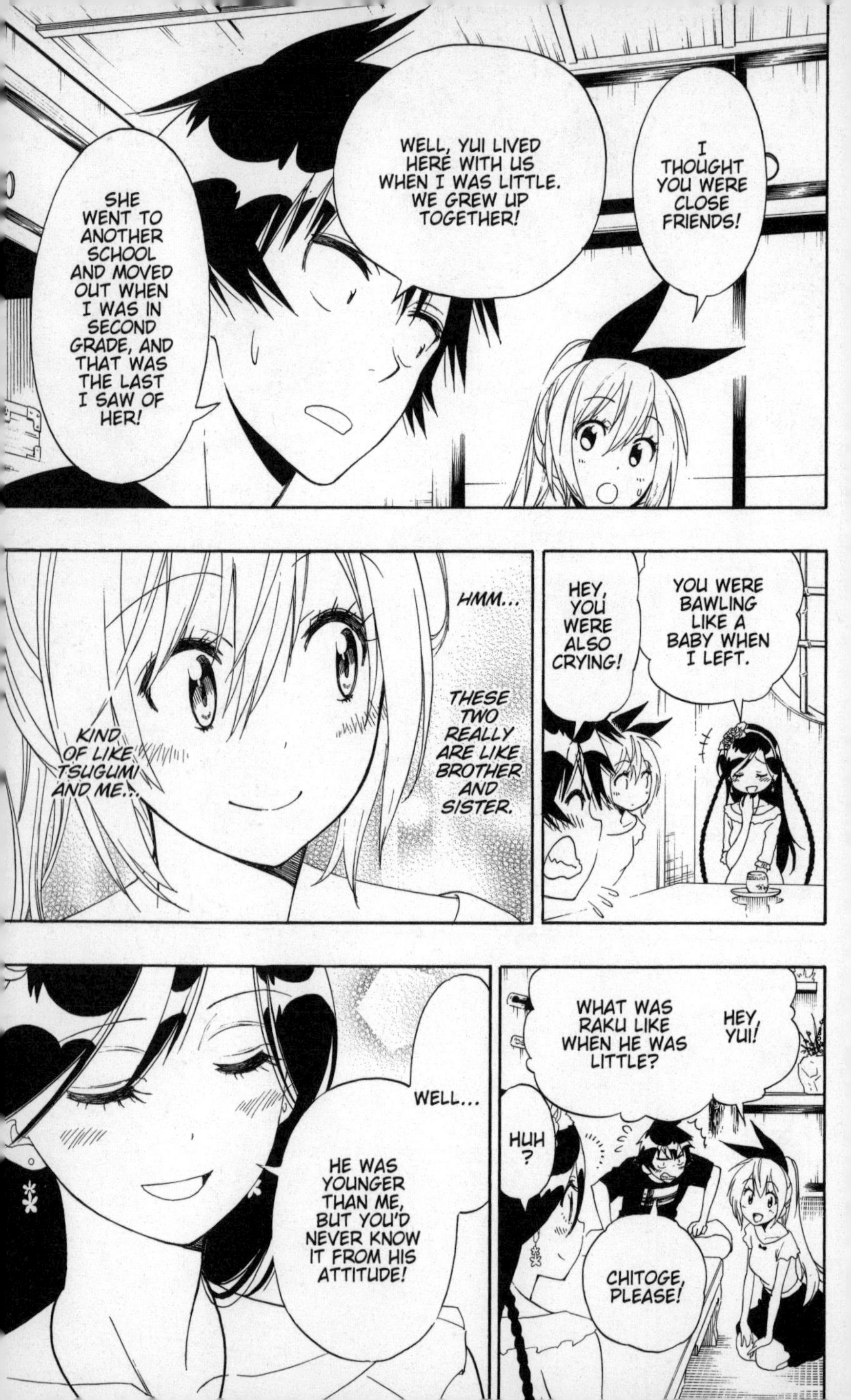
I THOUGHT YOU WERE CLOSE FRIENDS!
WELL, YUI LIVED HERE WITH US WHEN I WAS LITTLE. WE GREW UP TOGETHER!
SHE WENT TO ANOTHER SCHOOL AND MOVED OUT WHEN I WAS IN SECOND GRADE, AND THAT WAS THE LAST I SAW OF HER!
YOU WERE BAWLING LIKE A BABY WHEN I LEFT.
HEY, YOU WERE ALSO CRYING!
HMM...
THESE TWO REALLY ARE LIKE BROTHER AND SISTER.
KIND OF LIKE TSUGUMI AND ME...
HEY, YUI!
WHAT WAS RAKU LIKE WHEN HE WAS LITTLE?
HUH?
CHITOGE, PLEASE!
WELL...
HE WAS YOUNGER THAN ME, BUT YOU'D NEVER KNOW IT FROM HIS ATTITUDE!

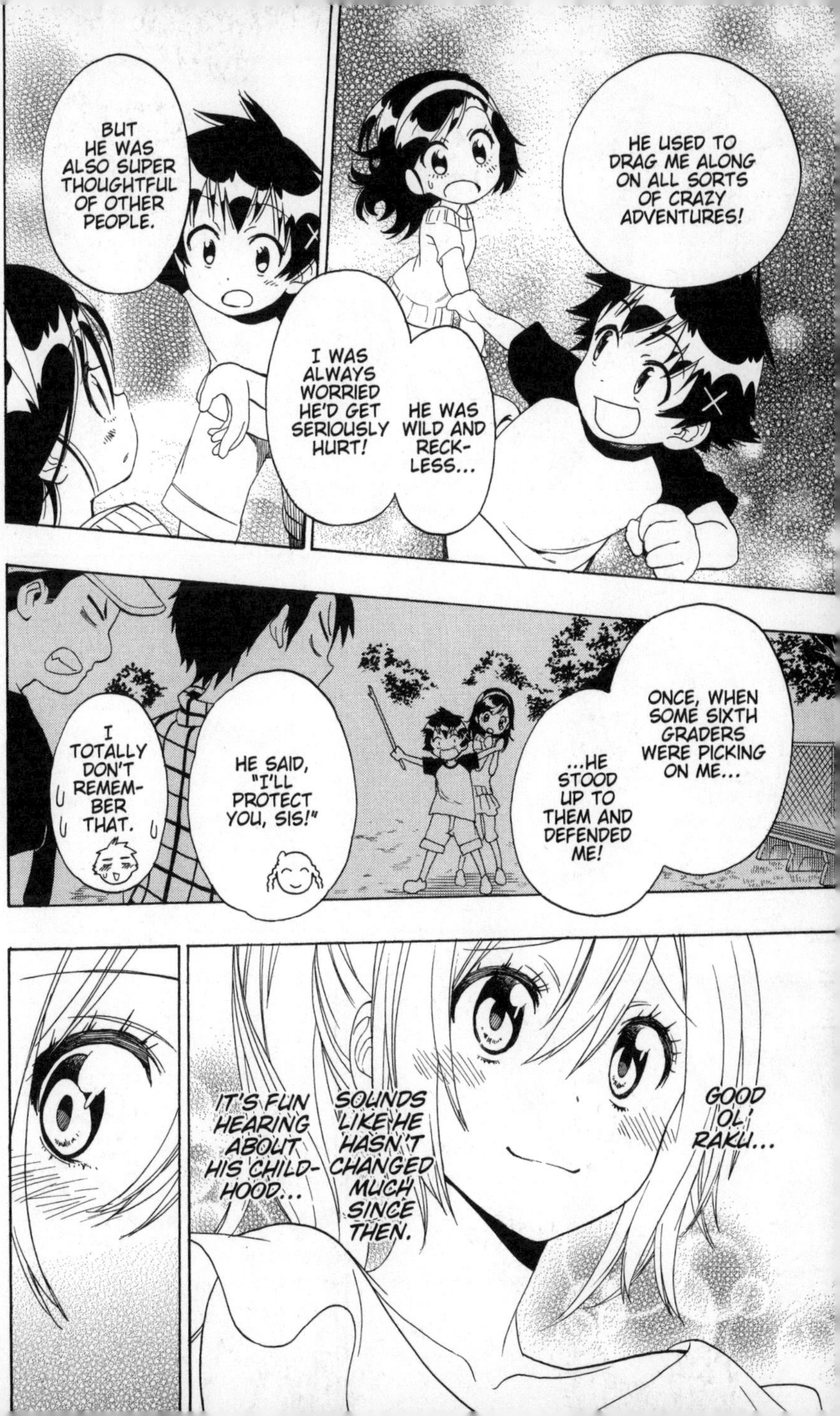
HE USED TO DRAG ME ALONG ON ALL SORTS OF CRAZY ADVENTURES!
HE WAS WILD AND RECK-LESS...
I WAS ALWAYS WORRIED HE'D GET SERIOUSLY HURT!
BUT HE WAS ALSO SUPER THOUGHTFUL OF OTHER PEOPLE.
ONCE, WHEN SOME SIXTH GRADERS WERE PICKING ON ME...
...HE STOOD UP TO THEM AND DEFENDED ME!
HE SAID, "I'LL PROTECT YOU, SIS!"
I TOTALLY DON'T REMEM-BER THAT.
GOOD OL' RAKU...
SOUNDS LIKE HE HASN'T CHANGED MUCH SINCE THEN.
IT'S FUN HEARING ABOUT HIS CHILD-HOOD...

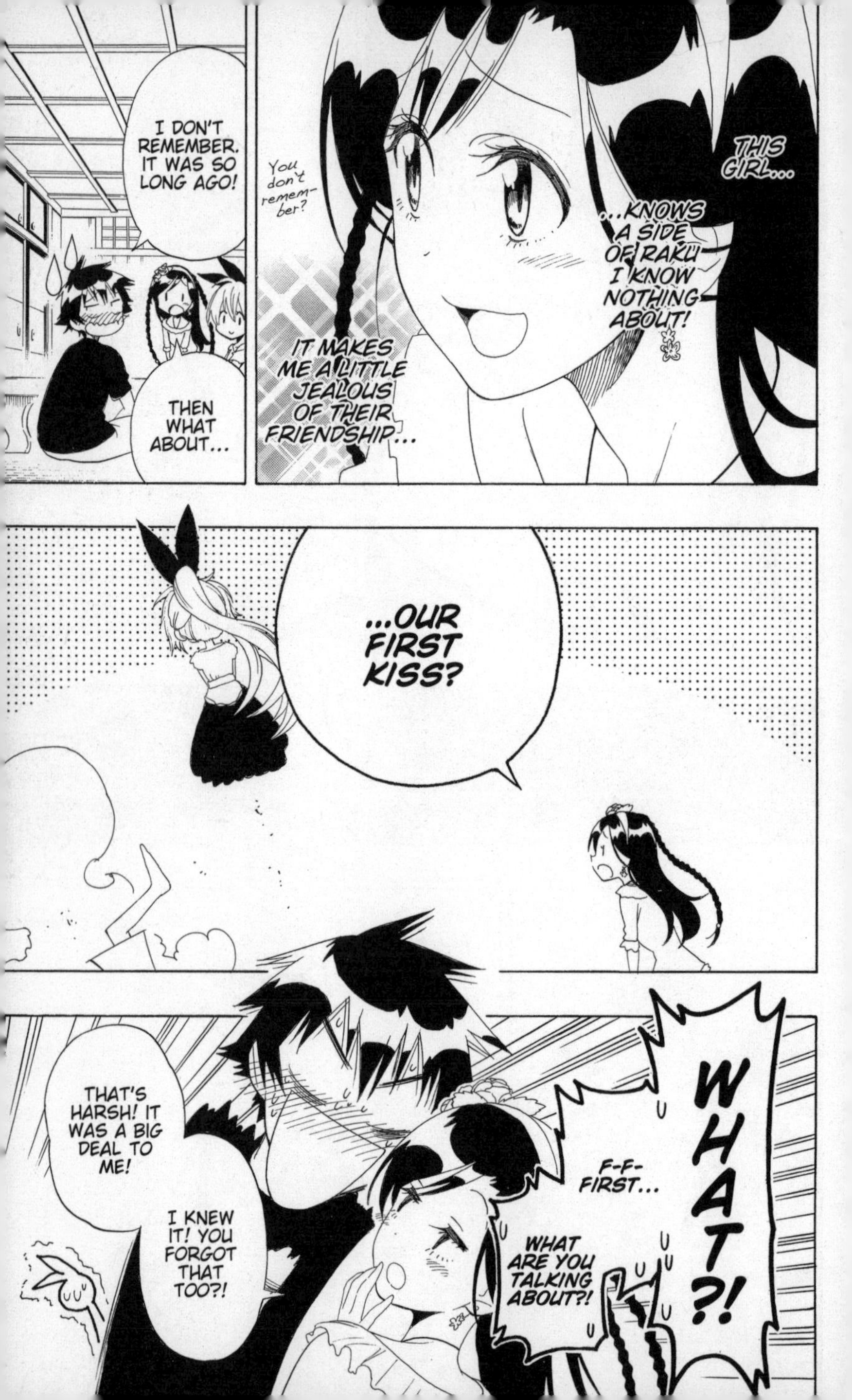
THIS GIRL...
...KNOWS A SIDE OF RAKU I KNOW NOTHING ABOUT!
You don't remember?
IT MAKES ME A LITTLE JEALOUS OF THEIR FRIENDSHIP...
I DON'T REMEMBER. IT WAS SO LONG AGO!
THEN WHAT ABOUT...
...OUR FIRST KISS?
WHAT?!
F-F-FIRST...
WHAT ARE YOU TALKING ABOUT?!
THAT'S HARSH! IT WAS A BIG DEAL TO ME!
I KNEW IT! YOU FORGOT THAT TOO?!

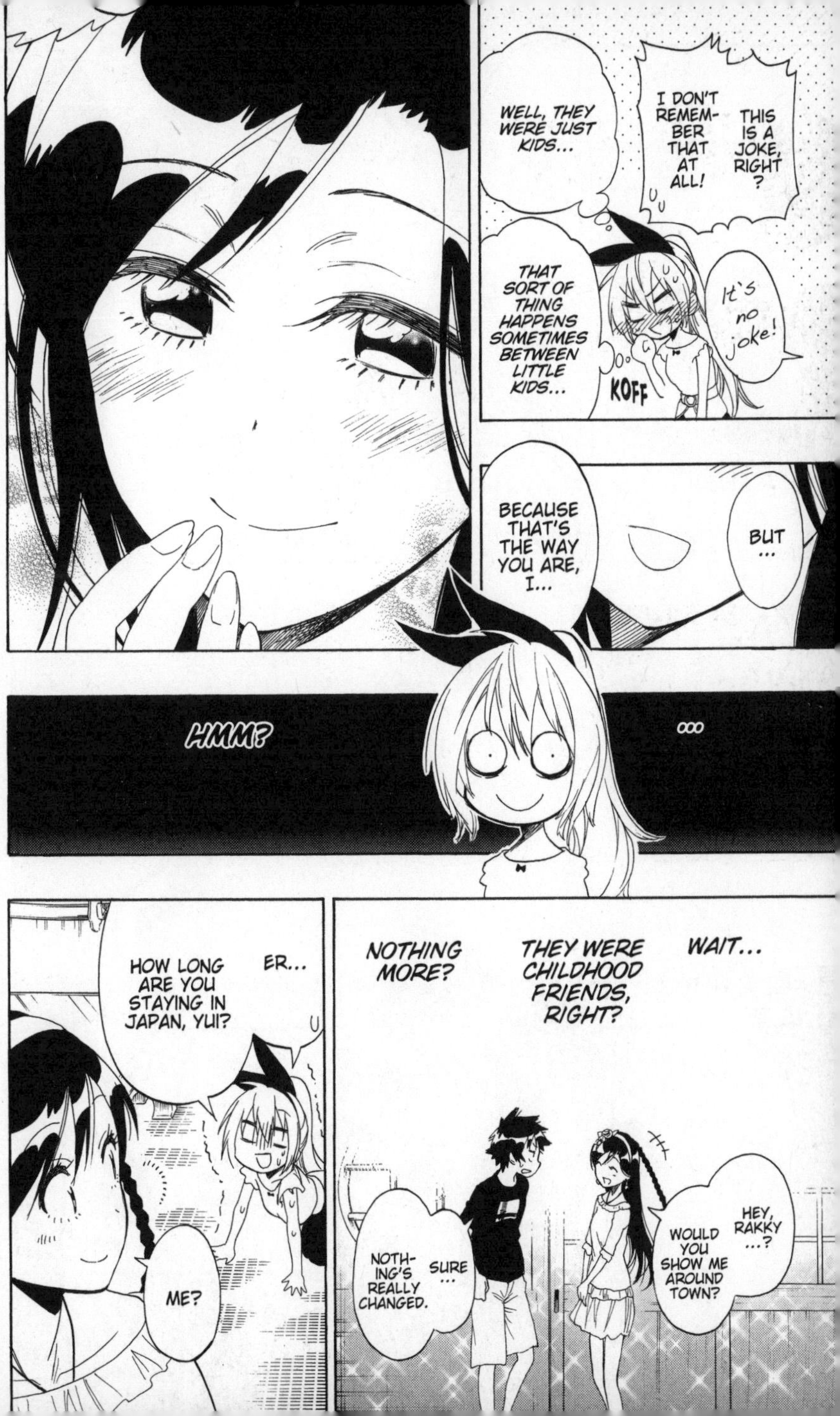
THIS IS A JOKE, RIGHT?
I DON'T REMEMBER THAT AT ALL!
WELL, THEY WERE JUST KIDS...
It's no joke!
THAT SORT OF THING HAPPENS SOMETIMES BETWEEN LITTLE KIDS...
KOFF
BUT...
BECAUSE THAT'S THE WAY YOU ARE, I...
ooo
HMM?
WAIT...
THEY WERE CHILDHOOD FRIENDS, RIGHT?
NOTHING MORE?
HEY, RAKKY...?
WOULD YOU SHOW ME AROUND TOWN?
SURE...
NOTHING'S REALLY CHANGED.
ER...
HOW LONG ARE YOU STAYING IN JAPAN, YUI?
ME?

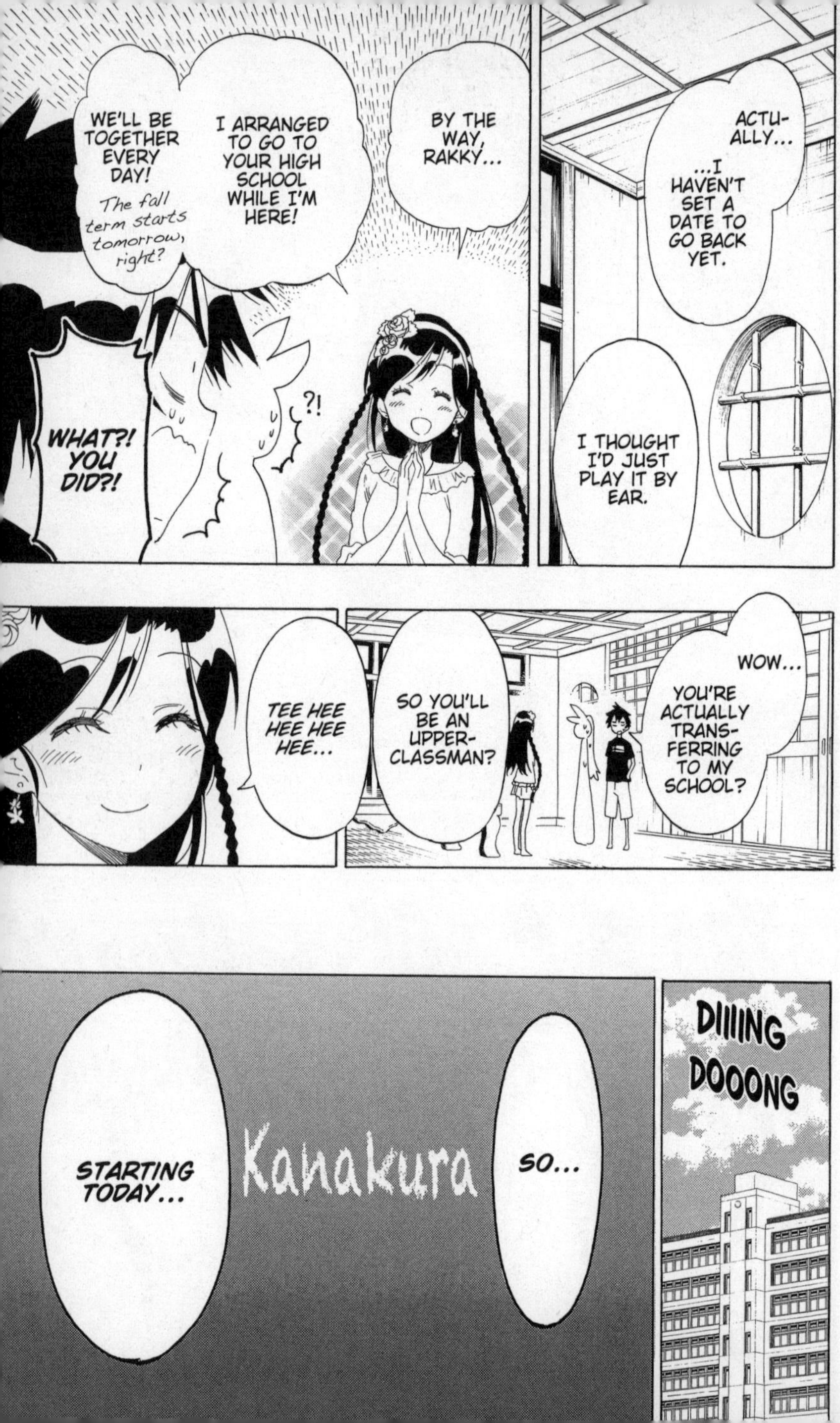
ACTUALLY... ...I HAVEN'T SET A DATE TO GO BACK YET.
I THOUGHT I'D JUST PLAY IT BY EAR.
BY THE WAY, RAKKY...
I ARRANGED TO GO TO YOUR HIGH SCHOOL WHILE I'M HERE!
WE'LL BE TOGETHER EVERY DAY!
The fall term starts tomorrow, right?
?!
WHAT?! YOU DID?!
WOW...
YOU'RE ACTUALLY TRANSFERRING TO MY SCHOOL?
SO YOU'LL BE AN UPPERCLASSMAN?
TEE HEE HEE HEE HEE...
DIIIING DOOONG
SO...
Kanakura
STARTING TODAY...

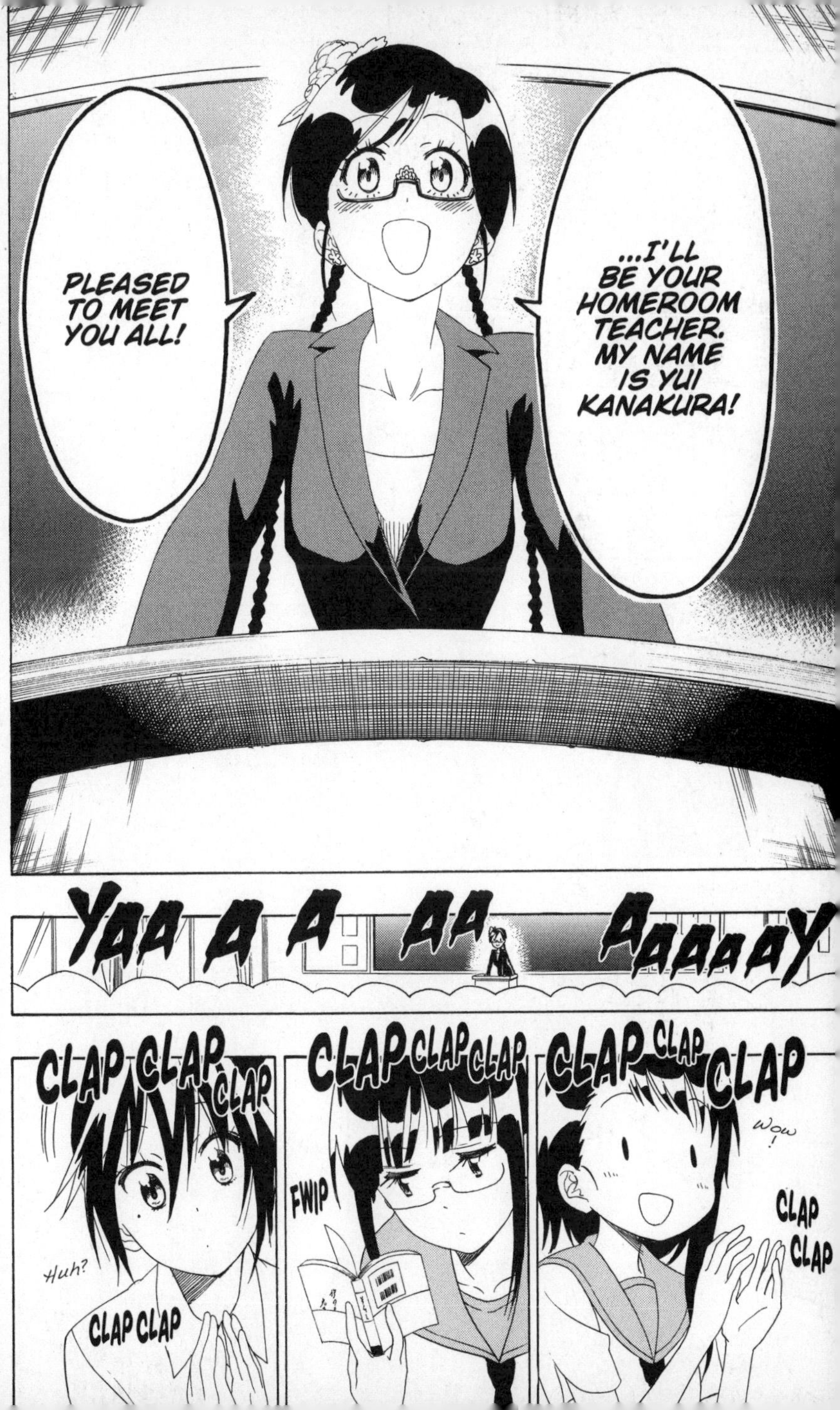
...I'LL BE YOUR HOMEROOM TEACHER. MY NAME IS YUI KANAKURA!
PLEASED TO MEET YOU ALL!
YAAAAAAAAAAAY
CLAP CLAP CLAP
Wow!
CLAP CLAP
CLAP CLAP CLAP
FWIP
CLAP CLAP CLAP
Huh?
CLAP CLAP

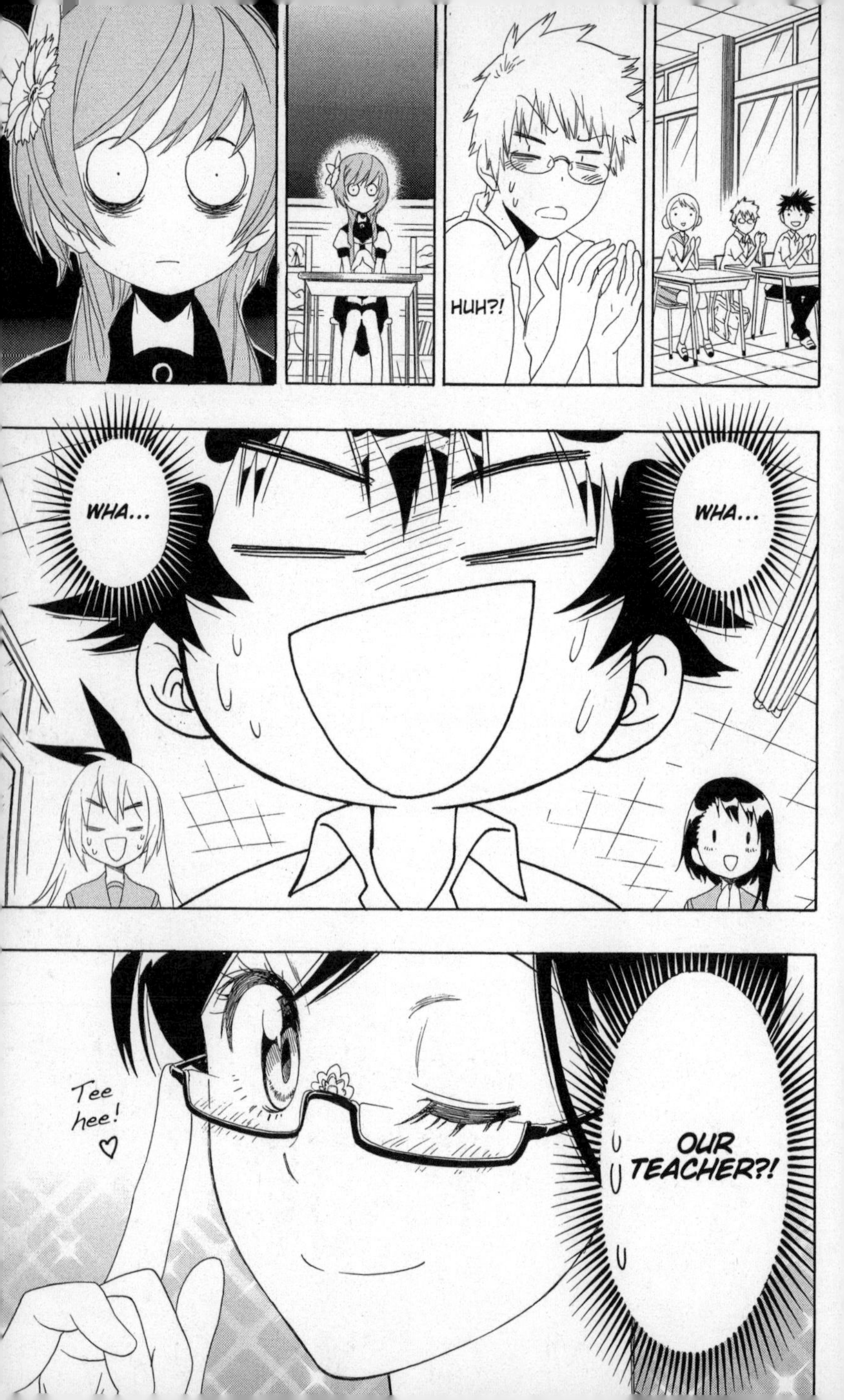
HUH?!
WHA...
WHA...
OUR TEACHER?!
Tee hee! ♡

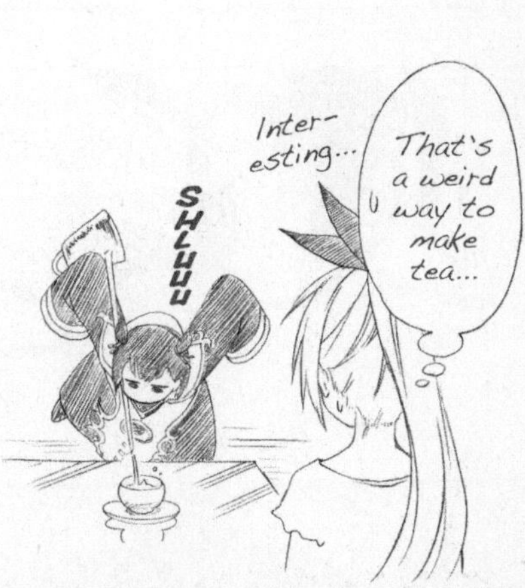
That's a weird way to make tea...
Inter-esting...
SHLUUU

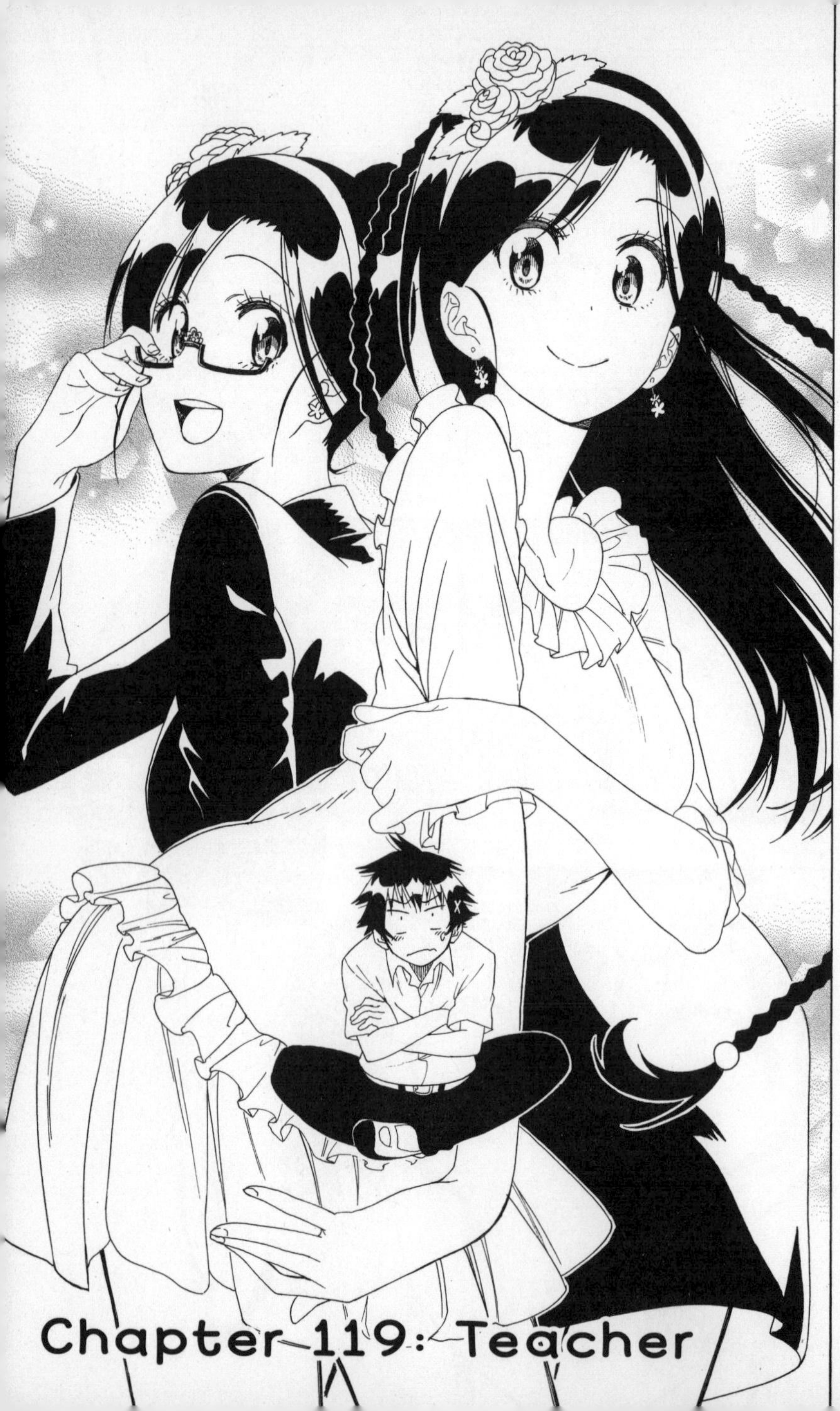

Chapter 119: Teacher

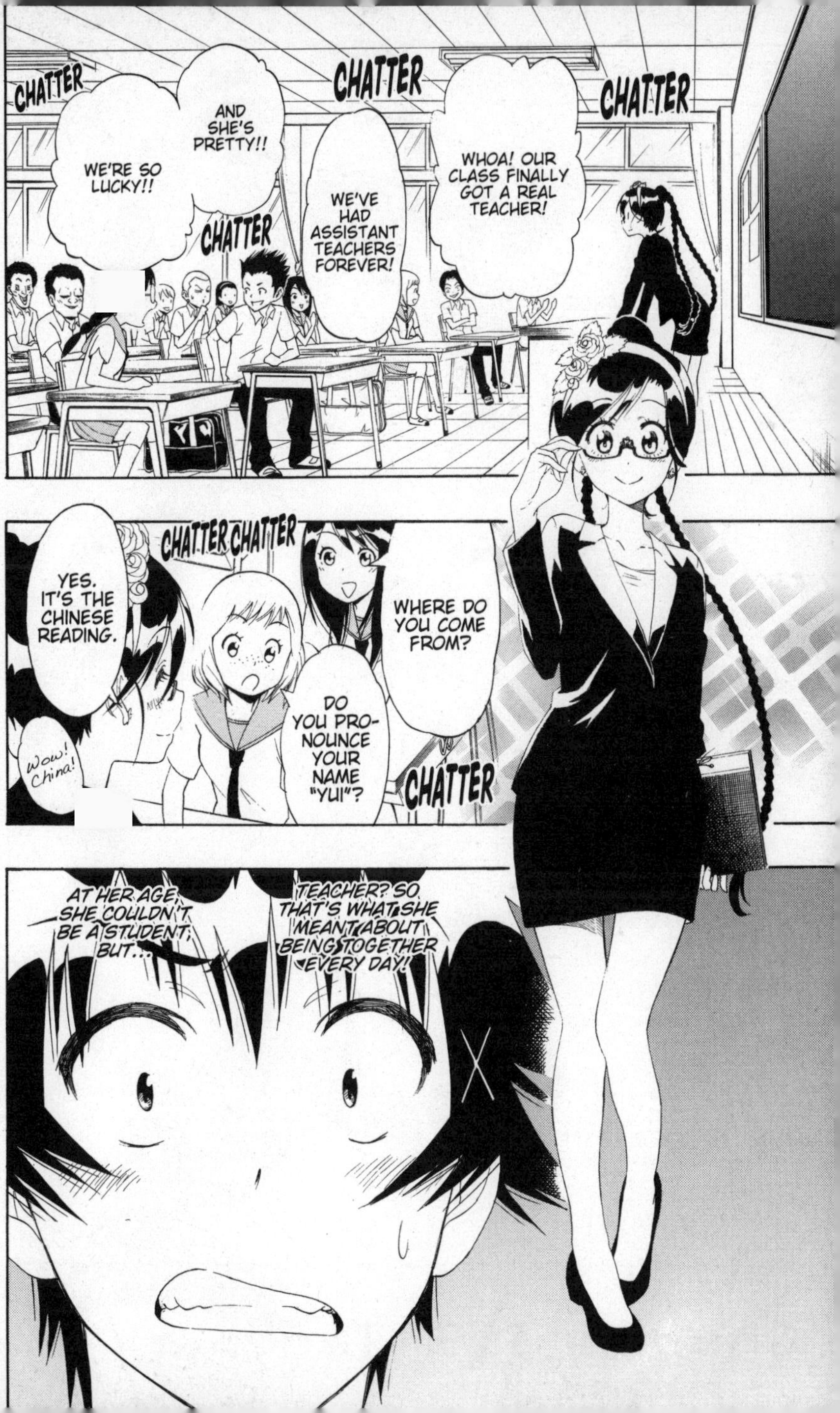
CHATTER
WHOA! OUR CLASS FINALLY GOT A REAL TEACHER!
CHATTER
WE'VE HAD ASSISTANT TEACHERS FOREVER!
AND SHE'S PRETTY!!
WE'RE SO LUCKY!!
CHATTER
CHATTER
WHERE DO YOU COME FROM?
DO YOU PRO-NOUNCE YOUR NAME "YUI"?
CHATTER
CHATTER CHATTER
YES. IT'S THE CHINESE READING.
Wow! China!
TEACHER? SO THAT'S WHAT SHE MEANT ABOUT BEING TOGETHER EVERY DAY!
AT HER AGE, SHE COULDN'T BE A STUDENT, BUT...

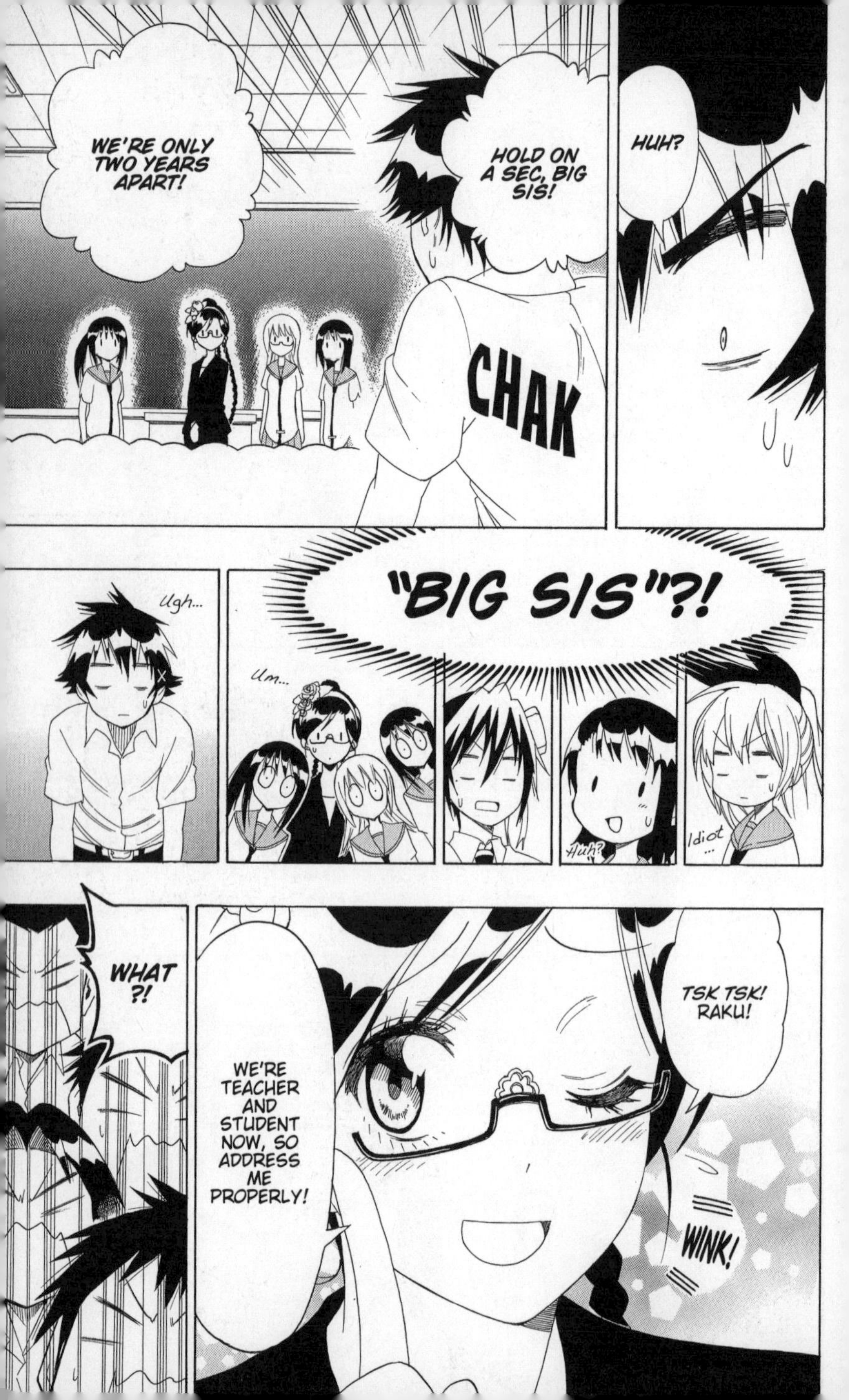
HUH?
HOLD ON A SEC, BIG SIS!
CHAK
WE'RE ONLY TWO YEARS APART!
"BIG SIS"?!
Idiot...
Huh?
Um...
Ugh...
TSK TSK! RAKU!
WE'RE TEACHER AND STUDENT NOW, SO ADDRESS ME PROPERLY!
WINK!
WHAT?!

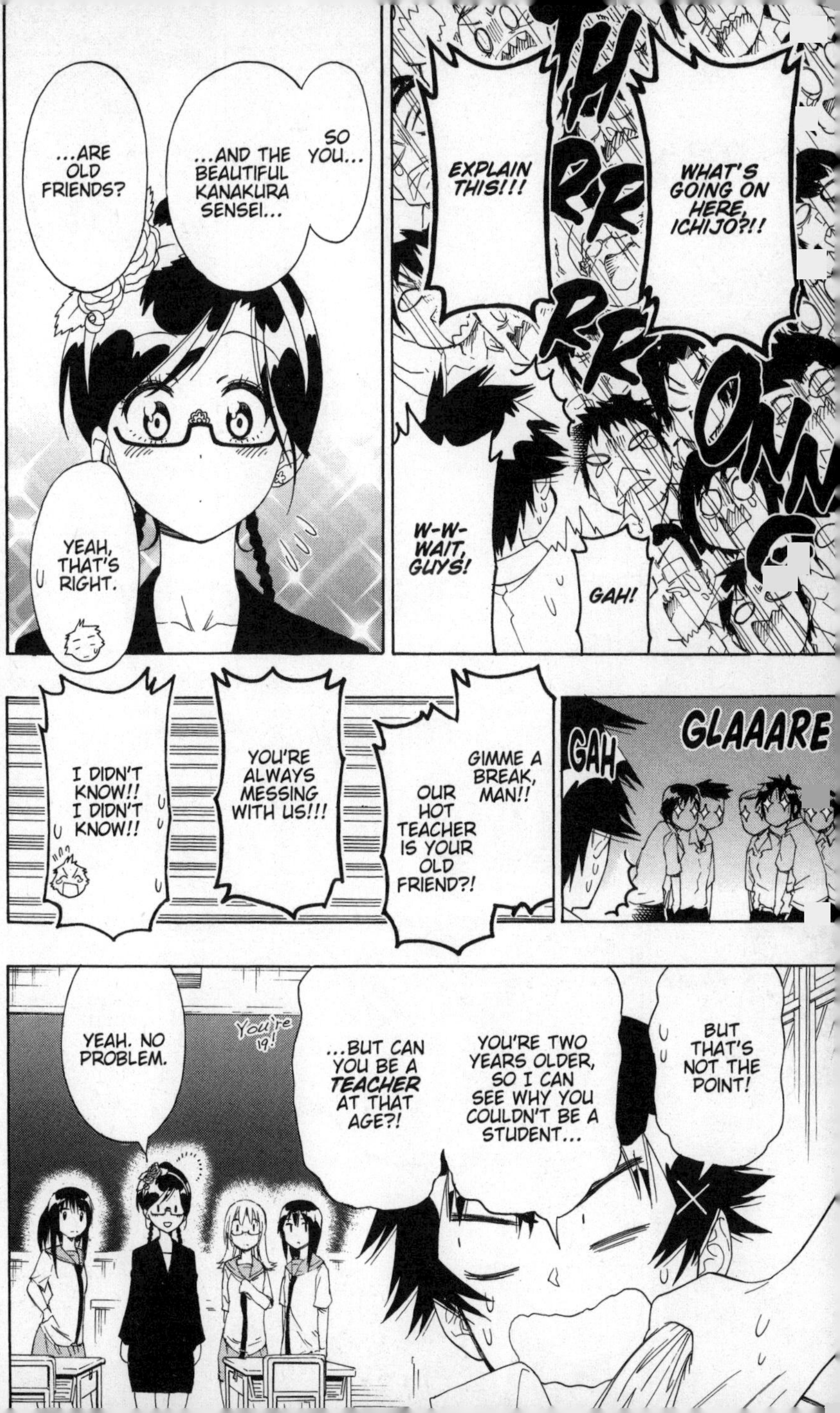
WHAT'S GOING ON HERE, ICHIJO?!!
EXPLAIN THIS!!!
GAH!
W-W-WAIT, GUYS!
SO YOU...
...AND THE BEAUTIFUL KANAKURA SENSEI...
...ARE OLD FRIENDS?
YEAH, THAT'S RIGHT.
GLAAARE
GAH
GIMME A BREAK, MAN!!
OUR HOT TEACHER IS YOUR OLD FRIEND?!
YOU'RE ALWAYS MESSING WITH US!!!
I DIDN'T KNOW!! I DIDN'T KNOW!!
BUT THAT'S NOT THE POINT!
YOU'RE TWO YEARS OLDER, SO I CAN SEE WHY YOU COULDN'T BE A STUDENT...
...BUT CAN YOU BE A TEACHER AT THAT AGE?!
You're 19!
YEAH. NO PROBLEM.

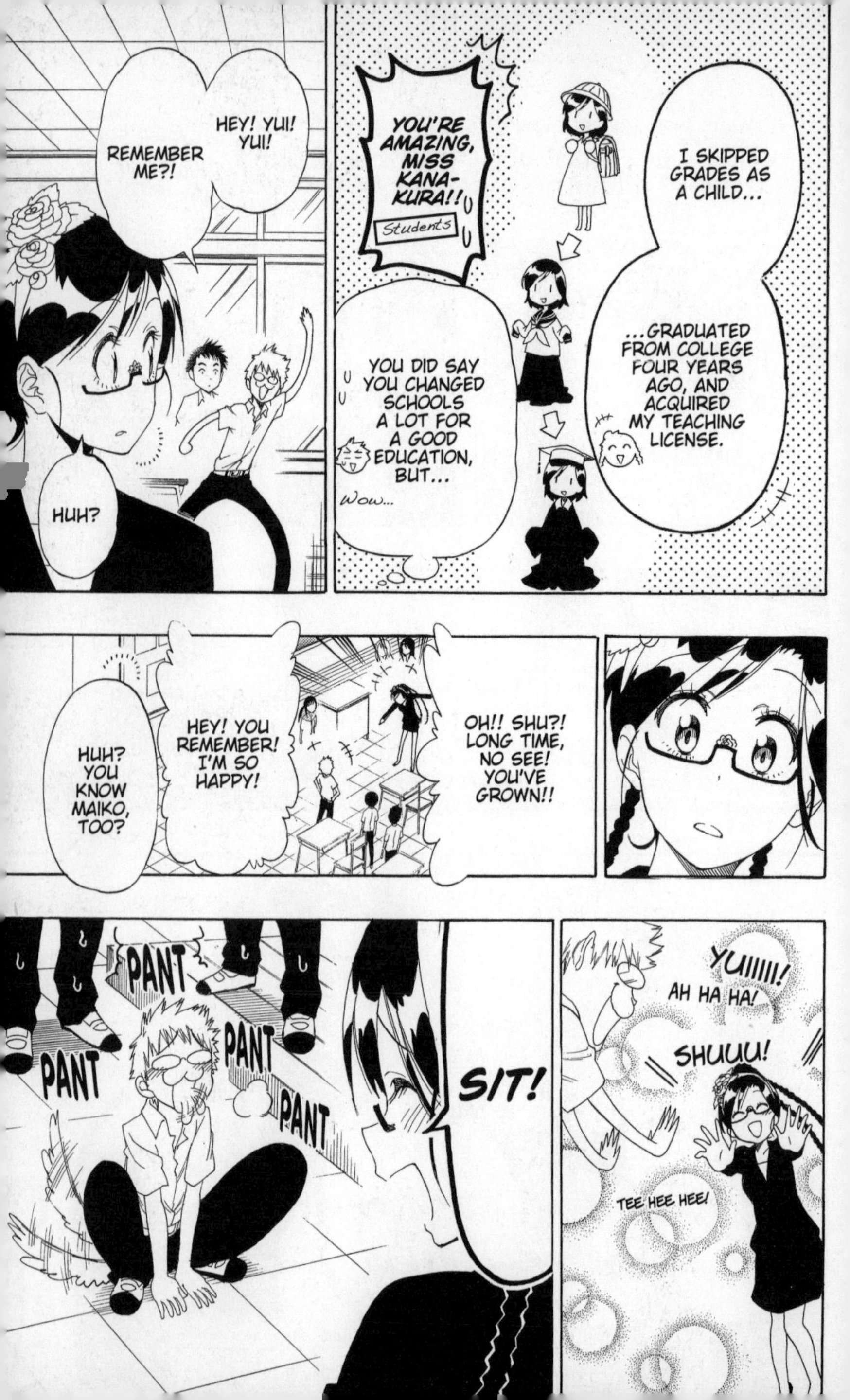
I SKIPPED GRADES AS A CHILD...
...GRADUATED FROM COLLEGE FOUR YEARS AGO, AND ACQUIRED MY TEACHING LICENSE.
YOU'RE AMAZING, MISS KANA-KURA!!
Students
YOU DID SAY YOU CHANGED SCHOOLS A LOT FOR A GOOD EDUCATION, BUT...
Wow...
HEY! YUI! YUI!
REMEMBER ME?!
HUH?
OH!! SHU?! LONG TIME, NO SEE! YOU'VE GROWN!!
HEY! YOU REMEMBER! I'M SO HAPPY!
HUH? YOU KNOW MAIKO, TOO?
YUIIIII!
AH HA HA!
SHUUU!
TEE HEE HEE!
SIT!
PANT
PANT
PANT
PANT

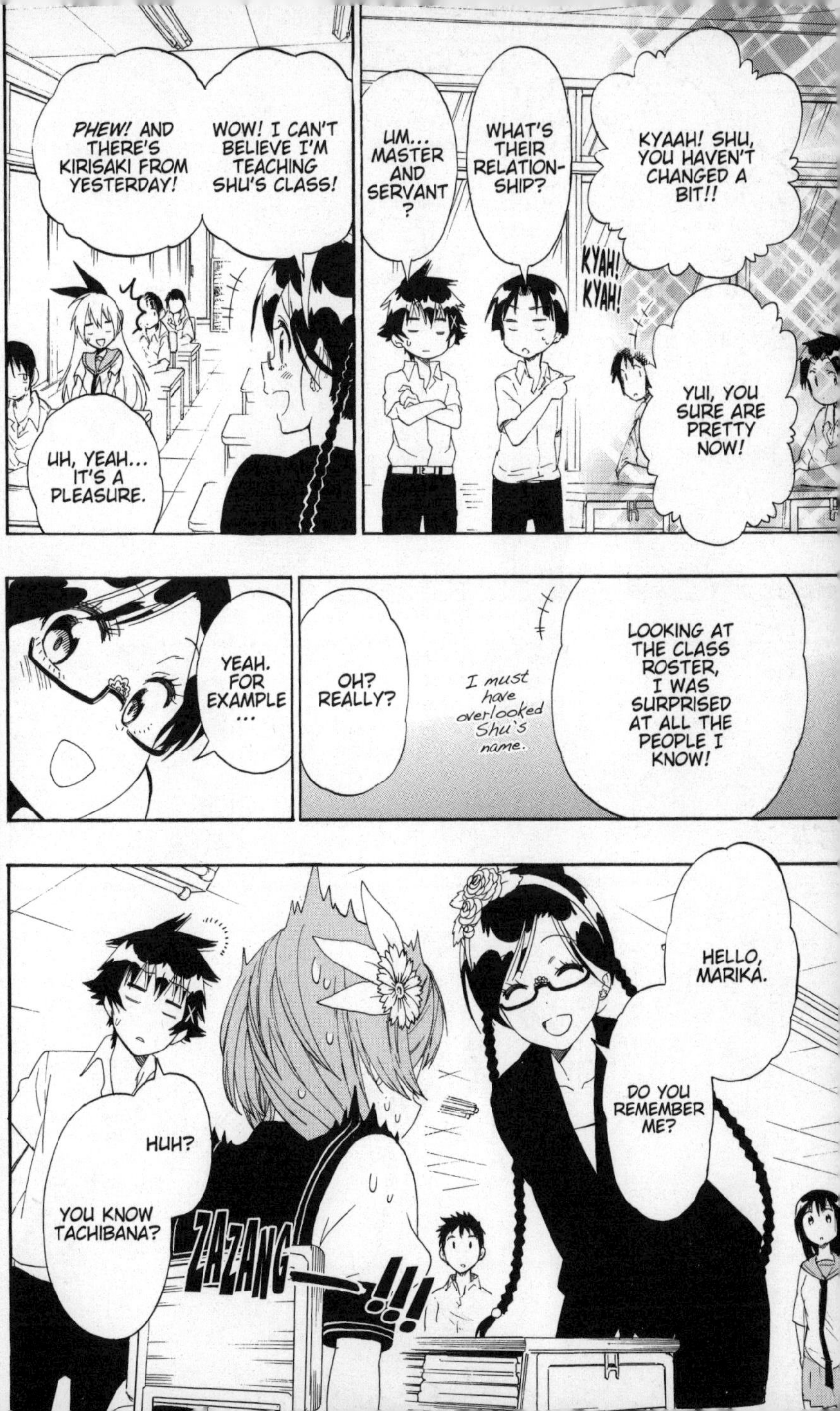
KYAAH! SHU, YOU HAVEN'T CHANGED A BIT!!
KYAH! KYAH!
YUI, YOU SURE ARE PRETTY NOW!
WHAT'S THEIR RELATION-SHIP?
UM... MASTER AND SERVANT?
WOW! I CAN'T BELIEVE I'M TEACHING SHU'S CLASS!
PHEW! AND THERE'S KIRISAKI FROM YESTERDAY!
UH, YEAH... IT'S A PLEASURE.
LOOKING AT THE CLASS ROSTER, I WAS SURPRISED AT ALL THE PEOPLE I KNOW!
I must have overlooked Shu's name.
OH? REALLY?
YEAH. FOR EXAMPLE...
HELLO, MARIKA.
DO YOU REMEMBER ME?
ZAZANG
!!!
HUH?
YOU KNOW TACHIBANA?

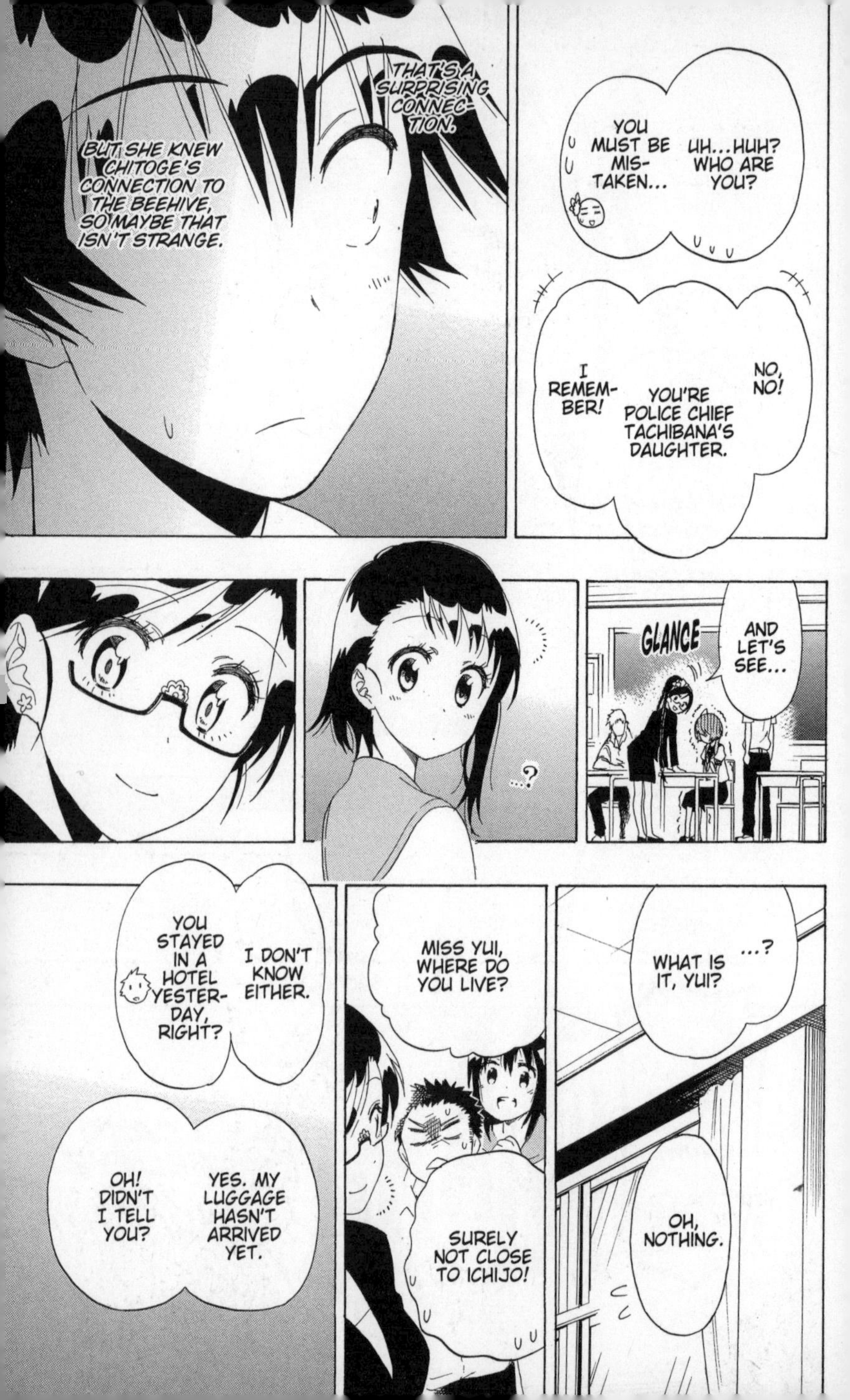
UH...HUH? WHO ARE YOU?
YOU MUST BE MIS-TAKEN...
NO, NO!
YOU'RE POLICE CHIEF TACHIBANA'S DAUGHTER.
I REMEM-BER!
THAT'S A SURPRISING CONNEC-TION.
BUT SHE KNEW CHITOGE'S CONNECTION TO THE BEEHIVE, SO MAYBE THAT ISN'T STRANGE.
AND LET'S SEE...
GLANCE
...?
...?
WHAT IS IT, YUI?
OH, NOTHING.
MISS YUI, WHERE DO YOU LIVE?
SURELY NOT CLOSE TO ICHIJO!
I DON'T KNOW EITHER.
YOU STAYED IN A HOTEL YESTER-DAY, RIGHT?
YES. MY LUGGAGE HASN'T ARRIVED YET.
OH! DIDN'T I TELL YOU?

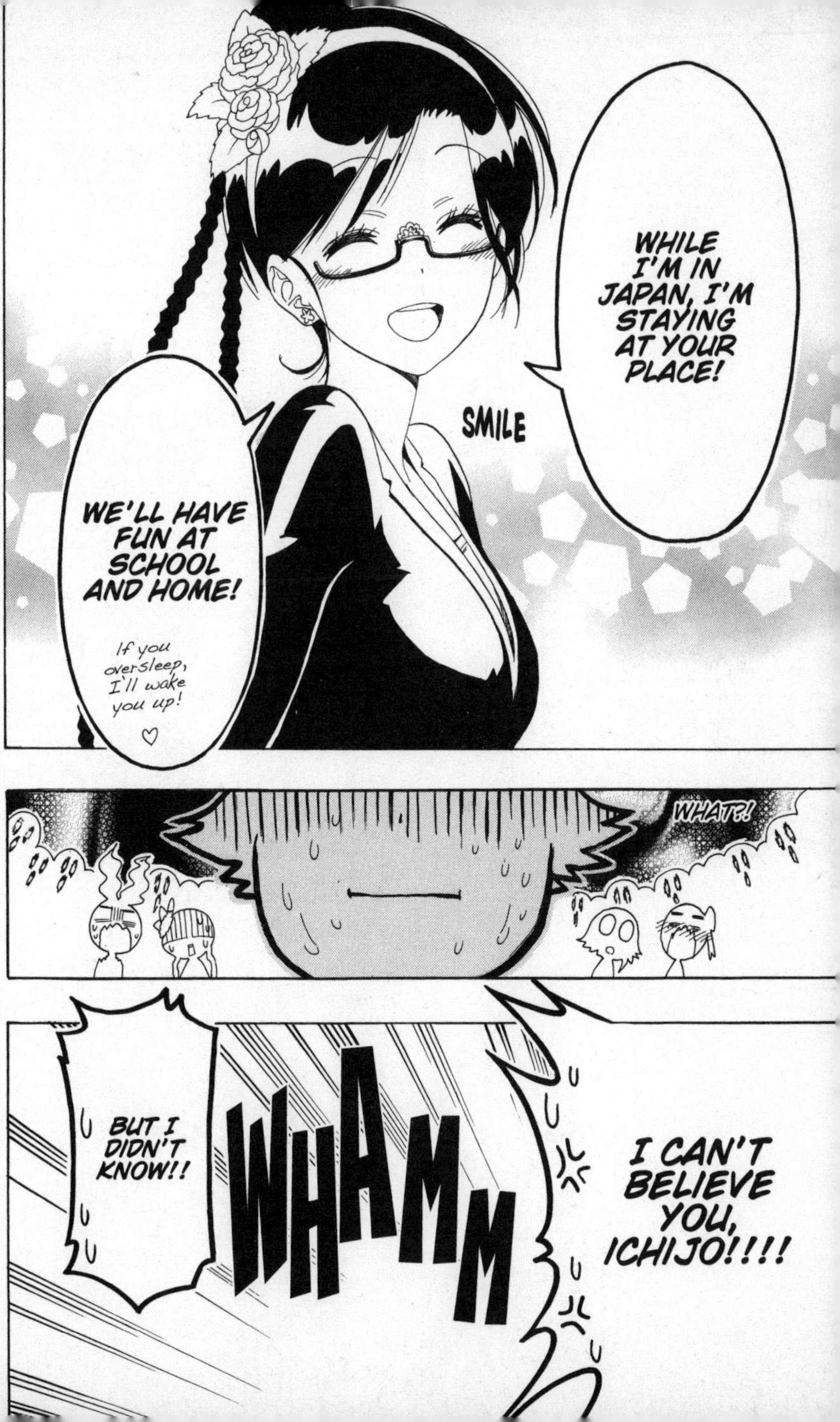
WHILE I'M IN JAPAN, I'M STAYING AT YOUR PLACE!
SMILE
WE'LL HAVE FUN AT SCHOOL AND HOME!
If you oversleep, I'll wake you up! ♡
WHAT?!
I CAN'T BELIEVE YOU, ICHIJO!!!!
WHAMM
BUT I DIDN'T KNOW!!

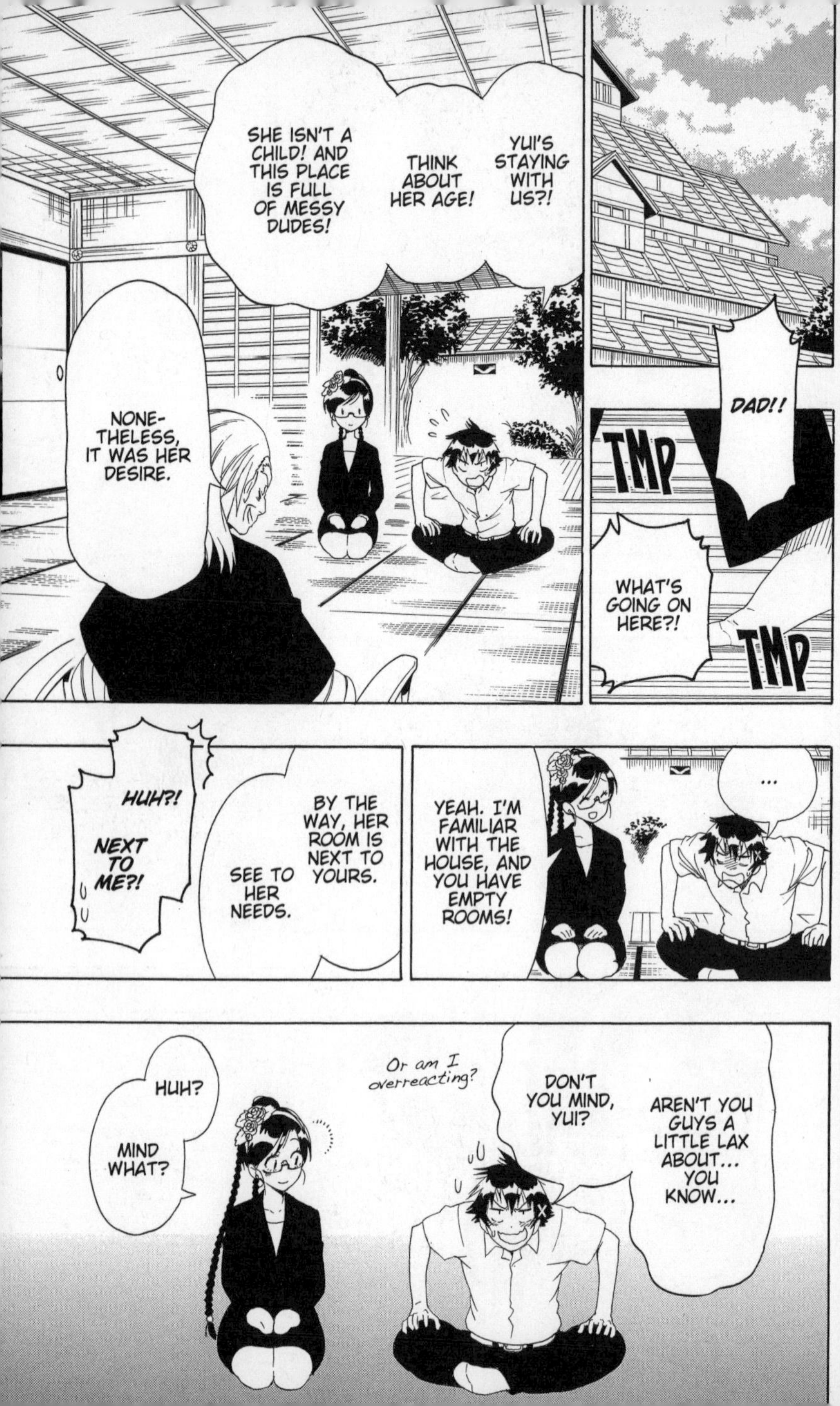
DAD!!
TMP
WHAT'S GOING ON HERE?!
TMP
YUI'S STAYING WITH US?!
THINK ABOUT HER AGE!
SHE ISN'T A CHILD! AND THIS PLACE IS FULL OF MESSY DUDES!
NONE-THELESS, IT WAS HER DESIRE.
...
YEAH. I'M FAMILIAR WITH THE HOUSE, AND YOU HAVE EMPTY ROOMS!
BY THE WAY, HER ROOM IS NEXT TO YOURS.
SEE TO HER NEEDS.
HUH?! NEXT TO ME?!
AREN'T YOU GUYS A LITTLE LAX ABOUT... YOU KNOW...
DON'T YOU MIND, YUI?
Or am I overreacting?
HUH?
MIND WHAT?

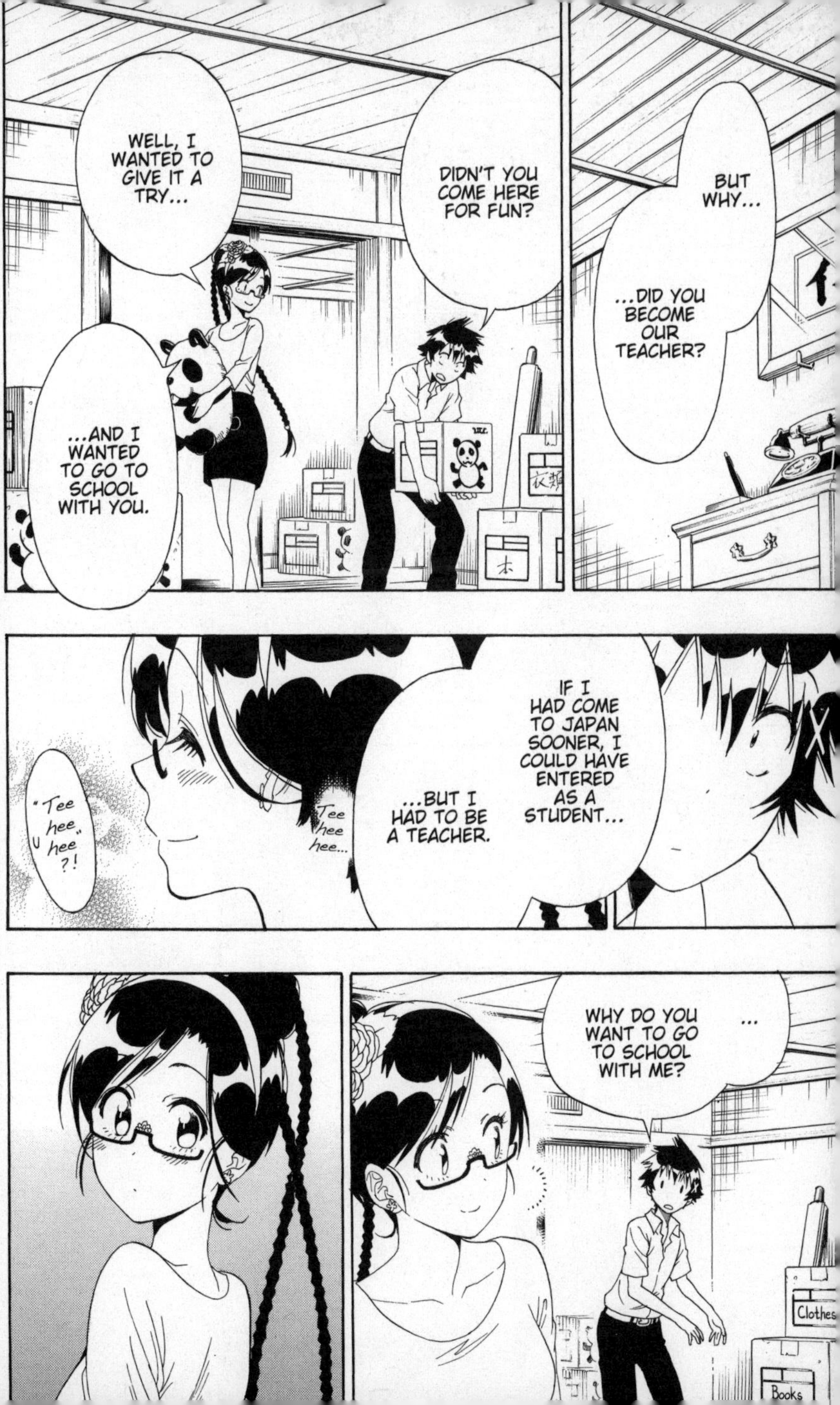
BUT WHY...
...DID YOU BECOME OUR TEACHER?
DIDN'T YOU COME HERE FOR FUN?
WELL, I WANTED TO GIVE IT A TRY...
...AND I WANTED TO GO TO SCHOOL WITH YOU.
衣類
本
IF I HAD COME TO JAPAN SOONER, I COULD HAVE ENTERED AS A STUDENT...
...BUT I HAD TO BE A TEACHER.
Tee hee hee...
"Tee hee hee"?!
...
WHY DO YOU WANT TO GO TO SCHOOL WITH ME?
Clothes
Books

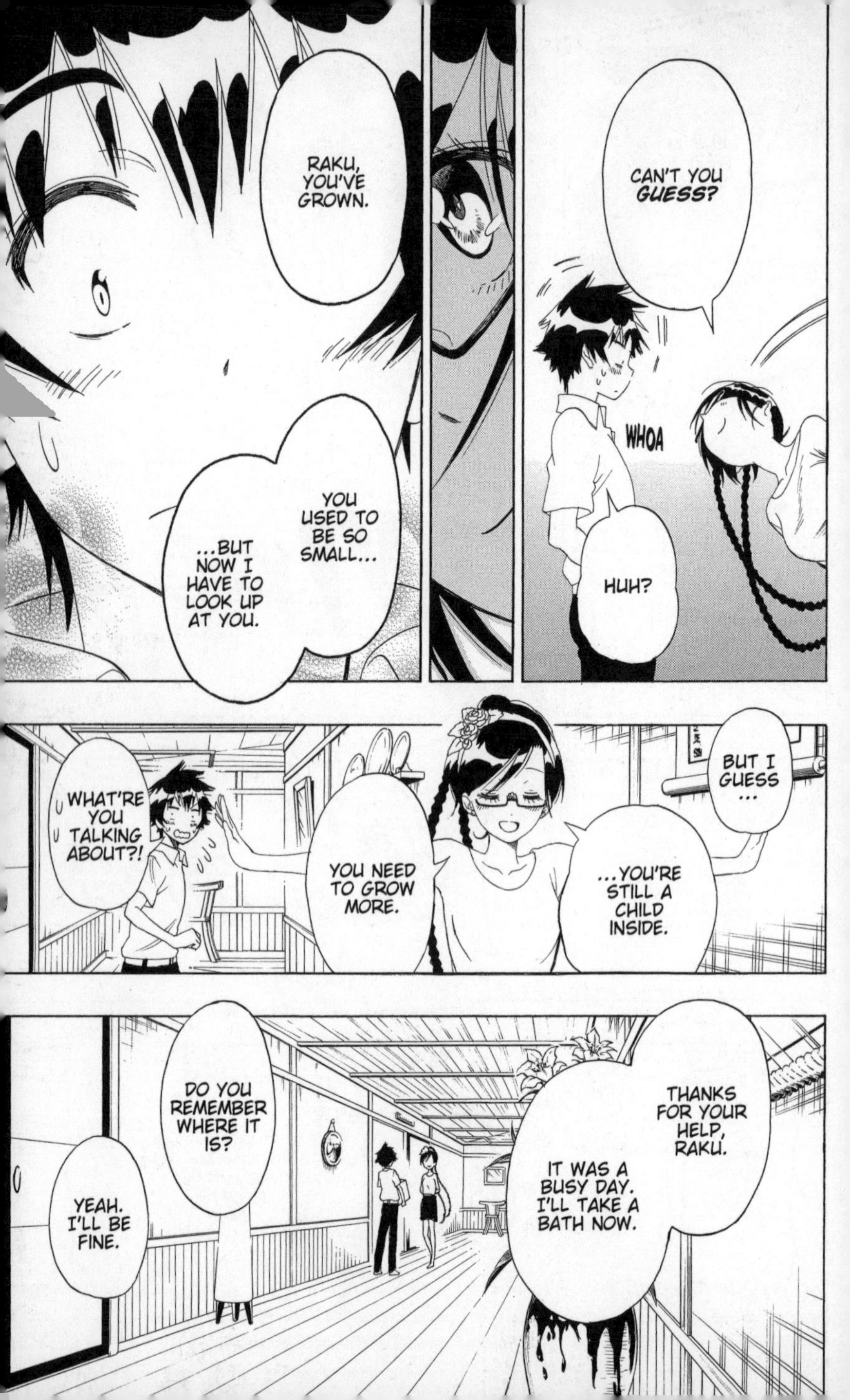
CAN'T YOU *GUESS?*
WHOA
HUH?
RAKU, YOU'VE GROWN.
YOU USED TO BE SO SMALL...
...BUT NOW I HAVE TO LOOK UP AT YOU.
BUT I GUESS...
...YOU'RE STILL A CHILD INSIDE.
YOU NEED TO GROW MORE.
WHAT'RE YOU TALKING ABOUT?!
THANKS FOR YOUR HELP, RAKU.
IT WAS A BUSY DAY. I'LL TAKE A BATH NOW.
DO YOU REMEMBER WHERE IT IS?
YEAH. I'LL BE FINE.

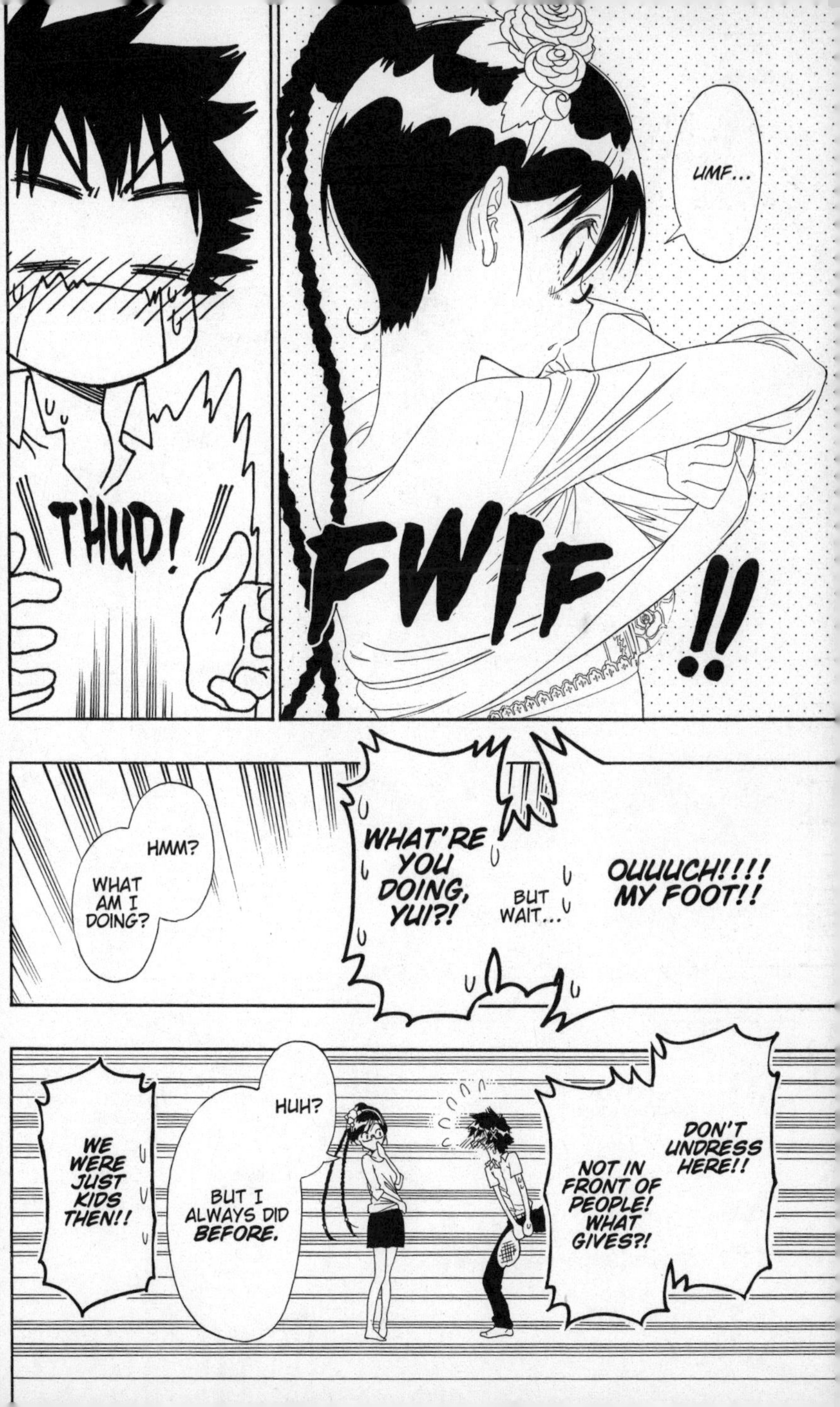
UMF...
FWIF!!
THUD!
OUUUCH!!!! MY FOOT!!
BUT WAIT...
WHAT'RE YOU DOING, YUI?!
HMM?
WHAT AM I DOING?
DON'T UNDRESS HERE!!
NOT IN FRONT OF PEOPLE! WHAT GIVES?!
HUH?
BUT I ALWAYS DID BEFORE.
WE WERE JUST KIDS THEN!!

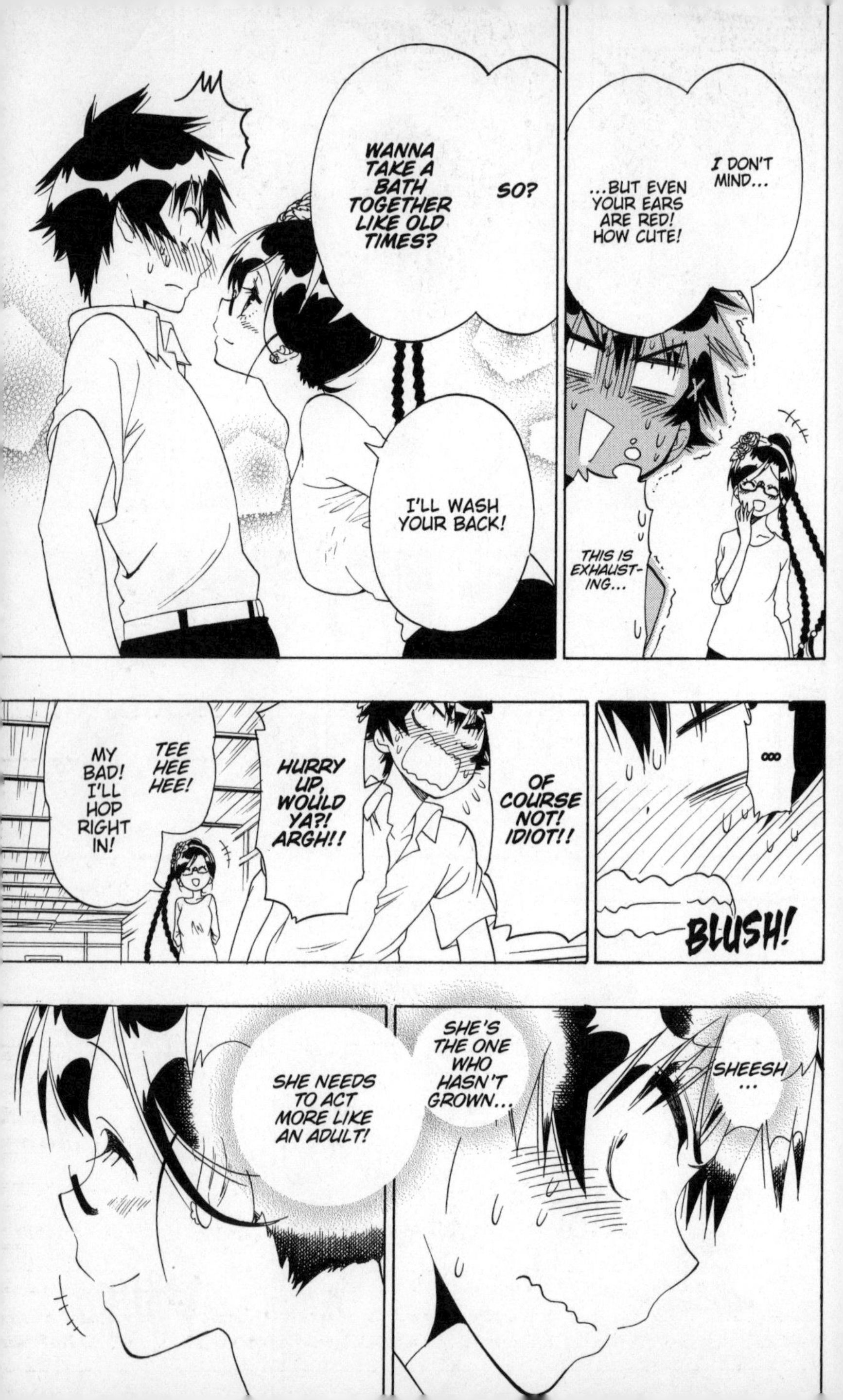
I DON'T MIND...
...BUT EVEN YOUR EARS ARE RED! HOW CUTE!
THIS IS EXHAUSTING...
SO?
WANNA TAKE A BATH TOGETHER LIKE OLD TIMES?
I'LL WASH YOUR BACK!
...
BLUSH!
OF COURSE NOT! IDIOT!!
HURRY UP, WOULD YA?! ARGH!!
TEE HEE HEE!
MY BAD! I'LL HOP RIGHT IN!
SHEESH...
SHE'S THE ONE WHO HASN'T GROWN...
SHE NEEDS TO ACT MORE LIKE AN ADULT!

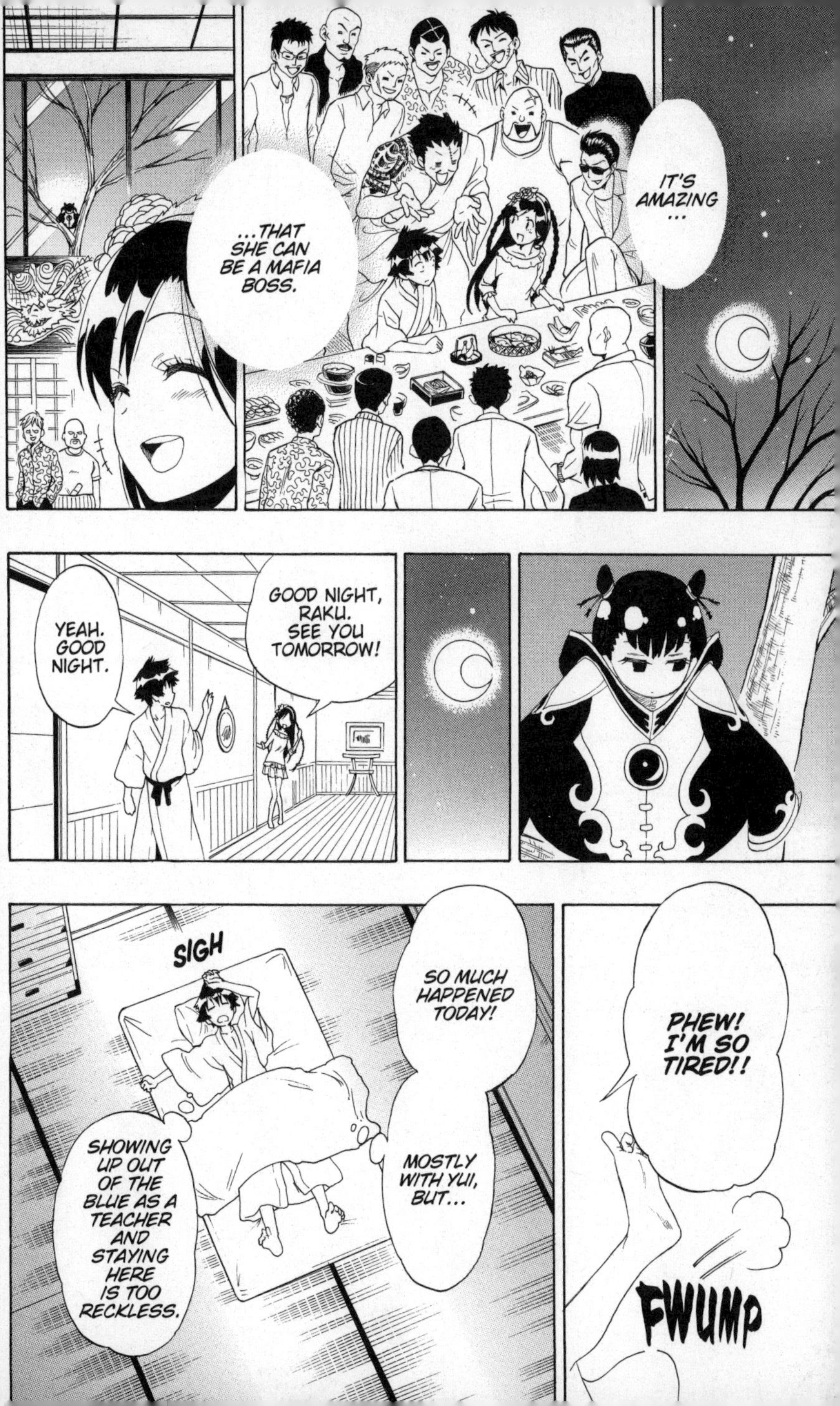
IT'S AMAZING...
...THAT SHE CAN BE A MAFIA BOSS.
GOOD NIGHT, RAKU. SEE YOU TOMORROW!
YEAH. GOOD NIGHT.
PHEW! I'M SO TIRED!!
FWUMP
SO MUCH HAPPENED TODAY!
SIGH
MOSTLY WITH YUI, BUT...
SHOWING UP OUT OF THE BLUE AS A TEACHER AND STAYING HERE IS TOO RECKLESS.

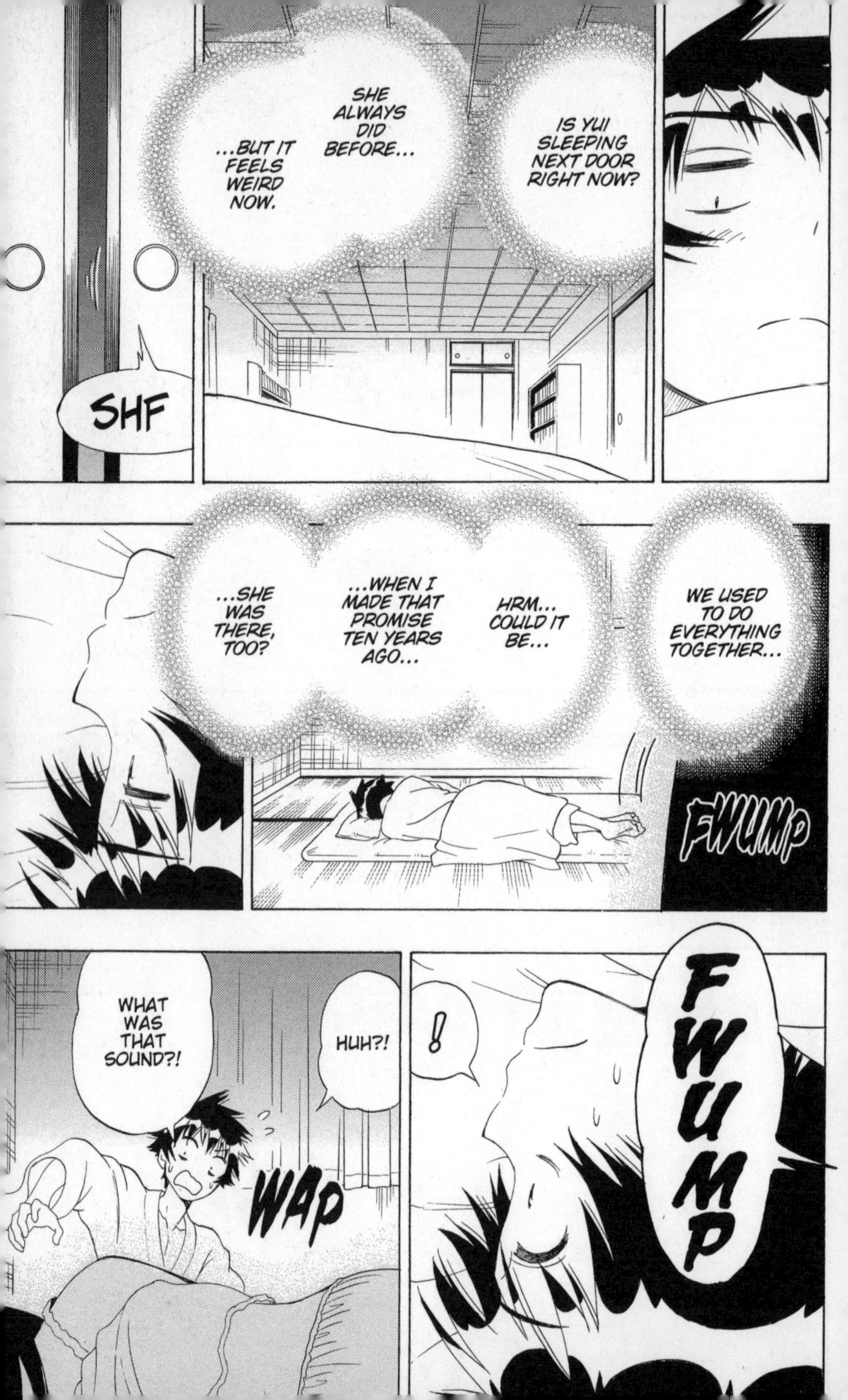
IS YUI SLEEPING NEXT DOOR RIGHT NOW?
SHE ALWAYS DID BEFORE…
…BUT IT FEELS WEIRD NOW.
SHF
WE USED TO DO EVERYTHING TOGETHER…
FWUMP
HRM… COULD IT BE…
…WHEN I MADE THAT PROMISE TEN YEARS AGO…
…SHE WAS THERE, TOO?
FWUMP
!
HUH?!
WHAT WAS THAT SOUND?!
WAP

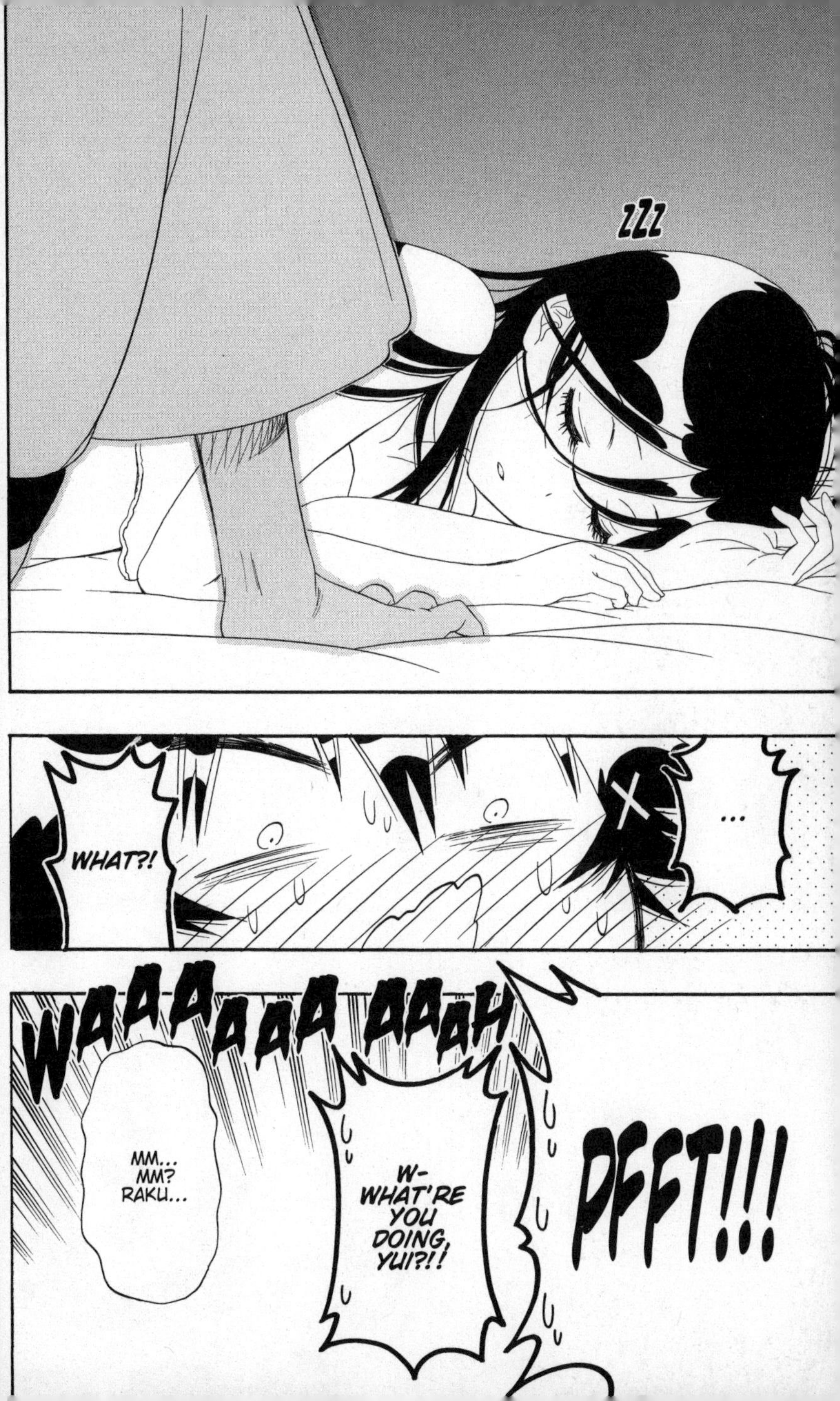
ZZZ
...
WHAT?!
PFFT!!!
WAAAAAAAA AAAH
W-WHAT'RE YOU DOING, YUI?!!
MM... MM? RAKU...

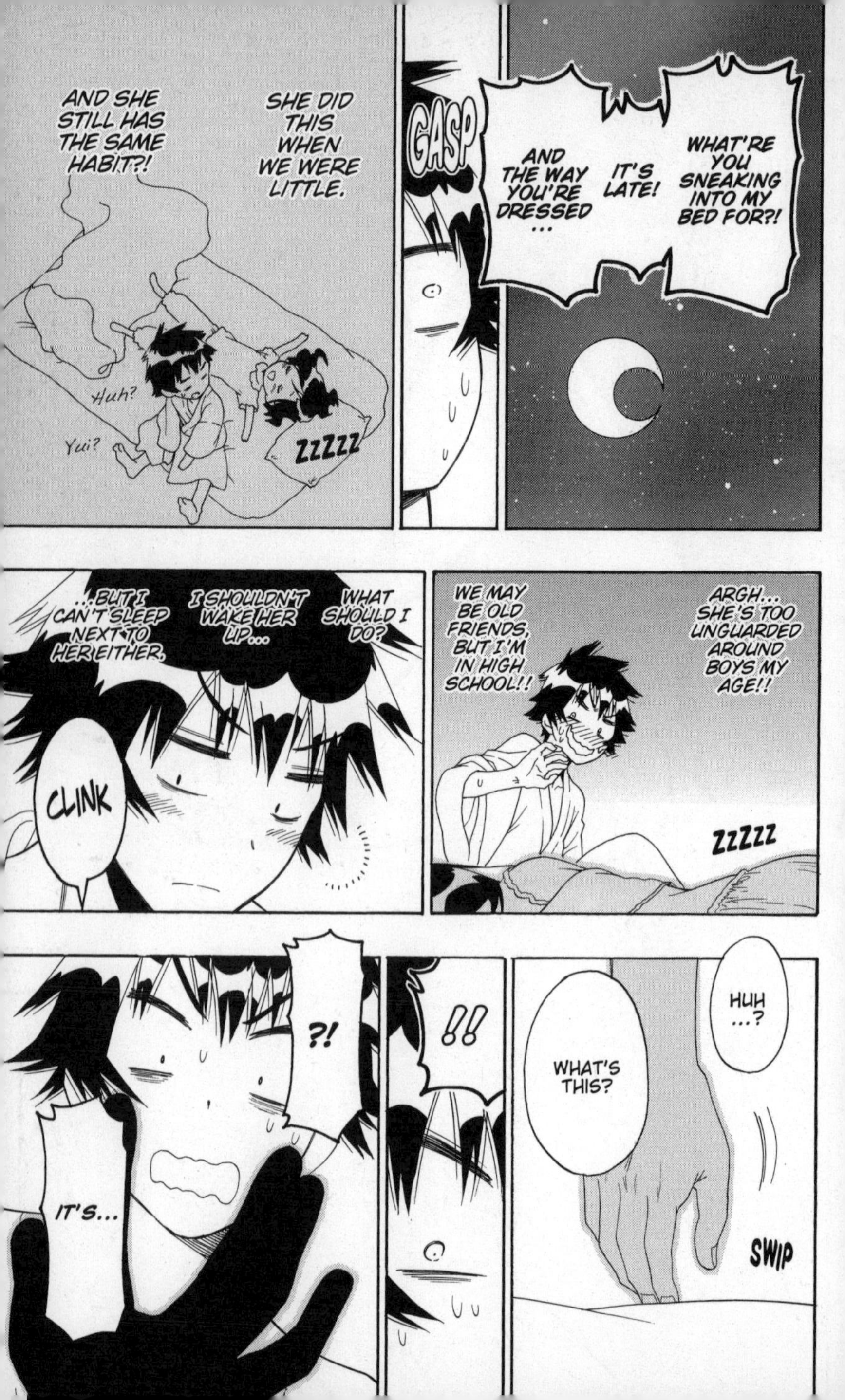
WHAT'RE YOU SNEAKING INTO MY BED FOR?!
IT'S LATE!
AND THE WAY YOU'RE DRESSED...
GASP
SHE DID THIS WHEN WE WERE LITTLE.
AND SHE STILL HAS THE SAME HABIT?!
Huh?
Yui?
ZZZZZ
ARGH... SHE'S TOO UNGUARDED AROUND BOYS MY AGE!!
WE MAY BE OLD FRIENDS, BUT I'M IN HIGH SCHOOL!!
ZZZZZ
WHAT SHOULD I DO?
I SHOULDN'T WAKE HER UP...
...BUT I CAN'T SLEEP NEXT TO HER EITHER.
CLINK
HUH...?
WHAT'S THIS?
SWIP
!!
?!
IT'S...

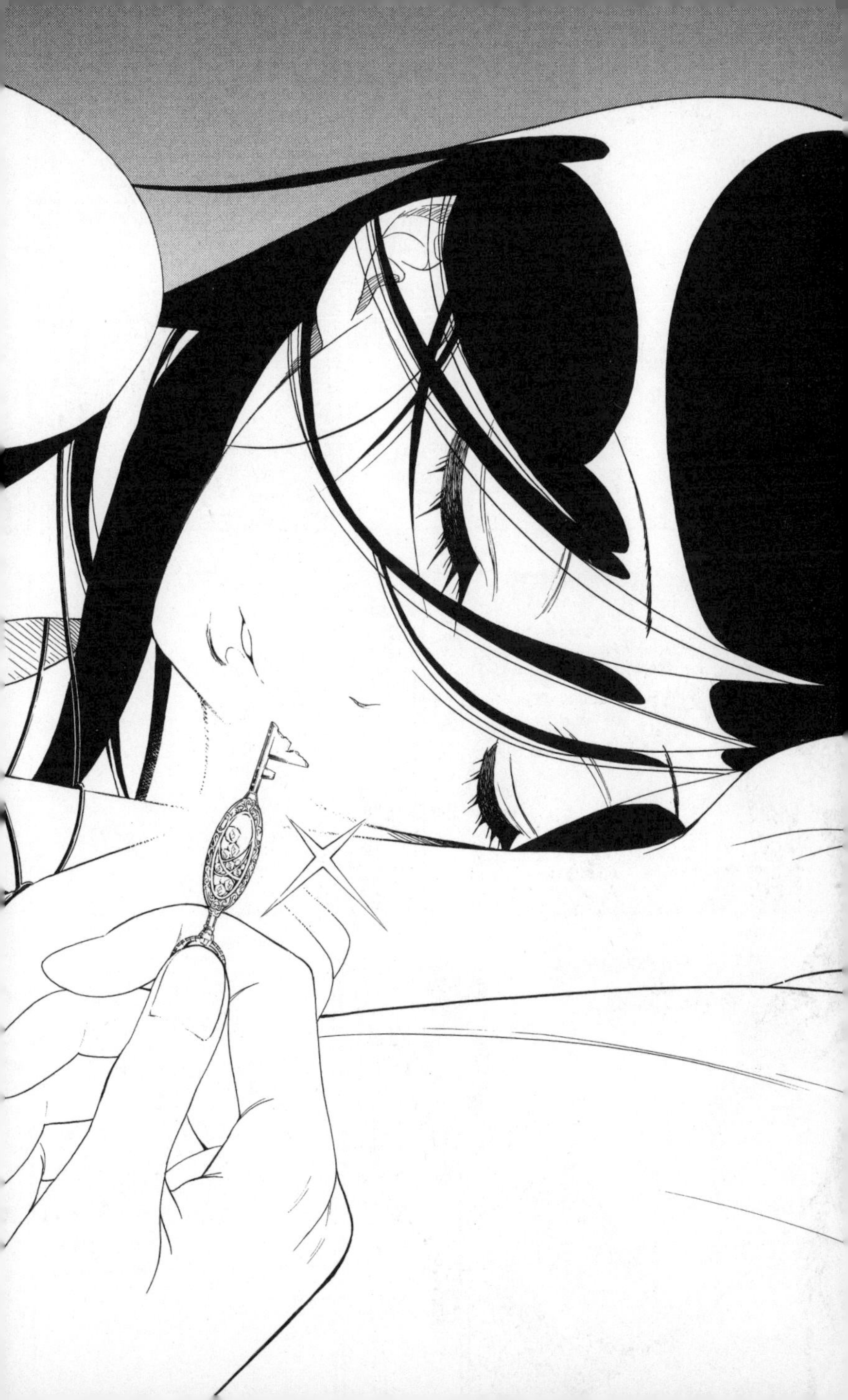

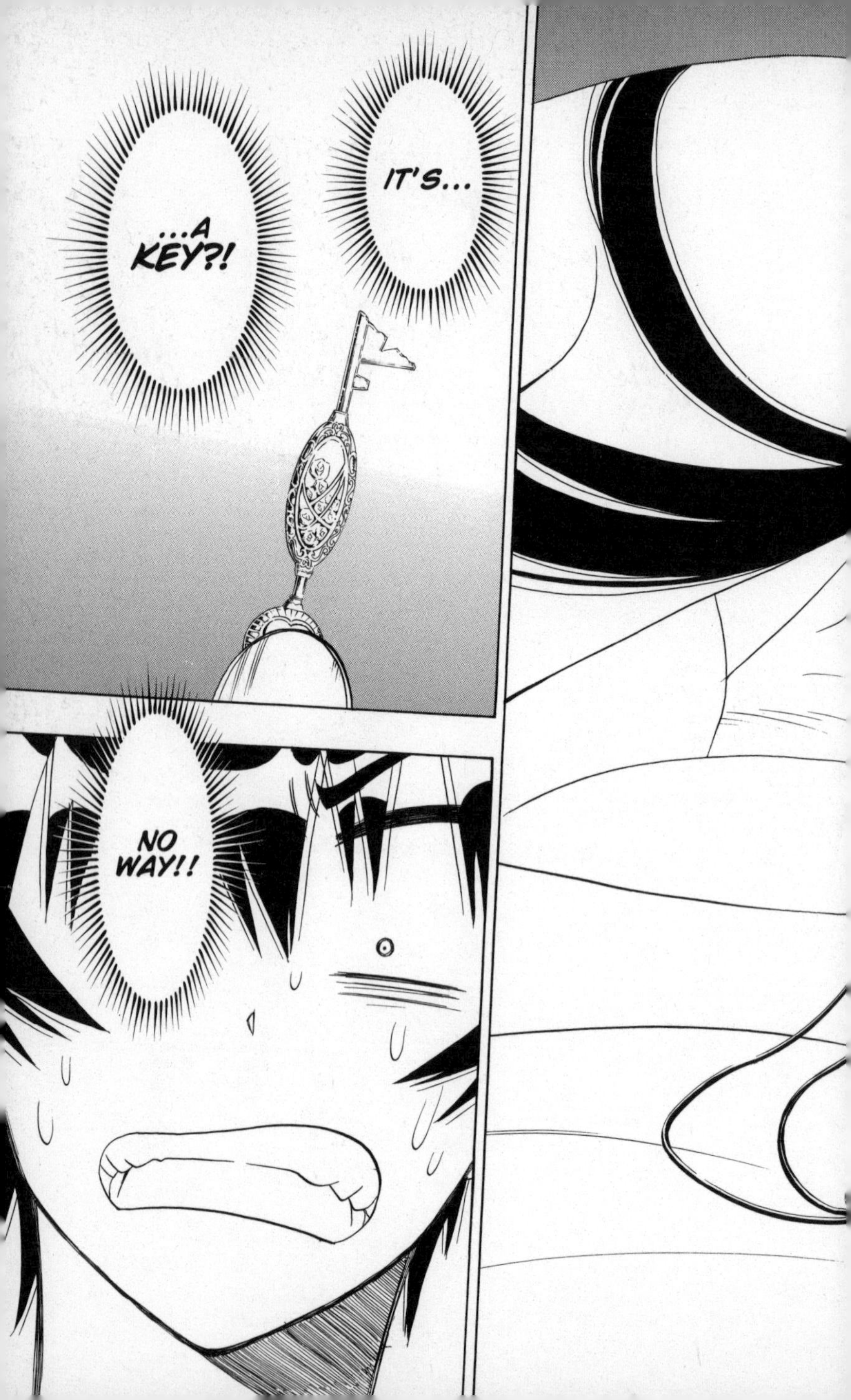
IT'S...
...A KEY?!
NO WAY!!

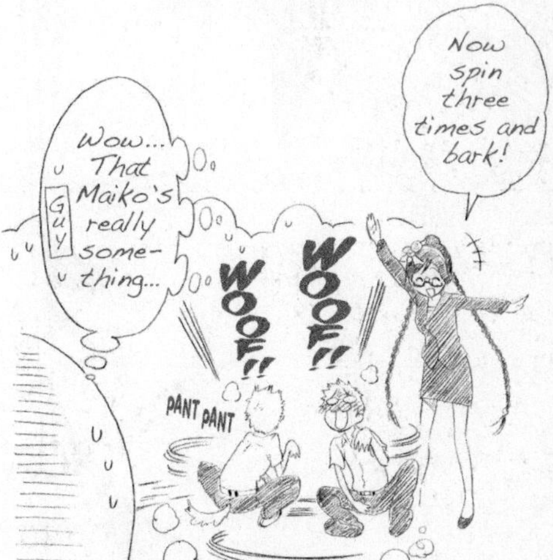
Now spin three times and bark!
WOOF!!
WOOF!!
Wow... That Maiko's really something...
GUY
PANT PANT
WHRR WHRR

Chapter 120: Need to Know

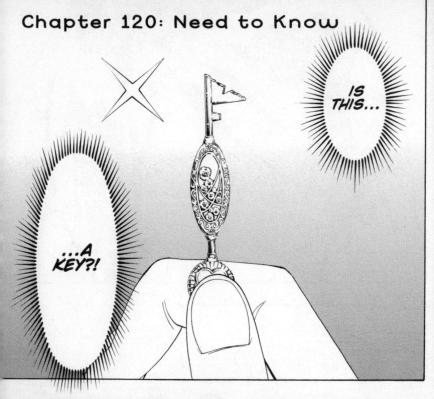

IS THIS...
...A KEY?!
WHAT DOES THIS MEAN?!
B-BMP
B-BMP
IT'S BROKEN AT THE TIP, BUT IT LOOKS ABOUT THE RIGHT SIZE FOR MY PENDANT LOCK...
COULD IT BE ...?!
HER TOO?!
ZZZZ
CHIRP
CHIRP

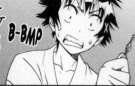

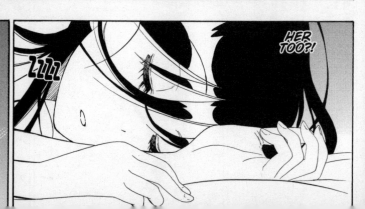

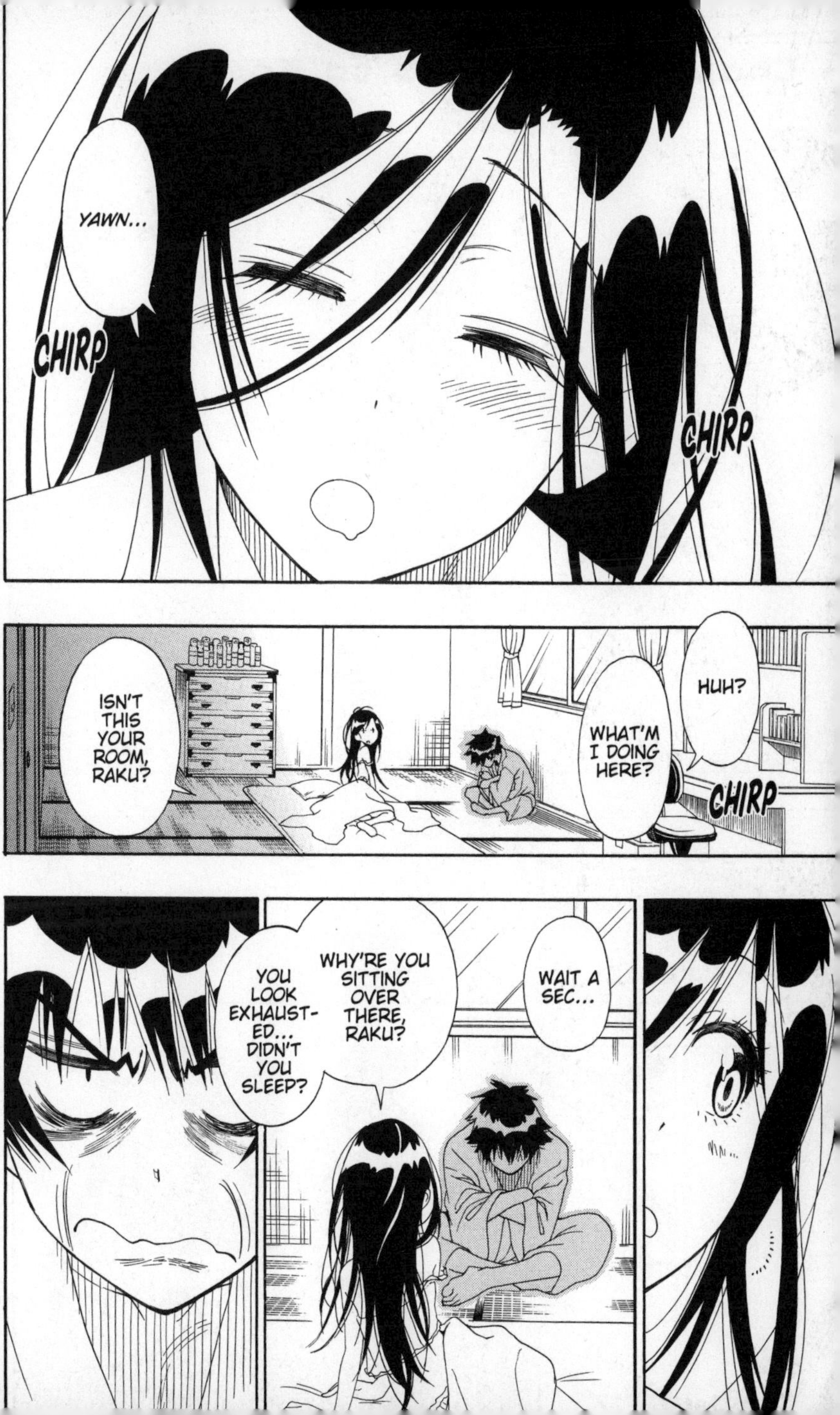
YAWN...
CHIRP
CHIRP
HUH?
WHAT'M I DOING HERE?
CHIRP
ISN'T THIS YOUR ROOM, RAKU?
WAIT A SEC...
WHY'RE YOU SITTING OVER THERE, RAKU?
YOU LOOK EXHAUSTED... DIDN'T YOU SLEEP?

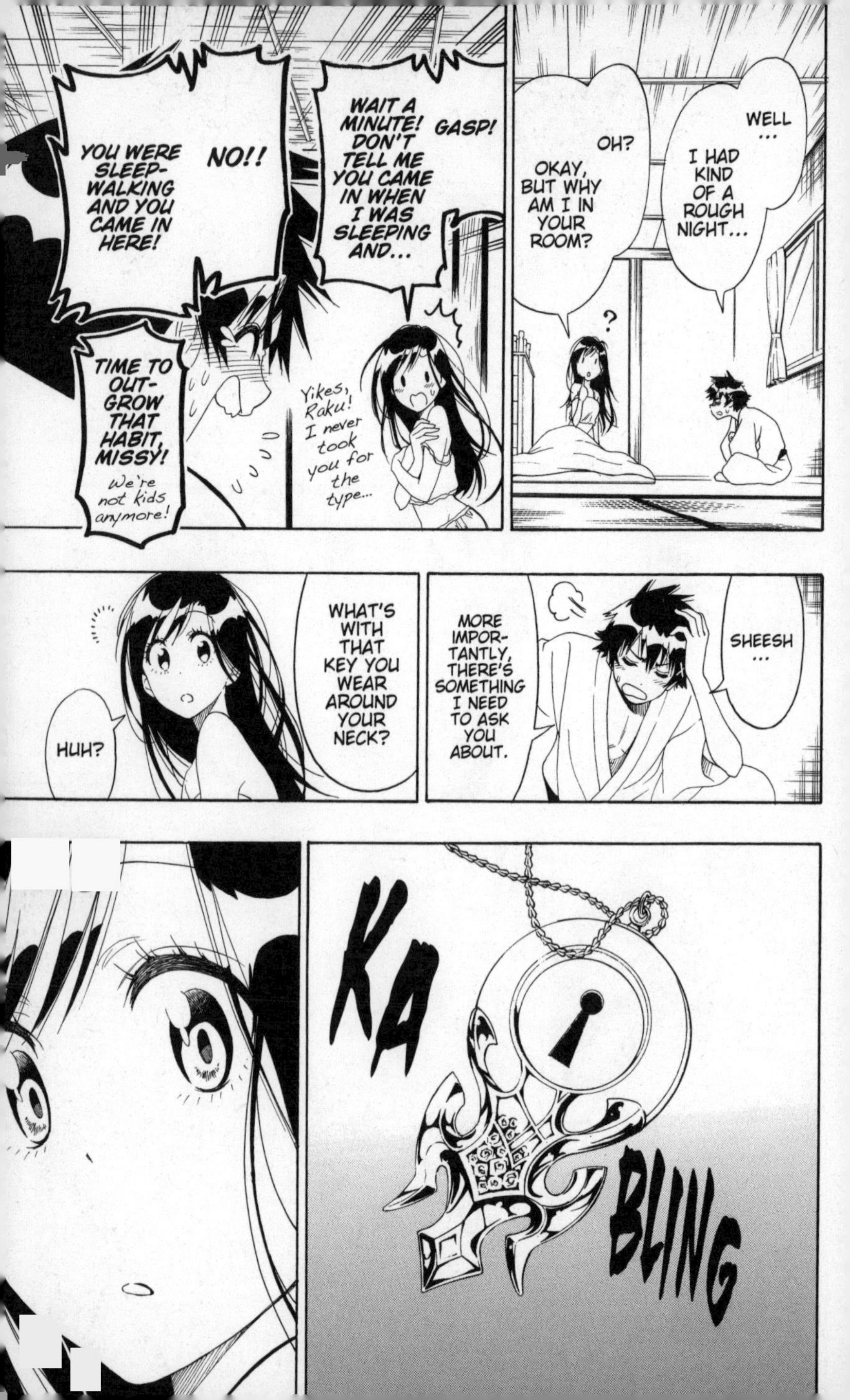
WELL... I HAD KIND OF A ROUGH NIGHT...
OH?
OKAY, BUT WHY AM I IN YOUR ROOM?
?
GASP!
WAIT A MINUTE! DON'T TELL ME YOU CAME IN WHEN I WAS SLEEPING AND...
Yikes, Raku! I never took you for the type...
NO!!
YOU WERE SLEEP-WALKING AND YOU CAME IN HERE!
TIME TO OUT-GROW THAT HABIT, MISSY!
We're not kids anymore!
SHEESH...
MORE IMPOR-TANTLY, THERE'S SOMETHING I NEED TO ASK YOU ABOUT.
WHAT'S WITH THAT KEY YOU WEAR AROUND YOUR NECK?
HUH?
KA
BLING

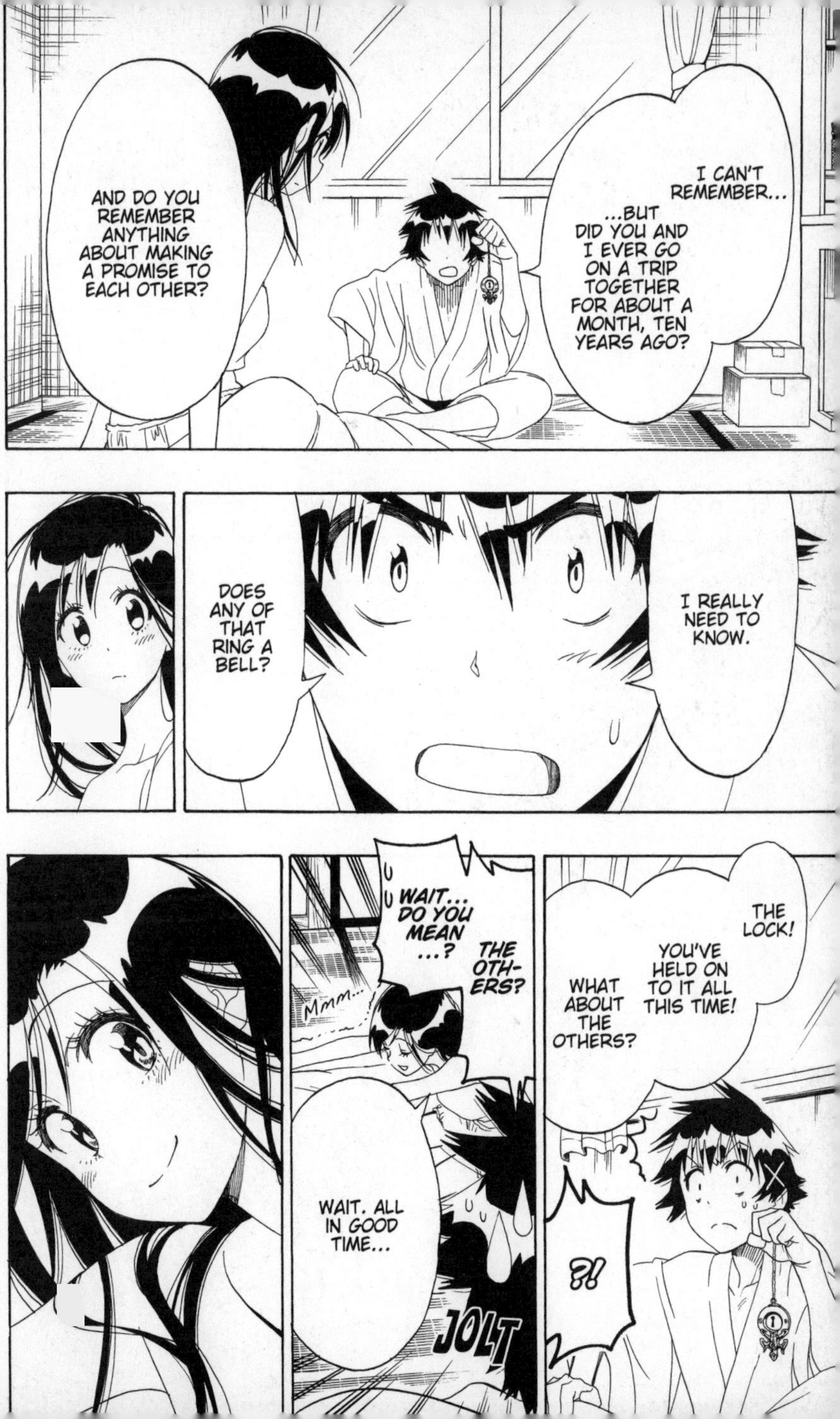
I CAN'T REMEMBER... ...BUT DID YOU AND I EVER GO ON A TRIP TOGETHER FOR ABOUT A MONTH, TEN YEARS AGO?
AND DO YOU REMEMBER ANYTHING ABOUT MAKING A PROMISE TO EACH OTHER?
I REALLY NEED TO KNOW.
DOES ANY OF THAT RING A BELL?
THE LOCK!
YOU'VE HELD ON TO IT ALL THIS TIME!
WHAT ABOUT THE OTHERS?
?!
THE OTH-ERS?
WAIT... DO YOU MEAN ...?
Mmm...
WAIT. ALL IN GOOD TIME...
JOLT

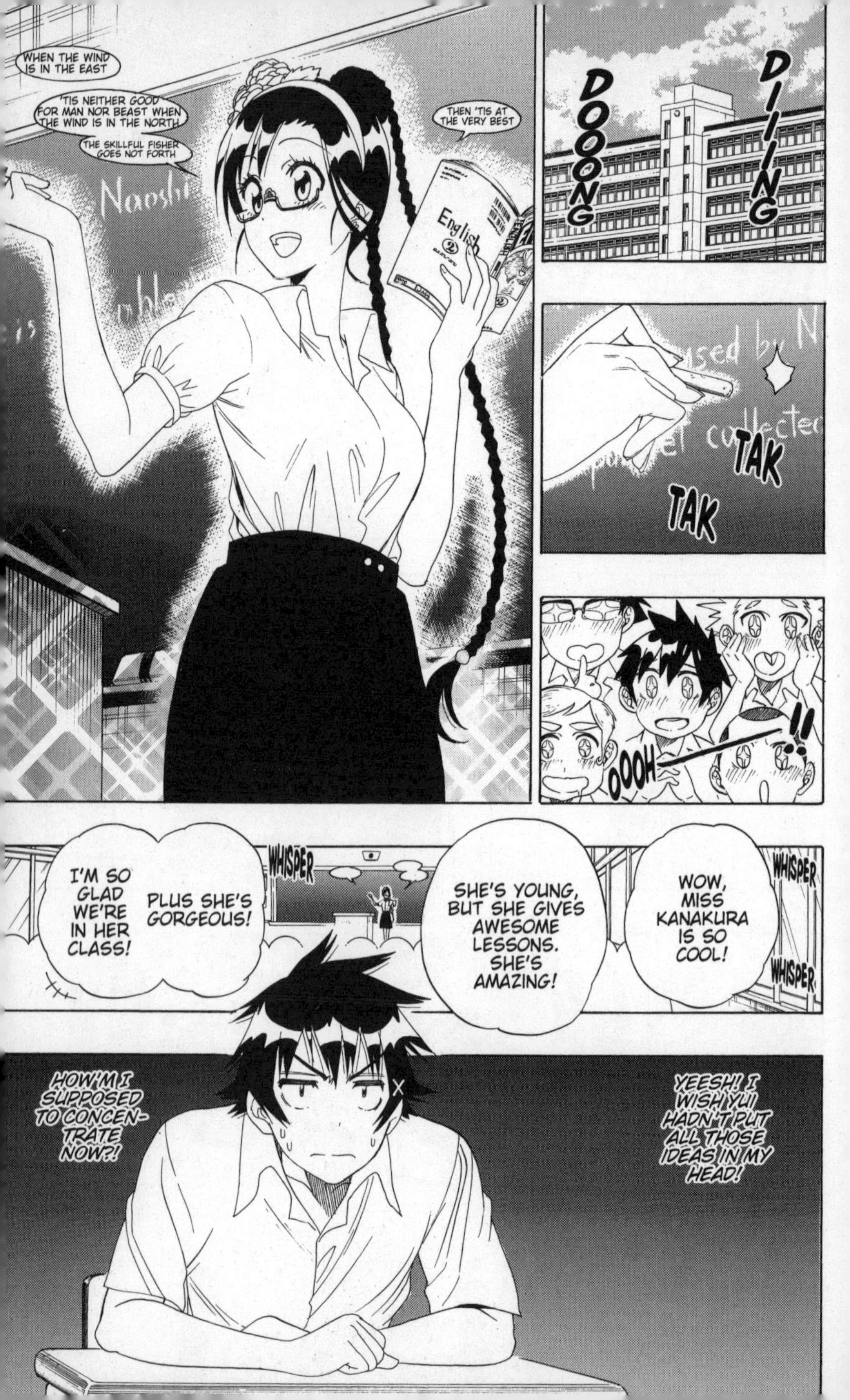
DIIING
DOOONG
TAK
TAK
!!
OOOH
WHEN THE WIND IS IN THE EAST
'TIS NEITHER GOOD FOR MAN NOR BEAST WHEN THE WIND IS IN THE NORTH
THE SKILLFUL FISHER GOES NOT FORTH
THEN 'TIS AT THE VERY BEST
WHISPER
WHISPER
WOW, MISS KANAKURA IS SO COOL!
SHE'S YOUNG, BUT SHE GIVES AWESOME LESSONS. SHE'S AMAZING!
WHISPER
PLUS SHE'S GORGEOUS!
I'M SO GLAD WE'RE IN HER CLASS!
YEESH! I WISH YUI HADN'T PUT ALL THOSE IDEAS IN MY HEAD!
HOW'M I SUPPOSED TO CONCEN-TRATE NOW?!

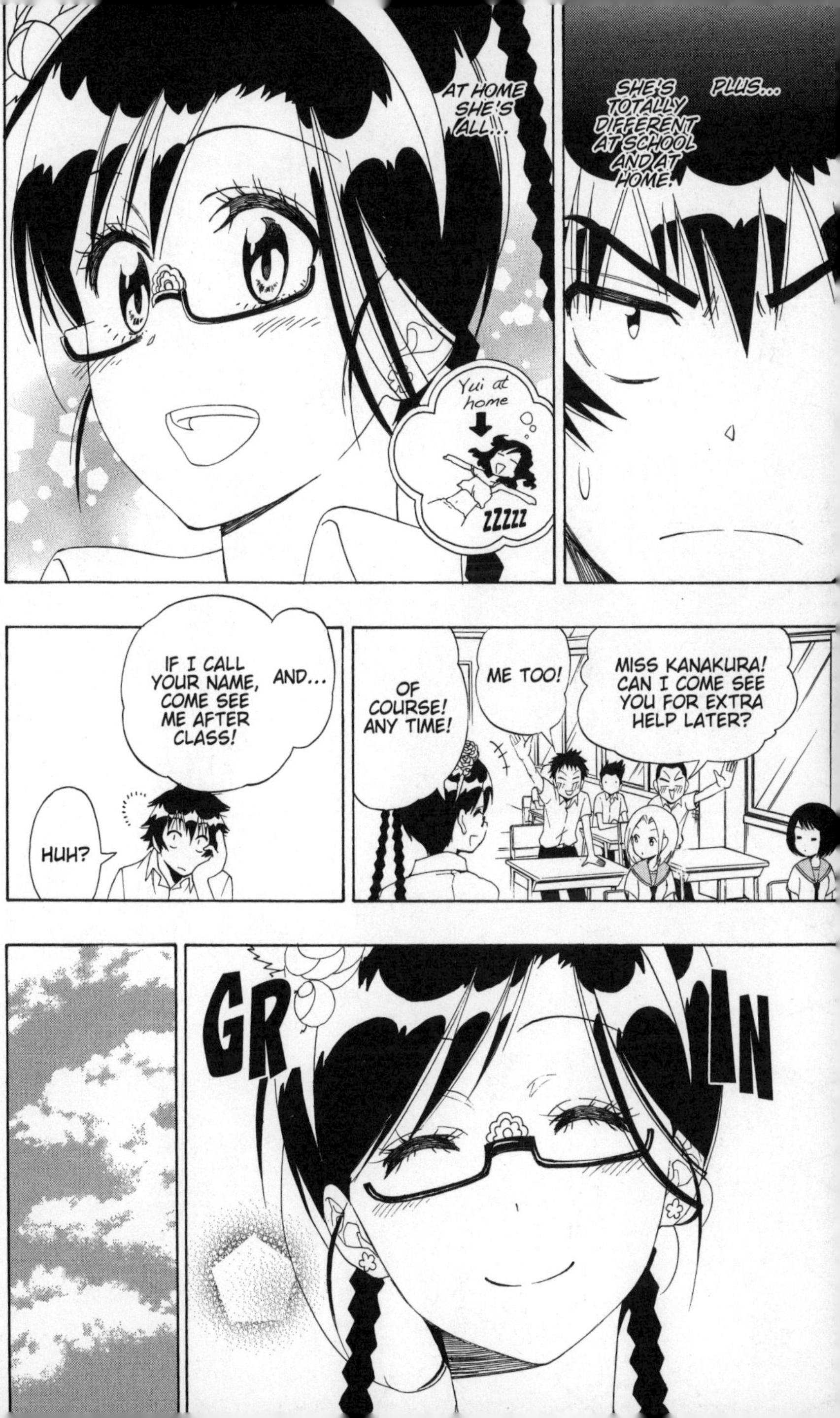
PLUS...
SHE'S TOTALLY DIFFERENT AT SCHOOL AND AT HOME.
AT HOME SHE'S ALL...
Yui at home
ZZZZZ
MISS KANAKURA! CAN I COME SEE YOU FOR EXTRA HELP LATER?
ME TOO!
OF COURSE! ANY TIME!
AND...
IF I CALL YOUR NAME, COME SEE ME AFTER CLASS!
HUH?
GRIN

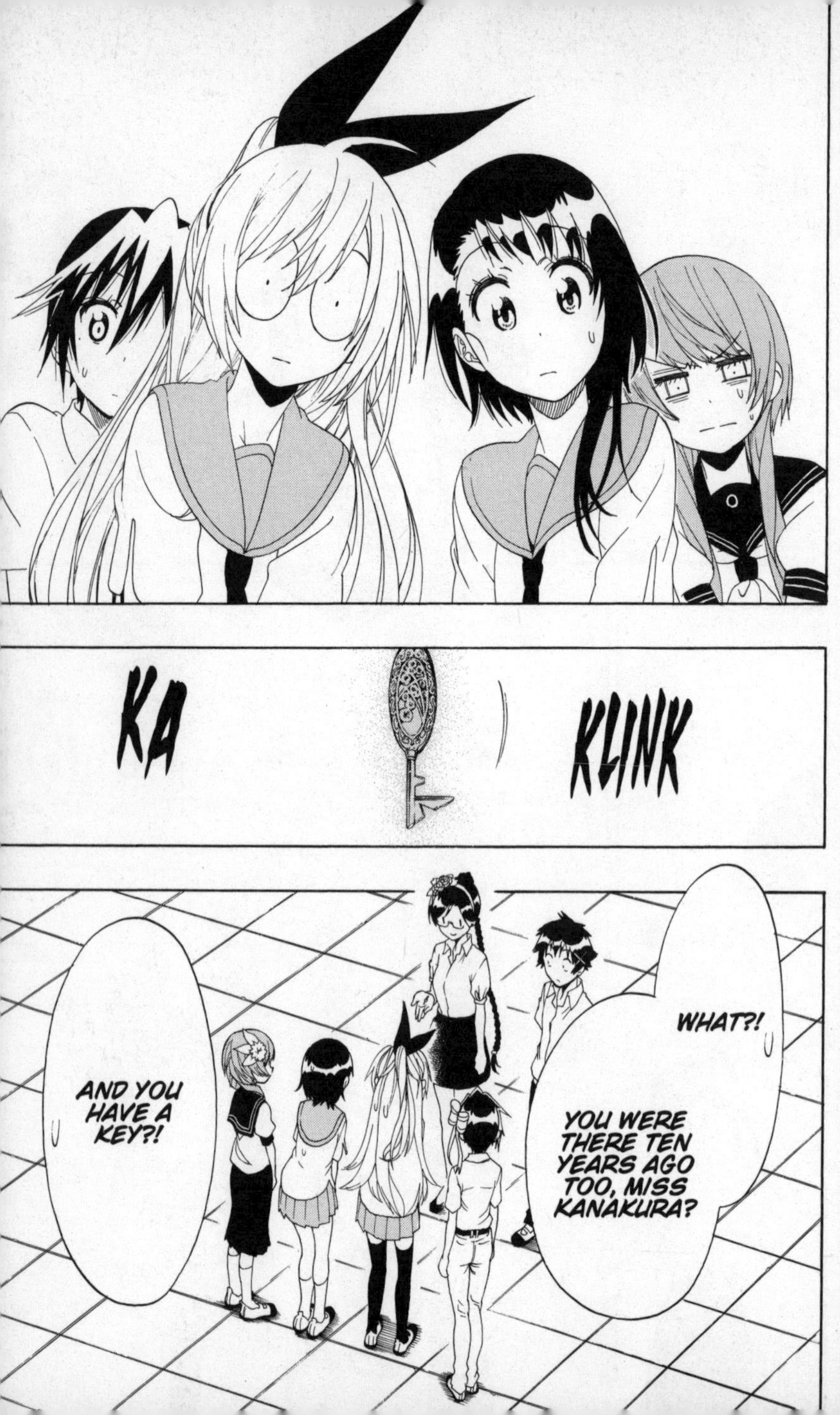
KA
KLINK
WHAT?!
YOU WERE THERE TEN YEARS AGO TOO, MISS KANAKURA?
AND YOU HAVE A KEY?!

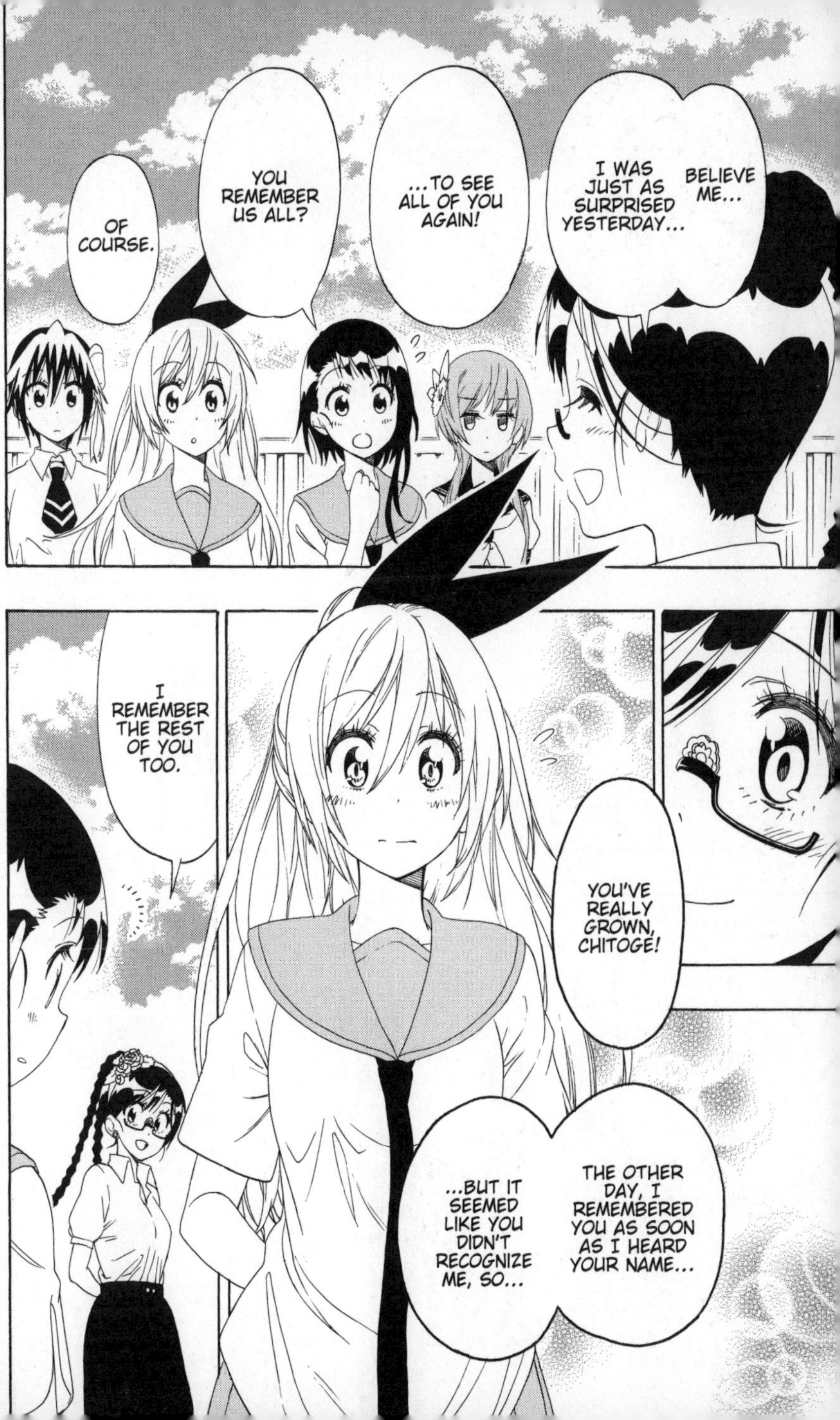
BELIEVE ME...
I WAS JUST AS SURPRISED YESTERDAY...
...TO SEE ALL OF YOU AGAIN!
YOU REMEMBER US ALL?
OF COURSE.
YOU'VE REALLY GROWN, CHITOGE!
THE OTHER DAY, I REMEMBERED YOU AS SOON AS I HEARD YOUR NAME...
...BUT IT SEEMED LIKE YOU DIDN'T RECOGNIZE ME, SO...
I REMEMBER THE REST OF YOU TOO.

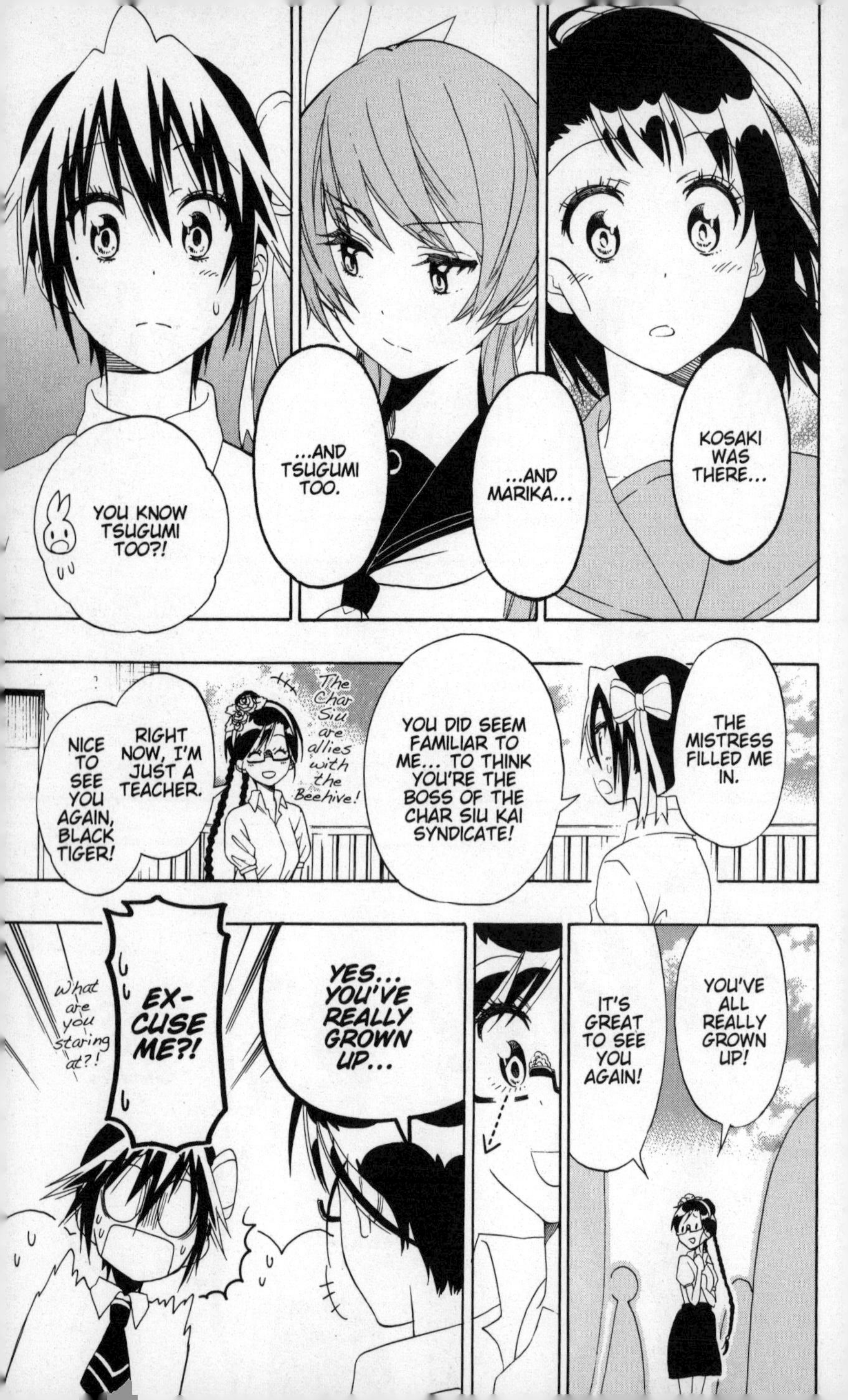
KOSAKI WAS THERE...
...AND MARIKA...
...AND TSUGUMI TOO.
YOU KNOW TSUGUMI TOO?!
THE MISTRESS FILLED ME IN.
YOU DID SEEM FAMILIAR TO ME... TO THINK YOU'RE THE BOSS OF THE CHAR SIU KAI SYNDICATE!
The Char Siu are allies with the Beehive!
RIGHT NOW, I'M JUST A TEACHER.
NICE TO SEE YOU AGAIN, BLACK TIGER!
YOU'VE ALL REALLY GROWN UP!
IT'S GREAT TO SEE YOU AGAIN!
YES... YOU'VE REALLY GROWN UP...
EX-CUSE ME?!
What are you staring at?!

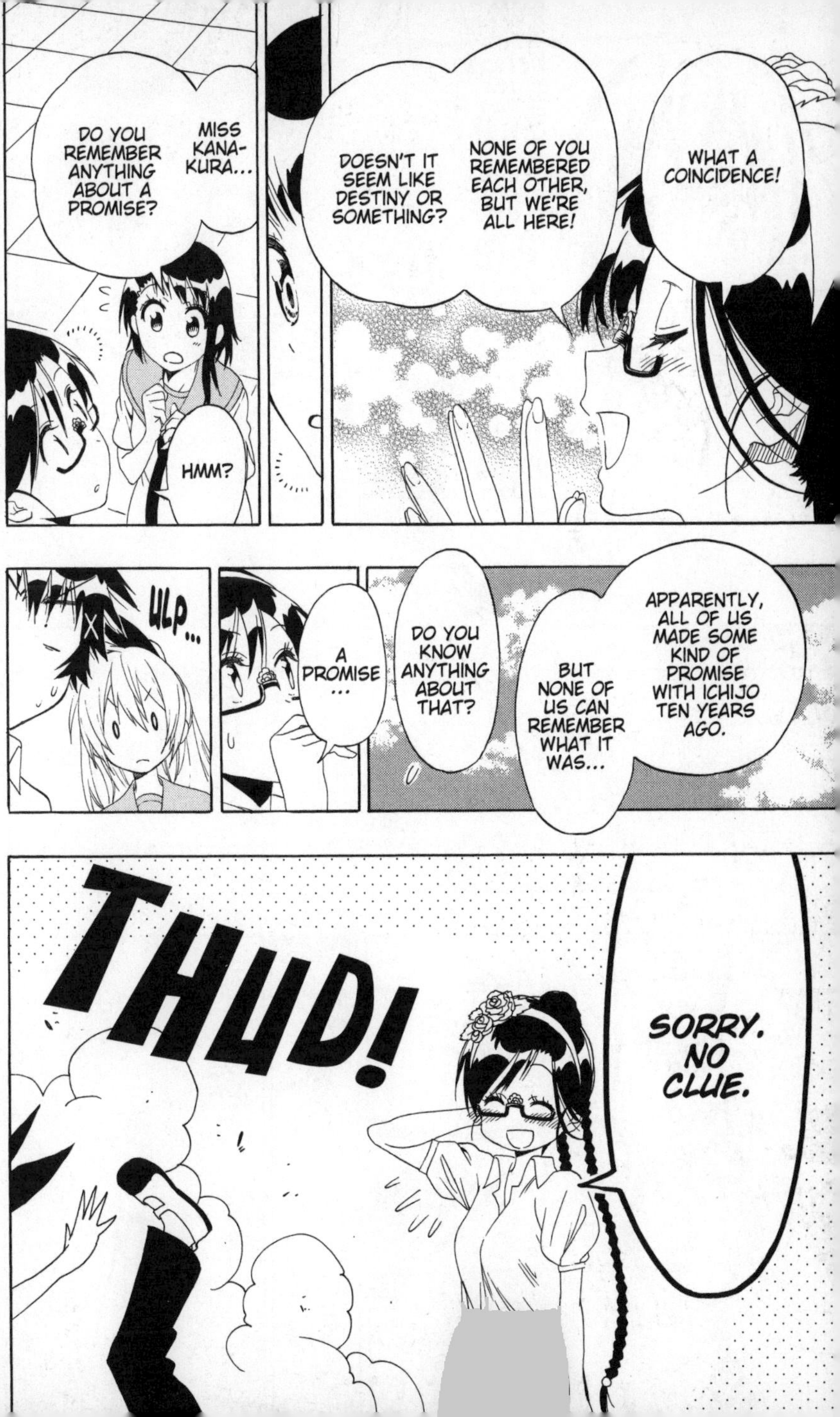
WHAT A COINCIDENCE!
NONE OF YOU REMEMBERED EACH OTHER, BUT WE'RE ALL HERE!
DOESN'T IT SEEM LIKE DESTINY OR SOMETHING?
MISS KANA-KURA...
DO YOU REMEMBER ANYTHING ABOUT A PROMISE?
HMM?
APPARENTLY, ALL OF US MADE SOME KIND OF PROMISE WITH ICHIJO TEN YEARS AGO.
BUT NONE OF US CAN REMEMBER WHAT IT WAS...
DO YOU KNOW ANYTHING ABOUT THAT?
A PROMISE ...
ULP...
SORRY. NO CLUE.
THUD!

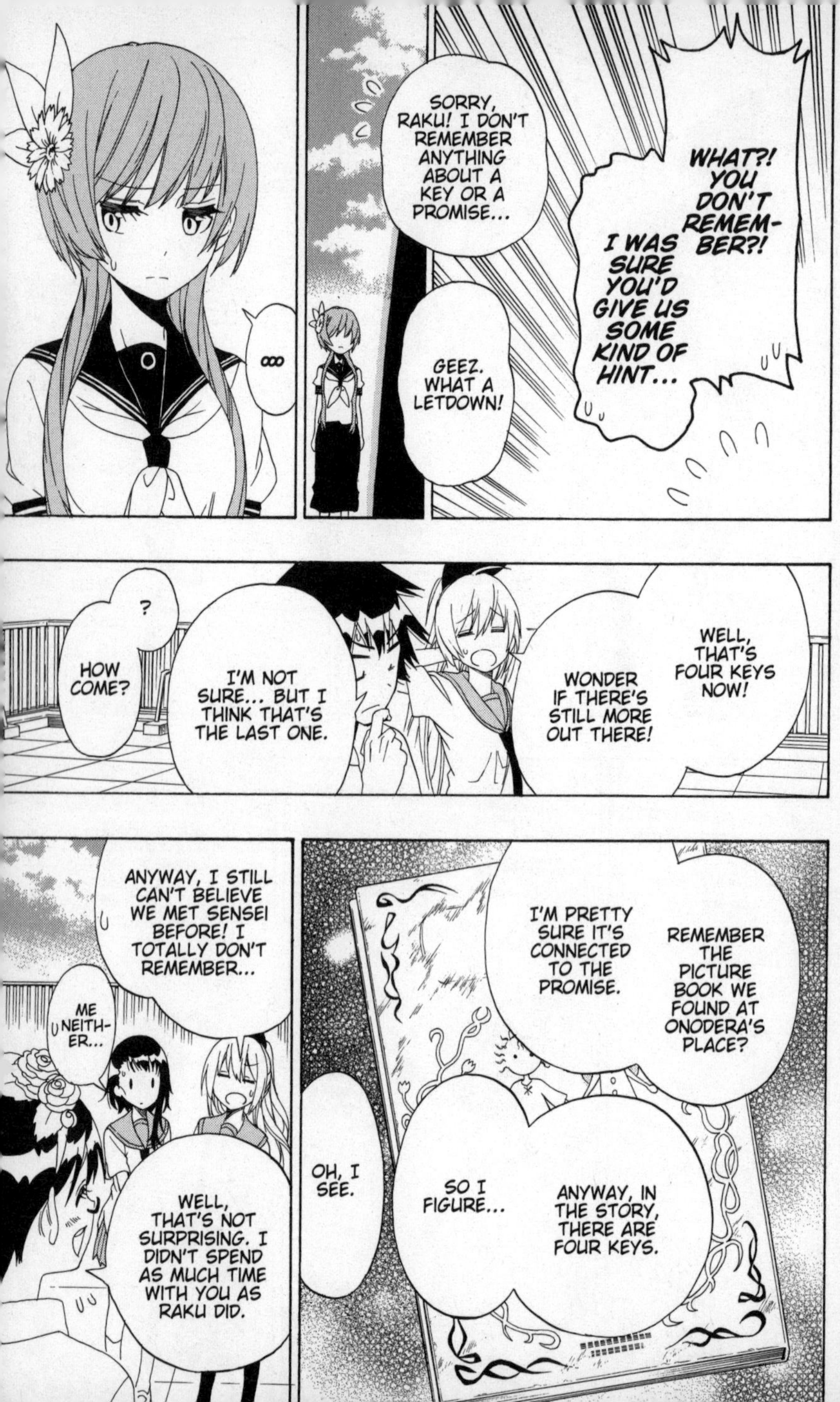
WHAT?! YOU DON'T REMEMBER?!
I WAS SURE YOU'D GIVE US SOME KIND OF HINT...
SORRY, RAKU! I DON'T REMEMBER ANYTHING ABOUT A KEY OR A PROMISE...
GEEZ. WHAT A LETDOWN!
ooo
WELL, THAT'S FOUR KEYS NOW!
WONDER IF THERE'S STILL MORE OUT THERE!
I'M NOT SURE... BUT I THINK THAT'S THE LAST ONE.
?
HOW COME?
REMEMBER THE PICTURE BOOK WE FOUND AT ONODERA'S PLACE?
I'M PRETTY SURE IT'S CONNECTED TO THE PROMISE.
ANYWAY, IN THE STORY, THERE ARE FOUR KEYS.
SO I FIGURE...
OH, I SEE.
ANYWAY, I STILL CAN'T BELIEVE WE MET SENSEI BEFORE! I TOTALLY DON'T REMEMBER...
ME NEITHER...
WELL, THAT'S NOT SURPRISING. I DIDN'T SPEND AS MUCH TIME WITH YOU AS RAKU DID.

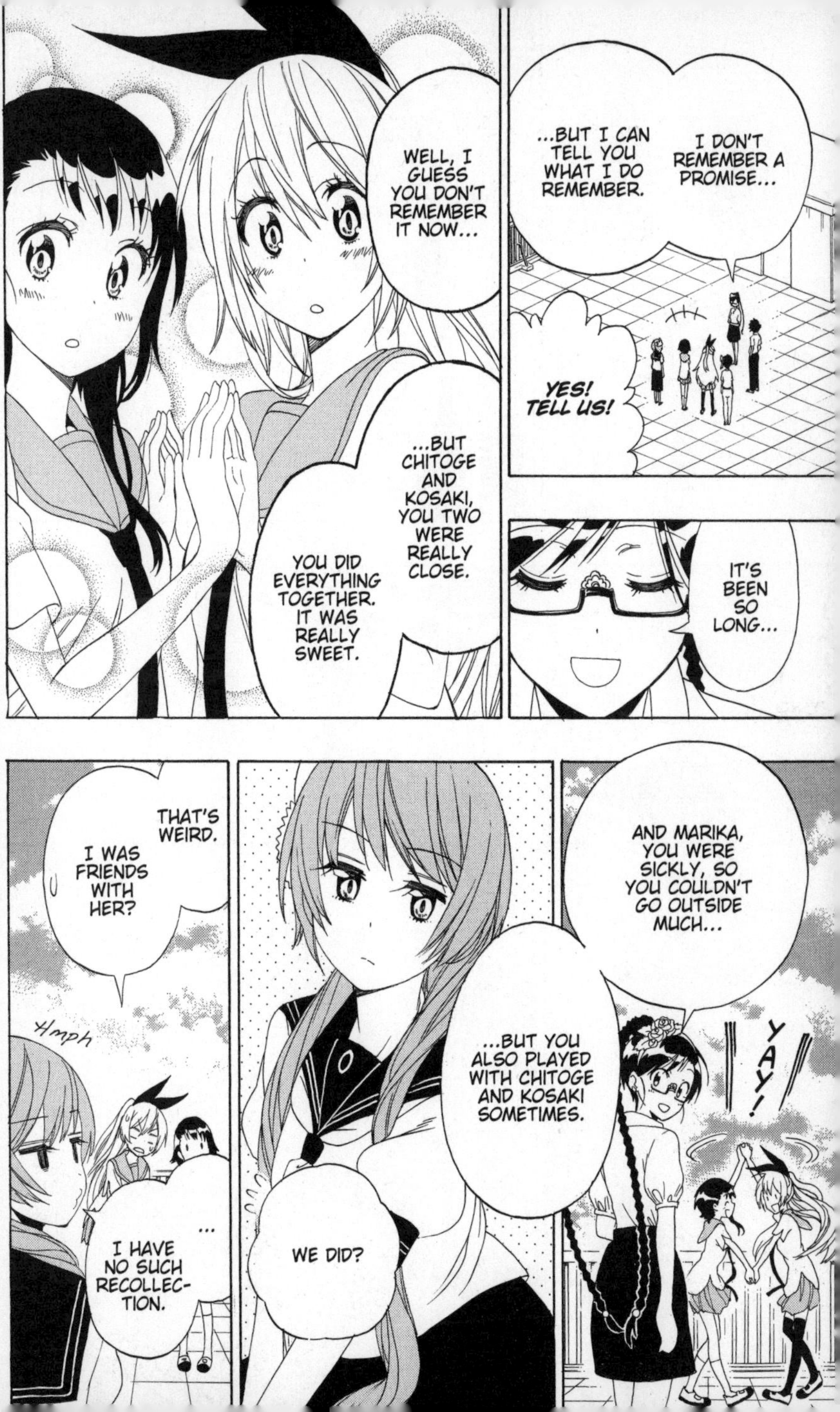
I DON'T REMEMBER A PROMISE...
...BUT I CAN TELL YOU WHAT I DO REMEMBER.
YES! TELL US!
IT'S BEEN SO LONG...
WELL, I GUESS YOU DON'T REMEMBER IT NOW...
...BUT CHITOGE AND KOSAKI, YOU TWO WERE REALLY CLOSE.
YOU DID EVERYTHING TOGETHER. IT WAS REALLY SWEET.
AND MARIKA, YOU WERE SICKLY, SO YOU COULDN'T GO OUTSIDE MUCH...
YAY!
...BUT YOU ALSO PLAYED WITH CHITOGE AND KOSAKI SOMETIMES.
WE DID?
THAT'S WEIRD.
I WAS FRIENDS WITH HER?
Hmph
...
I HAVE NO SUCH RECOLLEC-TION.

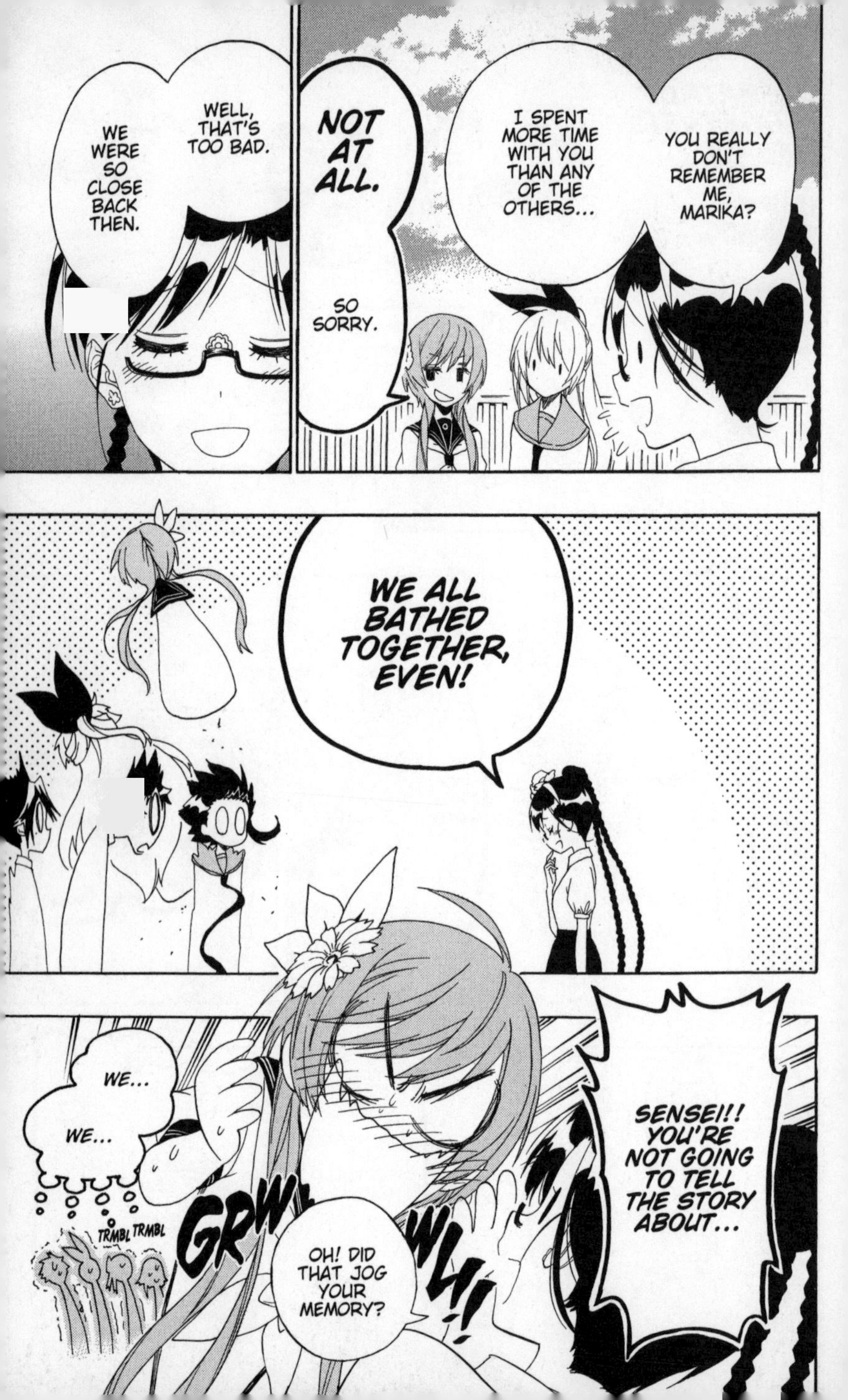
YOU REALLY DON'T REMEMBER ME, MARIKA?
I SPENT MORE TIME WITH YOU THAN ANY OF THE OTHERS...
NOT AT ALL.
SO SORRY.
WELL, THAT'S TOO BAD.
WE WERE SO CLOSE BACK THEN.
WE ALL BATHED TOGETHER, EVEN!
SENSEI!! YOU'RE NOT GOING TO TELL THE STORY ABOUT...
OH! DID THAT JOG YOUR MEMORY?
WE...
WE...
TRMBL TRMBL

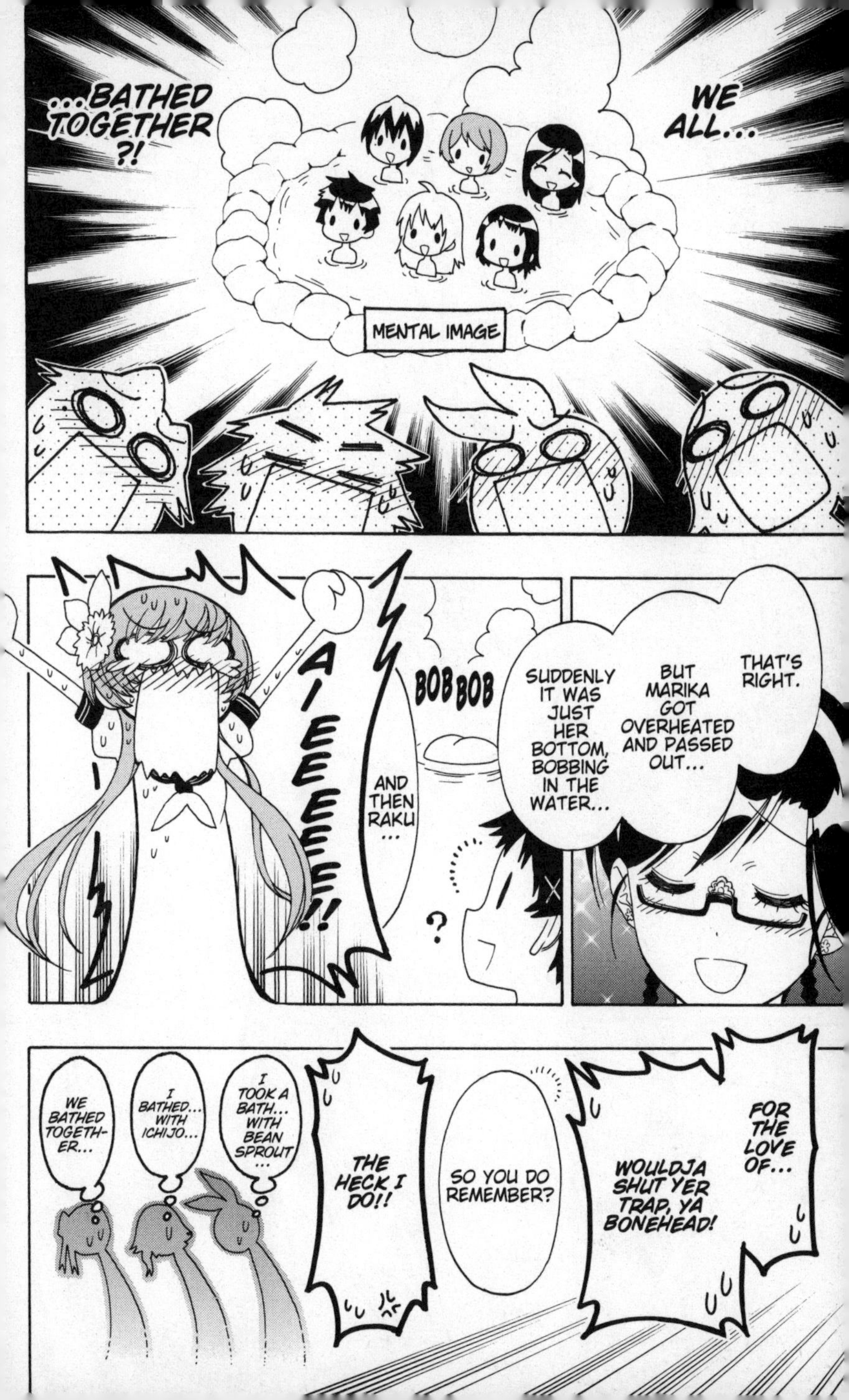
WE ALL...
...BATHED TOGETHER?!
MENTAL IMAGE
THAT'S RIGHT.
BUT MARIKA GOT OVERHEATED AND PASSED OUT...
SUDDENLY IT WAS JUST HER BOTTOM, BOBBING IN THE WATER...
BOB BOB
AND THEN RAKU...
AIEEEEEE!!
FOR THE LOVE OF...
WOULDJA SHUT YER TRAP, YA BONEHEAD!
SO YOU DO REMEMBER?
THE HECK I DO!!
I TOOK A BATH... WITH BEAN SPROUT...
I BATHED... WITH ICHIJO...
WE BATHED TOGETH-ER...

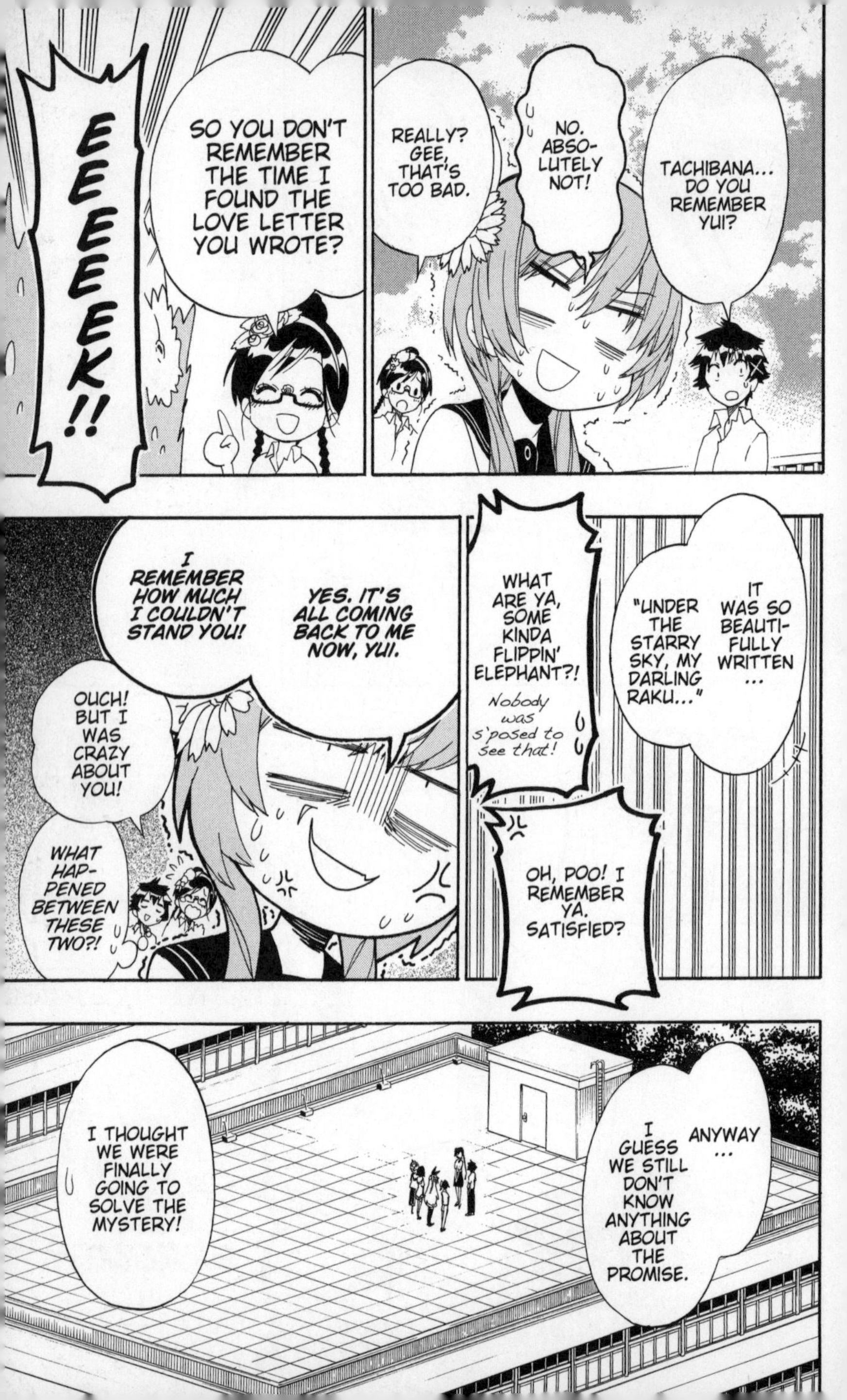
TACHIBANA... DO YOU REMEMBER YUI?
NO. ABSO-LUTELY NOT!
REALLY? GEE, THAT'S TOO BAD.
SO YOU DON'T REMEMBER THE TIME I FOUND THE LOVE LETTER YOU WROTE?
EEEEEK!!
IT WAS SO BEAUTI-FULLY WRITTEN...
"UNDER THE STARRY SKY, MY DARLING RAKU..."
WHAT ARE YA, SOME KINDA FLIPPIN' ELEPHANT?!
Nobody was s'posed to see that!
OH, POO! I REMEMBER YA. SATISFIED?
YES. IT'S ALL COMING BACK TO ME NOW, YUI.
I REMEMBER HOW MUCH I COULDN'T STAND YOU!
OUCH! BUT I WAS CRAZY ABOUT YOU!
WHAT HAP-PENED BETWEEN THESE TWO?!
ANYWAY...
I GUESS WE STILL DON'T KNOW ANYTHING ABOUT THE PROMISE.
I THOUGHT WE WERE FINALLY GOING TO SOLVE THE MYSTERY!

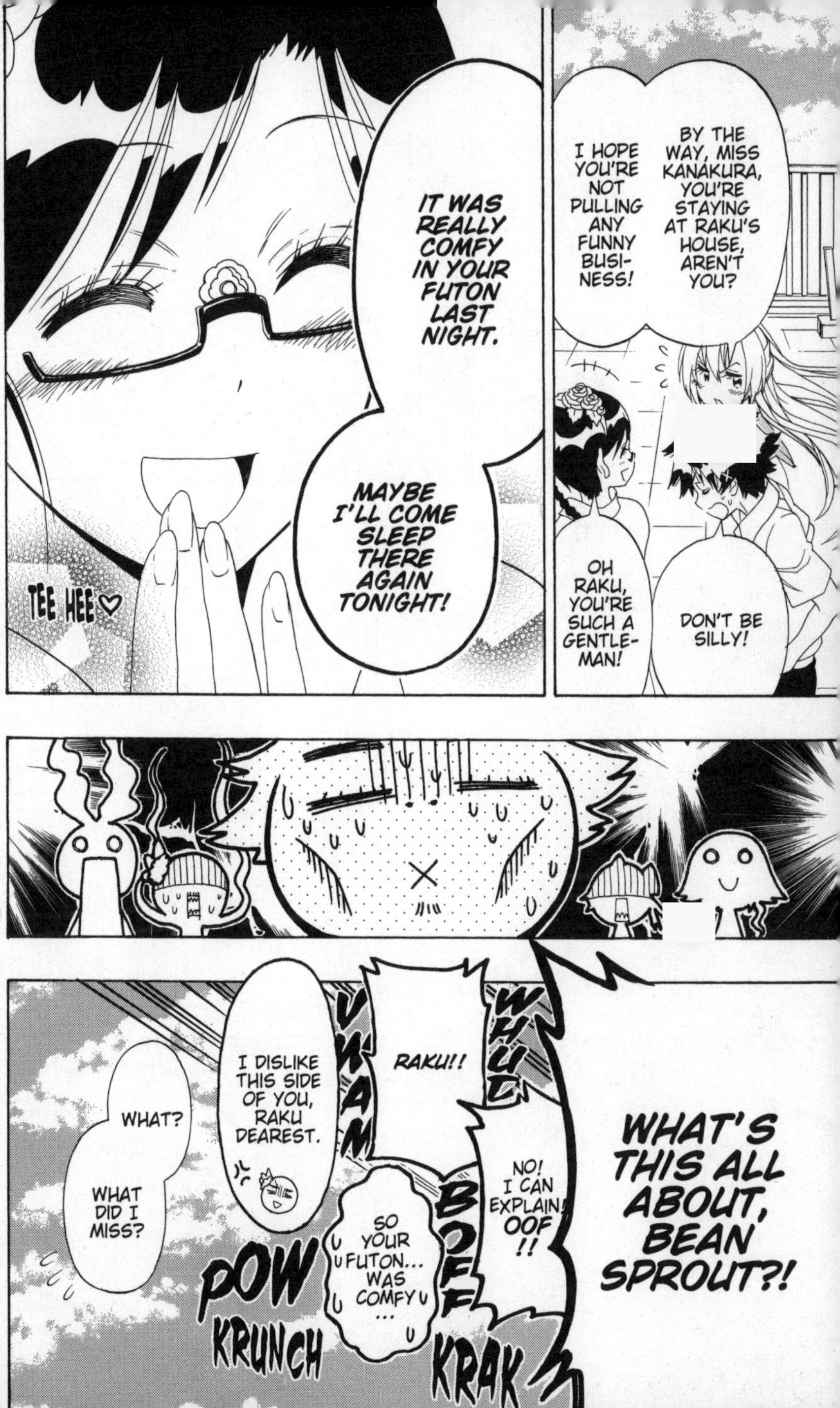
BY THE WAY, MISS KANAKURA, YOU'RE STAYING AT RAKU'S HOUSE, AREN'T YOU?
I HOPE YOU'RE NOT PULLING ANY FUNNY BUSI-NESS!
DON'T BE SILLY!
OH RAKU, YOU'RE SUCH A GENTLE-MAN!
IT WAS REALLY COMFY IN YOUR FUTON LAST NIGHT.
MAYBE I'LL COME SLEEP THERE AGAIN TONIGHT!
TEE HEE ♡
WHAT'S THIS ALL ABOUT, BEAN SPROUT?!
WHUD
NO! I CAN EXPLAIN! OOF!!
BOFF
KRAK
RAKU!!
WHAM
SO YOUR FUTON... WAS COMFY...
I DISLIKE THIS SIDE OF YOU, RAKU DEAREST.
POW
KRUNCH
WHAT?
WHAT DID I MISS?

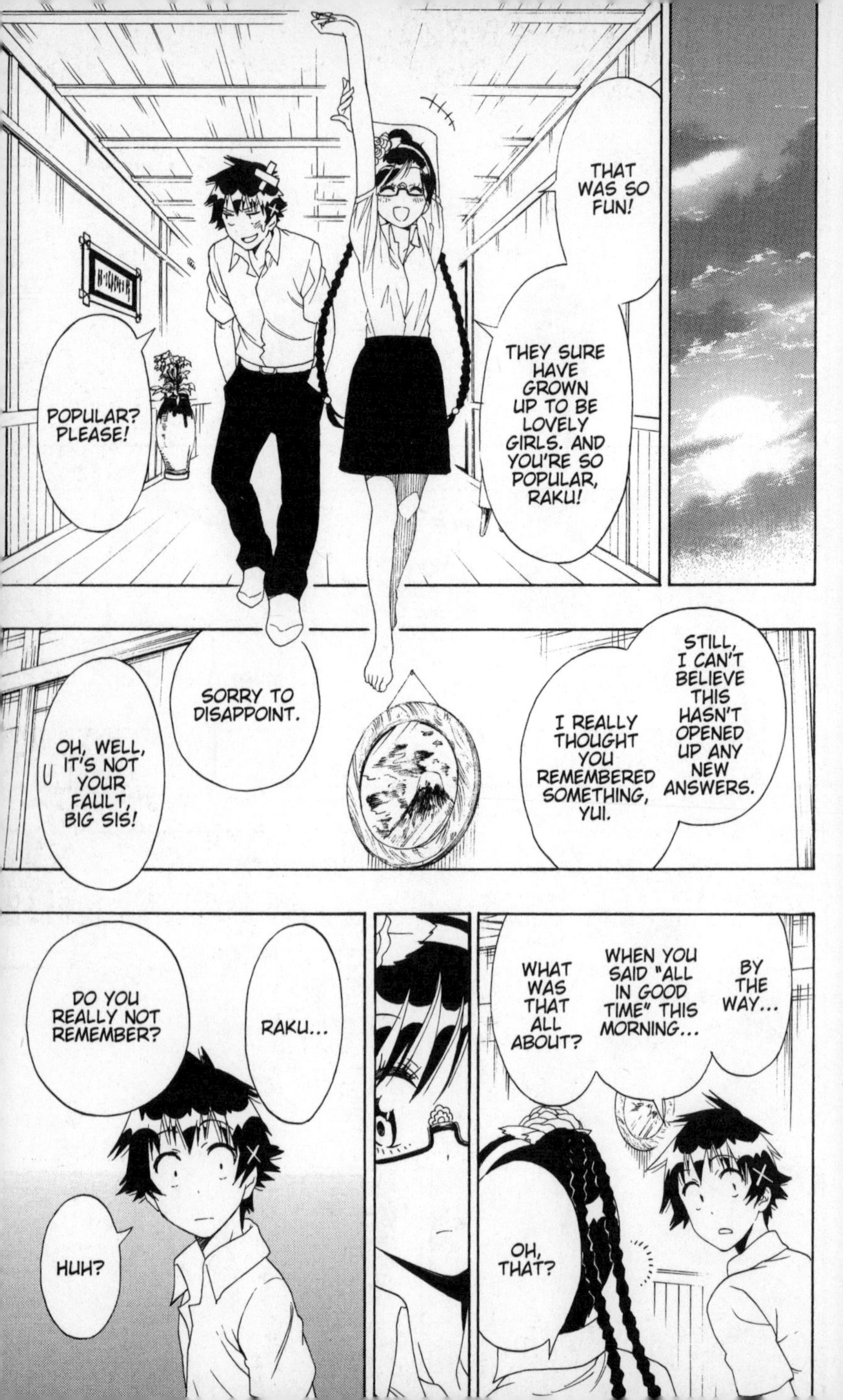
THAT WAS SO FUN!
THEY SURE HAVE GROWN UP TO BE LOVELY GIRLS. AND YOU'RE SO POPULAR, RAKU!
POPULAR? PLEASE!
STILL, I CAN'T BELIEVE THIS HASN'T OPENED UP ANY NEW ANSWERS.
I REALLY THOUGHT YOU REMEMBERED SOMETHING, YUI.
SORRY TO DISAPPOINT.
OH, WELL, IT'S NOT YOUR FAULT, BIG SIS!
BY THE WAY...
WHEN YOU SAID "ALL IN GOOD TIME" THIS MORNING...
WHAT WAS THAT ALL ABOUT?
OH, THAT?
RAKU...
DO YOU REALLY NOT REMEMBER?
HUH?

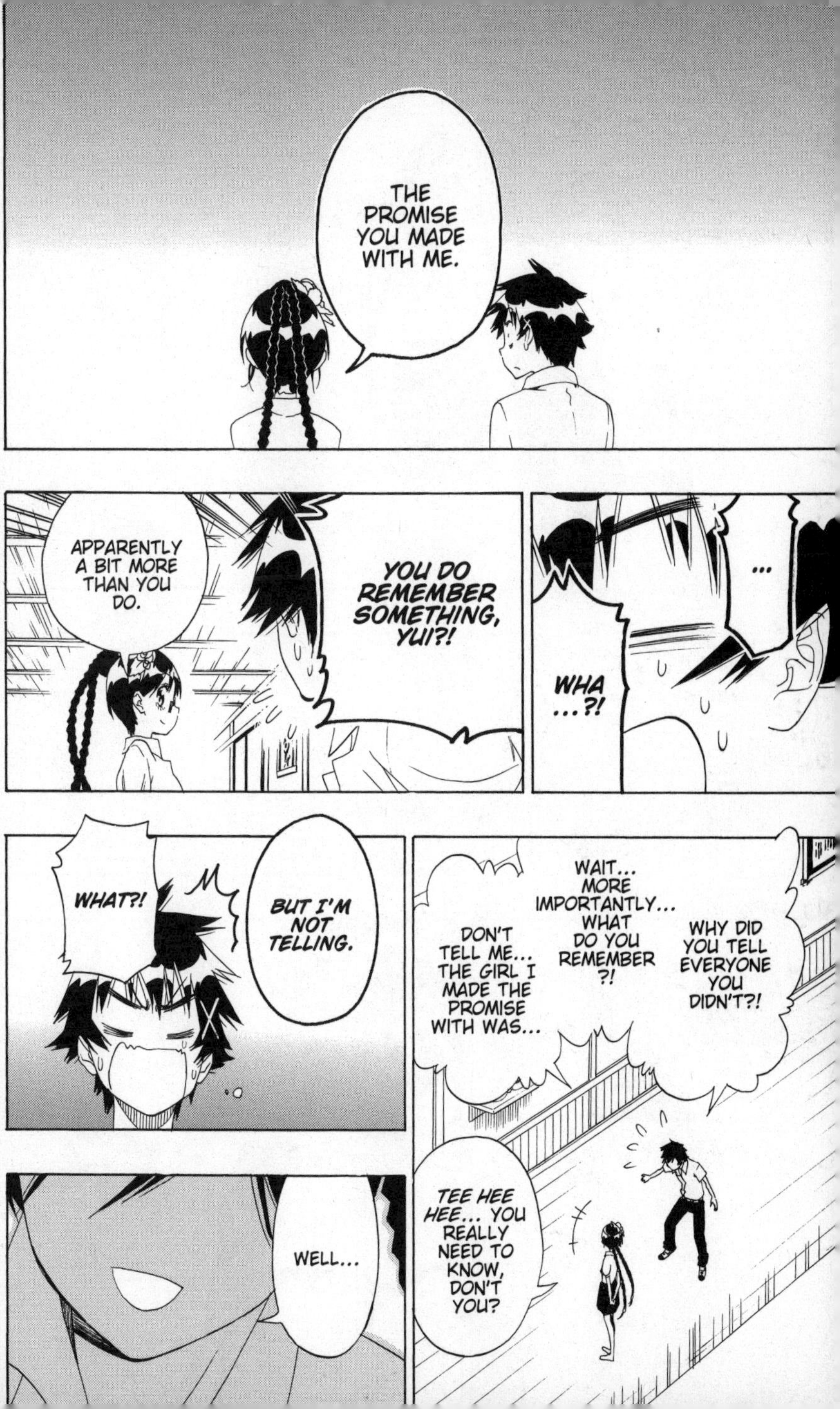
THE PROMISE YOU MADE WITH ME.
...
WHA...?!
YOU DO REMEMBER SOMETHING, YUI?!
APPARENTLY A BIT MORE THAN YOU DO.
WHY DID YOU TELL EVERYONE YOU DIDN'T?!
WAIT... MORE IMPORTANTLY... WHAT DO YOU REMEMBER?!
DON'T TELL ME... THE GIRL I MADE THE PROMISE WITH WAS...
TEE HEE HEE... YOU REALLY NEED TO KNOW, DON'T YOU?
BUT I'M NOT TELLING.
WHAT?!
WELL...

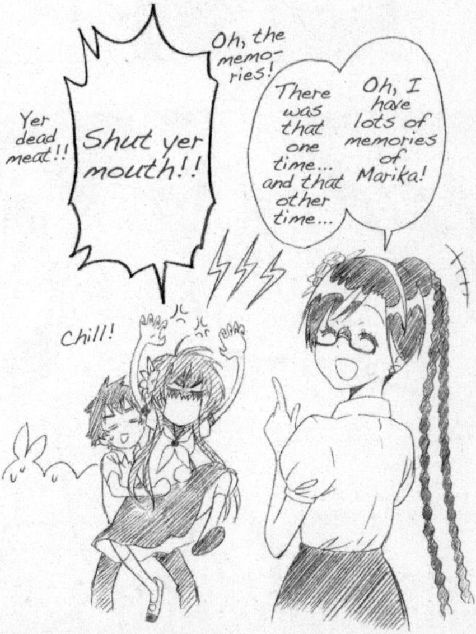
Oh, I have lots of memories of Marika!
There was that one time... and that other time...
Oh, the memories!
Shut yer mouth!!
Yer dead meat!!
Chill!

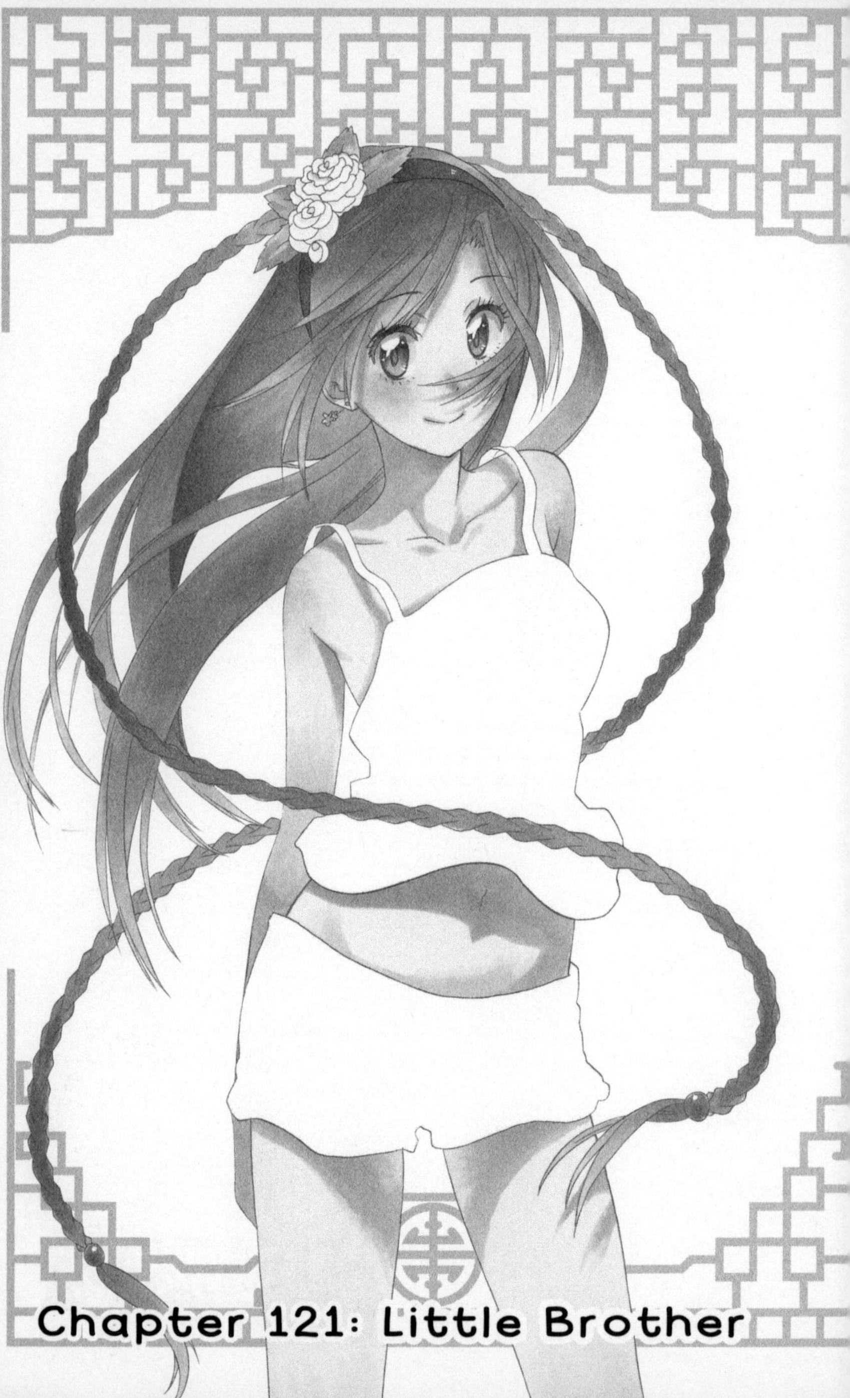

Chapter 121: Little Brother

NISEKOI
False Love

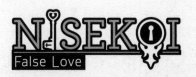

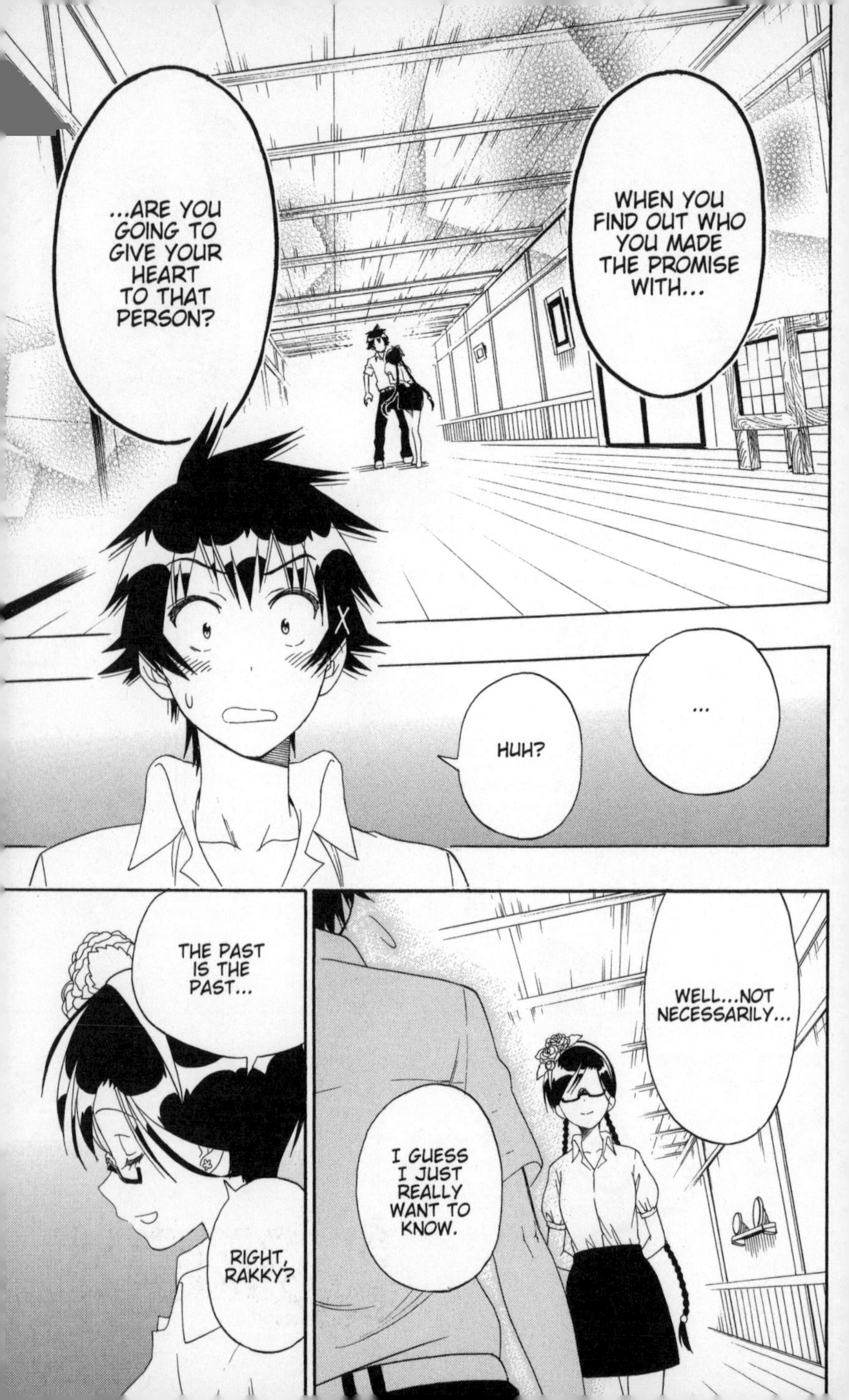
WHEN YOU FIND OUT WHO YOU MADE THE PROMISE WITH...
...ARE YOU GOING TO GIVE YOUR HEART TO THAT PERSON?
...
HUH?
WELL...NOT NECESSARILY...
I GUESS I JUST REALLY WANT TO KNOW.
THE PAST IS THE PAST...
RIGHT, RAKKY?

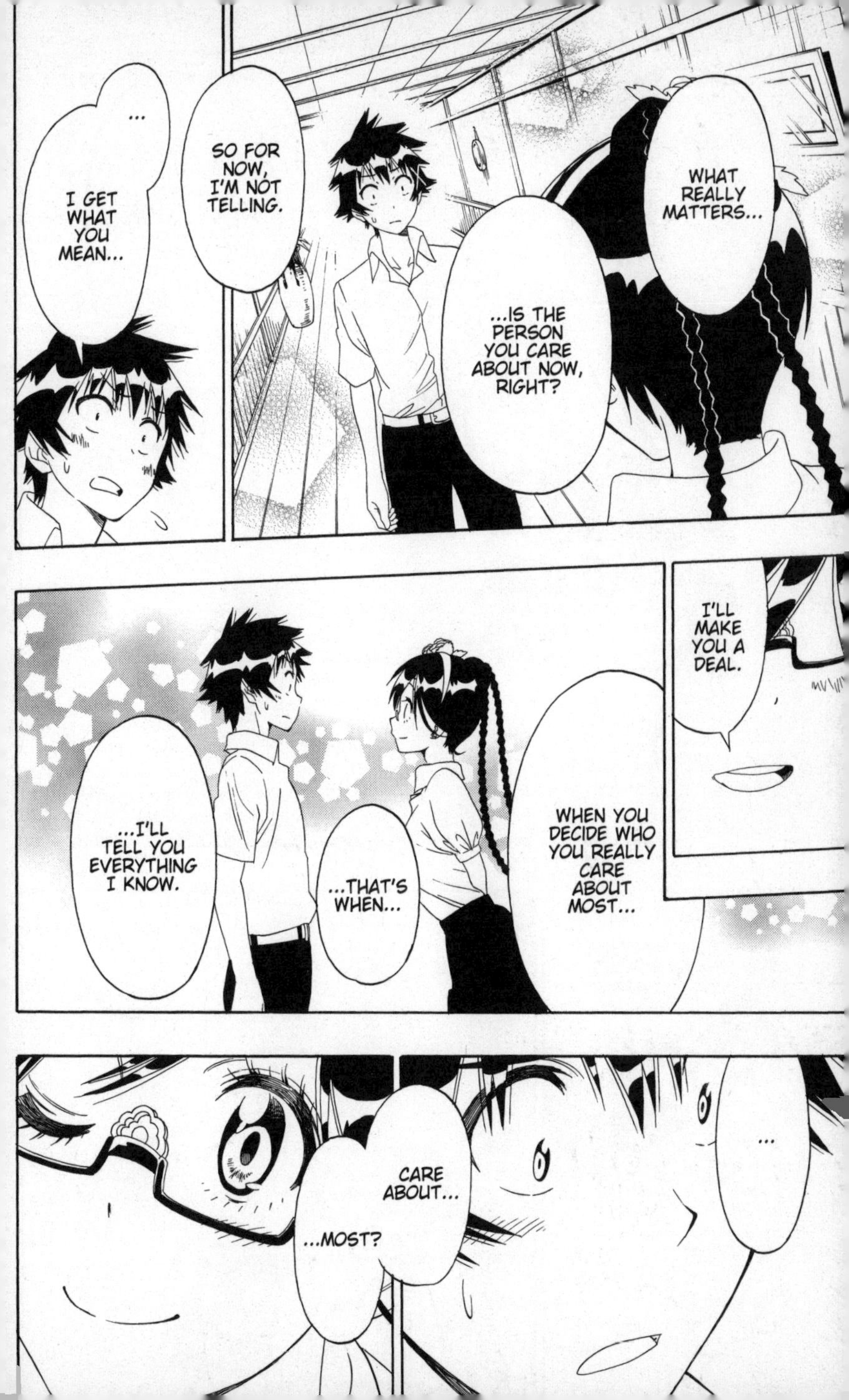
WHAT REALLY MATTERS...
...IS THE PERSON YOU CARE ABOUT NOW, RIGHT?
SO FOR NOW, I'M NOT TELLING.
...
I GET WHAT YOU MEAN...
I'LL MAKE YOU A DEAL.
WHEN YOU DECIDE WHO YOU REALLY CARE ABOUT MOST...
...THAT'S WHEN...
...I'LL TELL YOU EVERYTHING I KNOW.
...
CARE ABOUT...
...MOST?

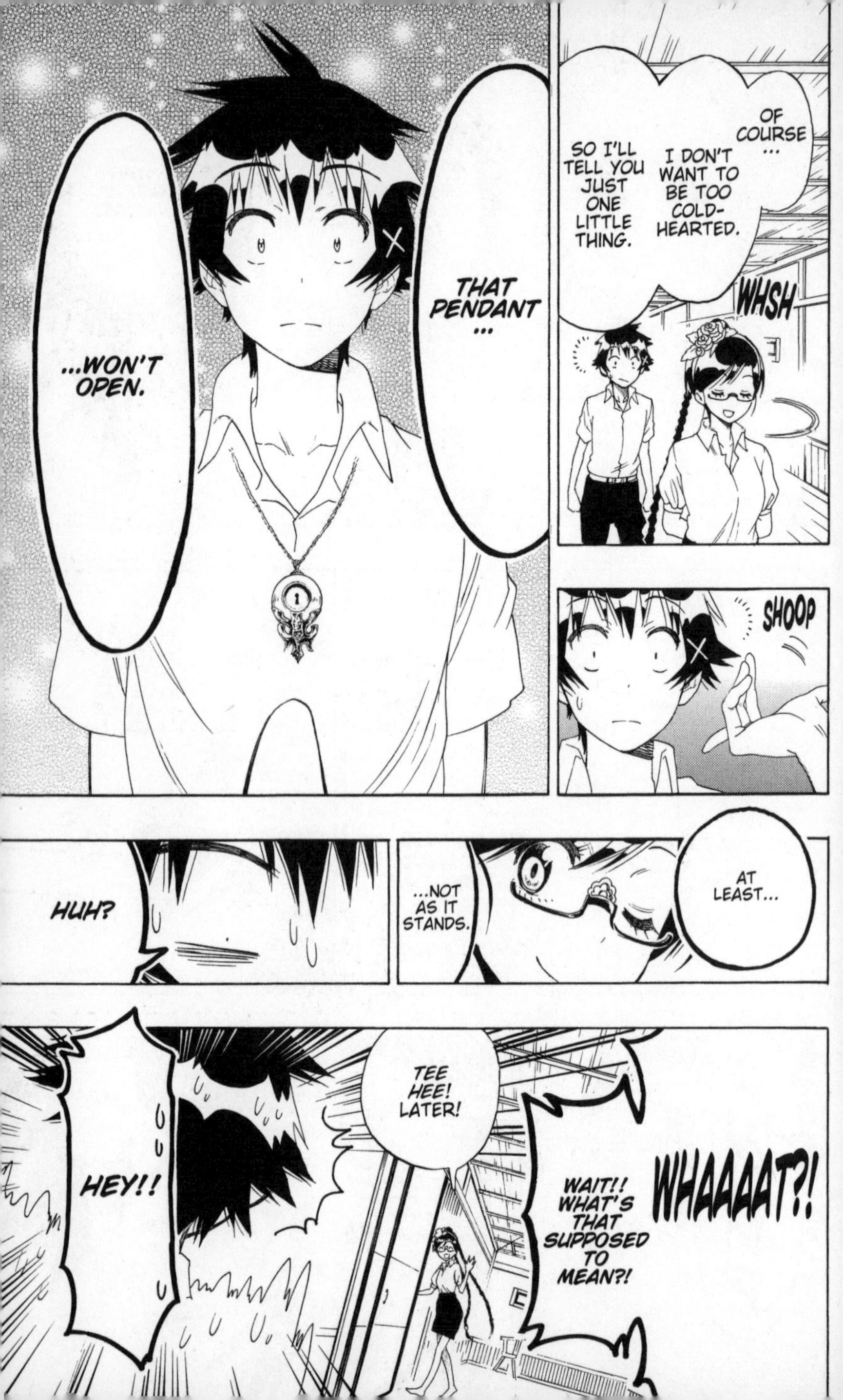
OF COURSE...
I DON'T WANT TO BE TOO COLD-HEARTED.
SO I'LL TELL YOU JUST ONE LITTLE THING.
WHSH
SHOOP
THAT PENDANT...
...WON'T OPEN.
AT LEAST...
...NOT AS IT STANDS.
HUH?
TEE HEE! LATER!
WHAAAAT?!
WAIT!! WHAT'S THAT SUPPOSED TO MEAN?!
HEY!!

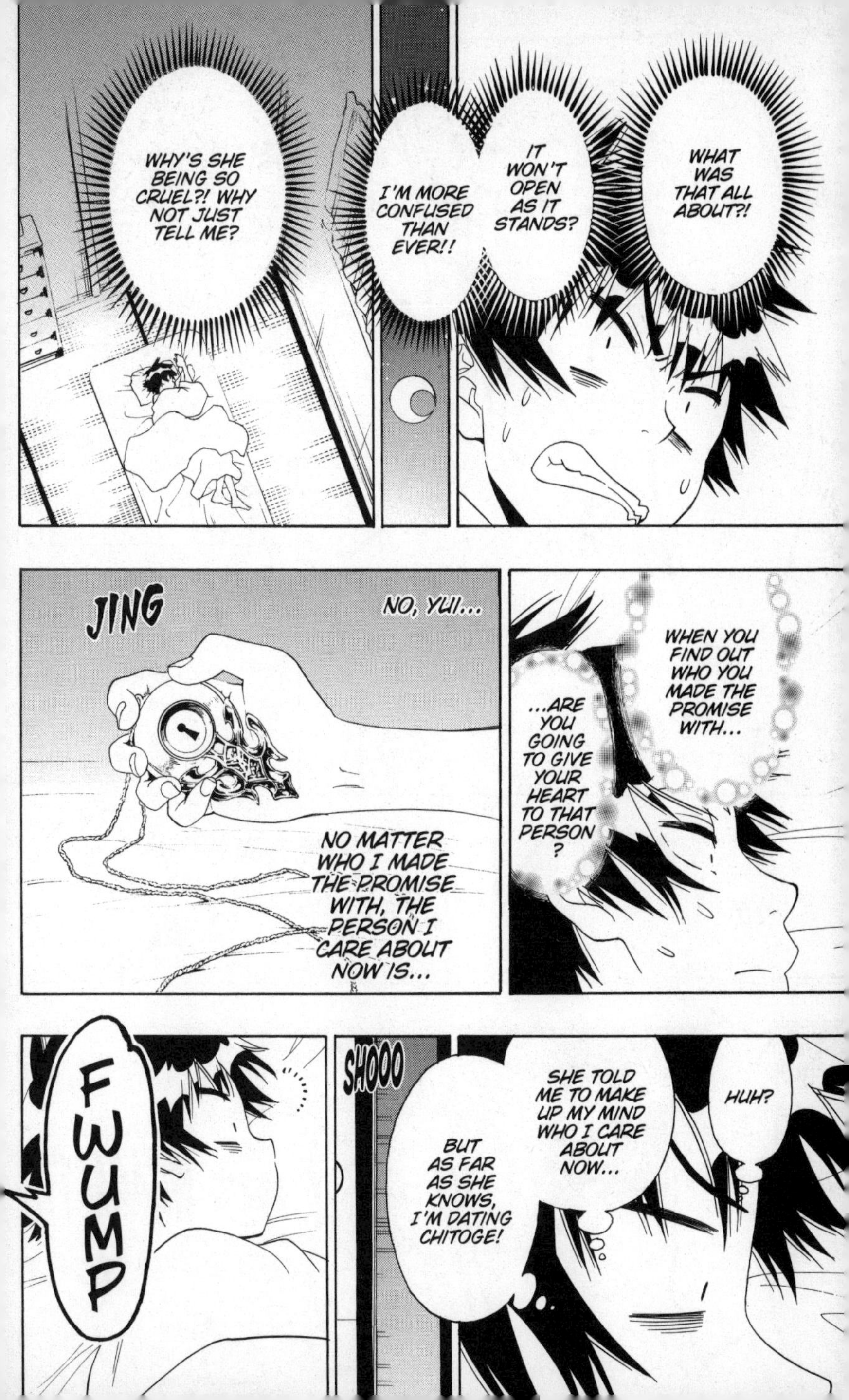
WHAT WAS THAT ALL ABOUT?!
IT WON'T OPEN AS IT STANDS?
I'M MORE CONFUSED THAN EVER!!
WHY'S SHE BEING SO CRUEL?! WHY NOT JUST TELL ME?
WHEN YOU FIND OUT WHO YOU MADE THE PROMISE WITH...
...ARE YOU GOING TO GIVE YOUR HEART TO THAT PERSON?
NO, YUI...
JING
NO MATTER WHO I MADE THE PROMISE WITH, THE PERSON I CARE ABOUT NOW IS...
HUH?
SHE TOLD ME TO MAKE UP MY MIND WHO I CARE ABOUT NOW...
BUT AS FAR AS SHE KNOWS, I'M DATING CHITOGE!
SHOOO
FWUMP

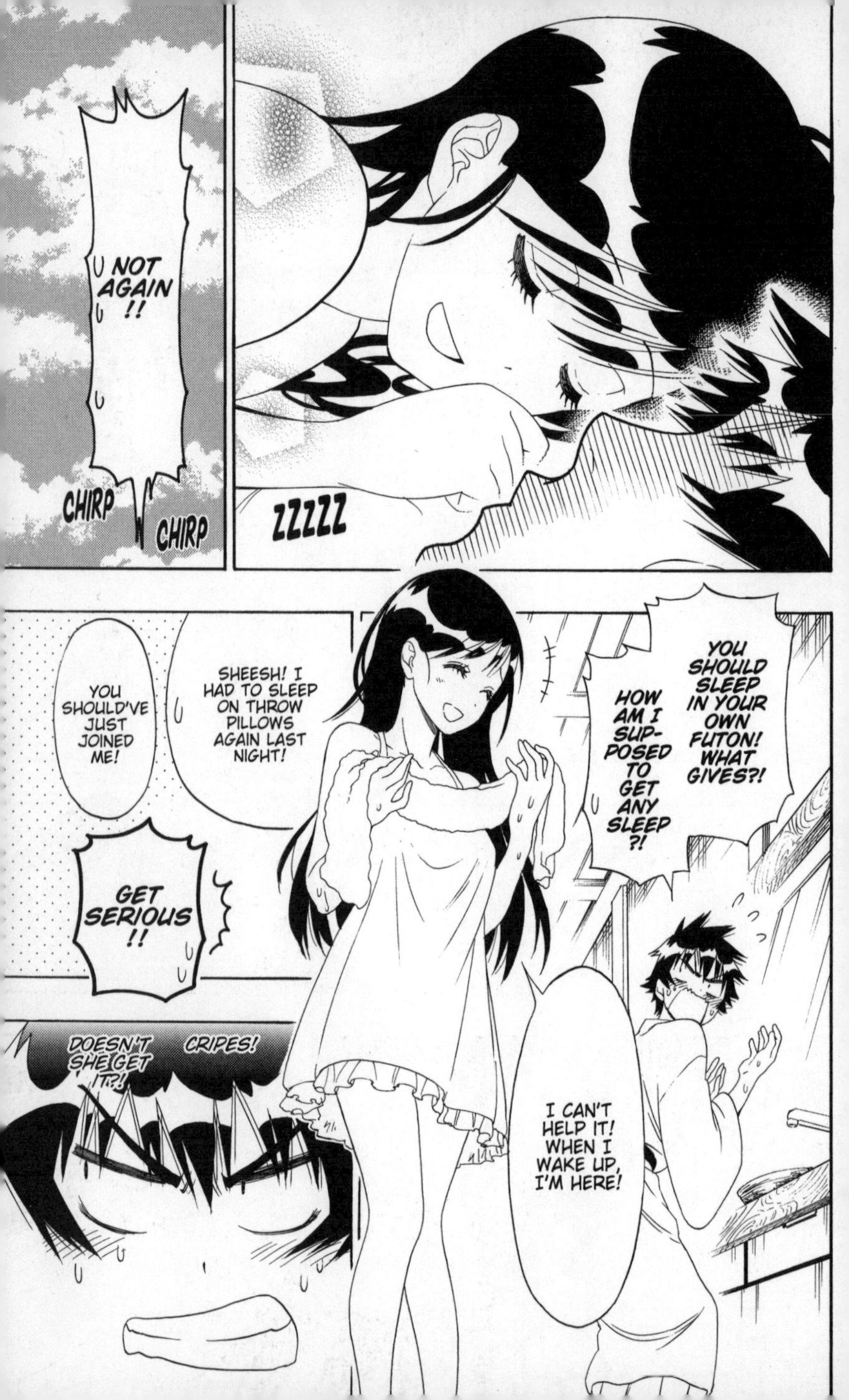
ZZZZZ
NOT AGAIN!!
CHIRP
CHIRP
YOU SHOULD SLEEP IN YOUR OWN FUTON! WHAT GIVES?!
HOW AM I SUP-POSED TO GET ANY SLEEP?!
I CAN'T HELP IT! WHEN I WAKE UP, I'M HERE!
SHEESH! I HAD TO SLEEP ON THROW PILLOWS AGAIN LAST NIGHT!
YOU SHOULD'VE JUST JOINED ME!
GET SERIOUS!!
CRIPES!
DOESN'T SHE GET IT?!

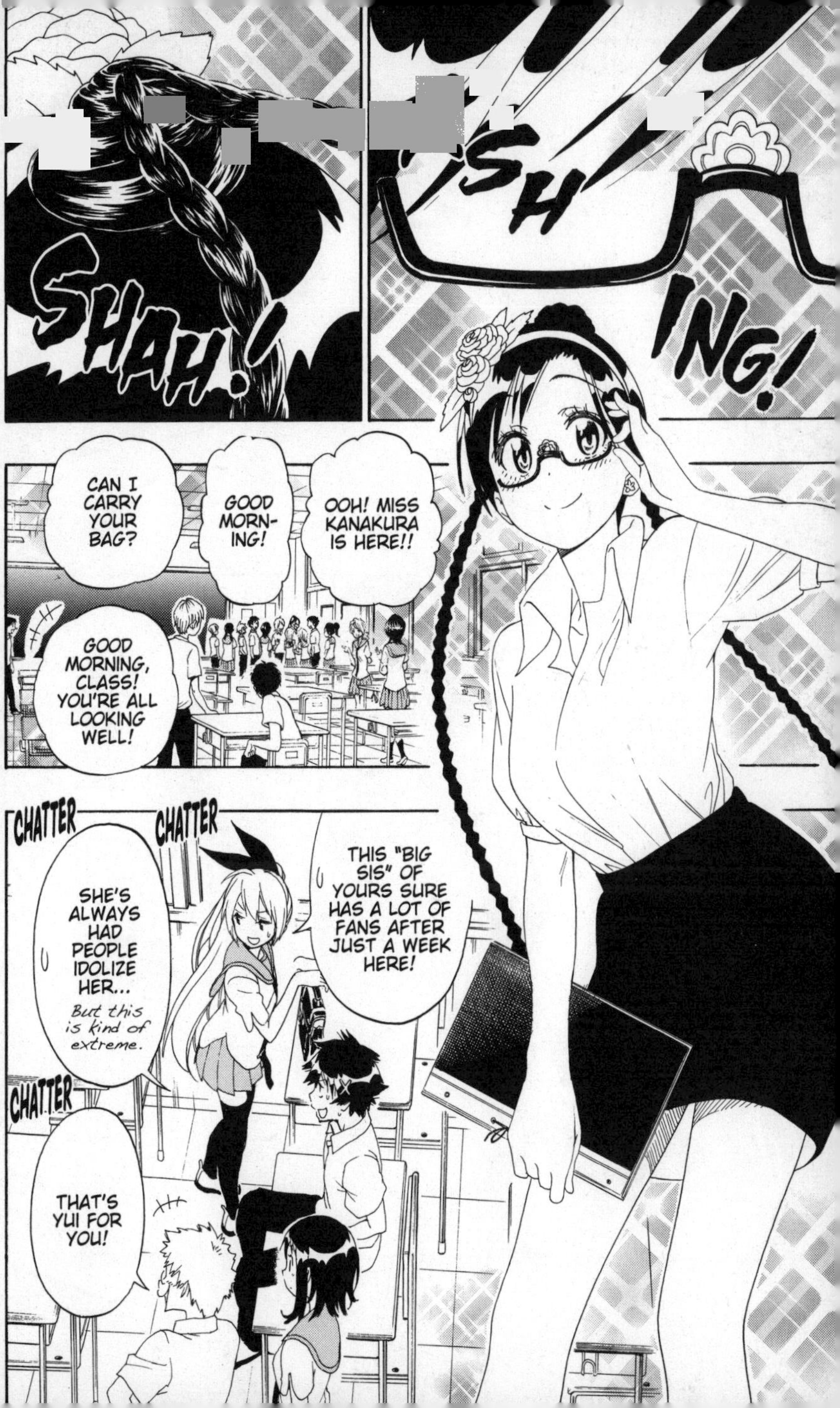
SHING!
SHAH!
OOH! MISS KANAKURA IS HERE!!
GOOD MORN-ING!
CAN I CARRY YOUR BAG?
GOOD MORNING, CLASS! YOU'RE ALL LOOKING WELL!
CHATTER
CHATTER
THIS "BIG SIS" OF YOURS SURE HAS A LOT OF FANS AFTER JUST A WEEK HERE!
SHE'S ALWAYS HAD PEOPLE IDOLIZE HER...
But this is kind of extreme.
CHATTER
THAT'S YUI FOR YOU!

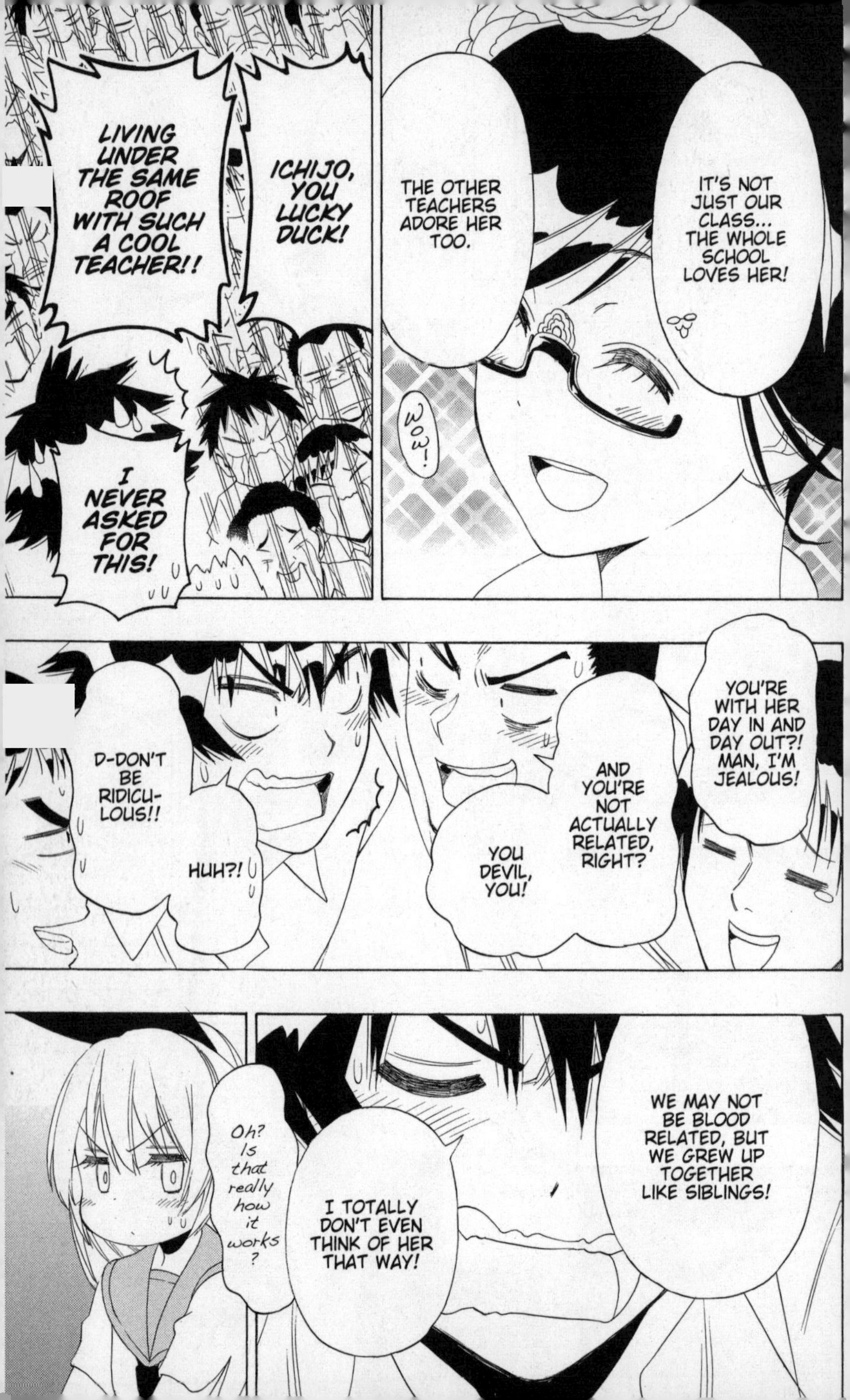
IT'S NOT JUST OUR CLASS... THE WHOLE SCHOOL LOVES HER!
THE OTHER TEACHERS ADORE HER TOO.
WOW!
ICHIJO, YOU LUCKY DUCK!
LIVING UNDER THE SAME ROOF WITH SUCH A COOL TEACHER!!
I NEVER ASKED FOR THIS!
YOU'RE WITH HER DAY IN AND DAY OUT?! MAN, I'M JEALOUS!
AND YOU'RE NOT ACTUALLY RELATED, RIGHT?
YOU DEVIL, YOU!
HUH?!
D-DON'T BE RIDICU-LOUS!!
WE MAY NOT BE BLOOD RELATED, BUT WE GREW UP TOGETHER LIKE SIBLINGS!
I TOTALLY DON'T EVEN THINK OF HER THAT WAY!
Oh? Is that really how it works?

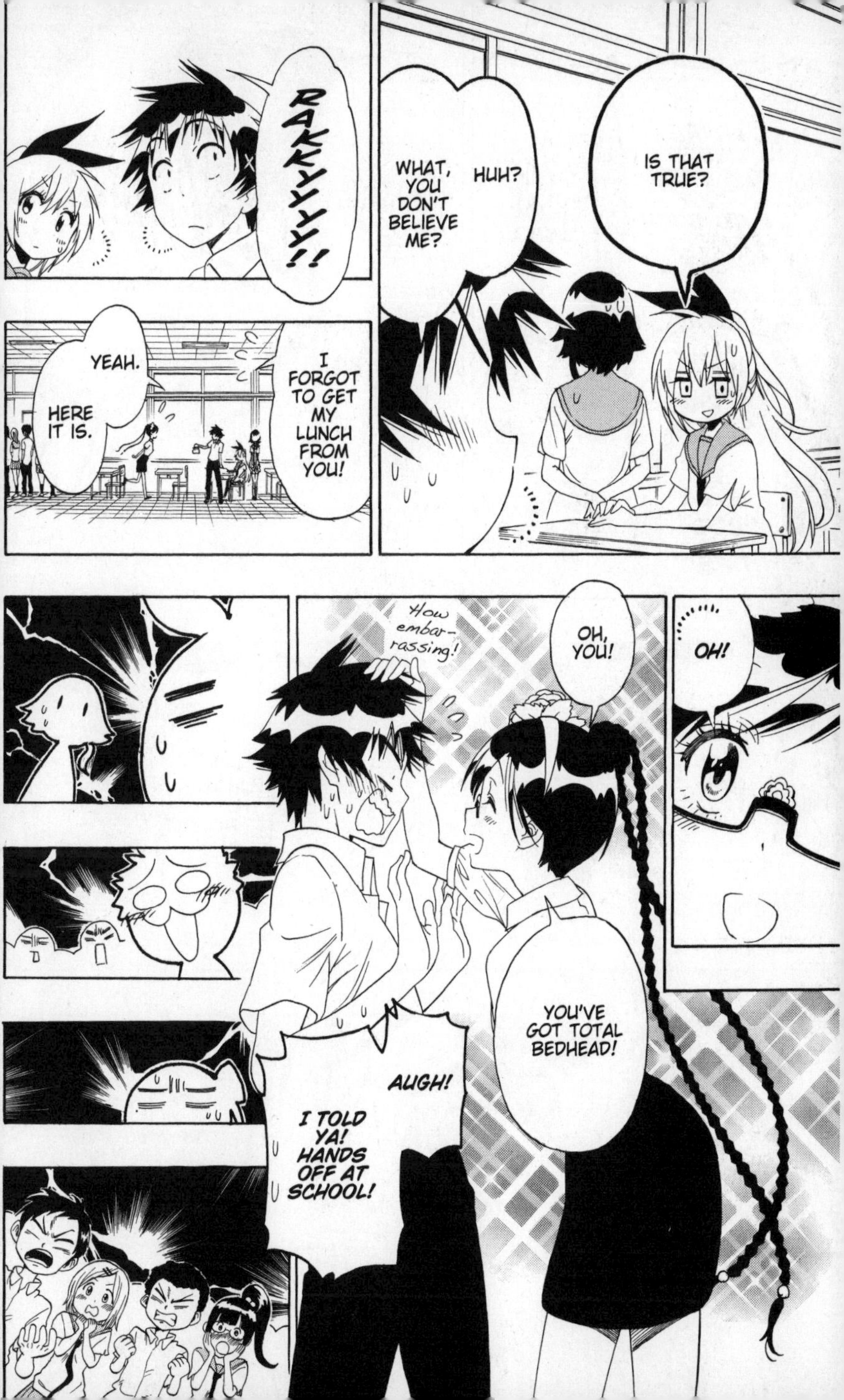
IS THAT TRUE?
HUH?
WHAT, YOU DON'T BELIEVE ME?
RAKKYYYY!!
I FORGOT TO GET MY LUNCH FROM YOU!
YEAH.
HERE IT IS.
OH!
OH, YOU!
How embarrassing!
YOU'VE GOT TOTAL BEDHEAD!
AUGH!
I TOLD YA! HANDS OFF AT SCHOOL!

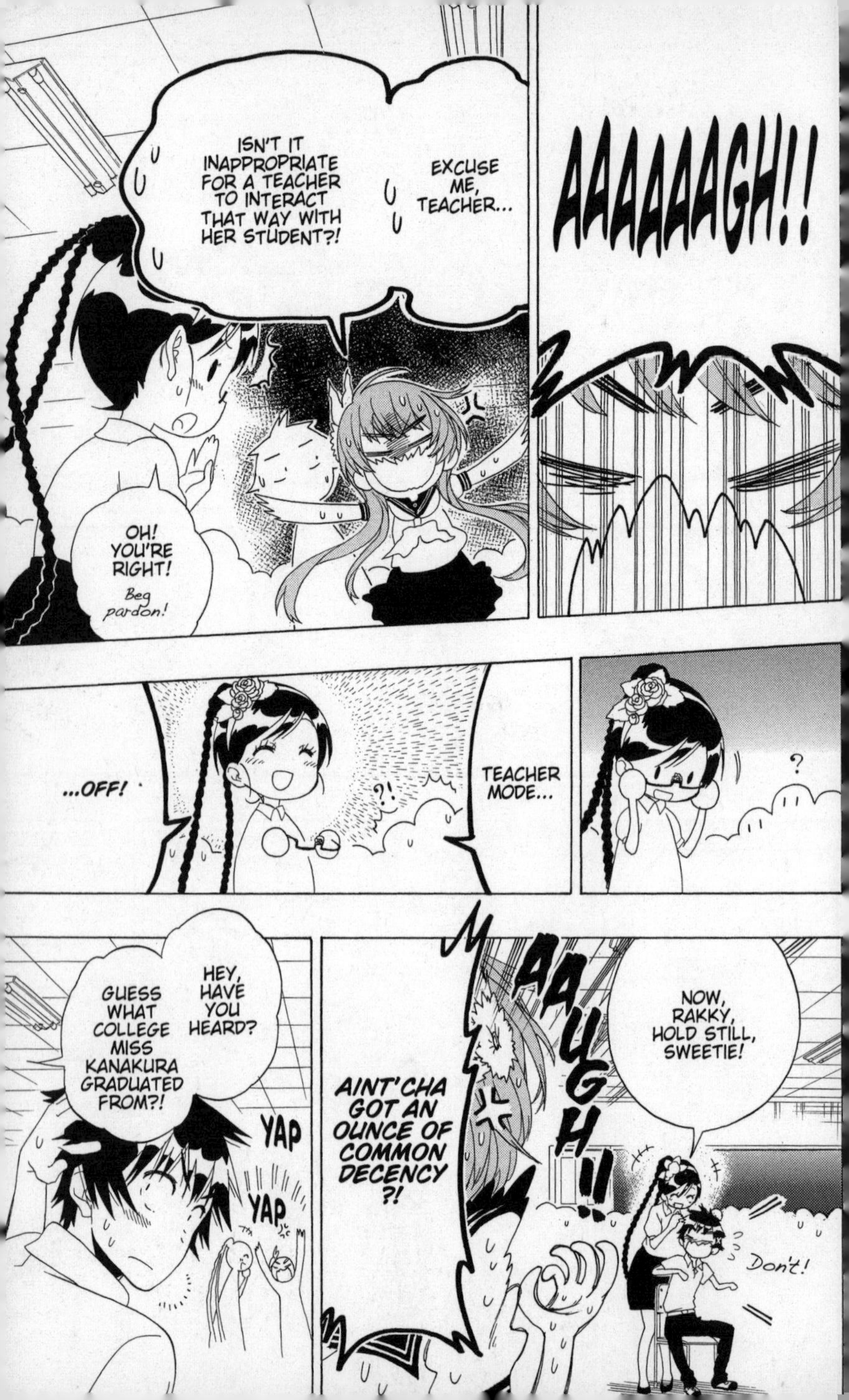
AAAAAAGH!!
EXCUSE ME, TEACHER...
ISN'T IT INAPPROPRIATE FOR A TEACHER TO INTERACT THAT WAY WITH HER STUDENT?!
OH! YOU'RE RIGHT!
Beg pardon!
?
TEACHER MODE...
?!
...OFF!
NOW, RAKKY, HOLD STILL, SWEETIE!
Don't!
AAUGH!!
AIN'T'CHA GOT AN OUNCE OF COMMON DECENCY?!
HEY, HAVE YOU HEARD?
GUESS WHAT COLLEGE MISS KANAKURA GRADUATED FROM?!
YAP
YAP

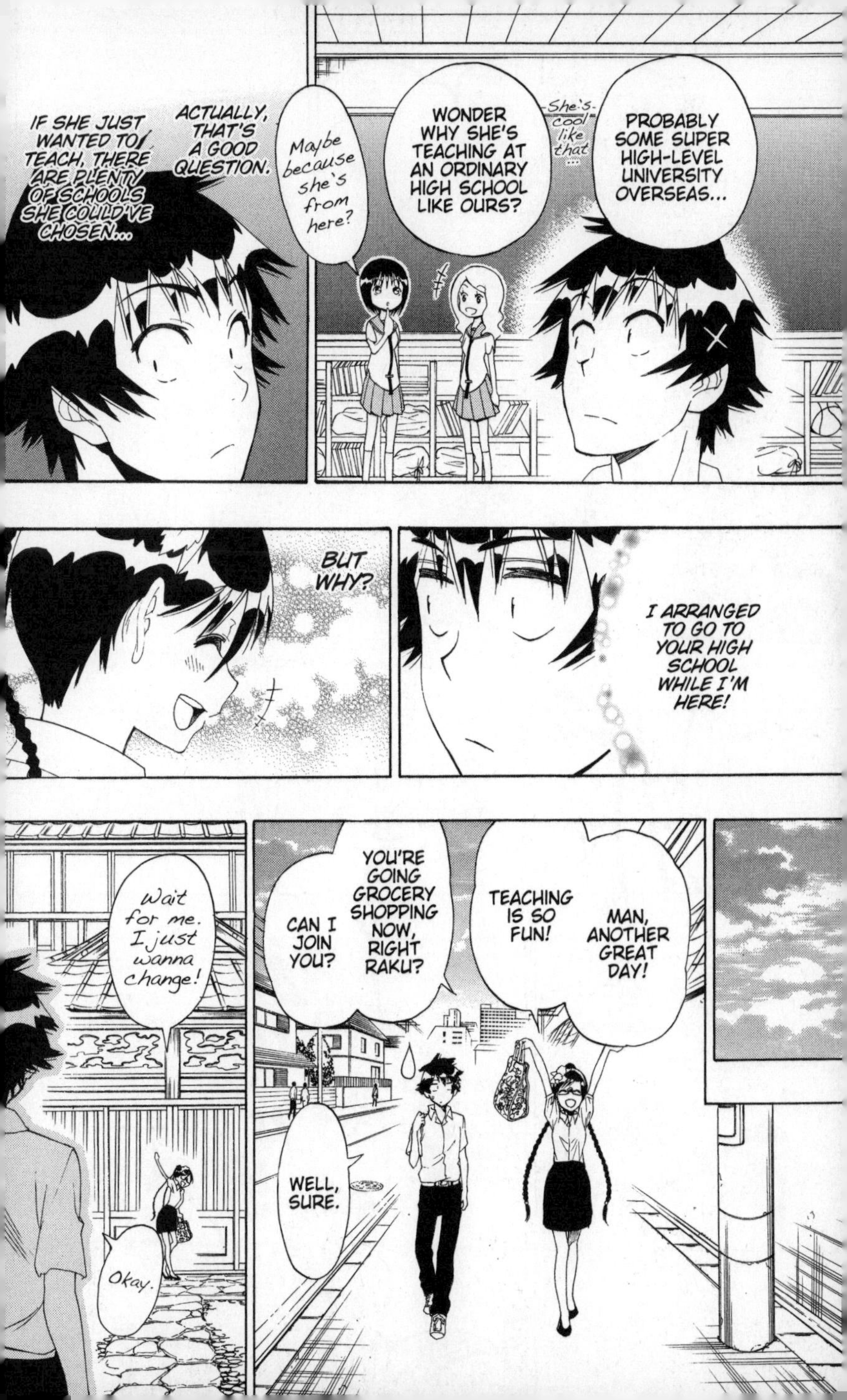
PROBABLY SOME SUPER HIGH-LEVEL UNIVERSITY OVERSEAS...
She's cool like that...
WONDER WHY SHE'S TEACHING AT AN ORDINARY HIGH SCHOOL LIKE OURS?
Maybe because she's from here?
ACTUALLY, THAT'S A GOOD QUESTION.
IF SHE JUST WANTED TO TEACH, THERE ARE PLENTY OF SCHOOLS SHE COULD'VE CHOSEN...
I ARRANGED TO GO TO YOUR HIGH SCHOOL WHILE I'M HERE!
BUT WHY?
MAN, ANOTHER GREAT DAY!
TEACHING IS SO FUN!
YOU'RE GOING GROCERY SHOPPING NOW, RIGHT RAKU?
CAN I JOIN YOU?
WELL, SURE.
Wait for me. I just wanna change!
Okay.

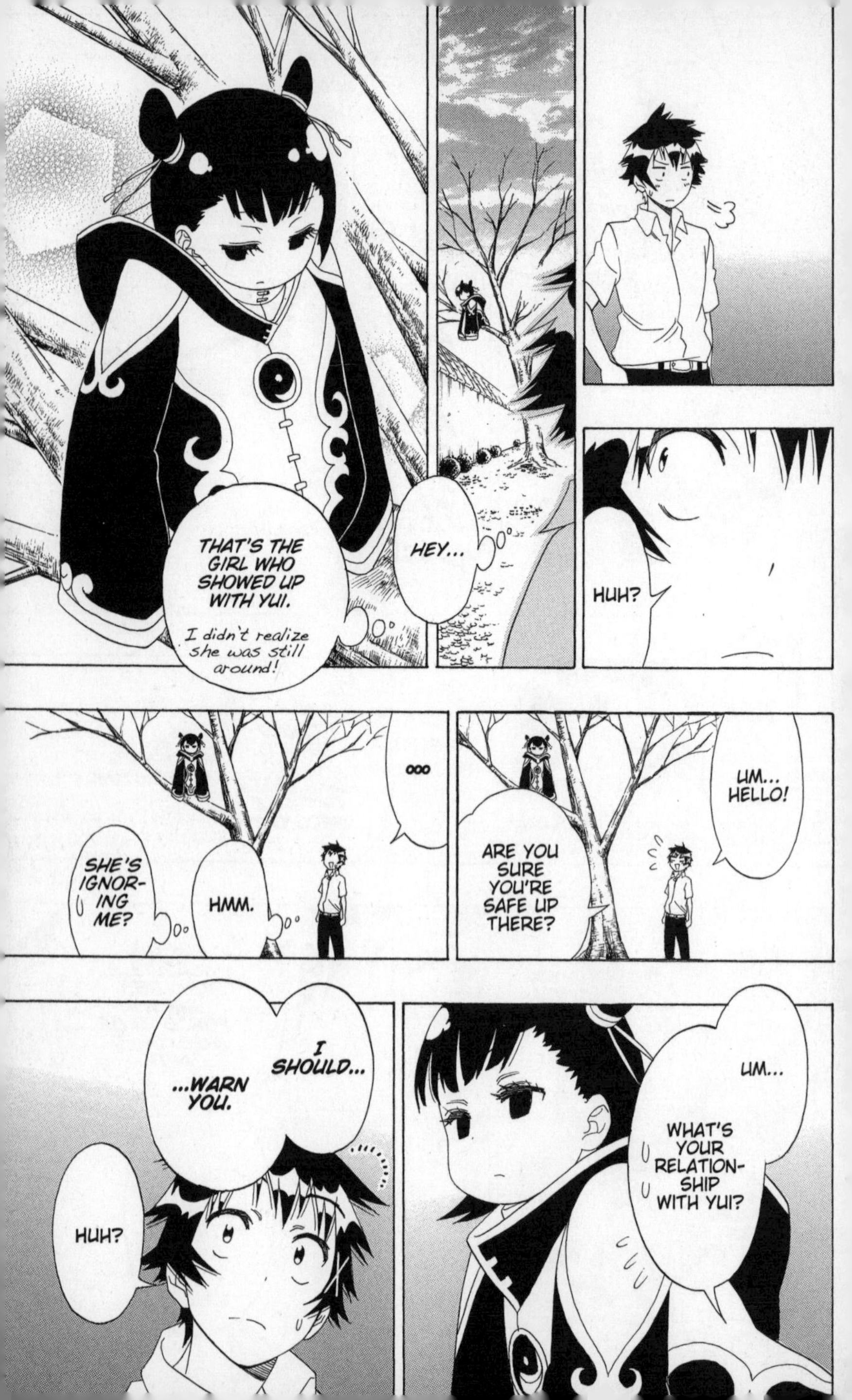
HUH?
HEY...
THAT'S THE GIRL WHO SHOWED UP WITH YUI.
I didn't realize she was still around!
UM... HELLO!
ARE YOU SURE YOU'RE SAFE UP THERE?
...
HMM.
SHE'S IGNOR-ING ME?
UM...
WHAT'S YOUR RELATION-SHIP WITH YUI?
I SHOULD...
...WARN YOU.
HUH?

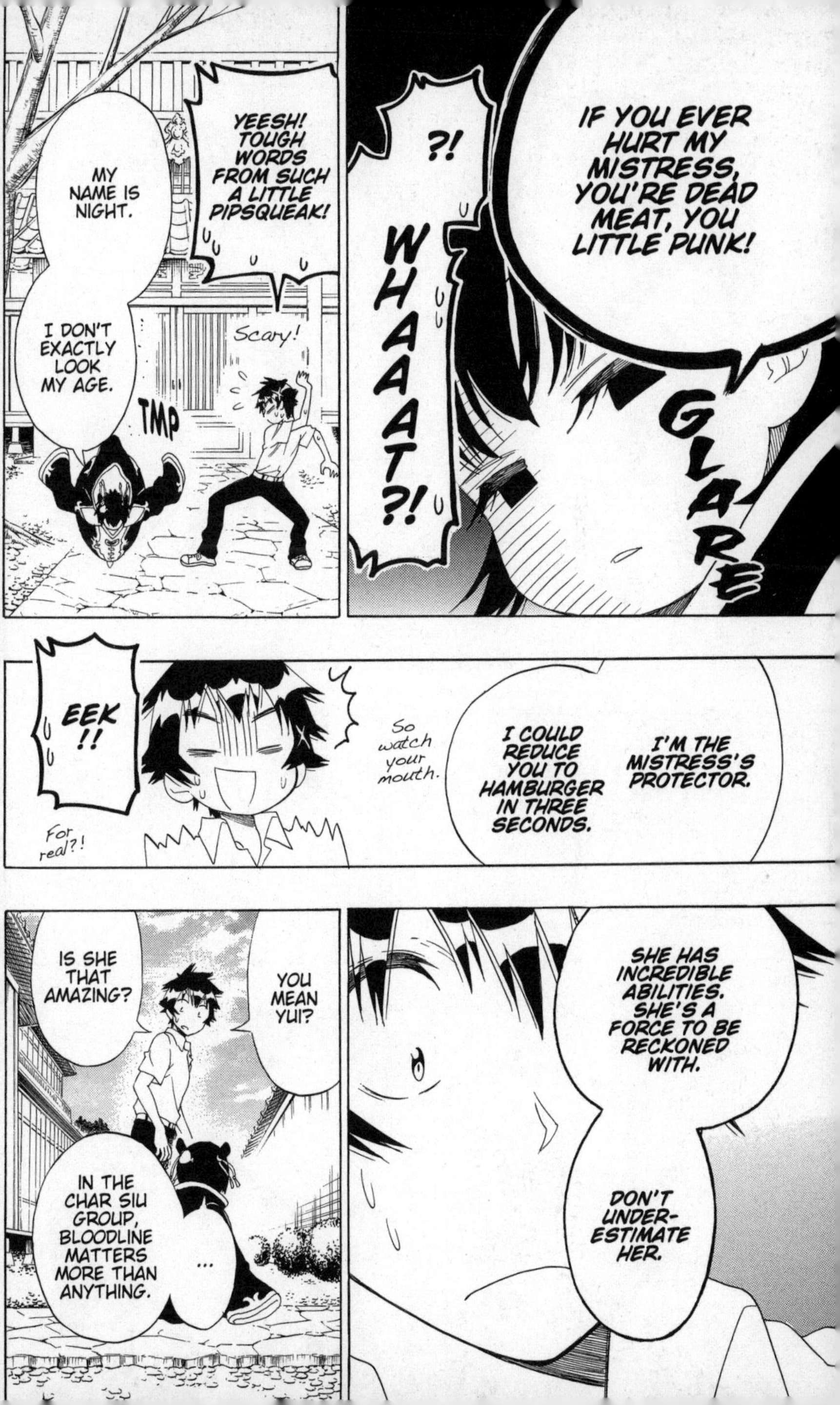
IF YOU EVER HURT MY MISTRESS, YOU'RE DEAD MEAT, YOU LITTLE PUNK!
?!
WHAAAT?!
GLARE
YEESH! TOUGH WORDS FROM SUCH A LITTLE PIPSQUEAK!
MY NAME IS NIGHT.
I DON'T EXACTLY LOOK MY AGE.
Scary!
TMP
I'M THE MISTRESS'S PROTECTOR.
I COULD REDUCE YOU TO HAMBURGER IN THREE SECONDS.
So watch your mouth.
EEK!!
For real?!
SHE HAS INCREDIBLE ABILITIES. SHE'S A FORCE TO BE RECKONED WITH.
DON'T UNDER-ESTIMATE HER.
YOU MEAN YUI?
IS SHE THAT AMAZING?
IN THE CHAR SIU GROUP, BLOODLINE MATTERS MORE THAN ANYTHING.
...

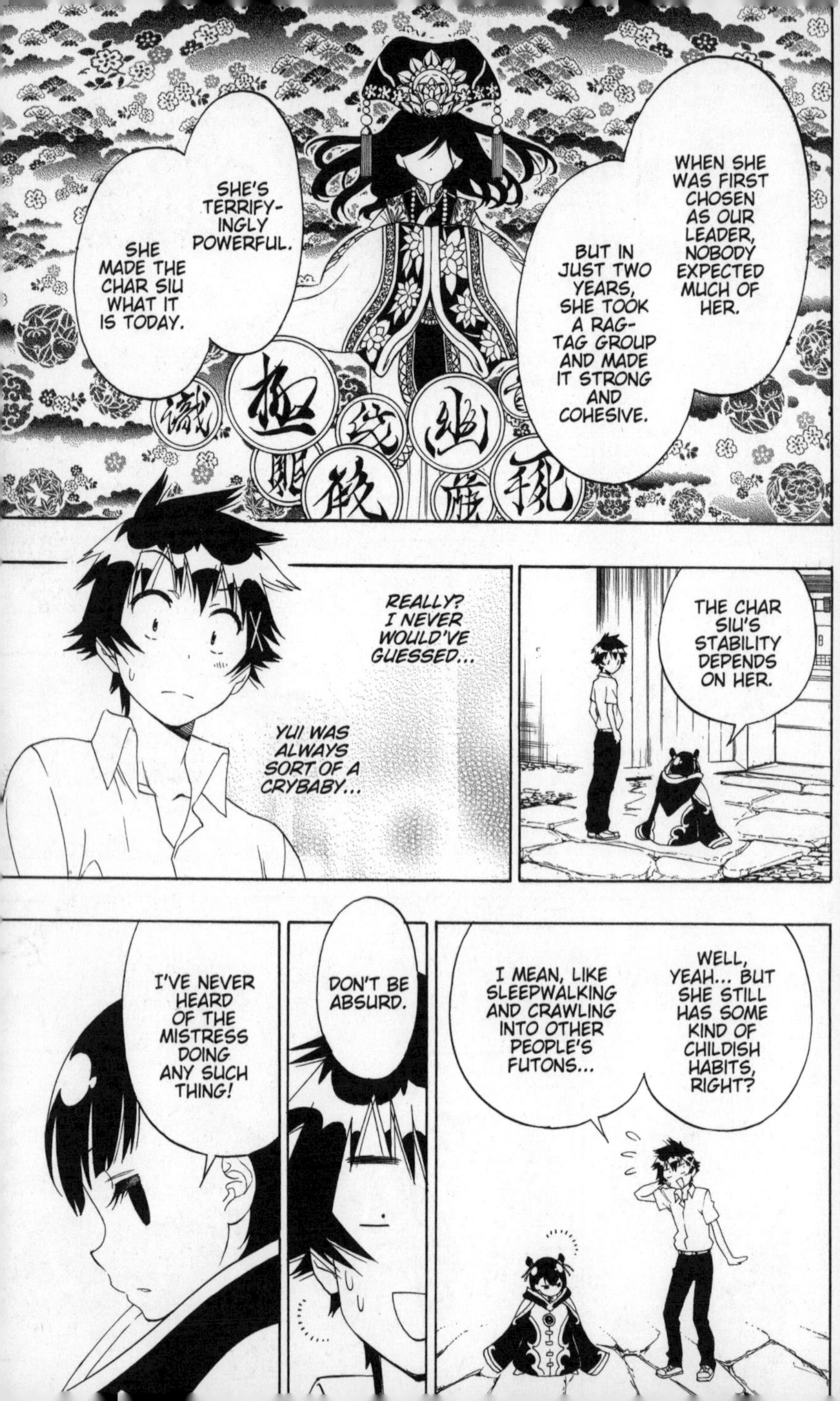
WHEN SHE WAS FIRST CHOSEN AS OUR LEADER, NOBODY EXPECTED MUCH OF HER.
BUT IN JUST TWO YEARS, SHE TOOK A RAG-TAG GROUP AND MADE IT STRONG AND COHESIVE.
SHE'S TERRIFYINGLY POWERFUL.
SHE MADE THE CHAR SIU WHAT IT IS TODAY.
THE CHAR SIU'S STABILITY DEPENDS ON HER.
REALLY? I NEVER WOULD'VE GUESSED...
YUI WAS ALWAYS SORT OF A CRYBABY...
WELL, YEAH... BUT SHE STILL HAS SOME KIND OF CHILDISH HABITS, RIGHT?
I MEAN, LIKE SLEEPWALKING AND CRAWLING INTO OTHER PEOPLE'S FUTONS...
DON'T BE ABSURD.
I'VE NEVER HEARD OF THE MISTRESS DOING ANY SUCH THING!

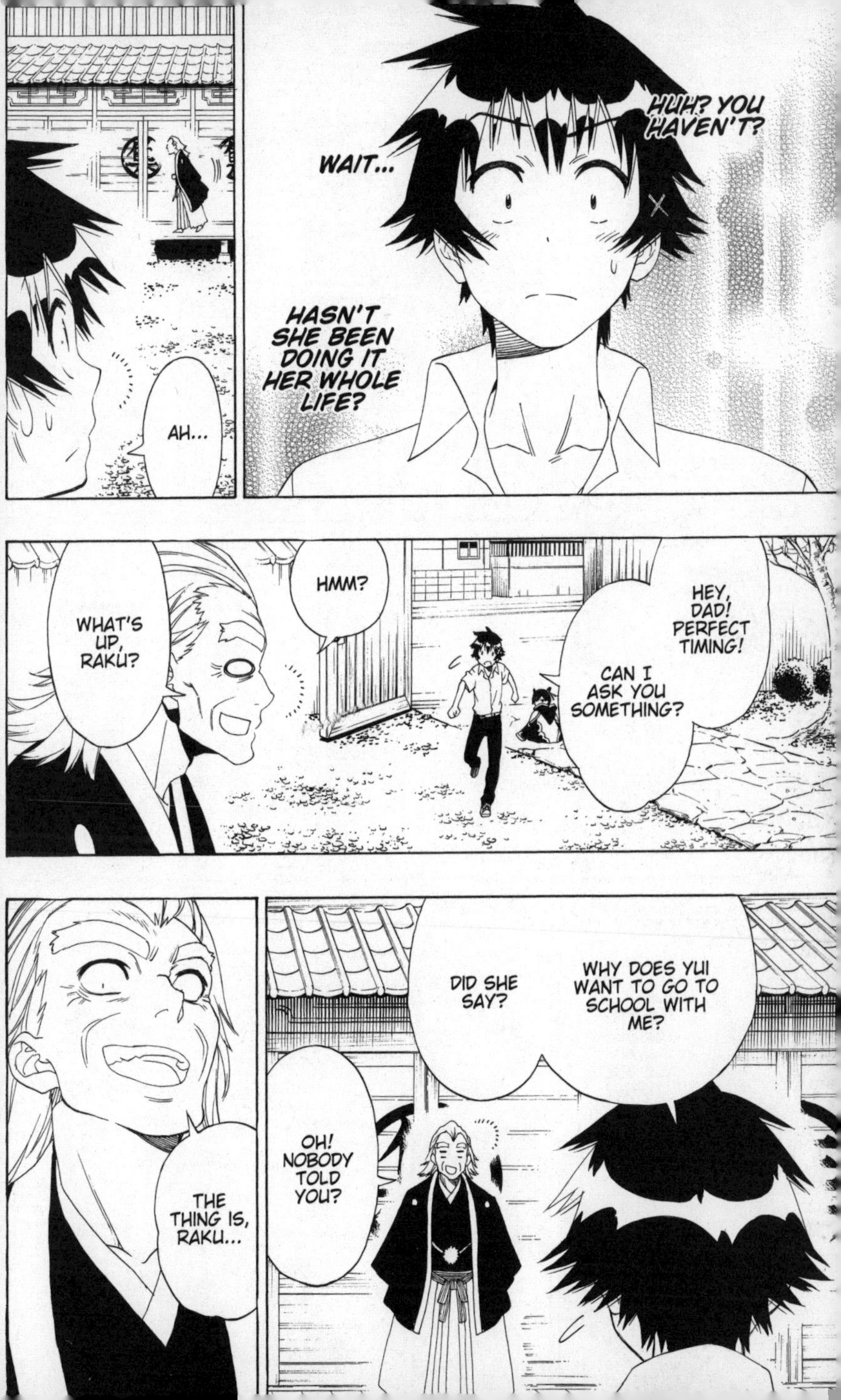
HUH? YOU HAVEN'T?
WAIT...
HASN'T SHE BEEN DOING IT HER WHOLE LIFE?
AH...
HEY, DAD! PERFECT TIMING!
CAN I ASK YOU SOMETHING?
HMM?
WHAT'S UP, RAKU?
WHY DOES YUI WANT TO GO TO SCHOOL WITH ME?
DID SHE SAY?
OH! NOBODY TOLD YOU?
THE THING IS, RAKU...

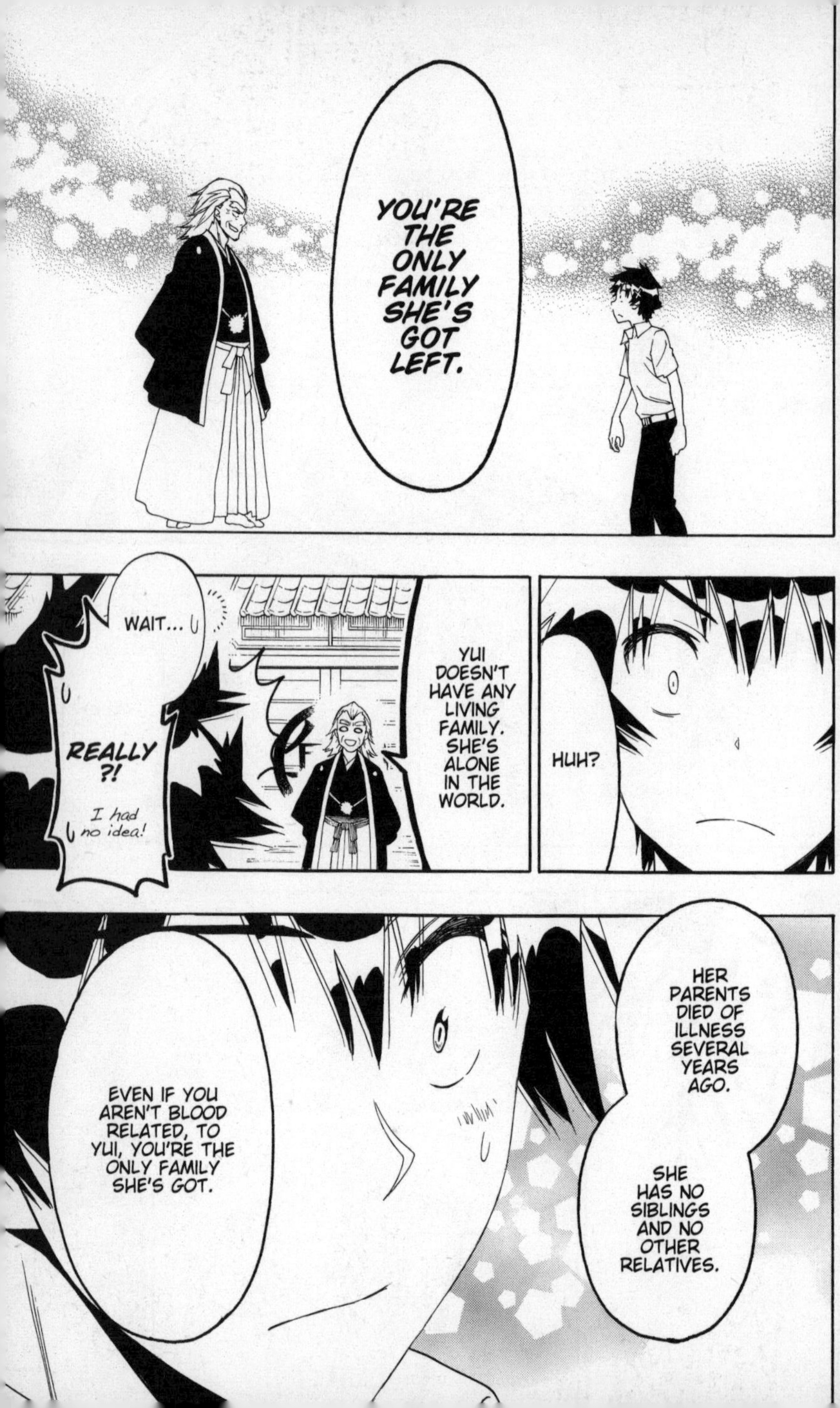
YOU'RE THE ONLY FAMILY SHE'S GOT LEFT.
HUH?
YUI DOESN'T HAVE ANY LIVING FAMILY. SHE'S ALONE IN THE WORLD.
WAIT...
REALLY ?!
I had no idea!
HER PARENTS DIED OF ILLNESS SEVERAL YEARS AGO.
SHE HAS NO SIBLINGS AND NO OTHER RELATIVES.
EVEN IF YOU AREN'T BLOOD RELATED, TO YUI, YOU'RE THE ONLY FAMILY SHE'S GOT.

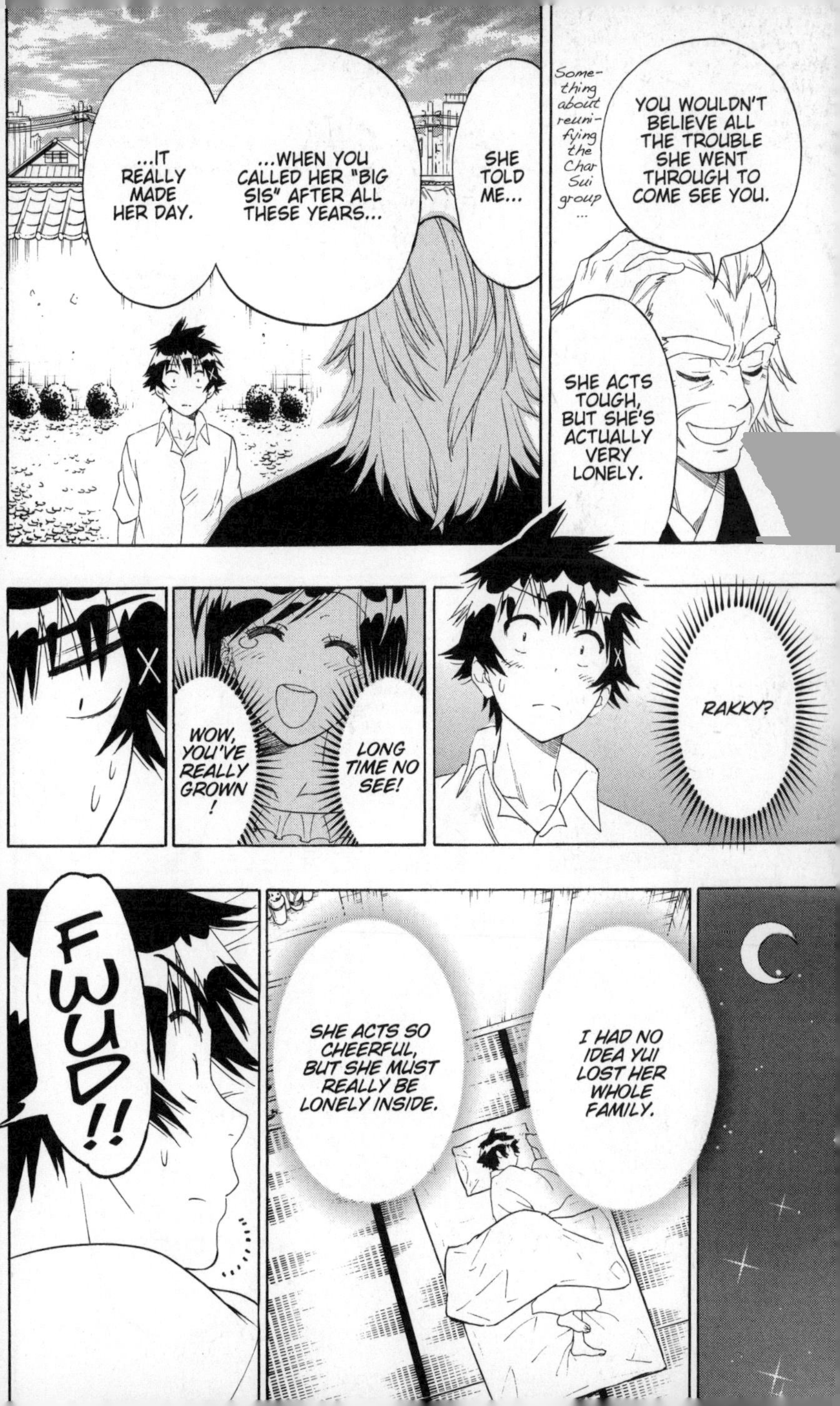
YOU WOULDN'T BELIEVE ALL THE TROUBLE SHE WENT THROUGH TO COME SEE YOU.
Something about reunifying the Char Sui group...
SHE ACTS TOUGH, BUT SHE'S ACTUALLY VERY LONELY.
SHE TOLD ME...
...WHEN YOU CALLED HER "BIG SIS" AFTER ALL THESE YEARS...
...IT REALLY MADE HER DAY.
RAKKY?
LONG TIME NO SEE!
WOW, YOU'VE REALLY GROWN!
I HAD NO IDEA YUI LOST HER WHOLE FAMILY.
SHE ACTS SO CHEERFUL, BUT SHE MUST REALLY BE LONELY INSIDE.
FWUD!!

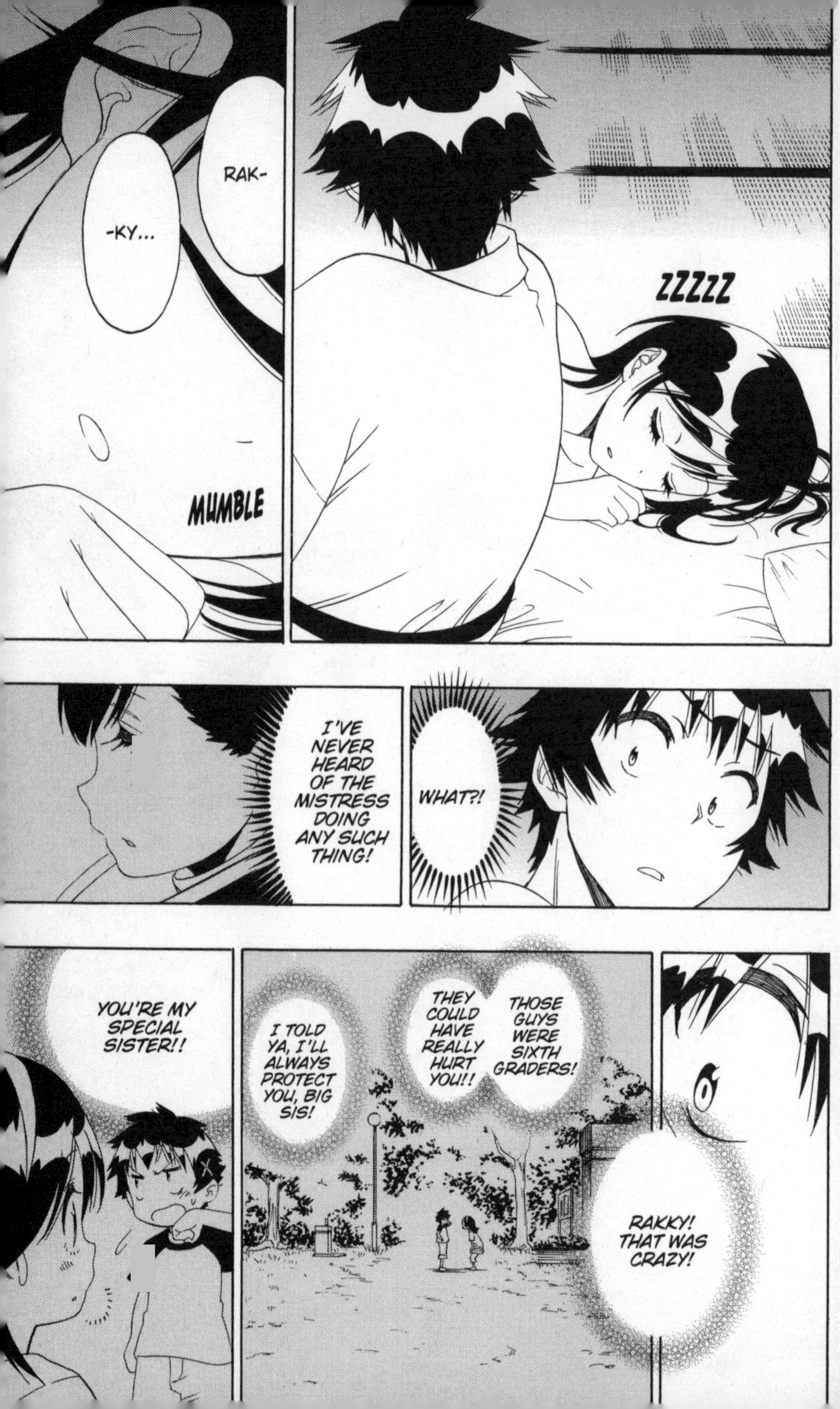
ZZZZZ
RAK-
-KY...
MUMBLE
WHAT?!
I'VE NEVER HEARD OF THE MISTRESS DOING ANY SUCH THING!
RAKKY! THAT WAS CRAZY!
THOSE GUYS WERE SIXTH GRADERS!
THEY COULD HAVE REALLY HURT YOU!!
I TOLD YA, I'LL ALWAYS PROTECT YOU, BIG SIS!
YOU'RE MY SPECIAL SISTER!!

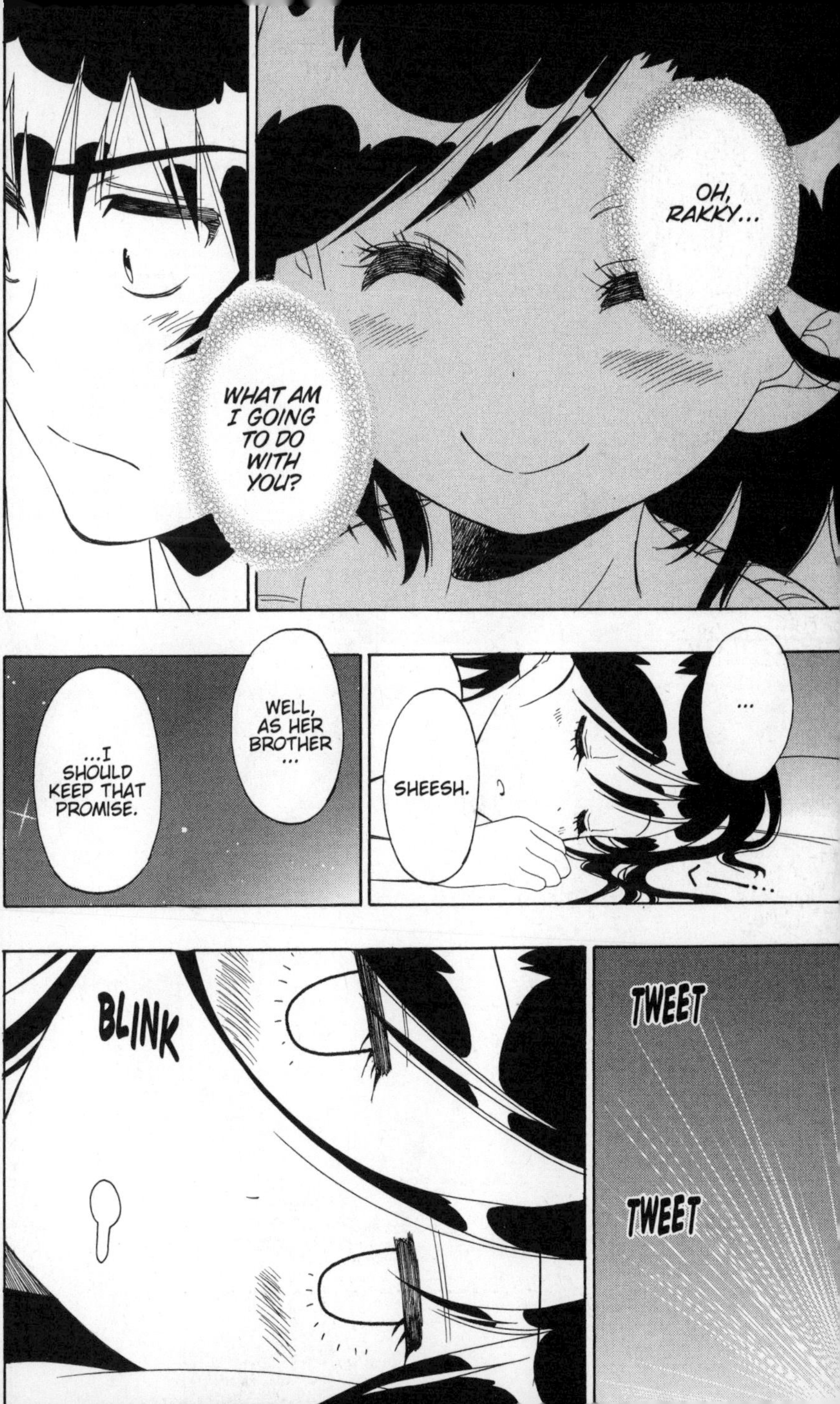
OH, RAKKY...
WHAT AM I GOING TO DO WITH YOU?
...
SHEESH.
WELL, AS HER BROTHER ...
...I SHOULD KEEP THAT PROMISE.
TWEET
TWEET
BLINK

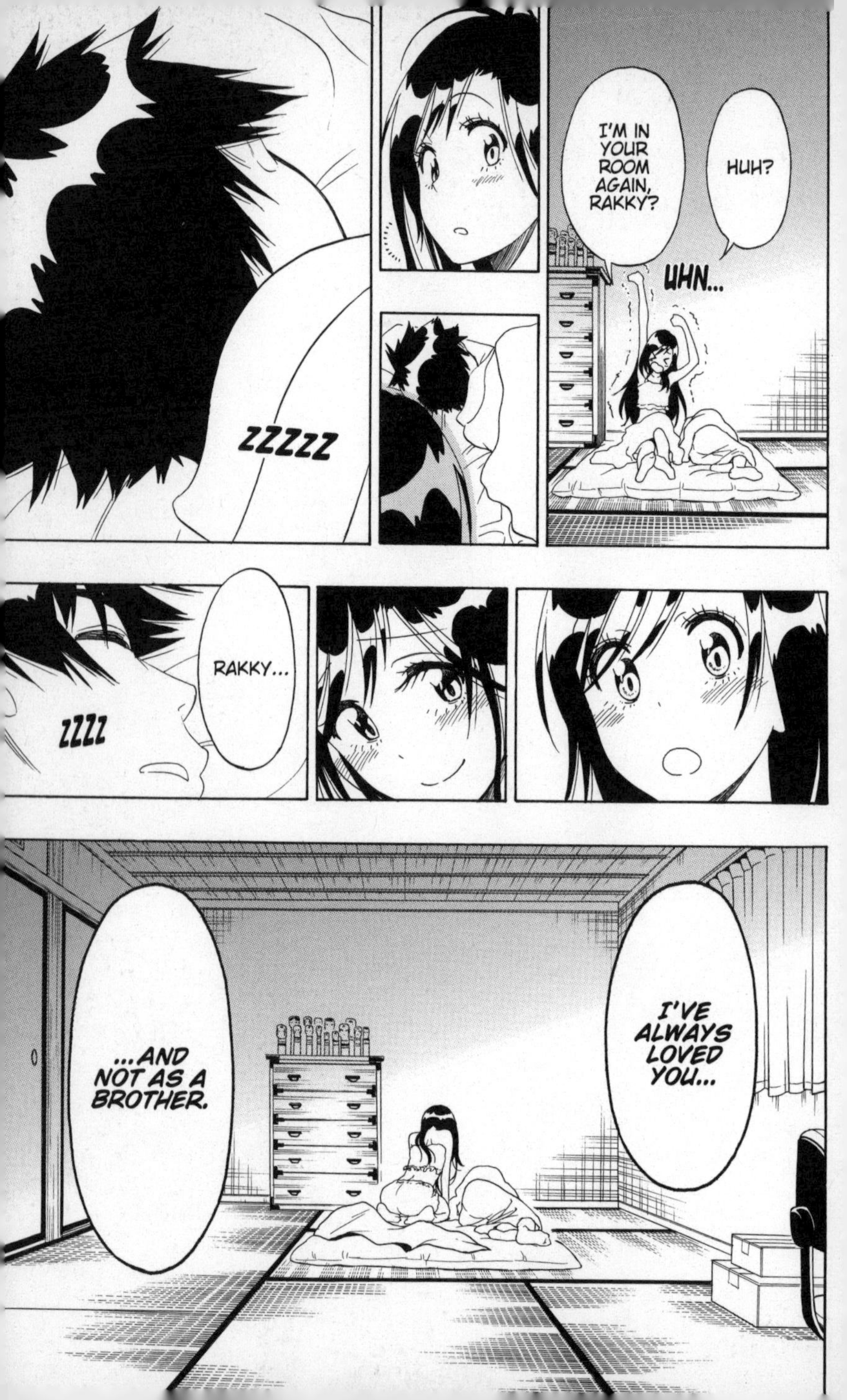
HUH?
I'M IN YOUR ROOM AGAIN, RAKKY?
UHN...
ZZZZZ
RAKKY...
ZZZZ
I'VE ALWAYS LOVED YOU...
...AND NOT AS A BROTHER.

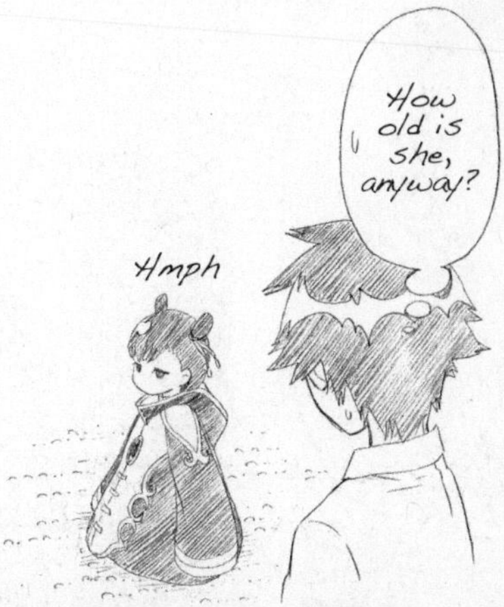
How old is she, anyway?
Hmph

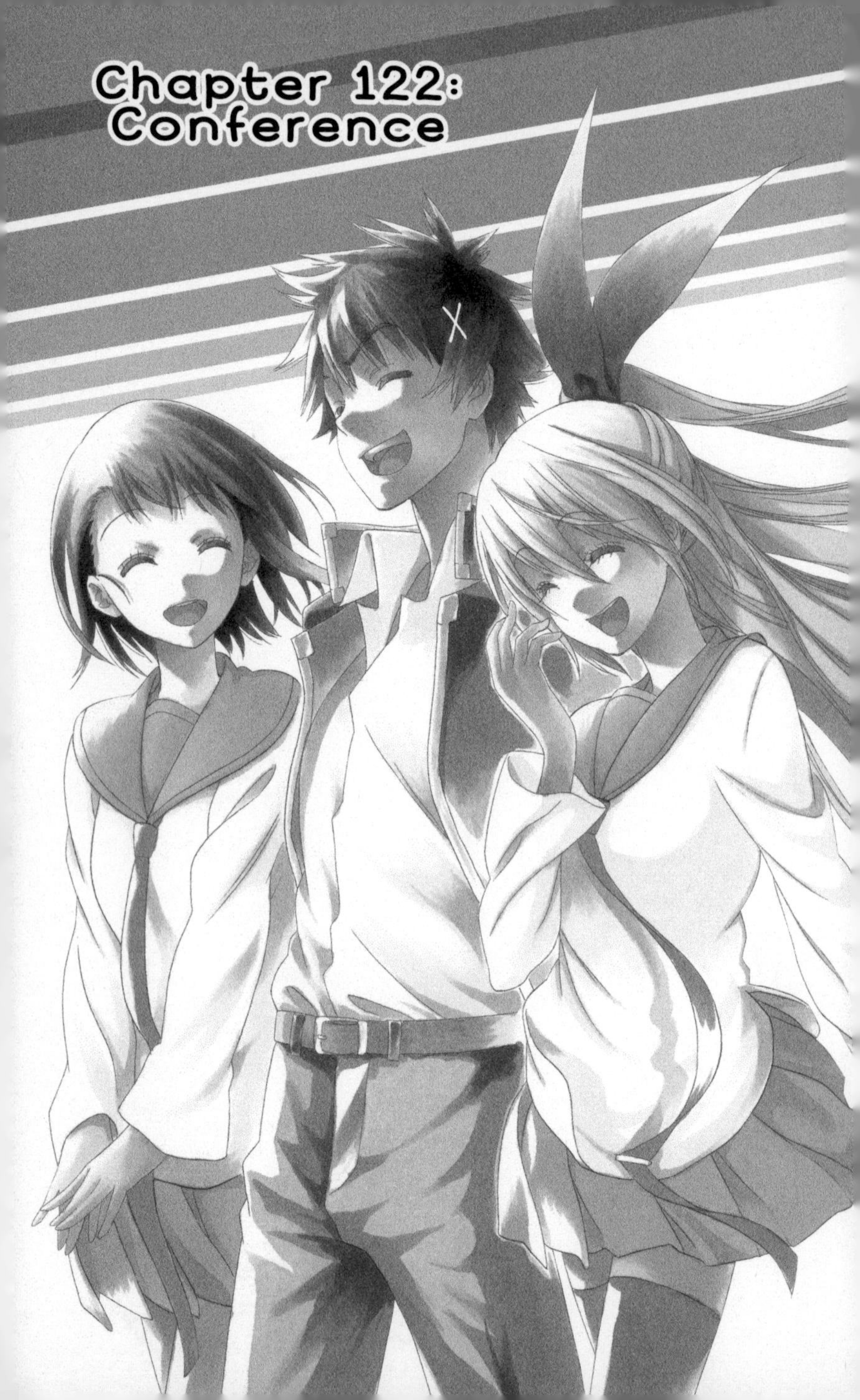
Chapter 122:
Conference

NISEKOI
False Love

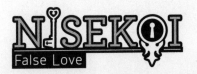

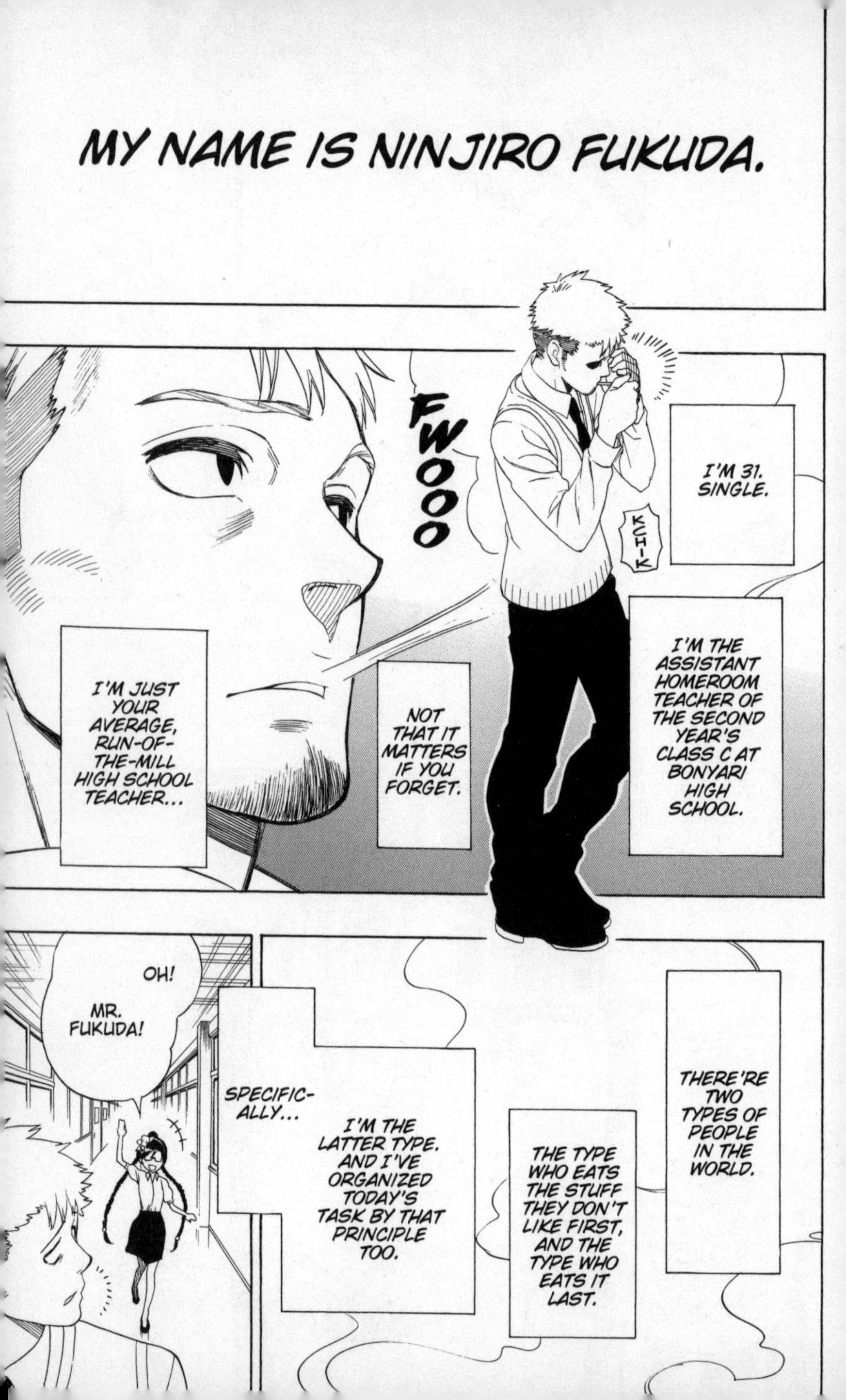
MY NAME IS NINJIRO FUKUDA.
I'M 31. SINGLE.
KCHIK
I'M THE ASSISTANT HOMEROOM TEACHER OF THE SECOND YEAR'S CLASS C AT BONYARI HIGH SCHOOL.
FWOOO
NOT THAT IT MATTERS IF YOU FORGET.
I'M JUST YOUR AVERAGE, RUN-OF-THE-MILL HIGH SCHOOL TEACHER...
THERE'RE TWO TYPES OF PEOPLE IN THE WORLD.
THE TYPE WHO EATS THE STUFF THEY DON'T LIKE FIRST, AND THE TYPE WHO EATS IT LAST.
I'M THE LATTER TYPE. AND I'VE ORGANIZED TODAY'S TASK BY THAT PRINCIPLE TOO.
SPECIFIC-ALLY...
OH!
MR. FUKUDA!

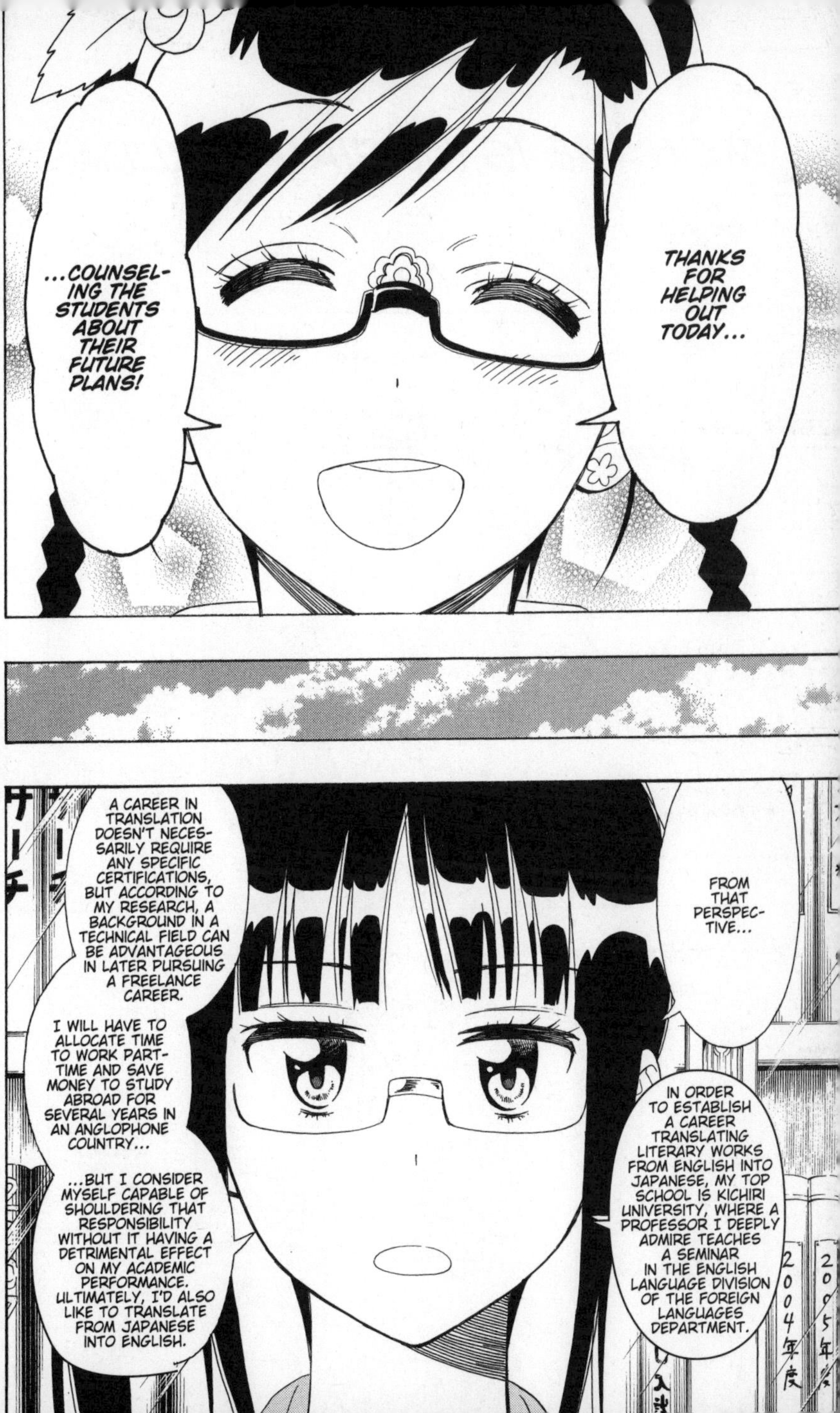

THANKS FOR HELPING OUT TODAY...
...COUNSELING THE STUDENTS ABOUT THEIR FUTURE PLANS!
FROM THAT PERSPECTIVE...
IN ORDER TO ESTABLISH A CAREER TRANSLATING LITERARY WORKS FROM ENGLISH INTO JAPANESE, MY TOP SCHOOL IS KICHIRI UNIVERSITY, WHERE A PROFESSOR I DEEPLY ADMIRE TEACHES A SEMINAR IN THE ENGLISH LANGUAGE DIVISION OF THE FOREIGN LANGUAGES DEPARTMENT.
A CAREER IN TRANSLATION DOESN'T NECESSARILY REQUIRE ANY SPECIFIC CERTIFICATIONS, BUT ACCORDING TO MY RESEARCH, A BACKGROUND IN A TECHNICAL FIELD CAN BE ADVANTAGEOUS IN LATER PURSUING A FREELANCE CAREER.
I WILL HAVE TO ALLOCATE TIME TO WORK PART-TIME AND SAVE MONEY TO STUDY ABROAD FOR SEVERAL YEARS IN AN ANGLOPHONE COUNTRY...
...BUT I CONSIDER MYSELF CAPABLE OF SHOULDERING THAT RESPONSIBILITY WITHOUT IT HAVING A DETRIMENTAL EFFECT ON MY ACADEMIC PERFORMANCE. ULTIMATELY, I'D ALSO LIKE TO TRANSLATE FROM JAPANESE INTO ENGLISH.
2004年度

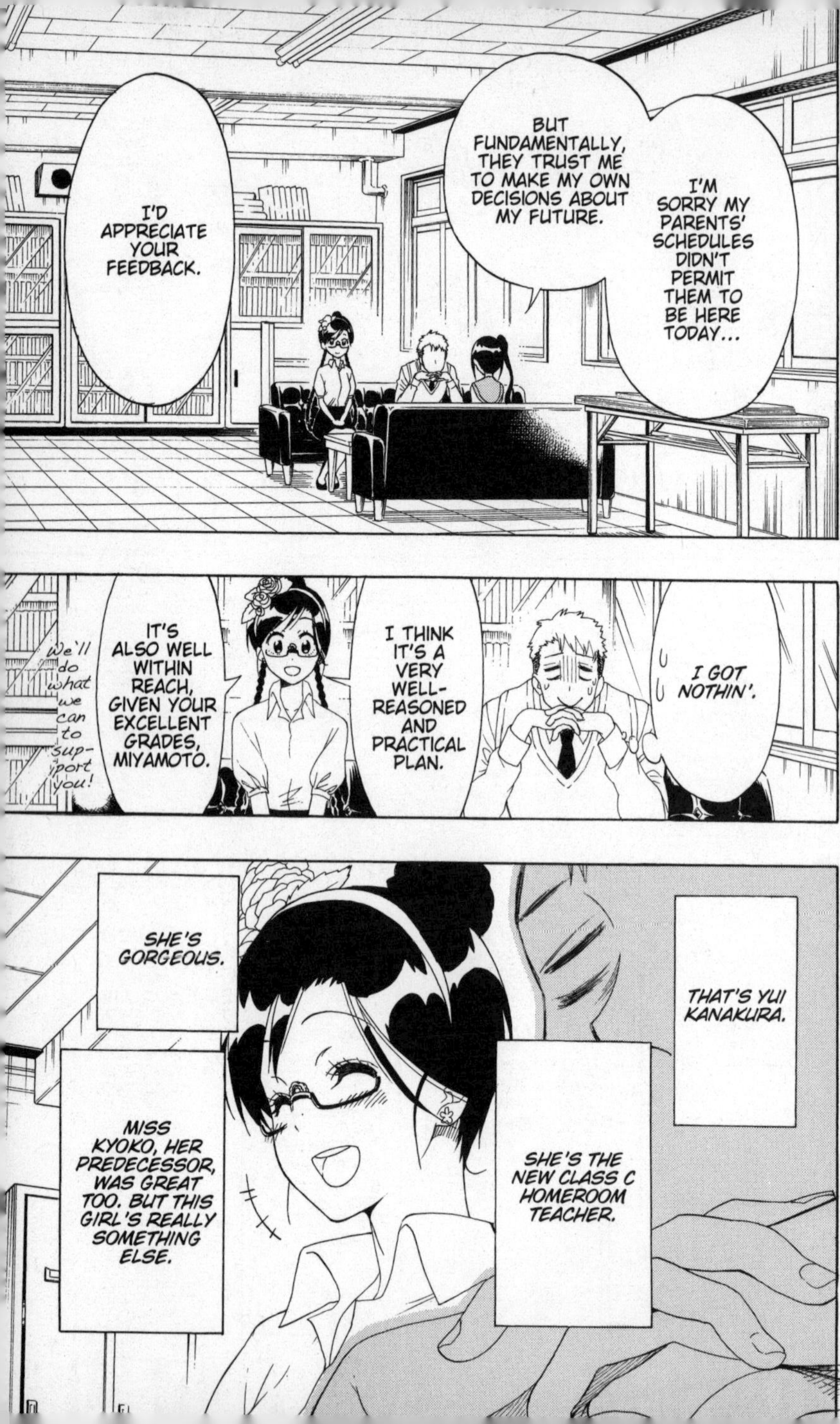
I'M SORRY MY PARENTS' SCHEDULES DIDN'T PERMIT THEM TO BE HERE TODAY...
BUT FUNDAMENTALLY, THEY TRUST ME TO MAKE MY OWN DECISIONS ABOUT MY FUTURE.
I'D APPRECIATE YOUR FEEDBACK.
I GOT NOTHIN'.
I THINK IT'S A VERY WELL-REASONED AND PRACTICAL PLAN.
IT'S ALSO WELL WITHIN REACH, GIVEN YOUR EXCELLENT GRADES, MIYAMOTO.
We'll do what we can to support you!
THAT'S YUI KANAKURA.
SHE'S THE NEW CLASS C HOMEROOM TEACHER.
SHE'S GORGEOUS.
MISS KYOKO, HER PREDECESSOR, WAS GREAT TOO. BUT THIS GIRL'S REALLY SOMETHING ELSE.

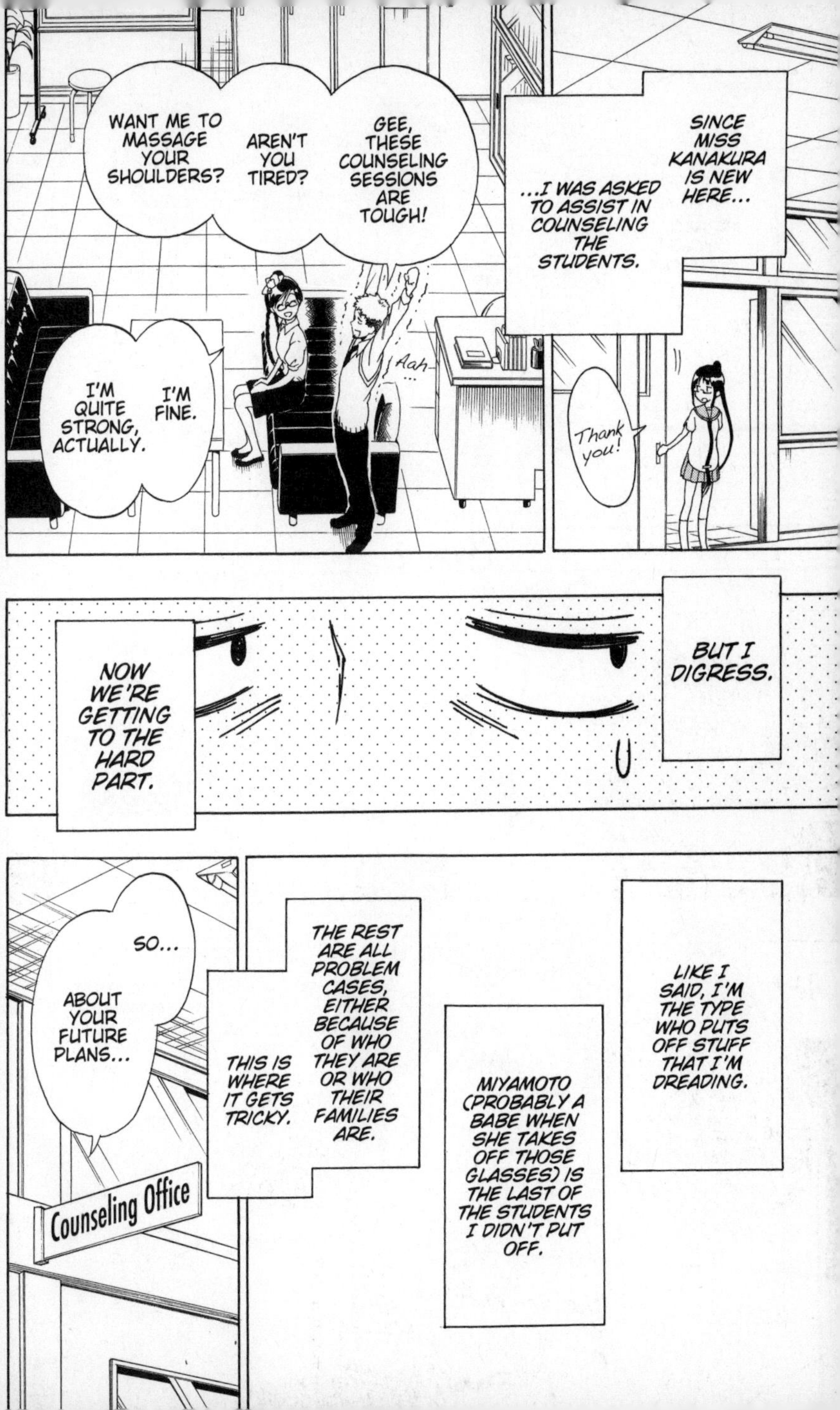
SINCE MISS KANAKURA IS NEW HERE...
...I WAS ASKED TO ASSIST IN COUNSELING THE STUDENTS.
Thank you!
GEE, THESE COUNSELING SESSIONS ARE TOUGH!
AREN'T YOU TIRED?
WANT ME TO MASSAGE YOUR SHOULDERS?
Aah...
I'M FINE.
I'M QUITE STRONG, ACTUALLY.
BUT I DIGRESS.
NOW WE'RE GETTING TO THE HARD PART.
LIKE I SAID, I'M THE TYPE WHO PUTS OFF STUFF THAT I'M DREADING.
MIYAMOTO (PROBABLY A BABE WHEN SHE TAKES OFF THOSE GLASSES) IS THE LAST OF THE STUDENTS I DIDN'T PUT OFF.
THE REST ARE ALL PROBLEM CASES, EITHER BECAUSE OF WHO THEY ARE OR WHO THEIR FAMILIES ARE.
THIS IS WHERE IT GETS TRICKY.
SO...
ABOUT YOUR FUTURE PLANS...
Counseling Office

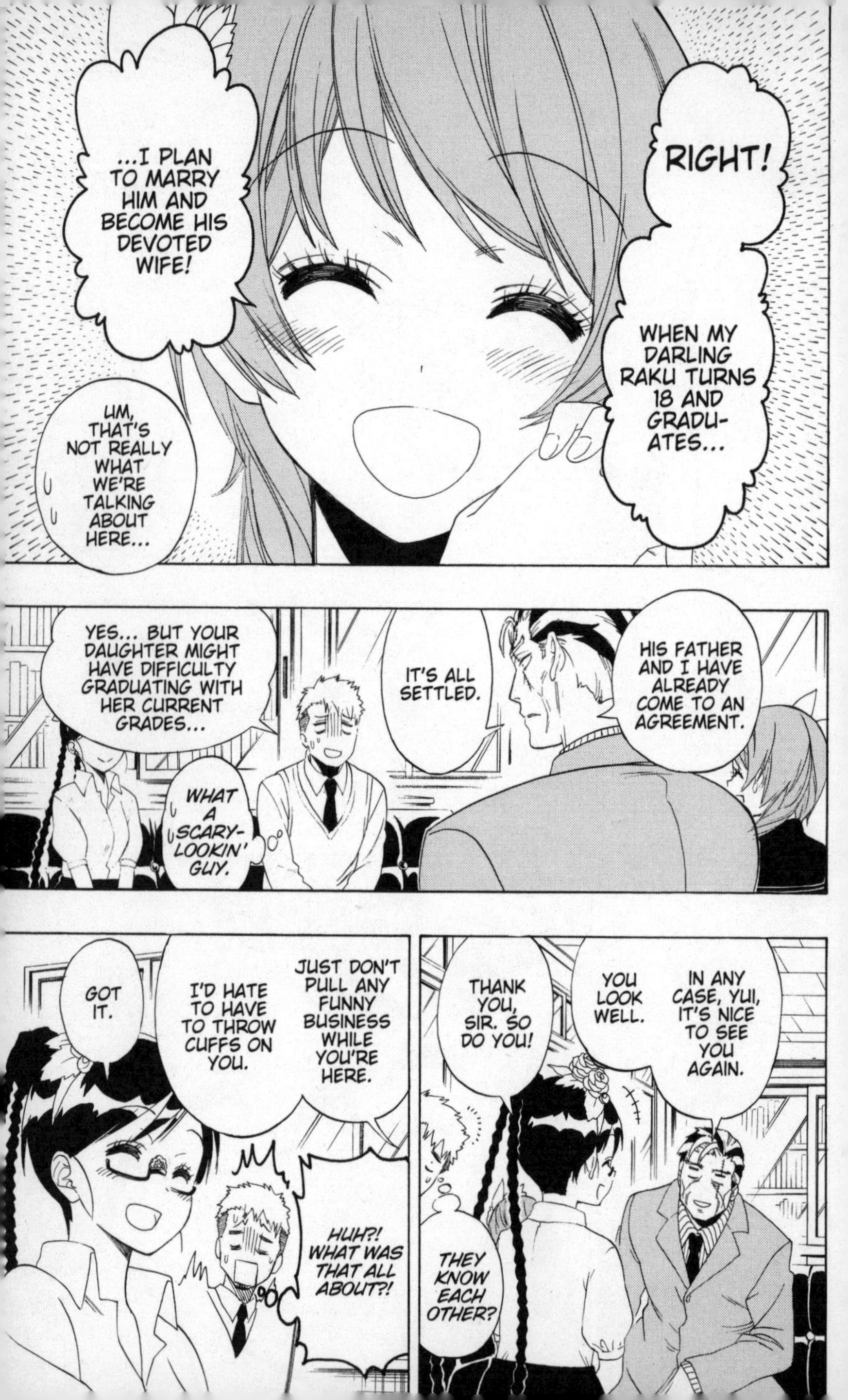
RIGHT!
WHEN MY DARLING RAKU TURNS 18 AND GRADUATES...
...I PLAN TO MARRY HIM AND BECOME HIS DEVOTED WIFE!
UM, THAT'S NOT REALLY WHAT WE'RE TALKING ABOUT HERE...
HIS FATHER AND I HAVE ALREADY COME TO AN AGREEMENT.
IT'S ALL SETTLED.
YES... BUT YOUR DAUGHTER MIGHT HAVE DIFFICULTY GRADUATING WITH HER CURRENT GRADES...
WHAT A SCARY-LOOKIN' GUY.
IN ANY CASE, YUI, IT'S NICE TO SEE YOU AGAIN.
YOU LOOK WELL.
THANK YOU, SIR. SO DO YOU!
THEY KNOW EACH OTHER?
JUST DON'T PULL ANY FUNNY BUSINESS WHILE YOU'RE HERE.
I'D HATE TO HAVE TO THROW CUFFS ON YOU.
GOT IT.
HUH?! WHAT WAS THAT ALL ABOUT?!

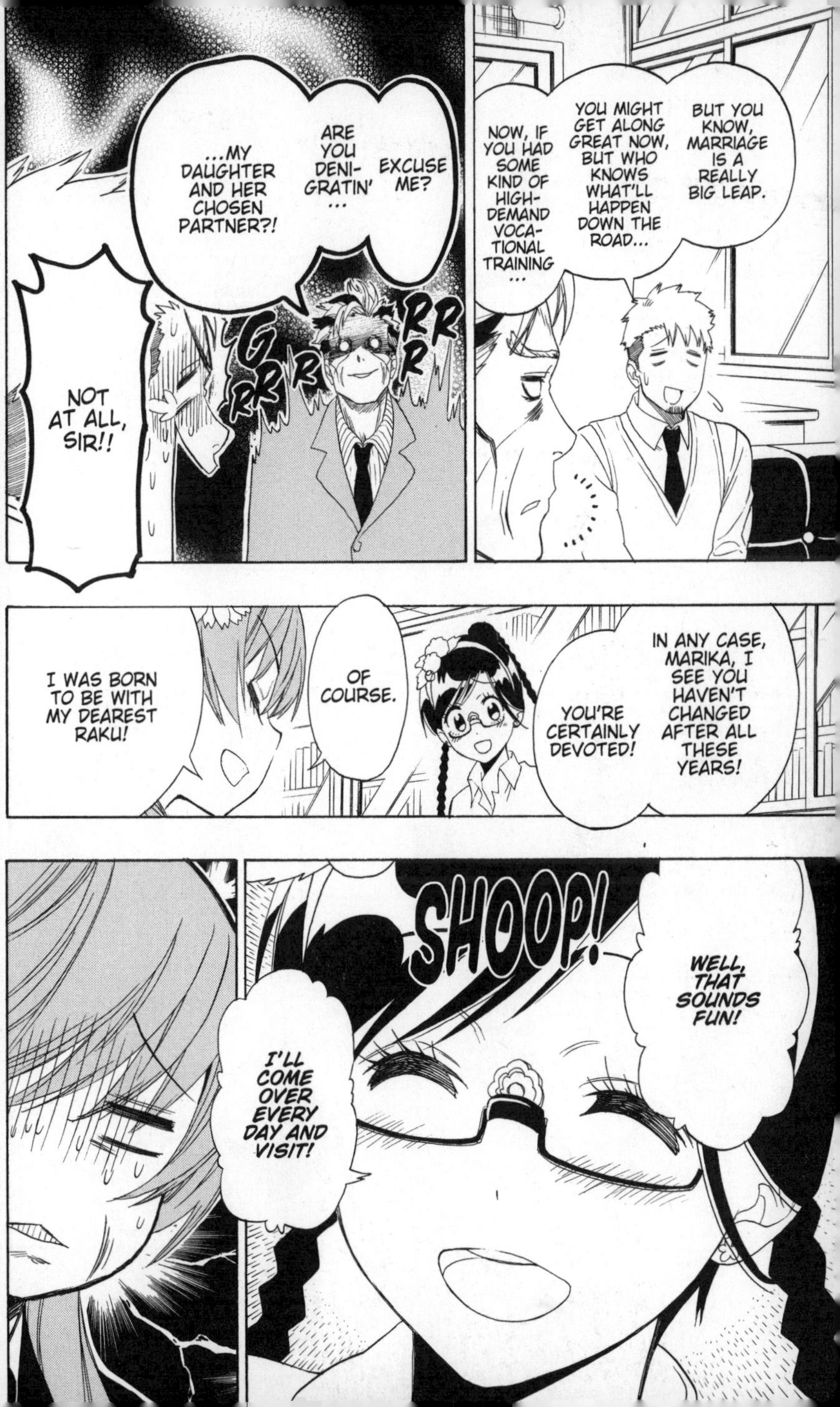
BUT YOU KNOW, MARRIAGE IS A REALLY BIG LEAP.
YOU MIGHT GET ALONG GREAT NOW, BUT WHO KNOWS WHAT'LL HAPPEN DOWN THE ROAD...
NOW, IF YOU HAD SOME KIND OF HIGH-DEMAND VOCATIONAL TRAINING...
EXCUSE ME?
ARE YOU DENIGRATIN'...
...MY DAUGHTER AND HER CHOSEN PARTNER?!
GRRRRRR
NOT AT ALL, SIR!!
IN ANY CASE, MARIKA, I SEE YOU HAVEN'T CHANGED AFTER ALL THESE YEARS!
YOU'RE CERTAINLY DEVOTED!
OF COURSE.
I WAS BORN TO BE WITH MY DEAREST RAKU!
SHOOP!
WELL, THAT SOUNDS FUN!
I'LL COME OVER EVERY DAY AND VISIT!

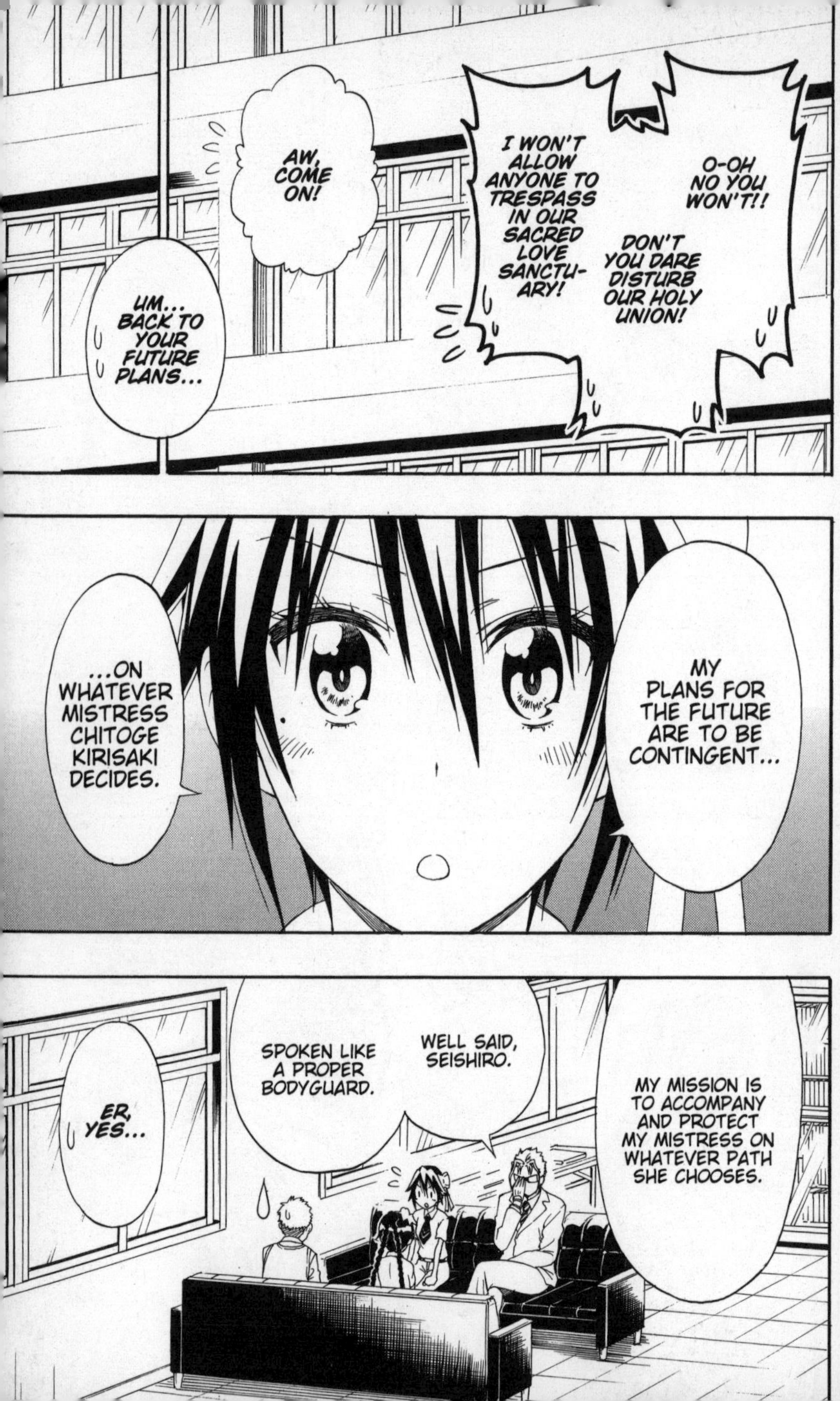
O-OH NO YOU WON'T!!
DON'T YOU DARE DISTURB OUR HOLY UNION!
I WON'T ALLOW ANYONE TO TRESPASS IN OUR SACRED LOVE SANCTUARY!
AW, COME ON!
UM... BACK TO YOUR FUTURE PLANS...
MY PLANS FOR THE FUTURE ARE TO BE CONTINGENT...
...ON WHATEVER MISTRESS CHITOGE KIRISAKI DECIDES.
MY MISSION IS TO ACCOMPANY AND PROTECT MY MISTRESS ON WHATEVER PATH SHE CHOOSES.
WELL SAID, SEISHIRO.
SPOKEN LIKE A PROPER BODYGUARD.
ER, YES...

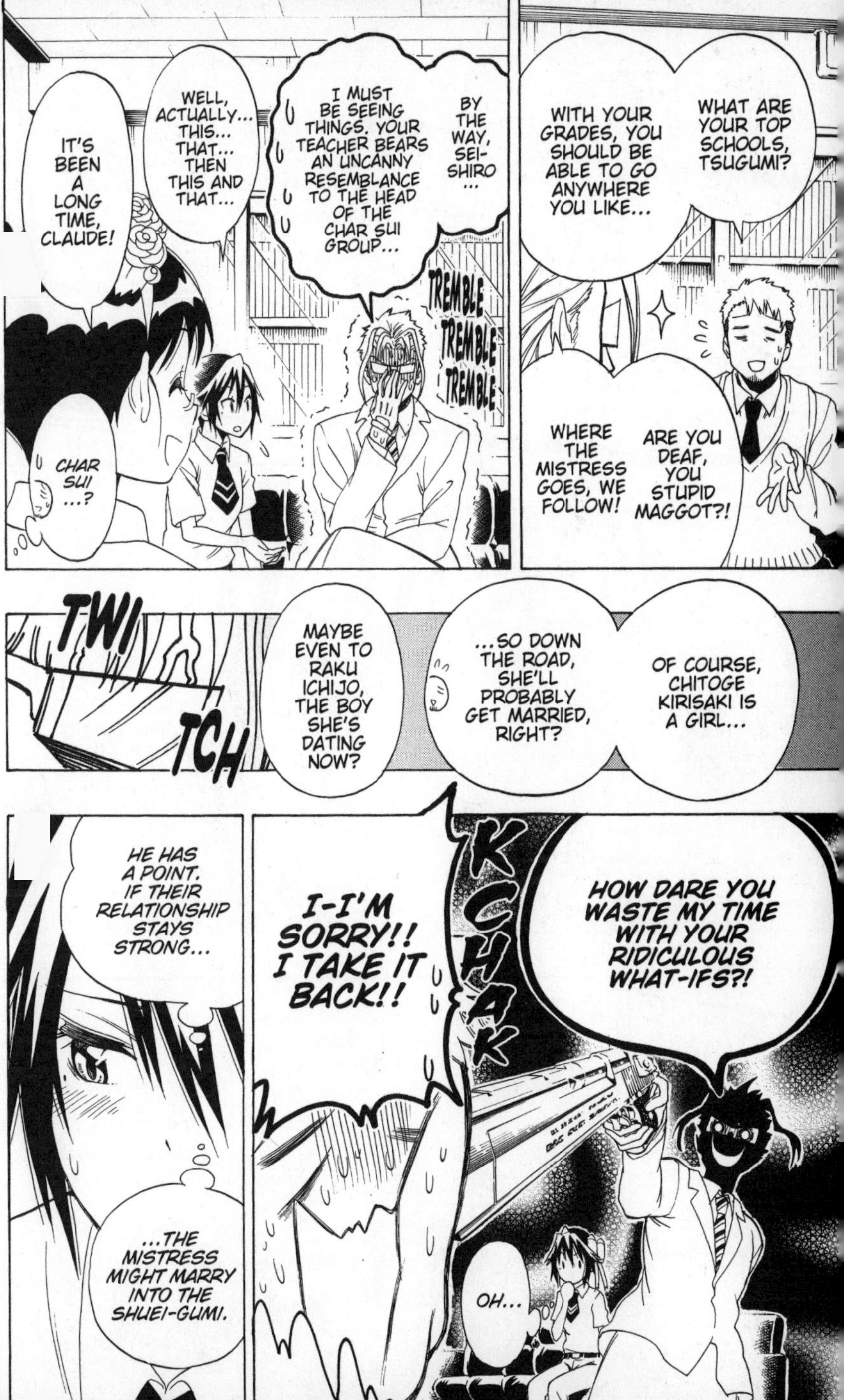
WHAT ARE YOUR TOP SCHOOLS, TSUGUMI?
WITH YOUR GRADES, YOU SHOULD BE ABLE TO GO ANYWHERE YOU LIKE...
ARE YOU DEAF, YOU STUPID MAGGOT?!
WHERE THE MISTRESS GOES, WE FOLLOW!
BY THE WAY, SEI-SHIRO...
I MUST BE SEEING THINGS. YOUR TEACHER BEARS AN UNCANNY RESEMBLANCE TO THE HEAD OF THE CHAR SUI GROUP...
TREMBLE TREMBLE TREMBLE
WELL, ACTUALLY... THIS... THAT... THEN THIS AND THAT...
IT'S BEEN A LONG TIME, CLAUDE!
CHAR SUI...?
OF COURSE, CHITOGE KIRISAKI IS A GIRL...
...SO DOWN THE ROAD, SHE'LL PROBABLY GET MARRIED, RIGHT?
MAYBE EVEN TO RAKU ICHIJO, THE BOY SHE'S DATING NOW?
TWITCH
HOW DARE YOU WASTE MY TIME WITH YOUR RIDICULOUS WHAT-IFS?!
KCHAK
I-I'M SORRY!! I TAKE IT BACK!!
OH...
HE HAS A POINT. IF THEIR RELATIONSHIP STAYS STRONG...
...THE MISTRESS MIGHT MARRY INTO THE SHUEI-GUMI.

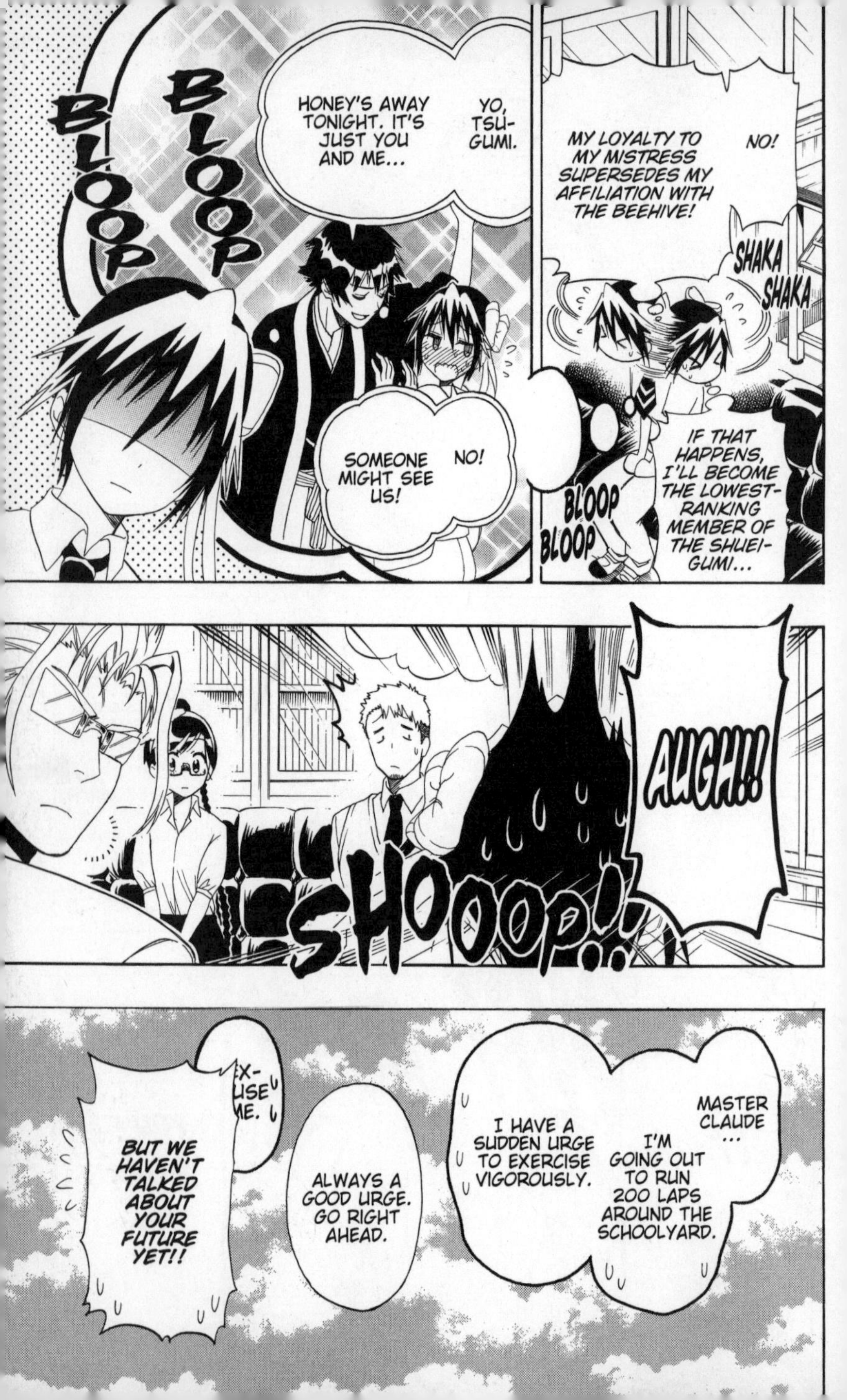
NO! MY LOYALTY TO MY MISTRESS SUPERSEDES MY AFFILIATION WITH THE BEEHIVE!
SHAKA SHAKA
IF THAT HAPPENS, I'LL BECOME THE LOWEST-RANKING MEMBER OF THE SHUEI-GUMI...
BLOOP BLOOP
YO, TSU-GUMI. HONEY'S AWAY TONIGHT. IT'S JUST YOU AND ME...
BLOOP BLOOP
NO! SOMEONE MIGHT SEE US!
AUGH!!
SHOOOP!!
MASTER CLAUDE... I'M GOING OUT TO RUN 200 LAPS AROUND THE SCHOOLYARD. I HAVE A SUDDEN URGE TO EXERCISE VIGOROUSLY.
ALWAYS A GOOD URGE. GO RIGHT AHEAD.
EX-CUSE ME.
BUT WE HAVEN'T TALKED ABOUT YOUR FUTURE YET!!

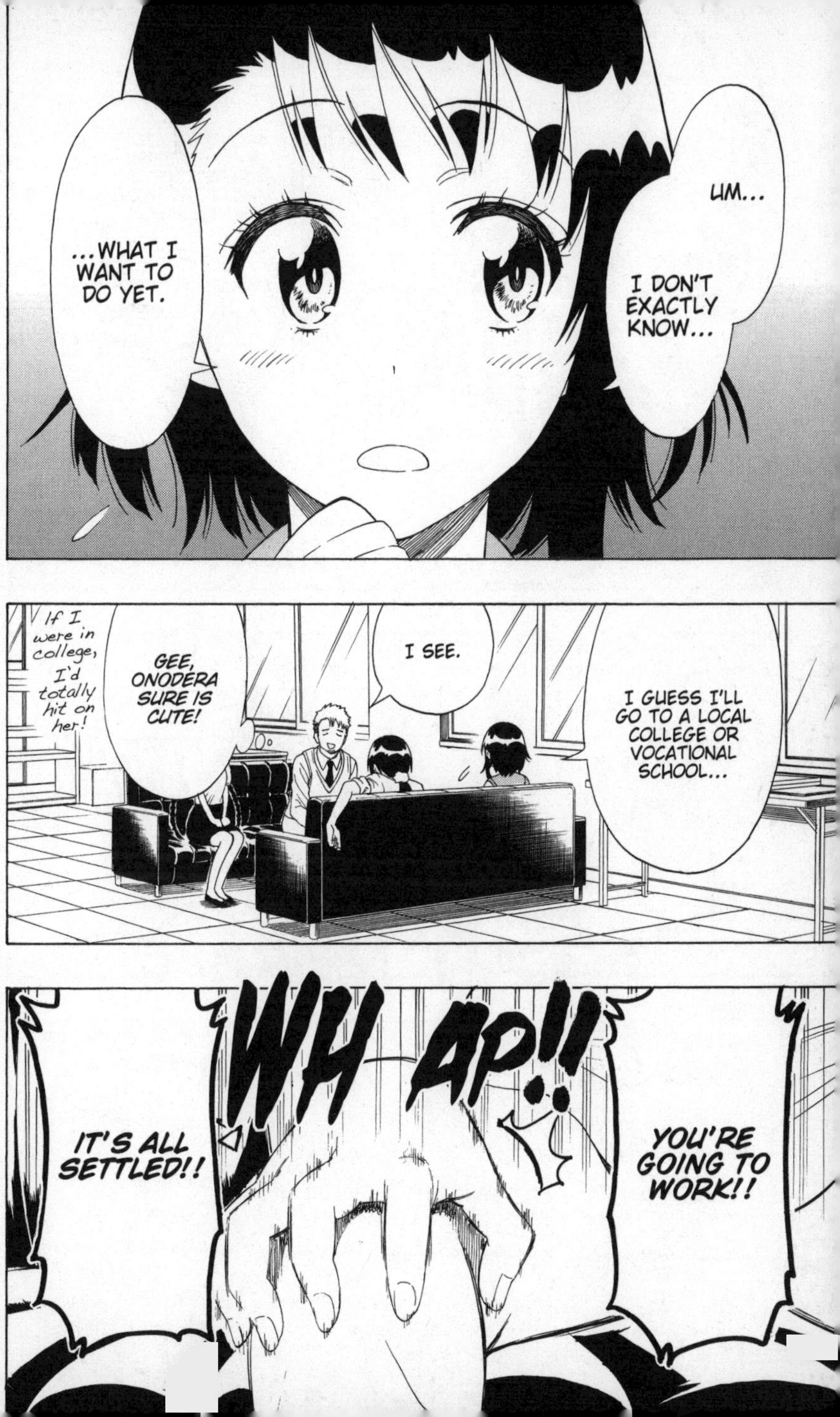
UM...
I DON'T EXACTLY KNOW...
...WHAT I WANT TO DO YET.
I GUESS I'LL GO TO A LOCAL COLLEGE OR VOCATIONAL SCHOOL...
I SEE.
GEE, ONODERA SURE IS CUTE!
If I were in college, I'd totally hit on her!
YOU'RE GOING TO WORK!!
WHAP!!
IT'S ALL SETTLED!!

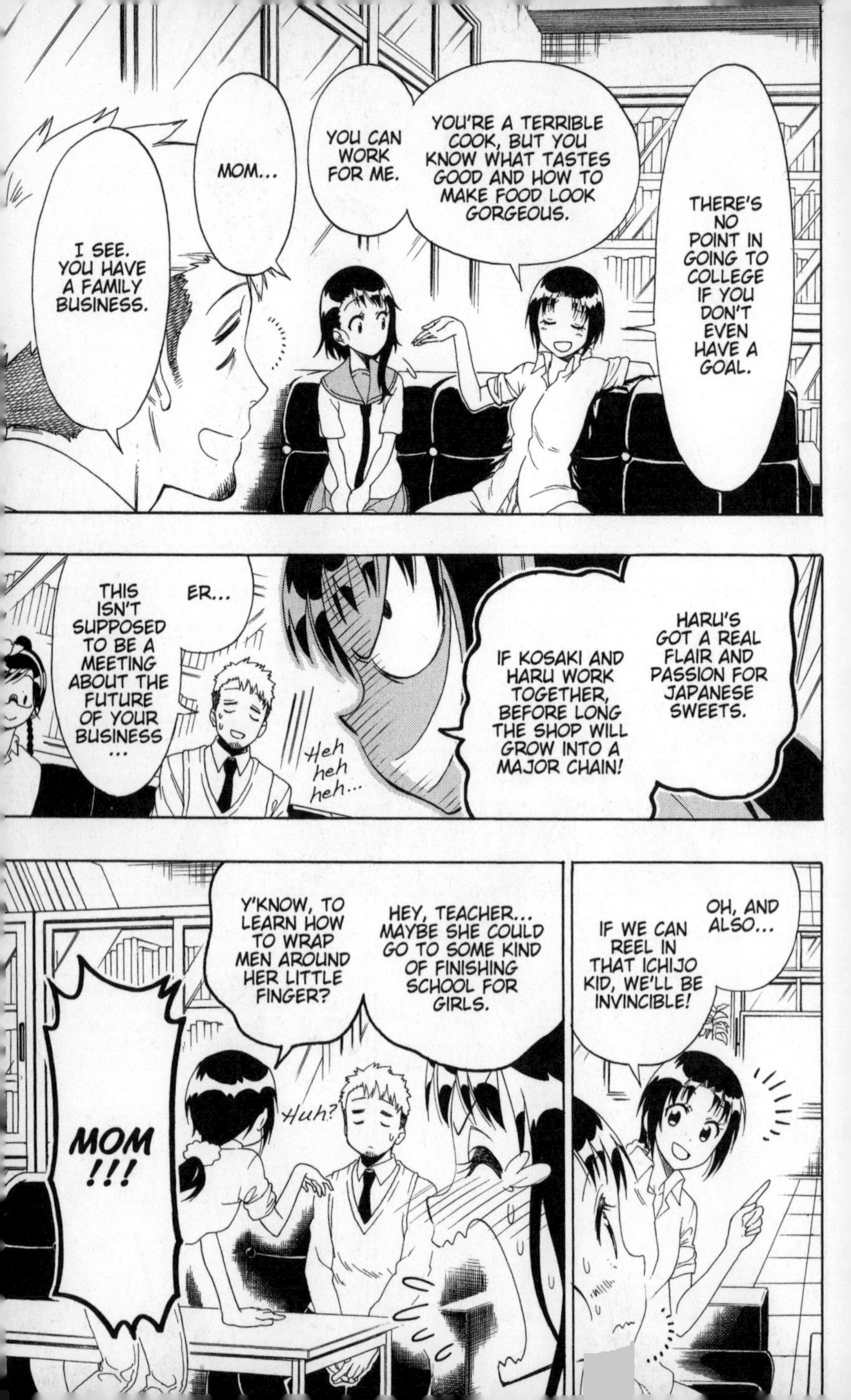
THERE'S NO POINT IN GOING TO COLLEGE IF YOU DON'T EVEN HAVE A GOAL.
YOU'RE A TERRIBLE COOK, BUT YOU KNOW WHAT TASTES GOOD AND HOW TO MAKE FOOD LOOK GORGEOUS.
YOU CAN WORK FOR ME.
MOM...
I SEE. YOU HAVE A FAMILY BUSINESS.
HARU'S GOT A REAL FLAIR AND PASSION FOR JAPANESE SWEETS.
IF KOSAKI AND HARU WORK TOGETHER, BEFORE LONG THE SHOP WILL GROW INTO A MAJOR CHAIN!
Heh heh heh...
ER...
THIS ISN'T SUPPOSED TO BE A MEETING ABOUT THE FUTURE OF YOUR BUSINESS...
OH, AND ALSO...
IF WE CAN REEL IN THAT ICHIJO KID, WE'LL BE INVINCIBLE!
HEY, TEACHER... MAYBE SHE COULD GO TO SOME KIND OF FINISHING SCHOOL FOR GIRLS.
Y'KNOW, TO LEARN HOW TO WRAP MEN AROUND HER LITTLE FINGER?
Huh?
MOM !!!

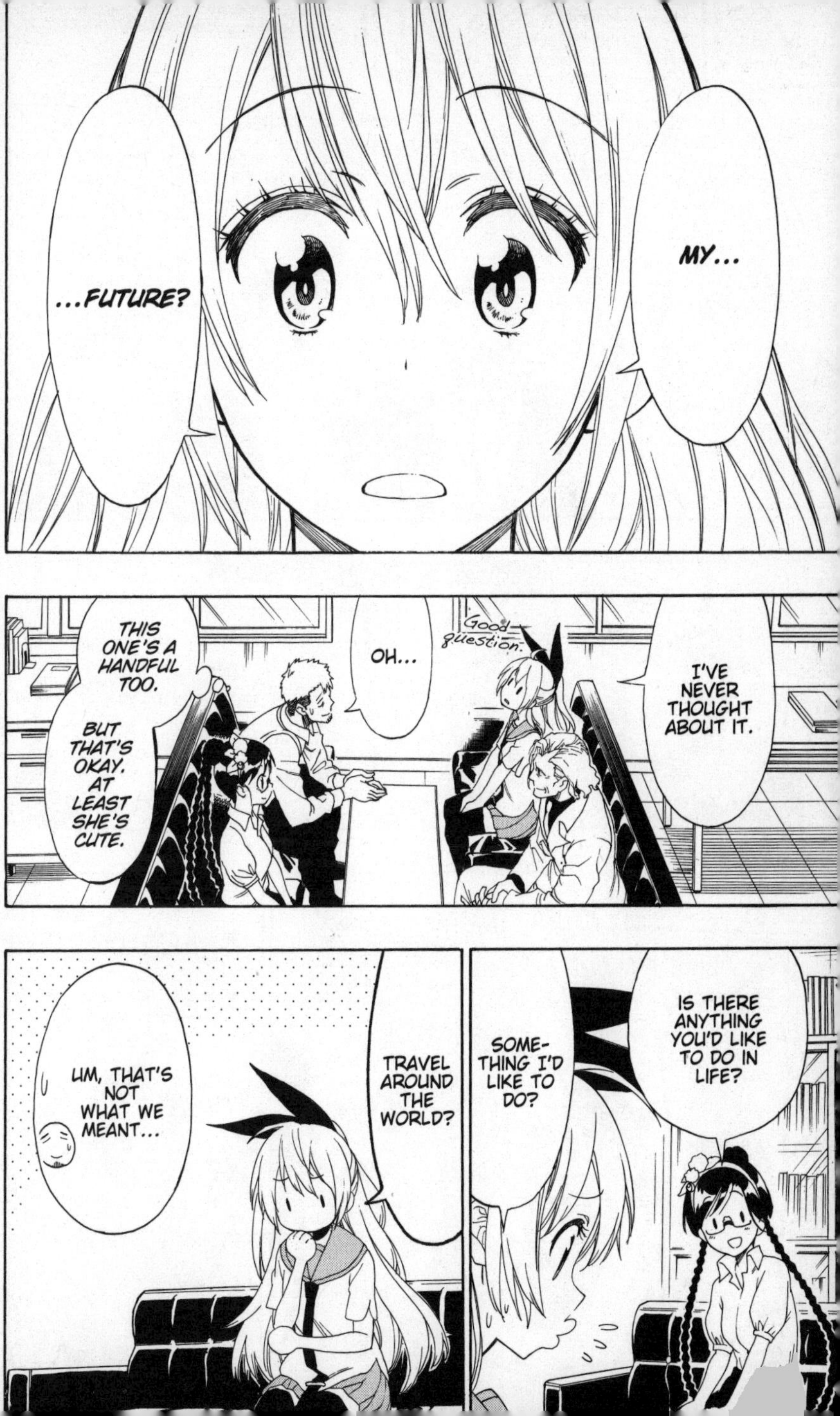
MY...
...FUTURE?
I'VE NEVER THOUGHT ABOUT IT.
Good question.
OH...
THIS ONE'S A HANDFUL TOO.
BUT THAT'S OKAY. AT LEAST SHE'S CUTE.
IS THERE ANYTHING YOU'D LIKE TO DO IN LIFE?
SOME-THING I'D LIKE TO DO?
TRAVEL AROUND THE WORLD?
UM, THAT'S NOT WHAT WE MEANT...

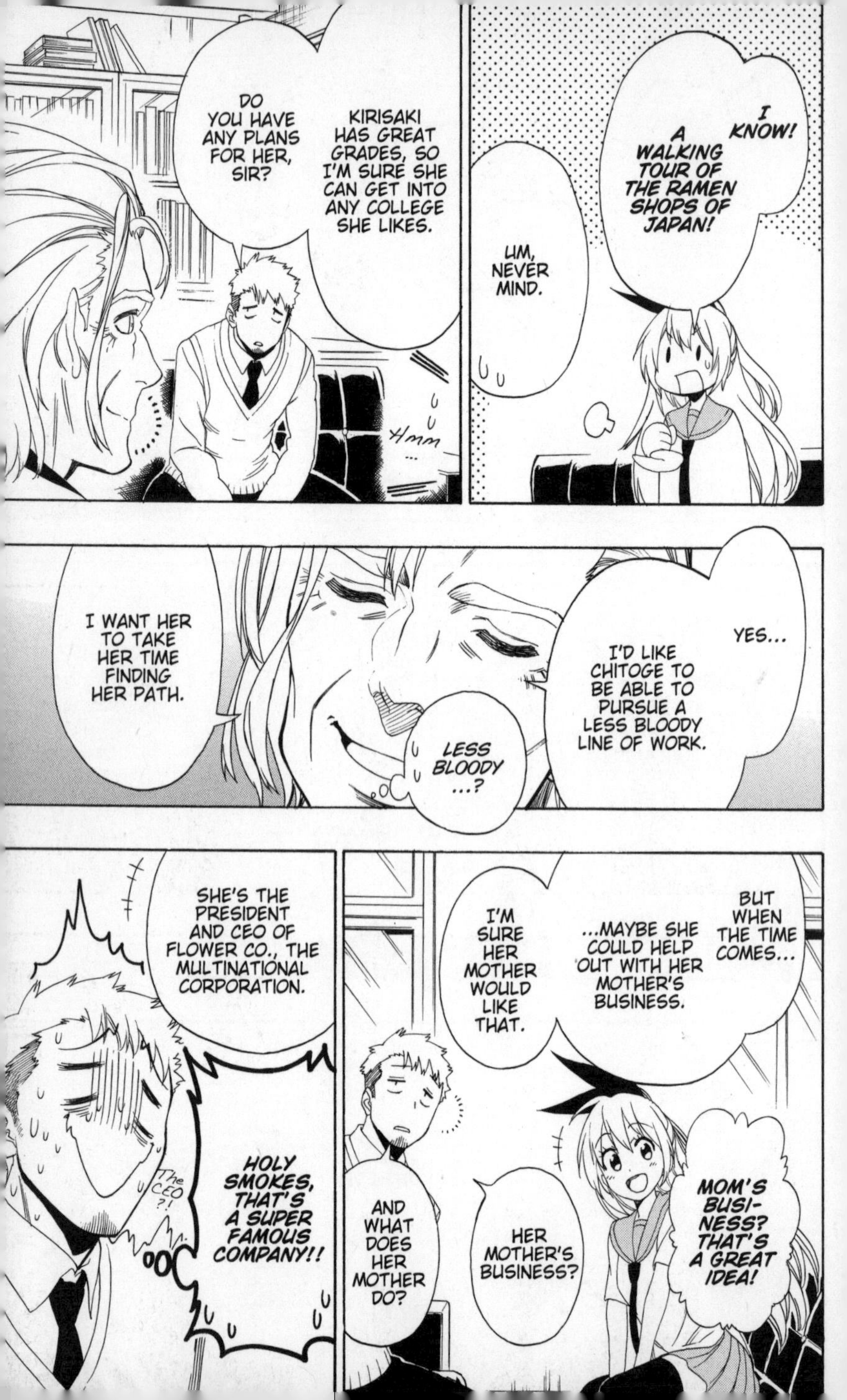
I KNOW!
A WALKING TOUR OF THE RAMEN SHOPS OF JAPAN!
UM, NEVER MIND.
KIRISAKI HAS GREAT GRADES, SO I'M SURE SHE CAN GET INTO ANY COLLEGE SHE LIKES.
DO YOU HAVE ANY PLANS FOR HER, SIR?
Hmm...
YES...
I'D LIKE CHITOGE TO BE ABLE TO PURSUE A LESS BLOODY LINE OF WORK.
LESS BLOODY...?
I WANT HER TO TAKE HER TIME FINDING HER PATH.
BUT WHEN THE TIME COMES...
...MAYBE SHE COULD HELP OUT WITH HER MOTHER'S BUSINESS.
I'M SURE HER MOTHER WOULD LIKE THAT.
MOM'S BUSI-NESS? THAT'S A GREAT IDEA!
HER MOTHER'S BUSINESS?
AND WHAT DOES HER MOTHER DO?
SHE'S THE PRESIDENT AND CEO OF FLOWER CO., THE MULTINATIONAL CORPORATION.
HOLY SMOKES, THAT'S A SUPER FAMOUS COMPANY!!
The CEO?!

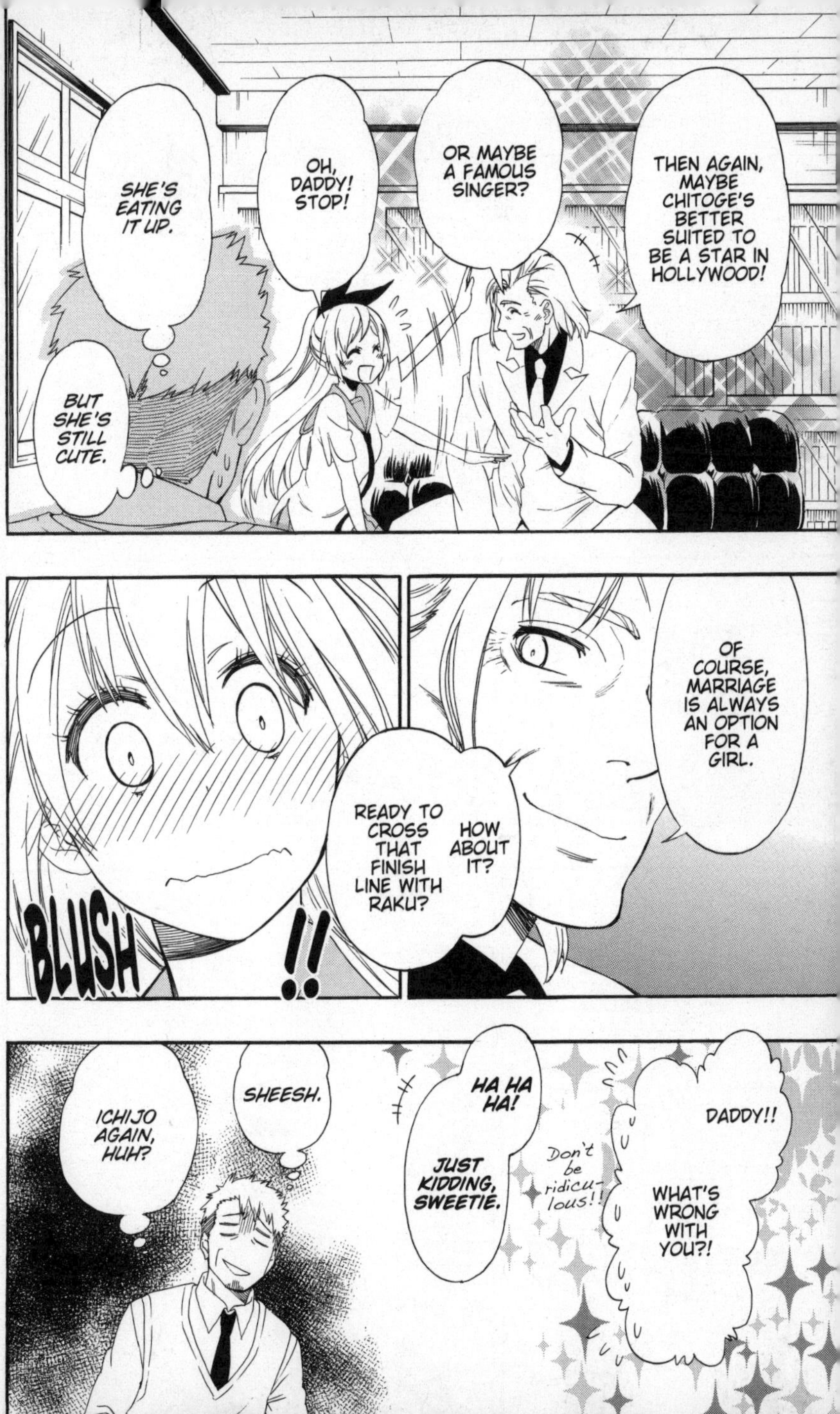
THEN AGAIN, MAYBE CHITOGE'S BETTER SUITED TO BE A STAR IN HOLLYWOOD!
OR MAYBE A FAMOUS SINGER?
OH, DADDY! STOP!
SHE'S EATING IT UP.
BUT SHE'S STILL CUTE.
OF COURSE, MARRIAGE IS ALWAYS AN OPTION FOR A GIRL.
HOW ABOUT IT?
READY TO CROSS THAT FINISH LINE WITH RAKU?
BLUSH
!!
DADDY!!
WHAT'S WRONG WITH YOU?!
Don't be ridiculous!!
HA HA HA!
JUST KIDDING, SWEETIE.
SHEESH.
ICHIJO AGAIN, HUH?

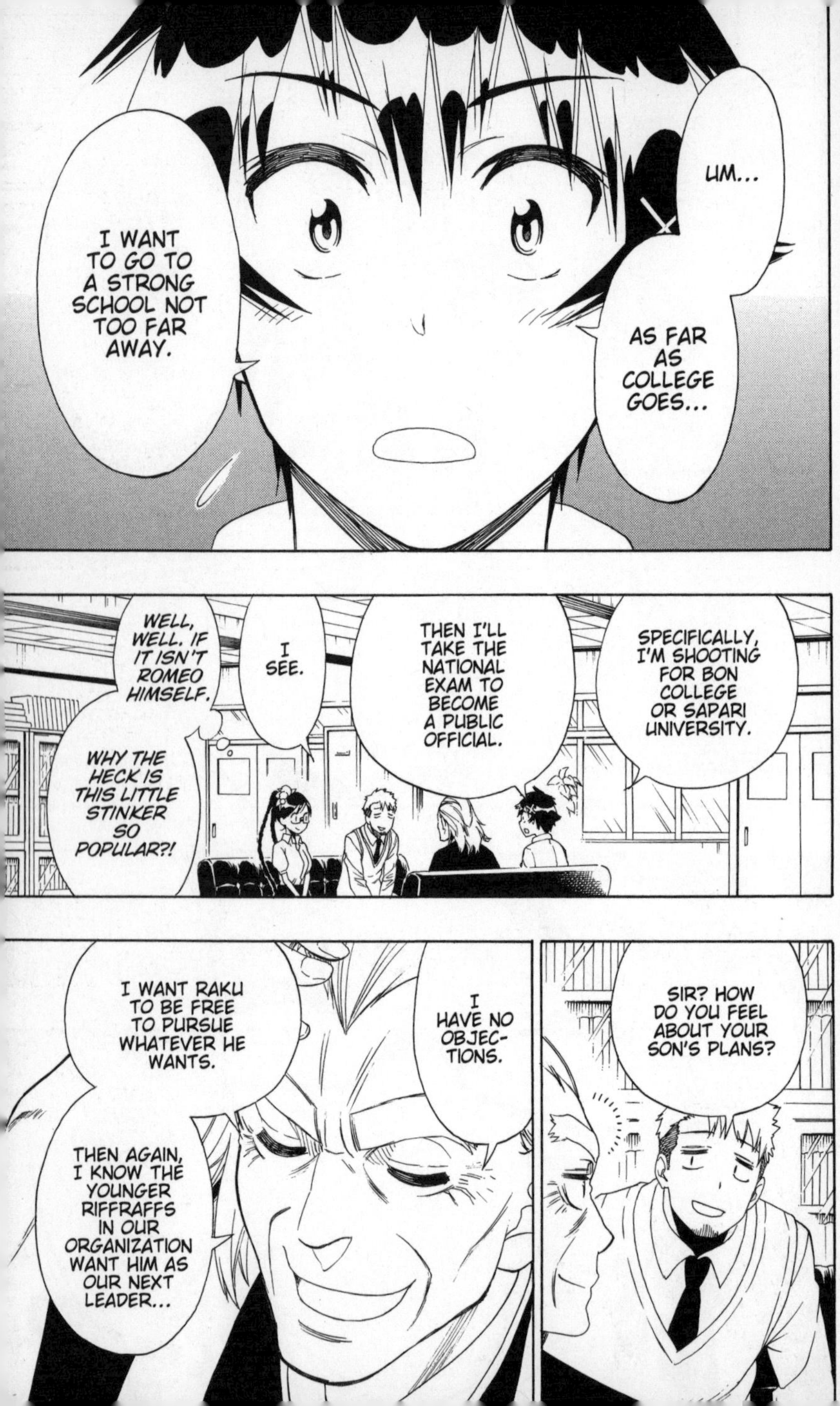
UM...
AS FAR AS COLLEGE GOES...
I WANT TO GO TO A STRONG SCHOOL NOT TOO FAR AWAY.
SPECIFICALLY, I'M SHOOTING FOR BON COLLEGE OR SAPARI UNIVERSITY.
THEN I'LL TAKE THE NATIONAL EXAM TO BECOME A PUBLIC OFFICIAL.
I SEE.
WELL, WELL. IF IT ISN'T ROMEO HIMSELF.
WHY THE HECK IS THIS LITTLE STINKER SO POPULAR?!
SIR? HOW DO YOU FEEL ABOUT YOUR SON'S PLANS?
I HAVE NO OBJECTIONS.
I WANT RAKU TO BE FREE TO PURSUE WHATEVER HE WANTS.
THEN AGAIN, I KNOW THE YOUNGER RIFFRAFFS IN OUR ORGANIZATION WANT HIM AS OUR NEXT LEADER...

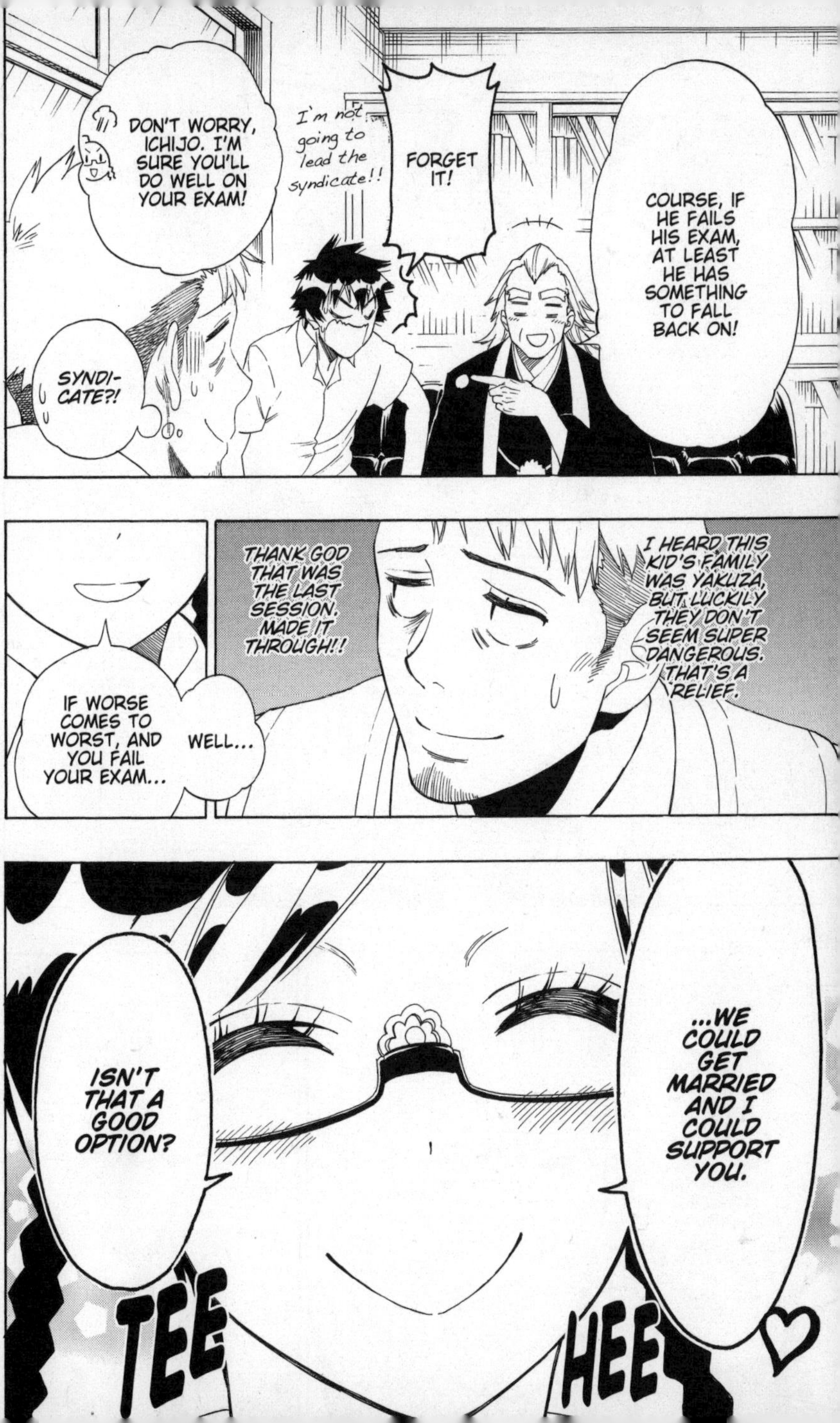
COURSE, IF HE FAILS HIS EXAM, AT LEAST HE HAS SOMETHING TO FALL BACK ON!
FORGET IT!
I'm not going to lead the syndicate!!
DON'T WORRY, ICHIJO. I'M SURE YOU'LL DO WELL ON YOUR EXAM!
SYNDI-CATE?!
I HEARD THIS KID'S FAMILY WAS YAKUZA, BUT LUCKILY THEY DON'T SEEM SUPER DANGEROUS. THAT'S A RELIEF.
THANK GOD THAT WAS THE LAST SESSION. MADE IT THROUGH!!
WELL...
IF WORSE COMES TO WORST, AND YOU FAIL YOUR EXAM...
...WE COULD GET MARRIED AND I COULD SUPPORT YOU.
ISN'T THAT A GOOD OPTION?
TEE HEE

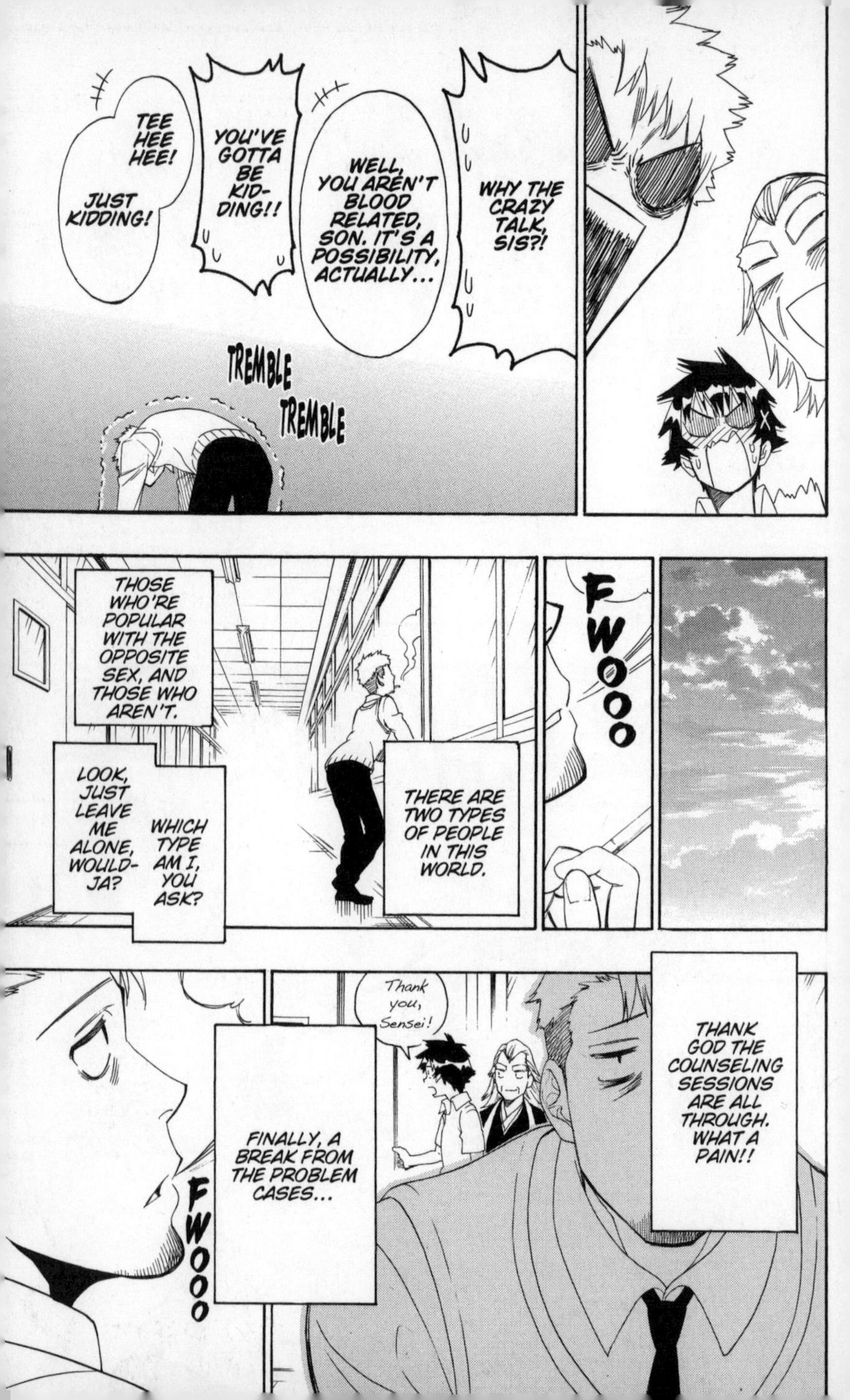
WHY THE CRAZY TALK, SIS?!
WELL, YOU AREN'T BLOOD RELATED, SON. IT'S A POSSIBILITY, ACTUALLY...
YOU'VE GOTTA BE KIDDING!!
TEE HEE HEE! JUST KIDDING!
TREMBLE TREMBLE
FWOOO
THERE ARE TWO TYPES OF PEOPLE IN THIS WORLD.
THOSE WHO'RE POPULAR WITH THE OPPOSITE SEX, AND THOSE WHO AREN'T.
WHICH TYPE AM I, YOU ASK?
LOOK, JUST LEAVE ME ALONE, WOULDJA?
THANK GOD THE COUNSELING SESSIONS ARE ALL THROUGH. WHAT A PAIN!!
Thank you, Sensei!
FINALLY, A BREAK FROM THE PROBLEM CASES...
FWOOO

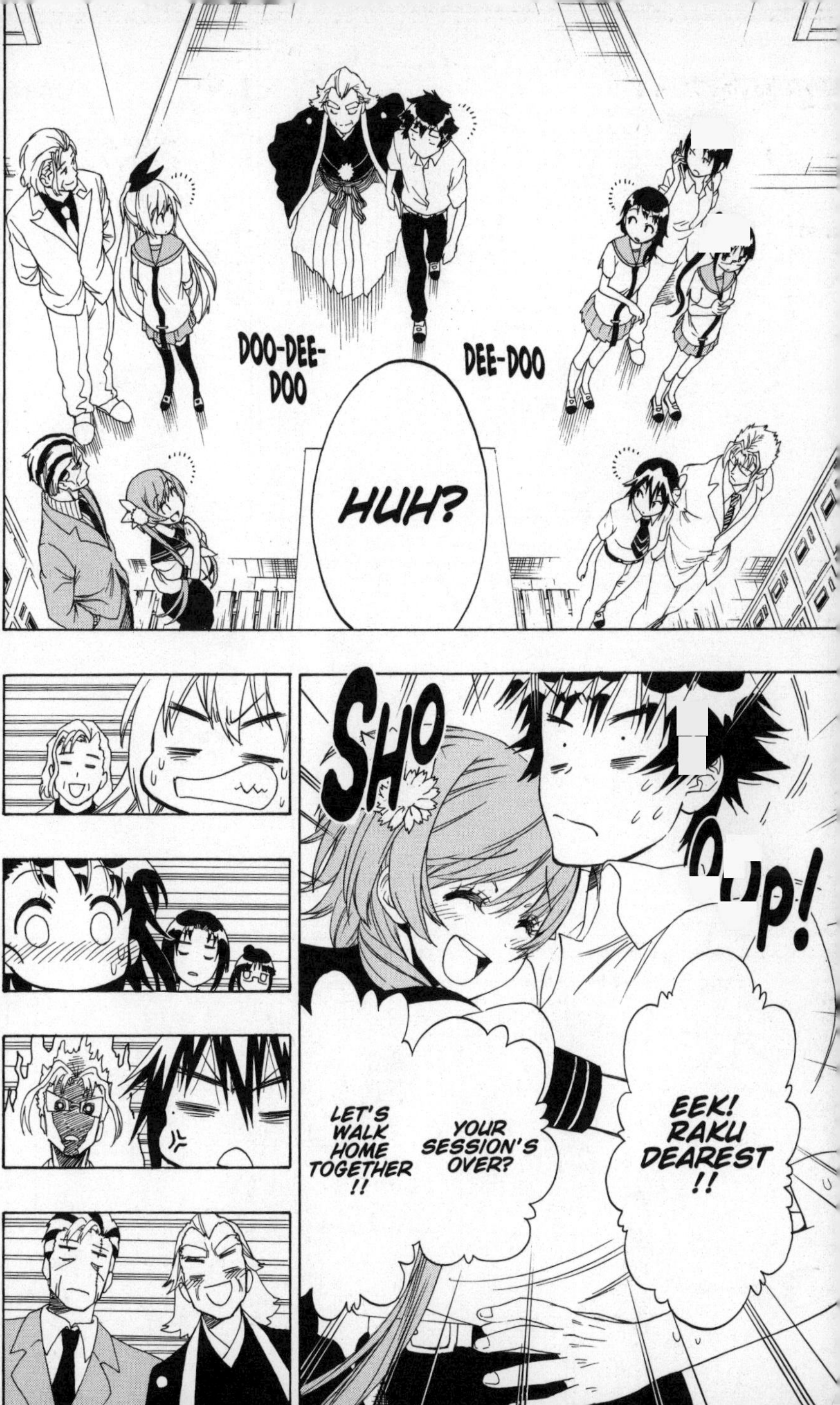
DEE-DOO
DOO-DEE-DOO
HUH?
SHO
UP!
EEK! RAKU DEAREST!!
YOUR SESSION'S OVER?
LET'S WALK HOME TOGETHER!!

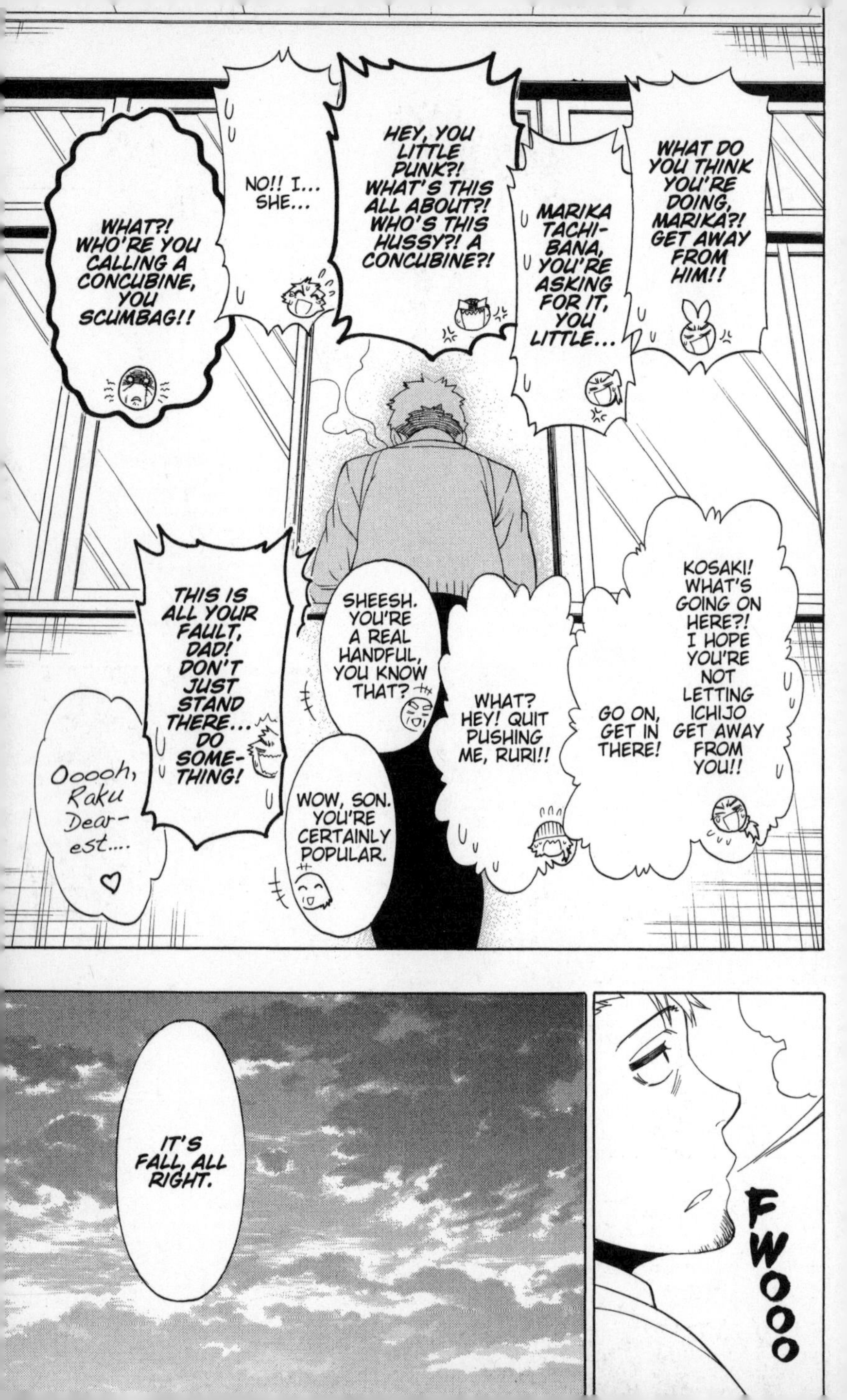
WHAT DO YOU THINK YOU'RE DOING, MARIKA?! GET AWAY FROM HIM!!
MARIKA TACHIBANA, YOU'RE ASKING FOR IT, YOU LITTLE...
HEY, YOU LITTLE PUNK?! WHAT'S THIS ALL ABOUT?! WHO'S THIS HUSSY?! A CONCUBINE?!
NO!! I... SHE...
WHAT?! WHO'RE YOU CALLING A CONCUBINE, YOU SCUMBAG!!
KOSAKI! WHAT'S GOING ON HERE?! I HOPE YOU'RE NOT LETTING ICHIJO GET AWAY FROM YOU!!
GO ON, GET IN THERE!
WHAT? HEY! QUIT PUSHING ME, RURI!!
SHEESH. YOU'RE A REAL HANDFUL, YOU KNOW THAT?
WOW, SON. YOU'RE CERTAINLY POPULAR.
THIS IS ALL YOUR FAULT, DAD! DON'T JUST STAND THERE... DO SOME-THING!
Ooooh, Raku Dear-est.... ♡
FWOOO
IT'S FALL, ALL RIGHT.

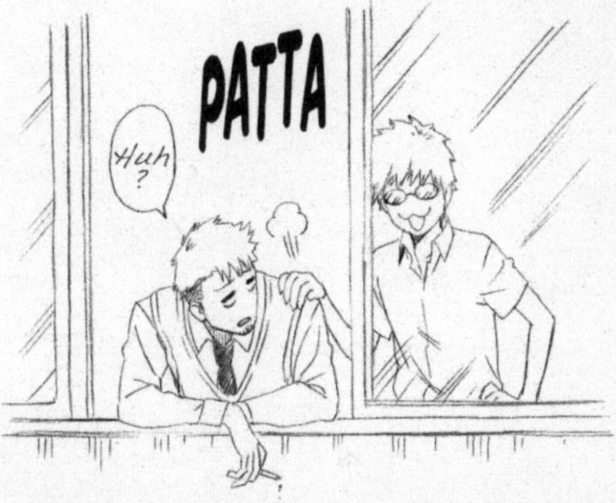
PATTA
Huh?

Chapter 123: Suitable

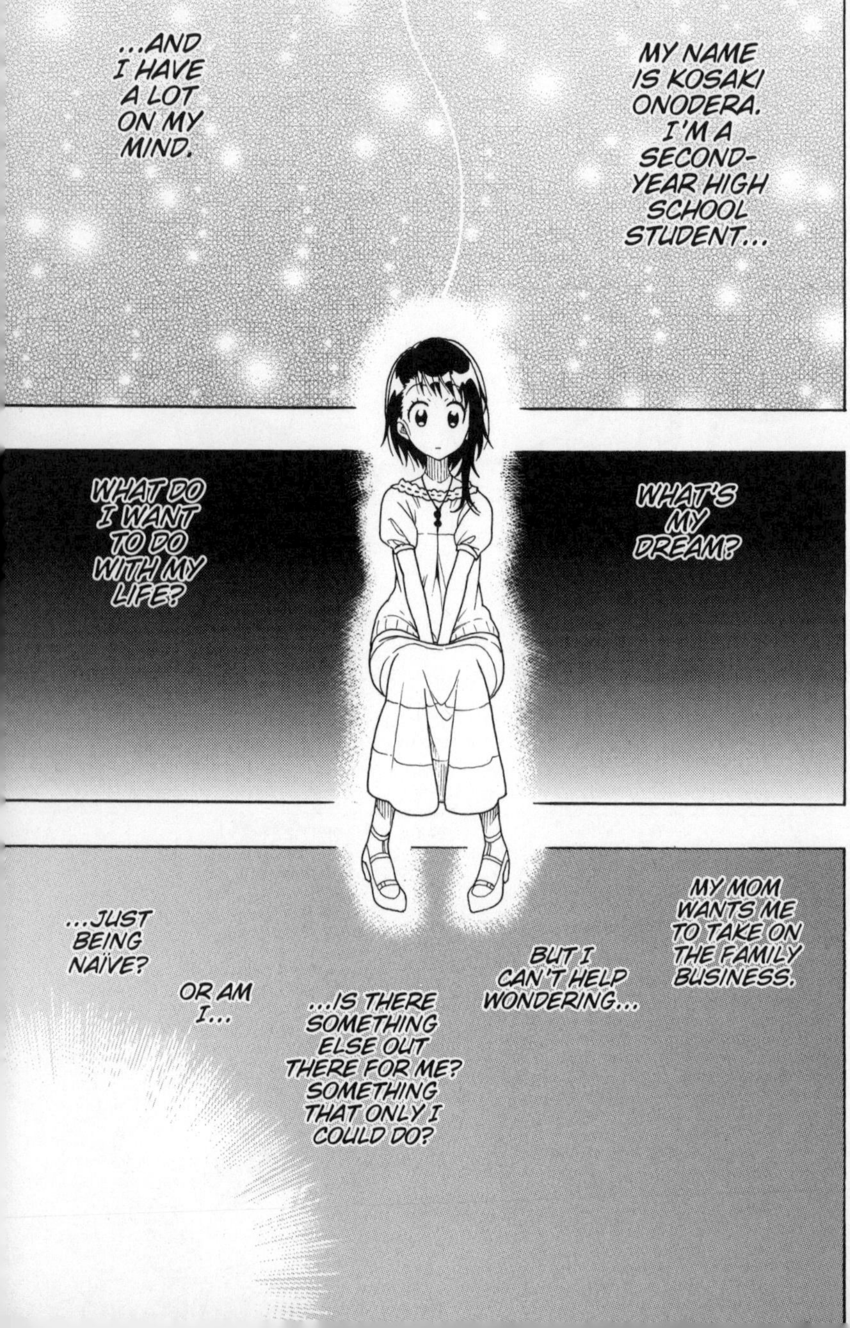
MY NAME IS KOSAKI ONODERA. I'M A SECOND-YEAR HIGH SCHOOL STUDENT...
...AND I HAVE A LOT ON MY MIND.
WHAT'S MY DREAM?
WHAT DO I WANT TO DO WITH MY LIFE?
MY MOM WANTS ME TO TAKE ON THE FAMILY BUSINESS.
BUT I CAN'T HELP WONDERING...
...IS THERE SOMETHING ELSE OUT THERE FOR ME? SOMETHING THAT ONLY I COULD DO?
OR AM I...
...JUST BEING NAÏVE?

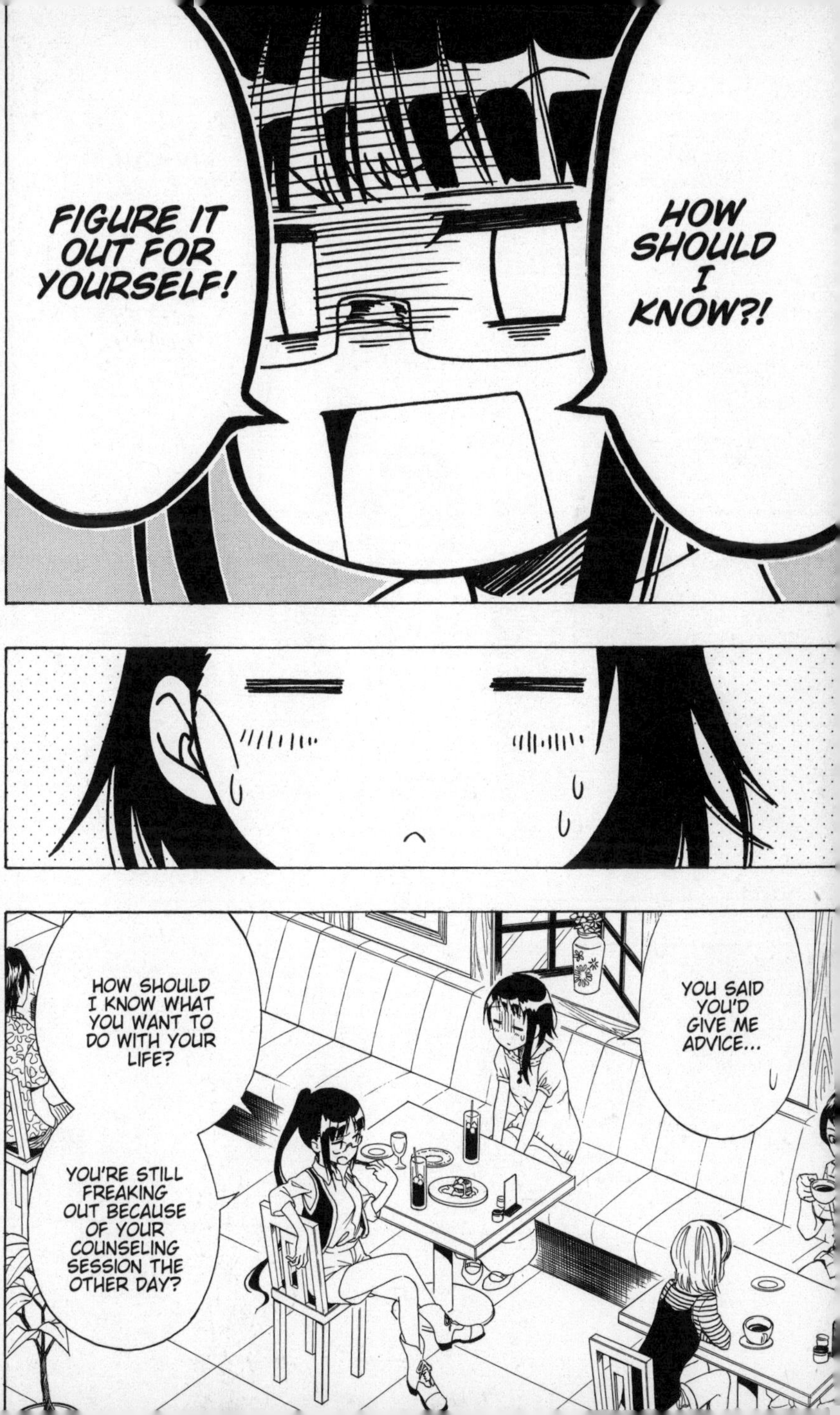
HOW SHOULD I KNOW?!
FIGURE IT OUT FOR YOURSELF!
YOU SAID YOU'D GIVE ME ADVICE...
HOW SHOULD I KNOW WHAT YOU WANT TO DO WITH YOUR LIFE?
YOU'RE STILL FREAKING OUT BECAUSE OF YOUR COUNSELING SESSION THE OTHER DAY?

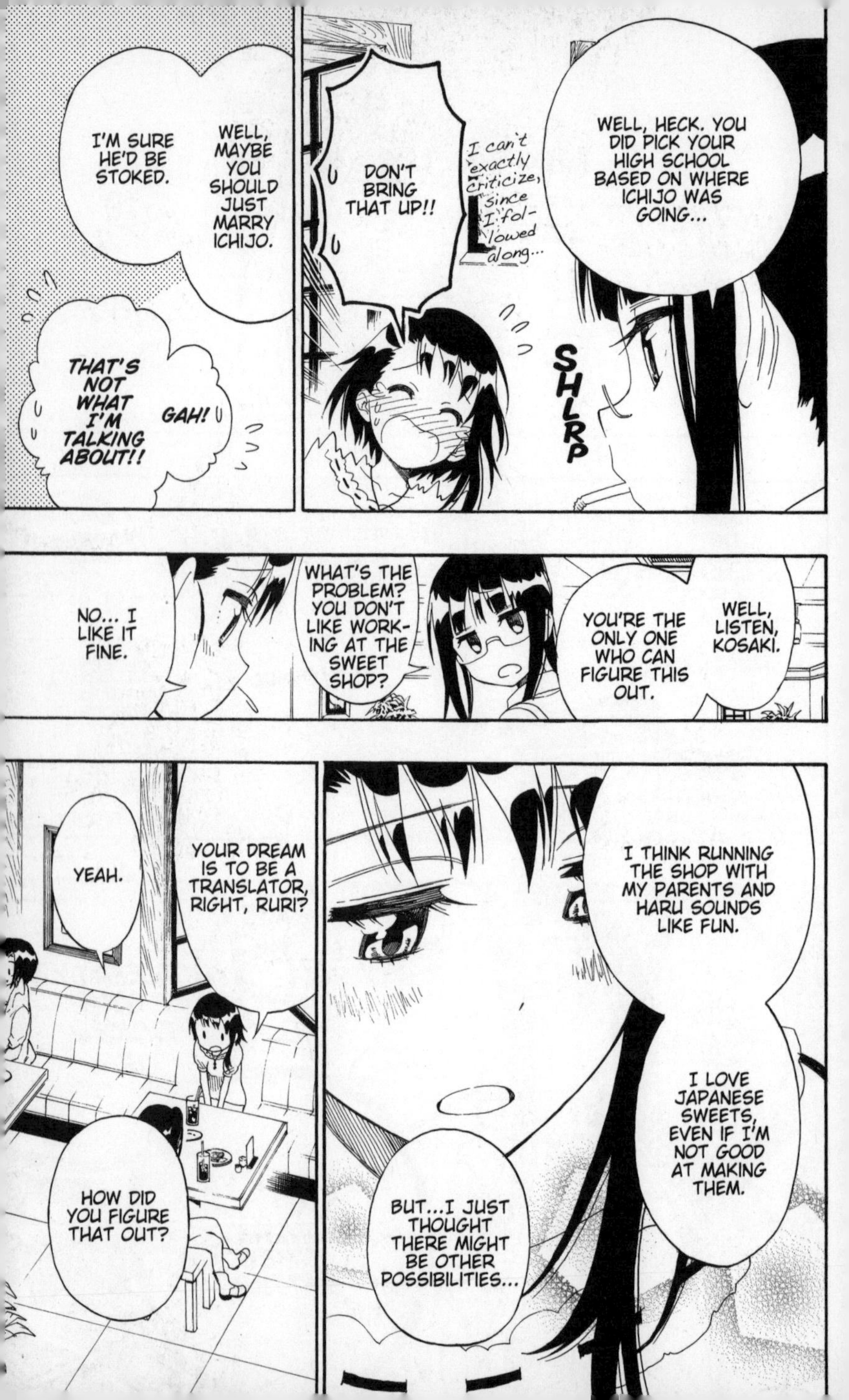
WELL, HECK. YOU DID PICK YOUR HIGH SCHOOL BASED ON WHERE ICHIJO WAS GOING...
I can't exactly criticize, since I followed along...
SHLRP
DON'T BRING THAT UP!!
WELL, MAYBE YOU SHOULD JUST MARRY ICHIJO.
I'M SURE HE'D BE STOKED.
GAH!
THAT'S NOT WHAT I'M TALKING ABOUT!!
WELL, LISTEN, KOSAKI.
YOU'RE THE ONLY ONE WHO CAN FIGURE THIS OUT.
WHAT'S THE PROBLEM? YOU DON'T LIKE WORKING AT THE SWEET SHOP?
NO... I LIKE IT FINE.
I THINK RUNNING THE SHOP WITH MY PARENTS AND HARU SOUNDS LIKE FUN.
I LOVE JAPANESE SWEETS, EVEN IF I'M NOT GOOD AT MAKING THEM.
BUT...I JUST THOUGHT THERE MIGHT BE OTHER POSSIBILITIES...
YOUR DREAM IS TO BE A TRANSLATOR, RIGHT, RURI?
YEAH.
HOW DID YOU FIGURE THAT OUT?

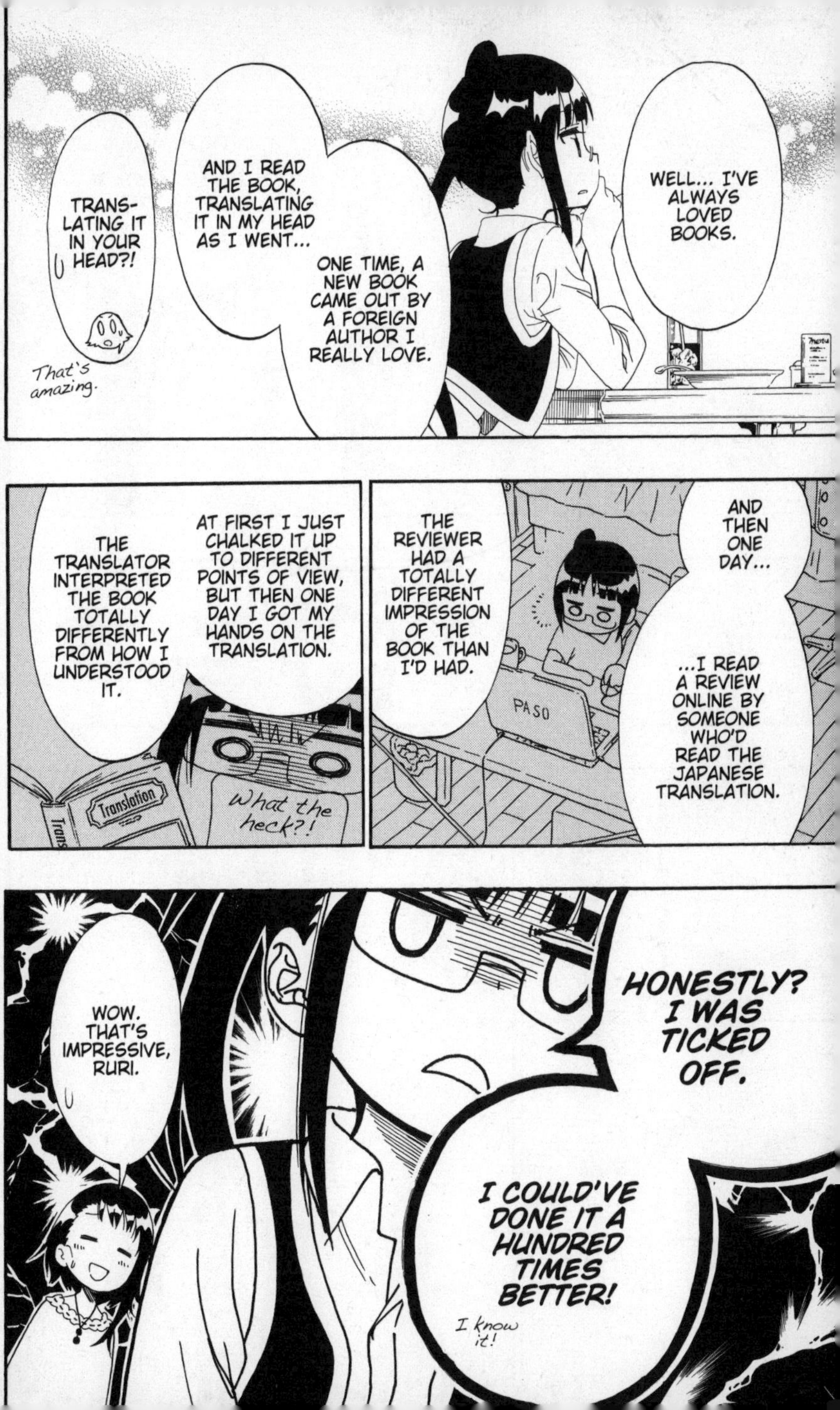
WELL... I'VE ALWAYS LOVED BOOKS.
ONE TIME, A NEW BOOK CAME OUT BY A FOREIGN AUTHOR I REALLY LOVE.
AND I READ THE BOOK, TRANSLATING IT IN MY HEAD AS I WENT...
TRANS-LATING IT IN YOUR HEAD?!
That's amazing.
AND THEN ONE DAY...
...I READ A REVIEW ONLINE BY SOMEONE WHO'D READ THE JAPANESE TRANSLATION.
THE REVIEWER HAD A TOTALLY DIFFERENT IMPRESSION OF THE BOOK THAN I'D HAD.
PASO
AT FIRST I JUST CHALKED IT UP TO DIFFERENT POINTS OF VIEW, BUT THEN ONE DAY I GOT MY HANDS ON THE TRANSLATION.
THE TRANSLATOR INTERPRETED THE BOOK TOTALLY DIFFERENTLY FROM HOW I UNDERSTOOD IT.
Translation
What the heck?!
HONESTLY? I WAS TICKED OFF.
I COULD'VE DONE IT A HUNDRED TIMES BETTER!
I know it!
WOW. THAT'S IMPRESSIVE, RURI.

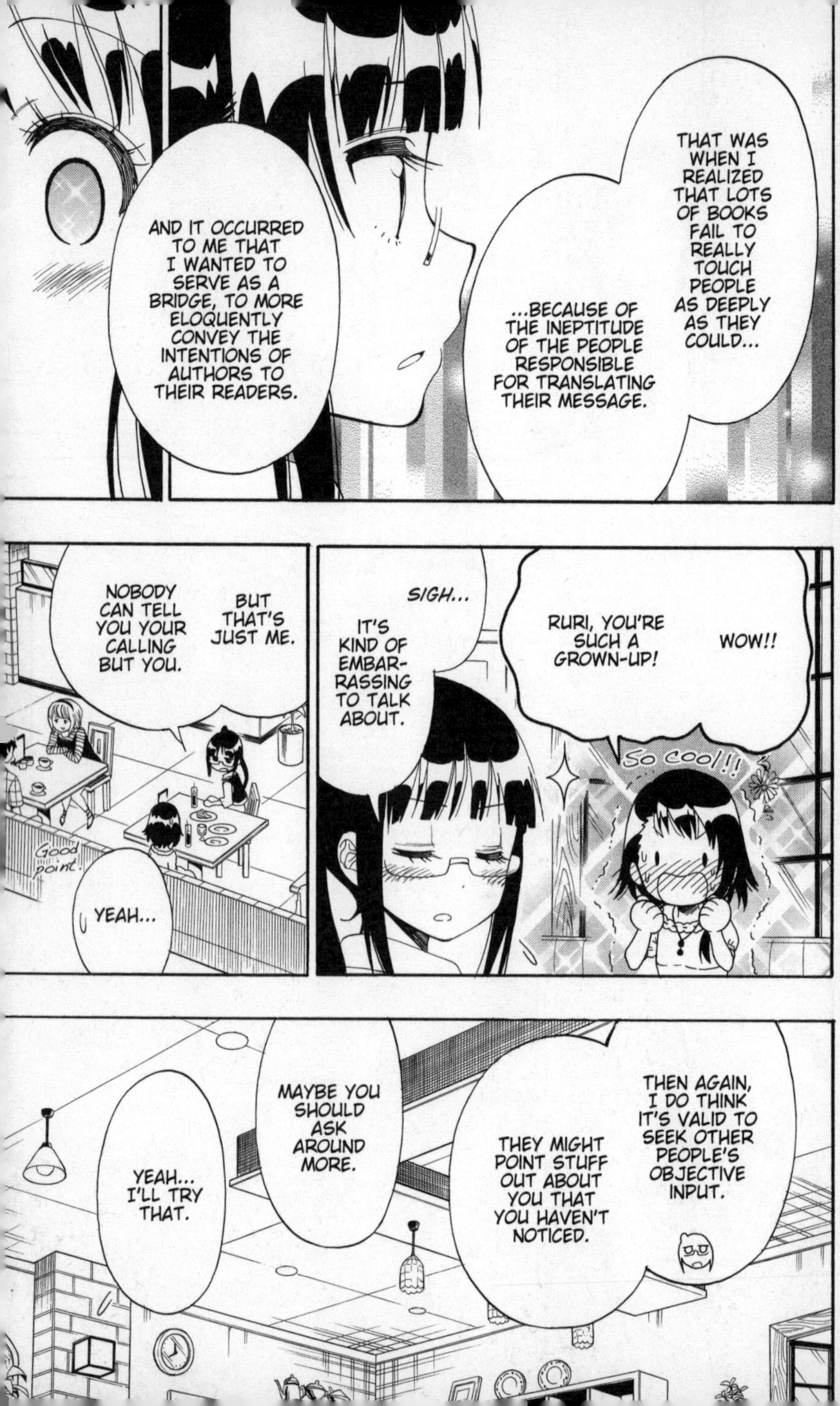
THAT WAS WHEN I REALIZED THAT LOTS OF BOOKS FAIL TO REALLY TOUCH PEOPLE AS DEEPLY AS THEY COULD...
...BECAUSE OF THE INEPTITUDE OF THE PEOPLE RESPONSIBLE FOR TRANSLATING THEIR MESSAGE.
AND IT OCCURRED TO ME THAT I WANTED TO SERVE AS A BRIDGE, TO MORE ELOQUENTLY CONVEY THE INTENTIONS OF AUTHORS TO THEIR READERS.
WOW!!
RURI, YOU'RE SUCH A GROWN-UP!
So cool!!
SIGH...
IT'S KIND OF EMBAR-RASSING TO TALK ABOUT.
BUT THAT'S JUST ME.
NOBODY CAN TELL YOU YOUR CALLING BUT YOU.
Good point.
YEAH...
THEN AGAIN, I DO THINK IT'S VALID TO SEEK OTHER PEOPLE'S OBJECTIVE INPUT.
THEY MIGHT POINT STUFF OUT ABOUT YOU THAT YOU HAVEN'T NOTICED.
MAYBE YOU SHOULD ASK AROUND MORE.
YEAH... I'LL TRY THAT.

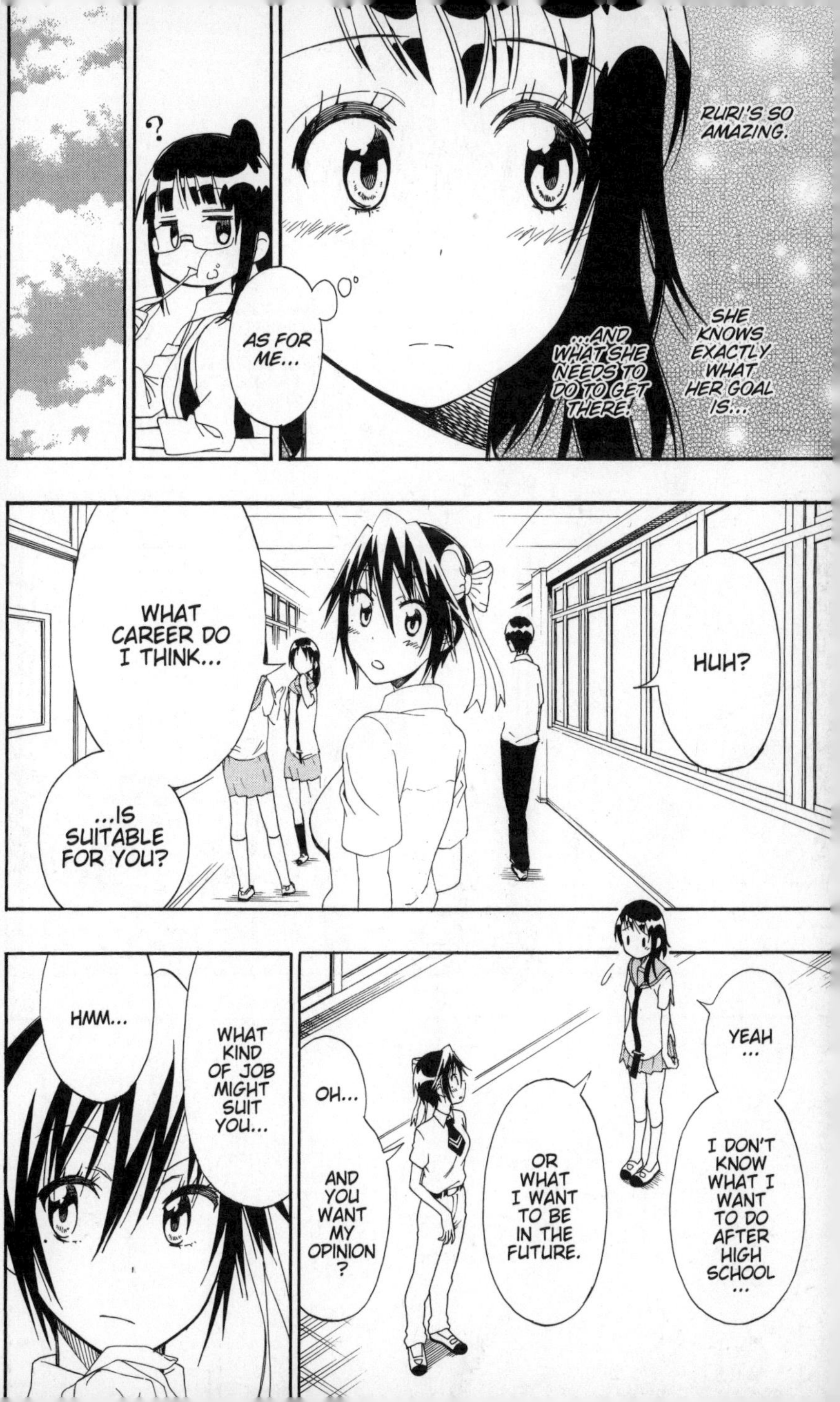
RURI'S SO AMAZING.
SHE KNOWS EXACTLY WHAT HER GOAL IS...
...AND WHAT SHE NEEDS TO DO TO GET THERE!
AS FOR ME...
?
HUH?
WHAT CAREER DO I THINK...
...IS SUITABLE FOR YOU?
YEAH... I DON'T KNOW WHAT I WANT TO DO AFTER HIGH SCHOOL...
OR WHAT I WANT TO BE IN THE FUTURE.
OH... AND YOU WANT MY OPINION?
WHAT KIND OF JOB MIGHT SUIT YOU...
HMM...

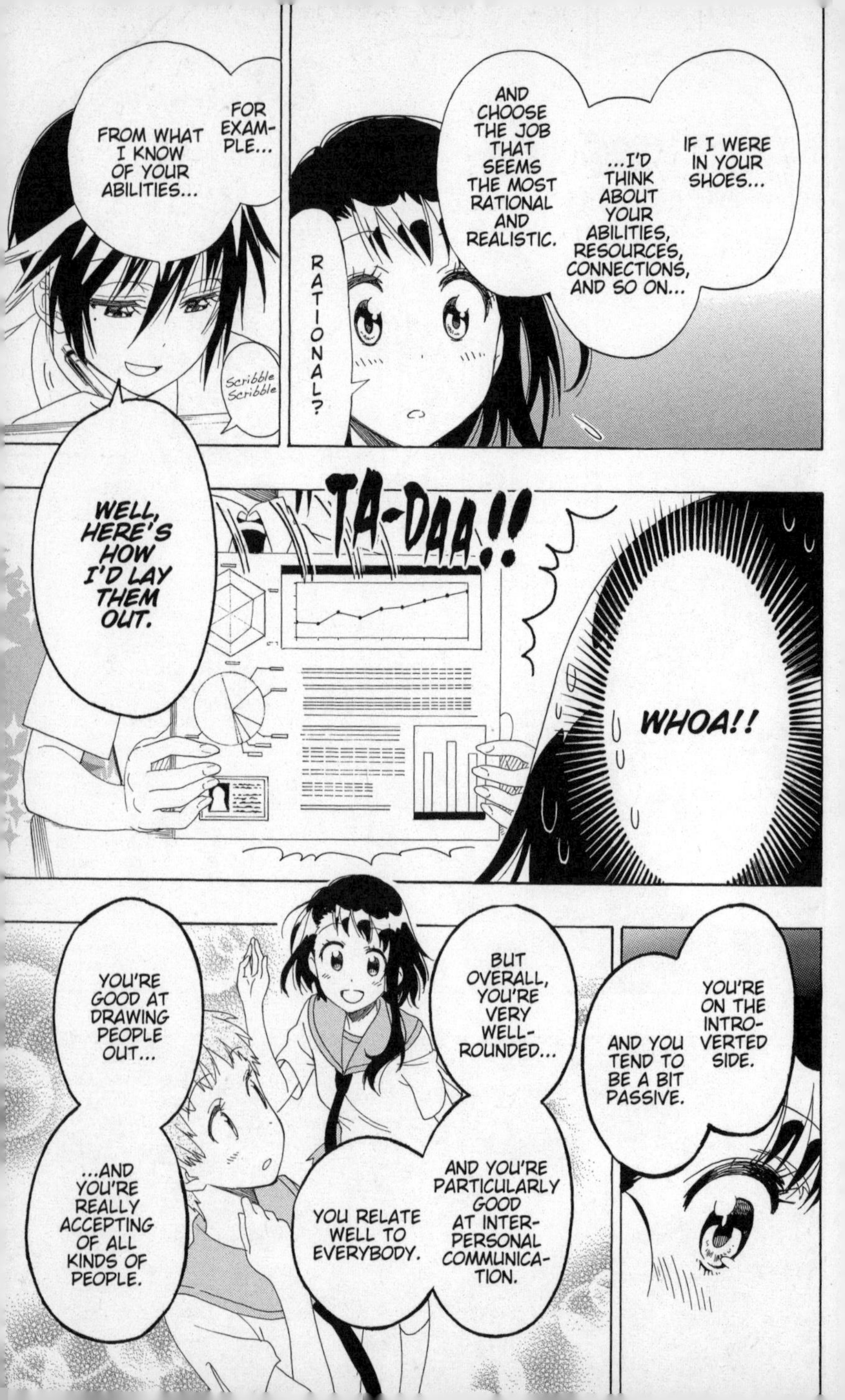
IF I WERE IN YOUR SHOES...
...I'D THINK ABOUT YOUR ABILITIES, RESOURCES, CONNECTIONS, AND SO ON...
AND CHOOSE THE JOB THAT SEEMS THE MOST RATIONAL AND REALISTIC.
RATIONAL?
FOR EXAMPLE...
FROM WHAT I KNOW OF YOUR ABILITIES...
Scribble Scribble
WELL, HERE'S HOW I'D LAY THEM OUT.
TA-DAA!!
WHOA!!
YOU'RE ON THE INTROVERTED SIDE.
AND YOU TEND TO BE A BIT PASSIVE.
BUT OVERALL, YOU'RE VERY WELL-ROUNDED...
YOU'RE GOOD AT DRAWING PEOPLE OUT...
AND YOU'RE PARTICULARLY GOOD AT INTERPERSONAL COMMUNICATION.
YOU RELATE WELL TO EVERYBODY.
...AND YOU'RE REALLY ACCEPTING OF ALL KINDS OF PEOPLE.

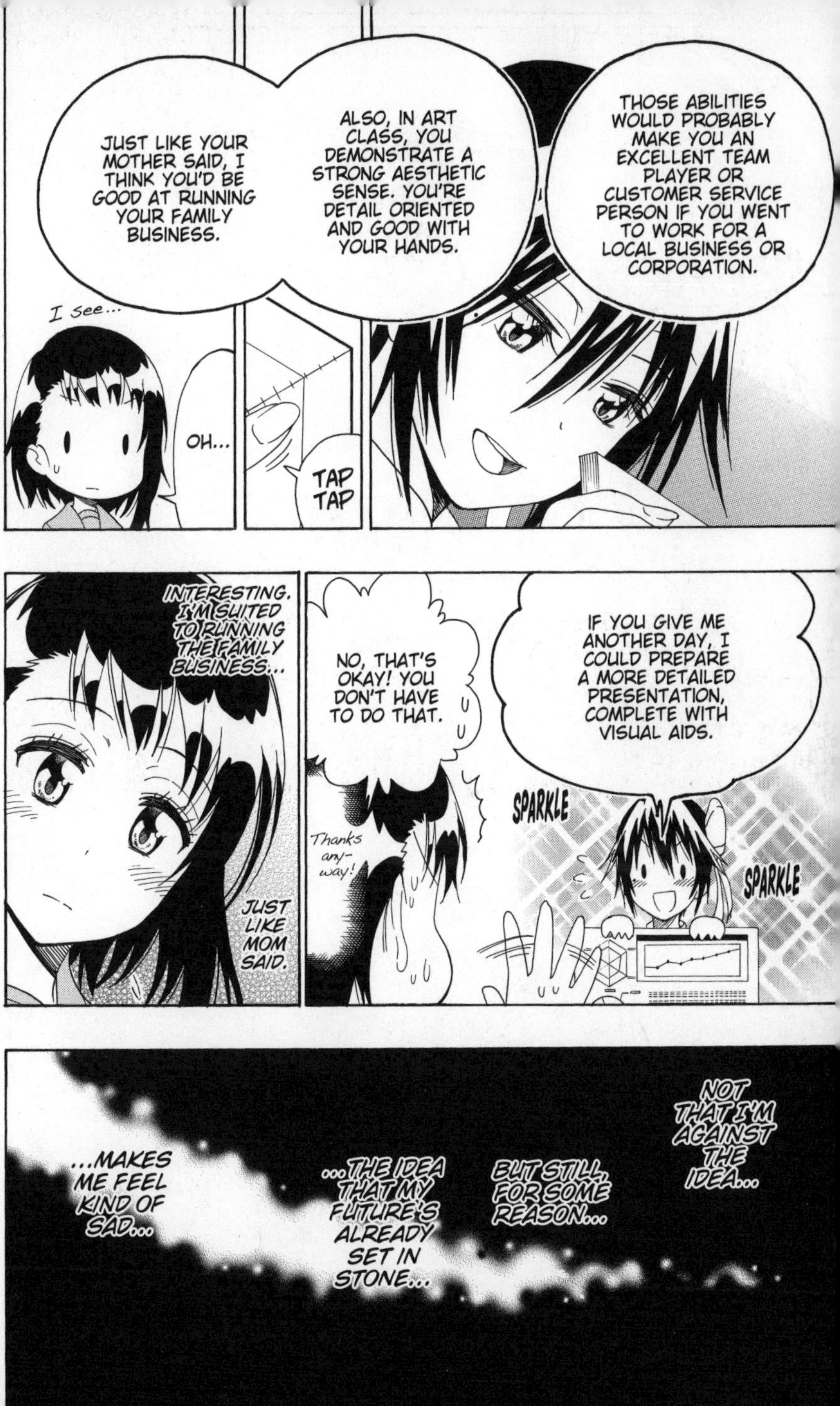
JUST LIKE YOUR MOTHER SAID, I THINK YOU'D BE GOOD AT RUNNING YOUR FAMILY BUSINESS.
ALSO, IN ART CLASS, YOU DEMONSTRATE A STRONG AESTHETIC SENSE. YOU'RE DETAIL ORIENTED AND GOOD WITH YOUR HANDS.
THOSE ABILITIES WOULD PROBABLY MAKE YOU AN EXCELLENT TEAM PLAYER OR CUSTOMER SERVICE PERSON IF YOU WENT TO WORK FOR A LOCAL BUSINESS OR CORPORATION.
TAP TAP
OH...
I see...
IF YOU GIVE ME ANOTHER DAY, I COULD PREPARE A MORE DETAILED PRESENTATION, COMPLETE WITH VISUAL AIDS.
SPARKLE
SPARKLE
NO, THAT'S OKAY! YOU DON'T HAVE TO DO THAT.
Thanks any-way!
INTERESTING. I'M SUITED TO RUNNING THE FAMILY BUSINESS...
JUST LIKE MOM SAID.
NOT THAT I'M AGAINST THE IDEA...
BUT STILL, FOR SOME REASON...
...THE IDEA THAT MY FUTURE'S ALREADY SET IN STONE...
...MAKES ME FEEL KIND OF SAD...

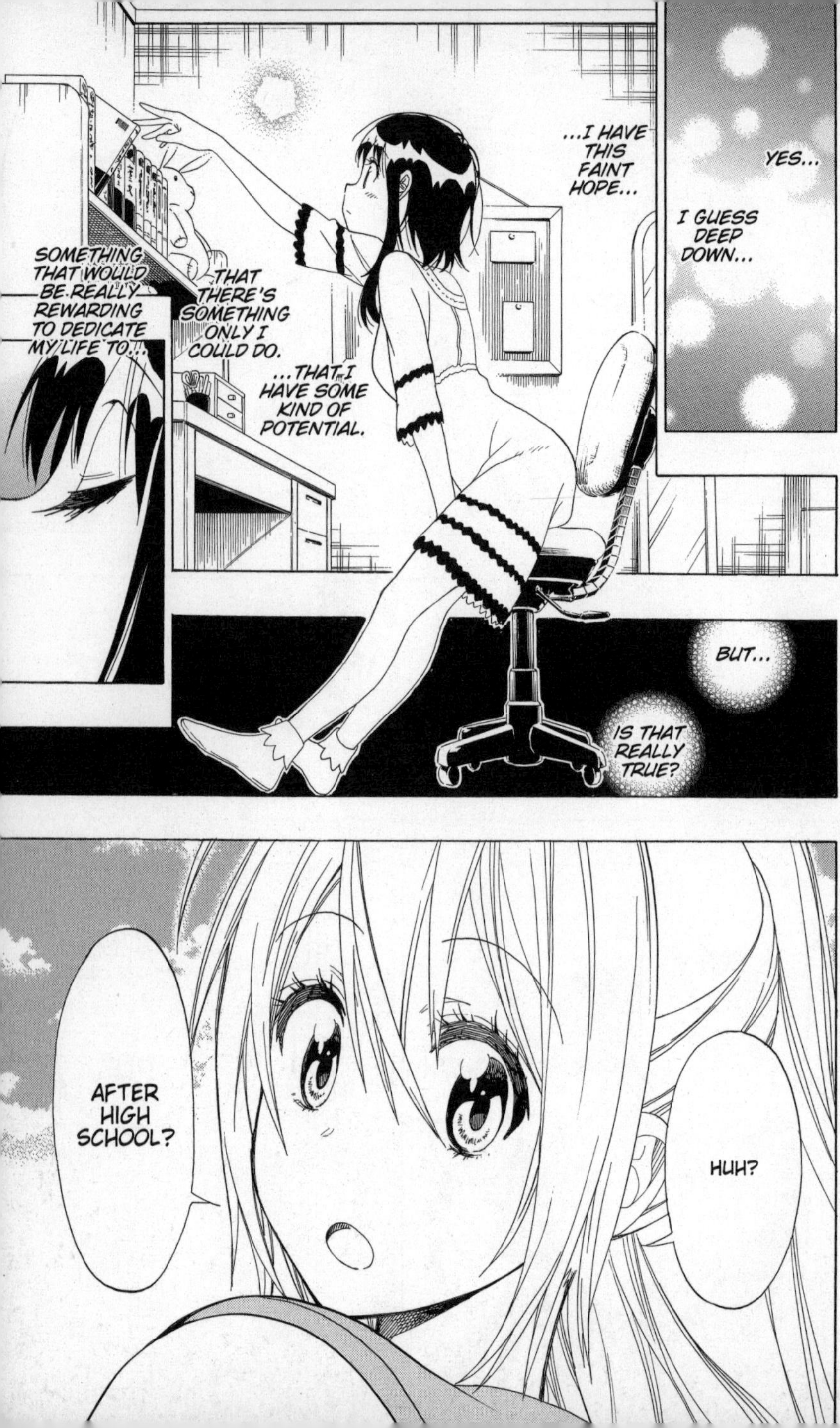
YES...
I GUESS DEEP DOWN...
...I HAVE THIS FAINT HOPE...
...THAT I HAVE SOME KIND OF POTENTIAL.
THAT THERE'S SOMETHING ONLY I COULD DO.
SOMETHING THAT WOULD BE REALLY REWARDING TO DEDICATE MY LIFE TO...
BUT...
IS THAT REALLY TRUE?
HUH?
AFTER HIGH SCHOOL?

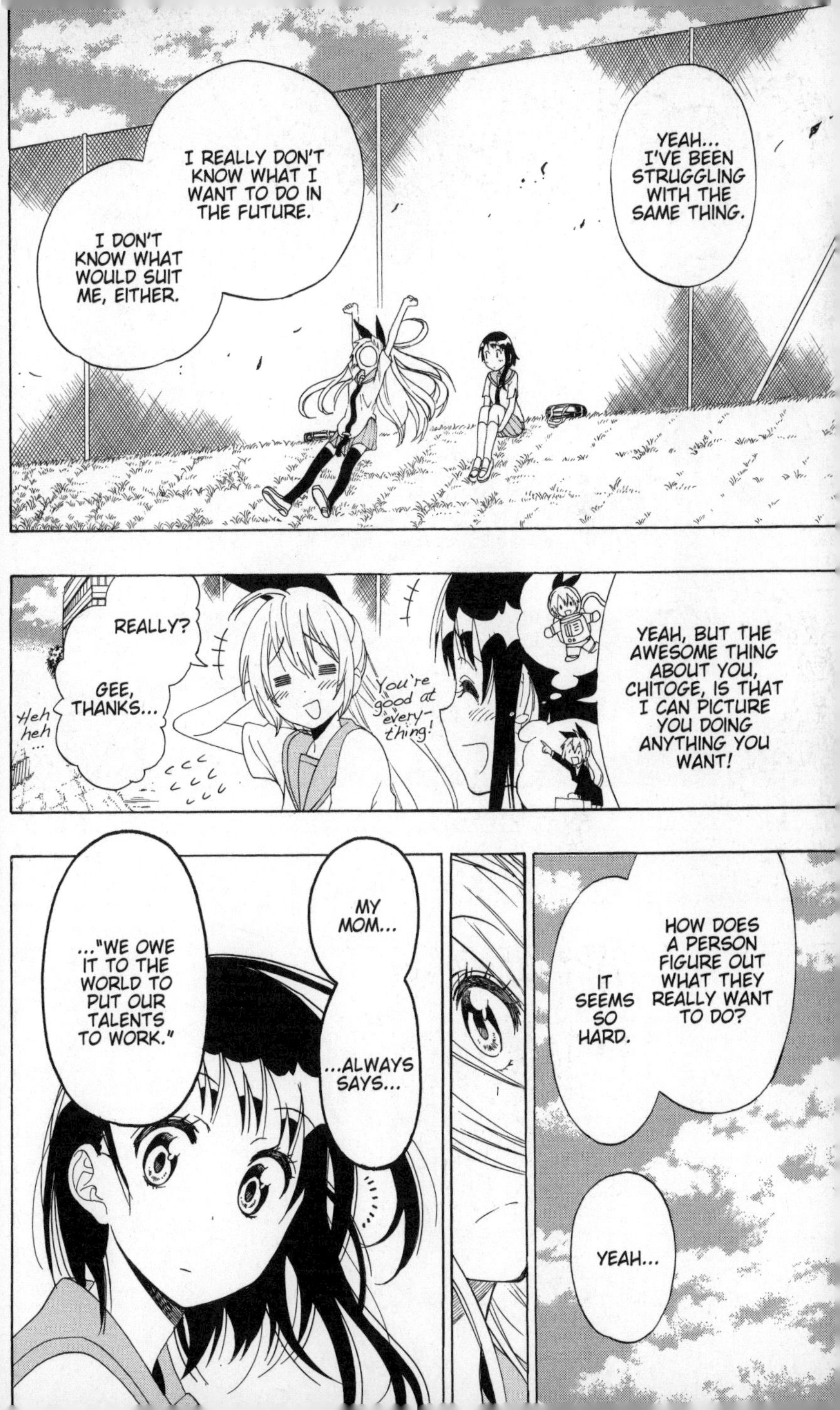
YEAH... I'VE BEEN STRUGGLING WITH THE SAME THING.
I REALLY DON'T KNOW WHAT I WANT TO DO IN THE FUTURE.
I DON'T KNOW WHAT WOULD SUIT ME, EITHER.
YEAH, BUT THE AWESOME THING ABOUT YOU, CHITOGE, IS THAT I CAN PICTURE YOU DOING ANYTHING YOU WANT!
You're good at every-thing!
REALLY?
GEE, THANKS...
Heh heh...
HOW DOES A PERSON FIGURE OUT WHAT THEY REALLY WANT TO DO?
IT SEEMS SO HARD.
YEAH...
MY MOM...
...ALWAYS SAYS...
..."WE OWE IT TO THE WORLD TO PUT OUR TALENTS TO WORK."

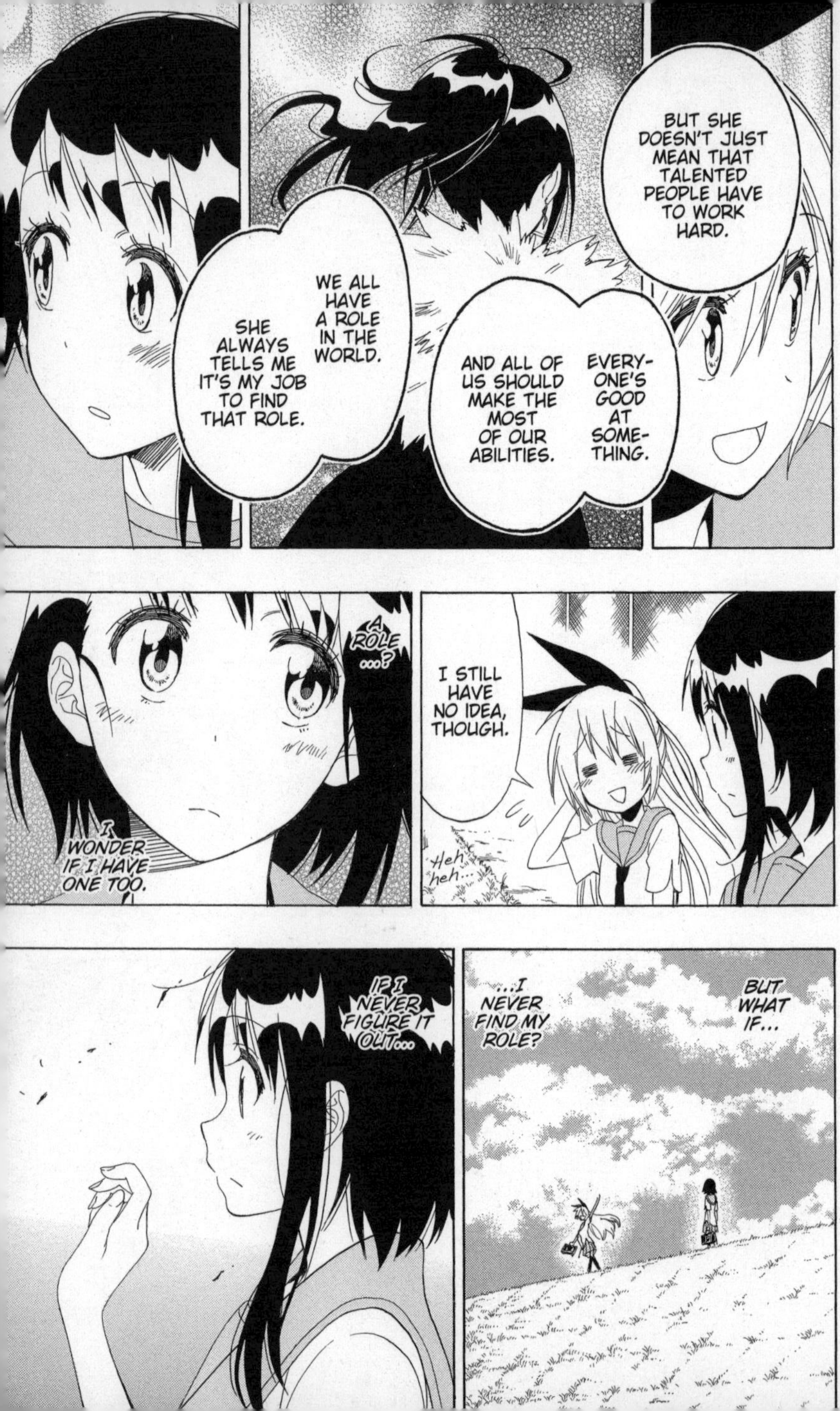
BUT SHE DOESN'T JUST MEAN THAT TALENTED PEOPLE HAVE TO WORK HARD.
EVERY-ONE'S GOOD AT SOME-THING.
AND ALL OF US SHOULD MAKE THE MOST OF OUR ABILITIES.
WE ALL HAVE A ROLE IN THE WORLD.
SHE ALWAYS TELLS ME IT'S MY JOB TO FIND THAT ROLE.
I STILL HAVE NO IDEA, THOUGH.
Heh heh...
A ROLE...?
I WONDER IF I HAVE ONE TOO.
BUT WHAT IF...
...I NEVER FIND MY ROLE?
IF I NEVER FIGURE IT OUT...

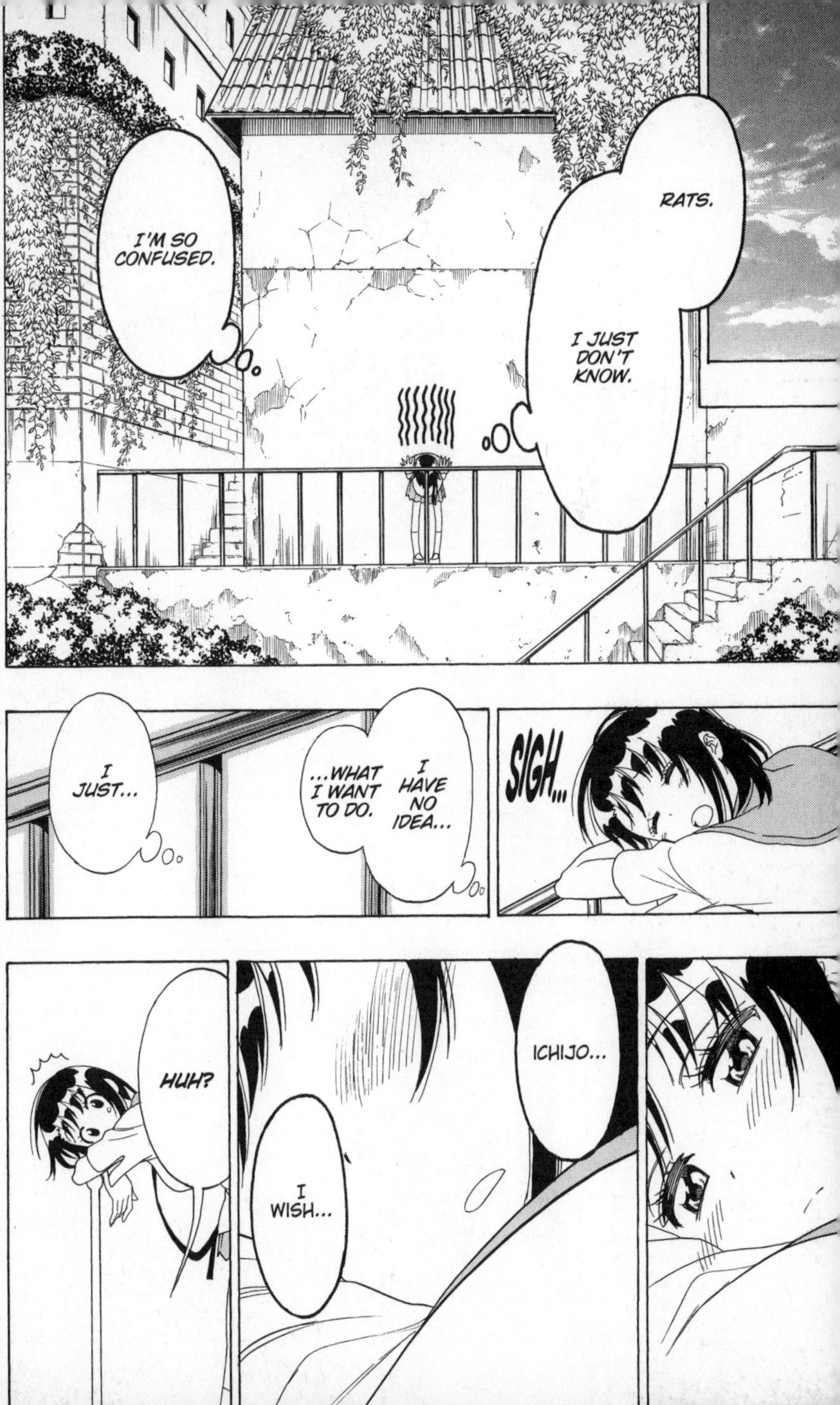
RATS.
I JUST DON'T KNOW.
I'M SO CONFUSED.
SIGH...
I HAVE NO IDEA...
...WHAT I WANT TO DO.
I JUST...
ICHIJO...
I WISH...
HUH?

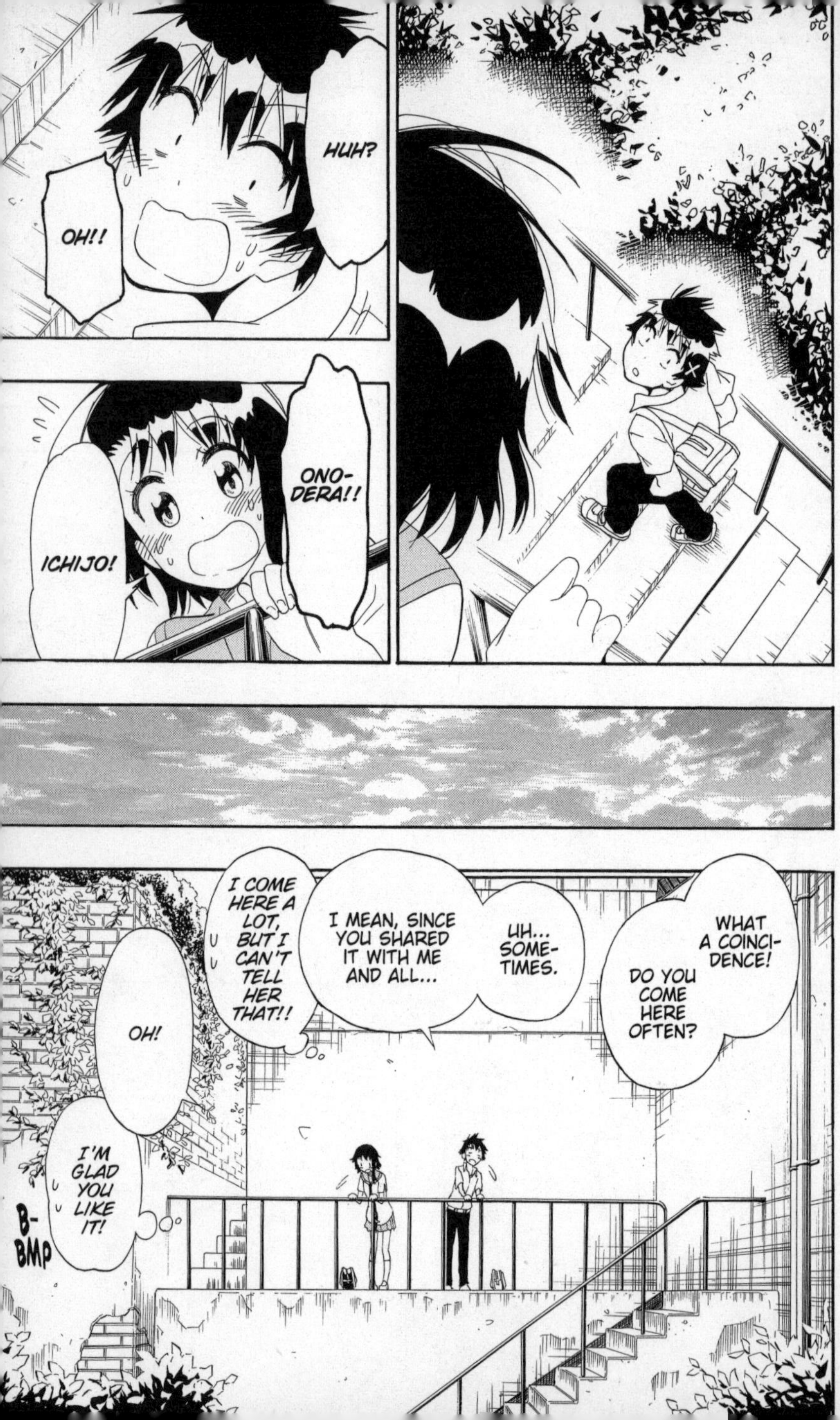
HUH?
OH!!
ONO-DERA!!
ICHIJO!
WHAT A COINCI-DENCE!
DO YOU COME HERE OFTEN?
UH... SOME-TIMES.
I MEAN, SINCE YOU SHARED IT WITH ME AND ALL...
I COME HERE A LOT, BUT I CAN'T TELL HER THAT!!
OH!
I'M GLAD YOU LIKE IT!
B-BMP

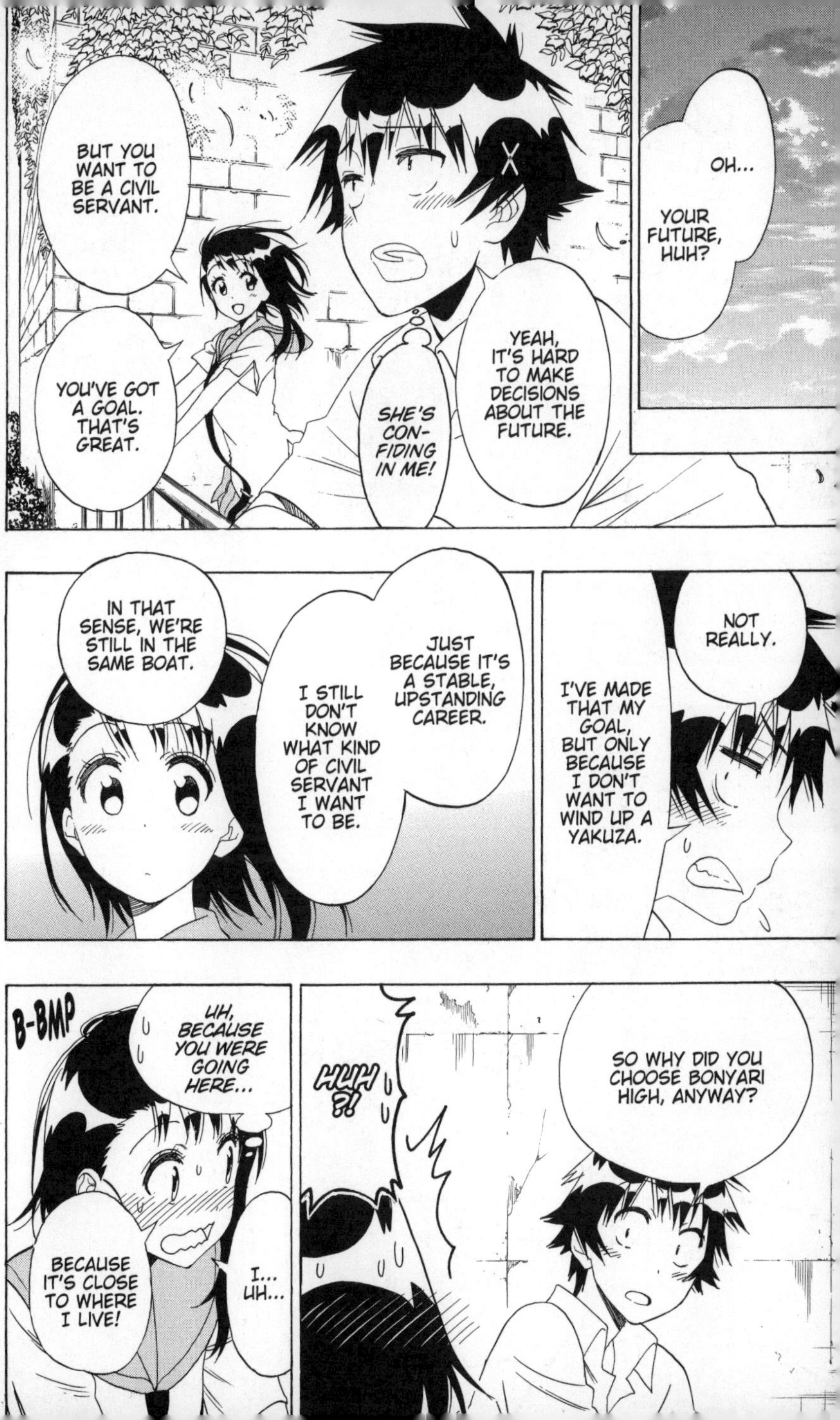
OH...
YOUR FUTURE, HUH?
YEAH, IT'S HARD TO MAKE DECISIONS ABOUT THE FUTURE.
SHE'S CON-FIDING IN ME!
BUT YOU WANT TO BE A CIVIL SERVANT.
YOU'VE GOT A GOAL. THAT'S GREAT.
NOT REALLY.
I'VE MADE THAT MY GOAL, BUT ONLY BECAUSE I DON'T WANT TO WIND UP A YAKUZA.
JUST BECAUSE IT'S A STABLE, UPSTANDING CAREER.
I STILL DON'T KNOW WHAT KIND OF CIVIL SERVANT I WANT TO BE.
IN THAT SENSE, WE'RE STILL IN THE SAME BOAT.
SO WHY DID YOU CHOOSE BONYARI HIGH, ANYWAY?
HUH ?!
B-BMP
UH, BECAUSE YOU WERE GOING HERE...
I... UH...
BECAUSE IT'S CLOSE TO WHERE I LIVE!

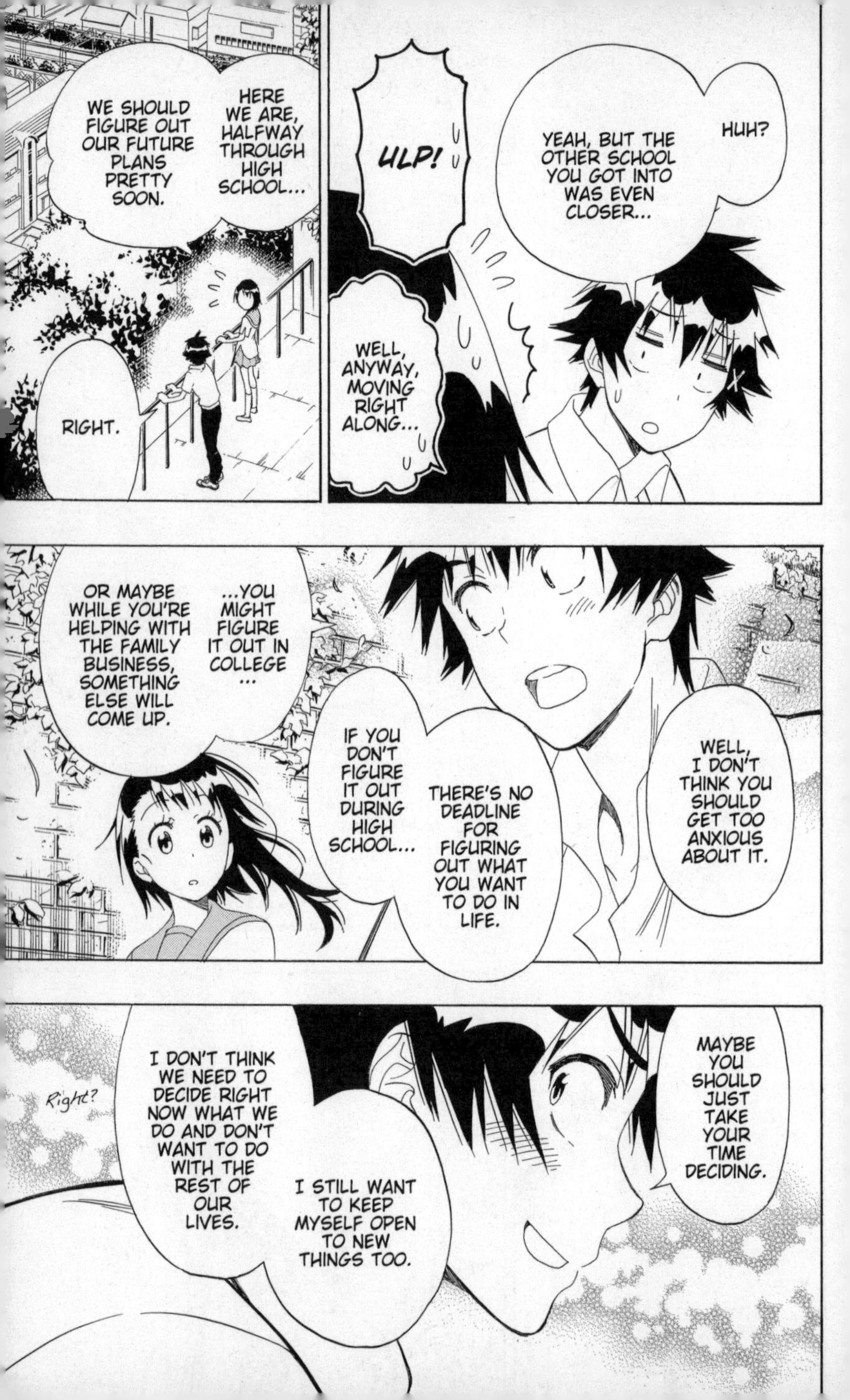
HUH?
YEAH, BUT THE OTHER SCHOOL YOU GOT INTO WAS EVEN CLOSER...
ULP!
WELL, ANYWAY, MOVING RIGHT ALONG...
HERE WE ARE, HALFWAY THROUGH HIGH SCHOOL...
WE SHOULD FIGURE OUT OUR FUTURE PLANS PRETTY SOON.
RIGHT.
WELL, I DON'T THINK YOU SHOULD GET TOO ANXIOUS ABOUT IT.
THERE'S NO DEADLINE FOR FIGURING OUT WHAT YOU WANT TO DO IN LIFE.
IF YOU DON'T FIGURE IT OUT DURING HIGH SCHOOL...
...YOU MIGHT FIGURE IT OUT IN COLLEGE...
OR MAYBE WHILE YOU'RE HELPING WITH THE FAMILY BUSINESS, SOMETHING ELSE WILL COME UP.
MAYBE YOU SHOULD JUST TAKE YOUR TIME DECIDING.
I STILL WANT TO KEEP MYSELF OPEN TO NEW THINGS TOO.
I DON'T THINK WE NEED TO DECIDE RIGHT NOW WHAT WE DO AND DON'T WANT TO DO WITH THE REST OF OUR LIVES.
Right?

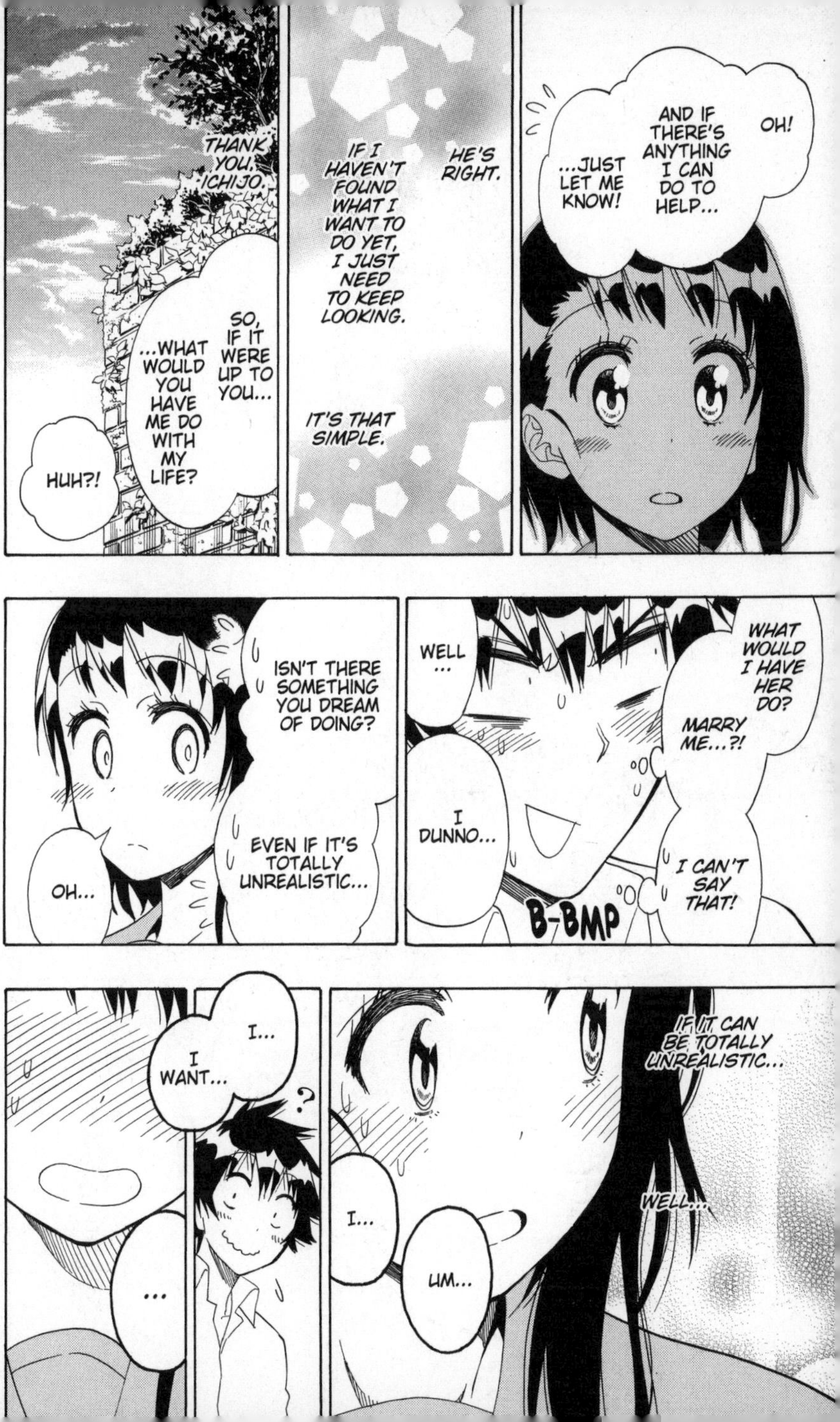
OH!
AND IF THERE'S ANYTHING I CAN DO TO HELP...
...JUST LET ME KNOW!
HE'S RIGHT.
IF I HAVEN'T FOUND WHAT I WANT TO DO YET, I JUST NEED TO KEEP LOOKING.
IT'S THAT SIMPLE.
THANK YOU, ICHIJO.
SO, IF IT WERE UP TO YOU...
...WHAT WOULD YOU HAVE ME DO WITH MY LIFE?
HUH?!
WHAT WOULD I HAVE HER DO?
MARRY ME...?!
WELL...
I DUNNO...
I CAN'T SAY THAT!
B-BMP
ISN'T THERE SOMETHING YOU DREAM OF DOING?
EVEN IF IT'S TOTALLY UNREALISTIC...
OH...
IF IT CAN BE TOTALLY UNREALISTIC...
WELL...
I...
UM...
I...
I WANT...
?
...

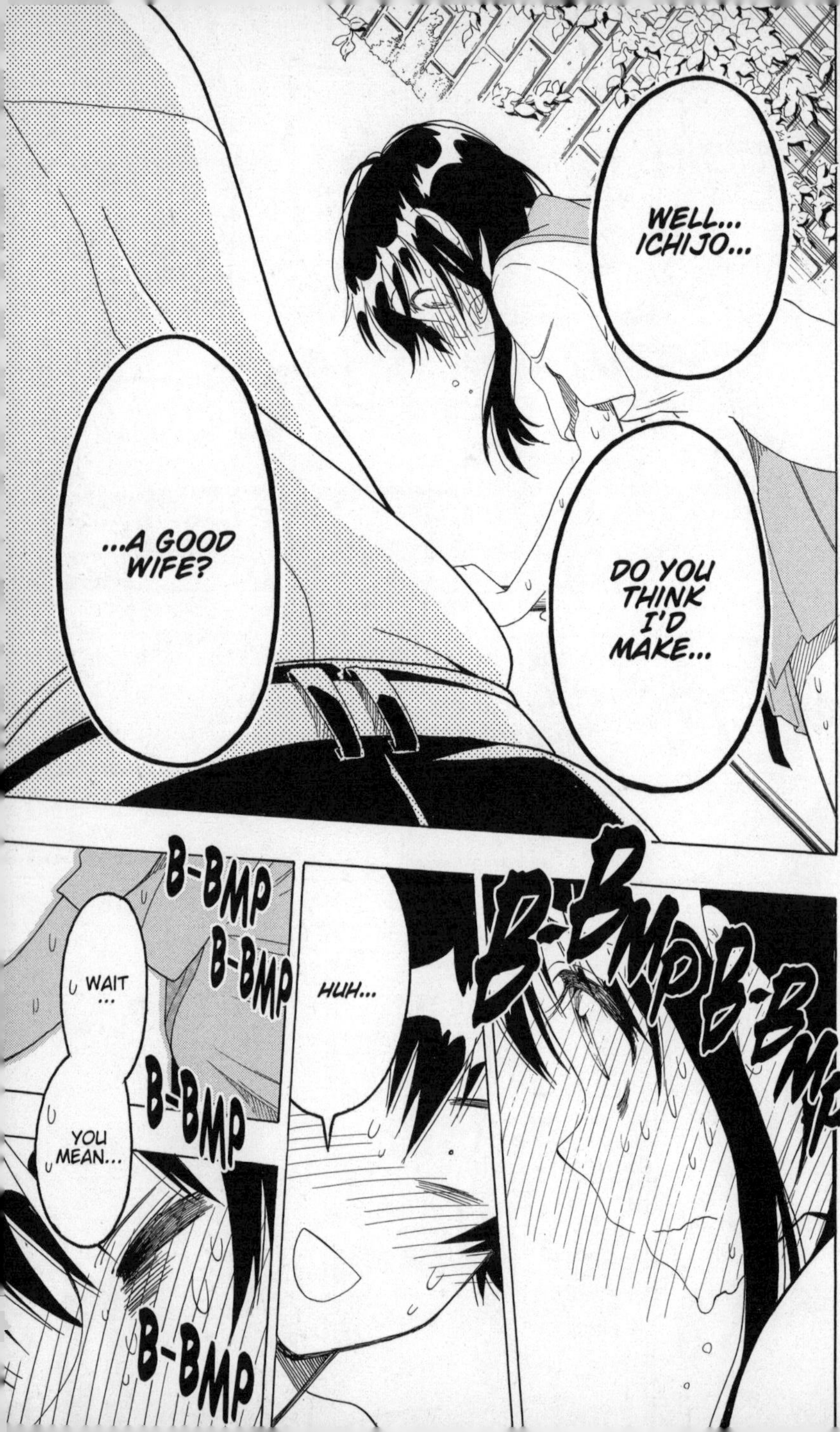
WELL... ICHIJO...
DO YOU THINK I'D MAKE...
...A GOOD WIFE?
B-BMP B-BMP
HUH...
B-BMP
B-BMP
WAIT ...
B-BMP
YOU MEAN...
B-BMP

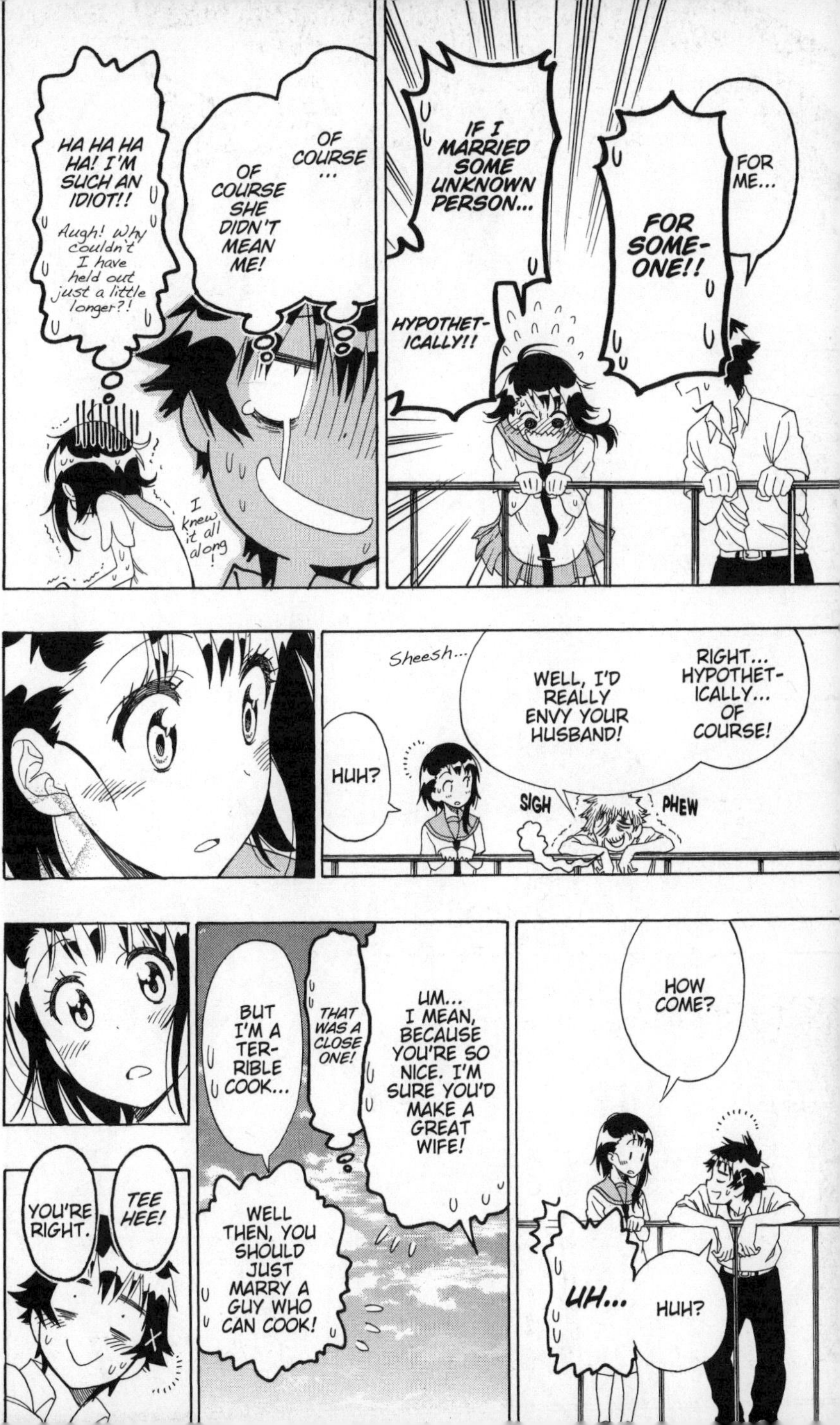
FOR ME...
FOR SOMEONE!!
IF I MARRIED SOME UNKNOWN PERSON...
HYPOTHETICALLY!!
OF COURSE...
OF COURSE SHE DIDN'T MEAN ME!
HA HA HA HA! I'M SUCH AN IDIOT!!
Augh! Why couldn't I have held out just a little longer?!
I knew it all along!
RIGHT... HYPOTHETICALLY... OF COURSE!
WELL, I'D REALLY ENVY YOUR HUSBAND!
Sheesh...
PHEW
SIGH
HUH?
HOW COME?
HUH?
UH...
UM... I MEAN, BECAUSE YOU'RE SO NICE. I'M SURE YOU'D MAKE A GREAT WIFE!
THAT WAS A CLOSE ONE!
BUT I'M A TERRIBLE COOK...
WELL THEN, YOU SHOULD JUST MARRY A GUY WHO CAN COOK!
TEE HEE!
YOU'RE RIGHT.

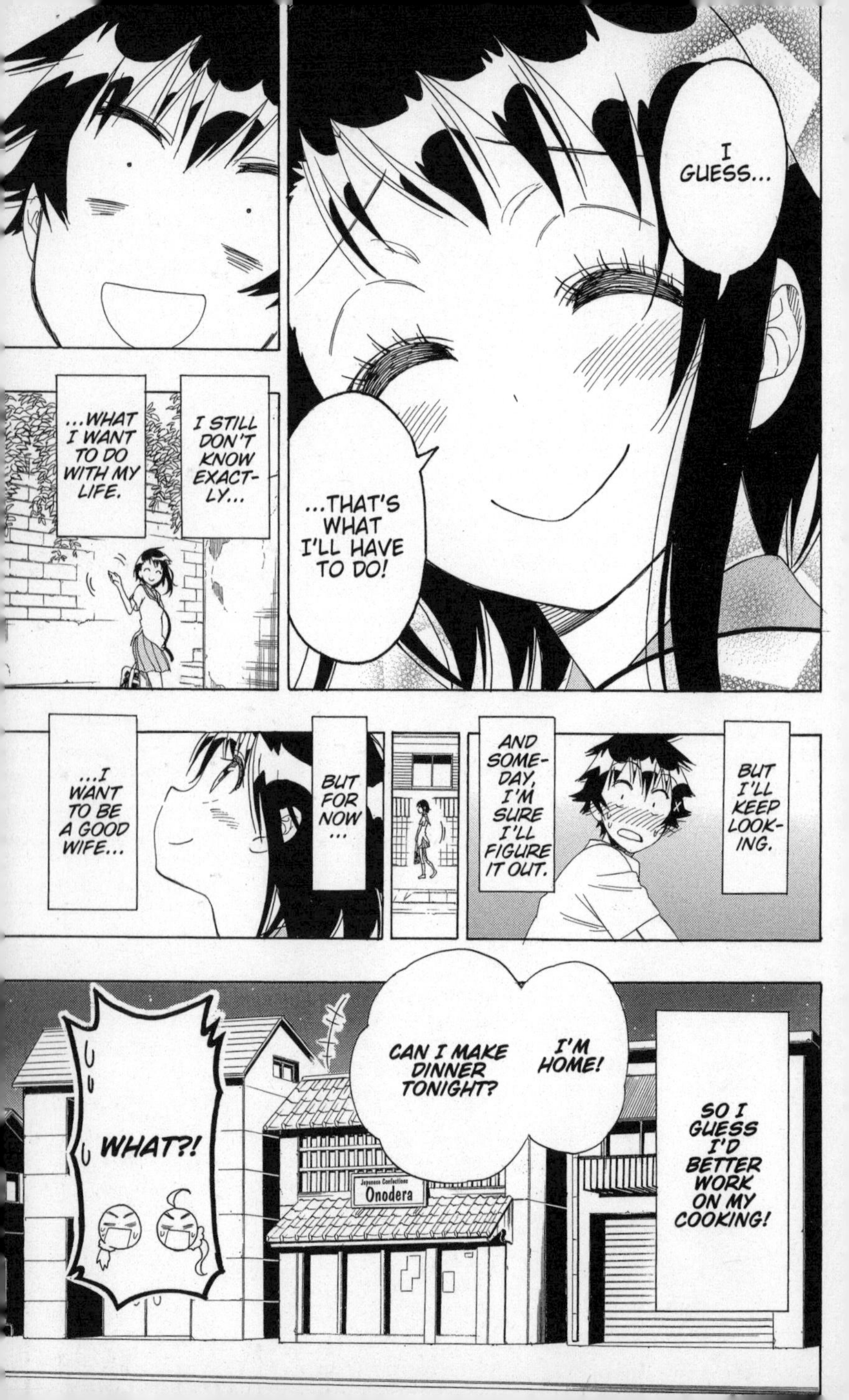
I GUESS...
...THAT'S WHAT I'LL HAVE TO DO!
I STILL DON'T KNOW EXACTLY...
...WHAT I WANT TO DO WITH MY LIFE.
BUT I'LL KEEP LOOKING.
AND SOMEDAY, I'M SURE I'LL FIGURE IT OUT.
BUT FOR NOW...
...I WANT TO BE A GOOD WIFE...
SO I GUESS I'D BETTER WORK ON MY COOKING!
I'M HOME!
CAN I MAKE DINNER TONIGHT?
Japanese Confections
Onodera
WHAT?!

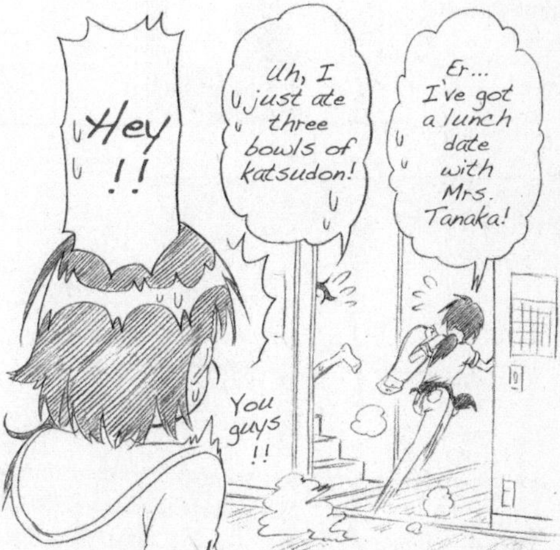
Er... I've got a lunch date with Mrs. Tanaka!
Uh, I just ate three bowls of katsudon!
Hey !!
You guys !!

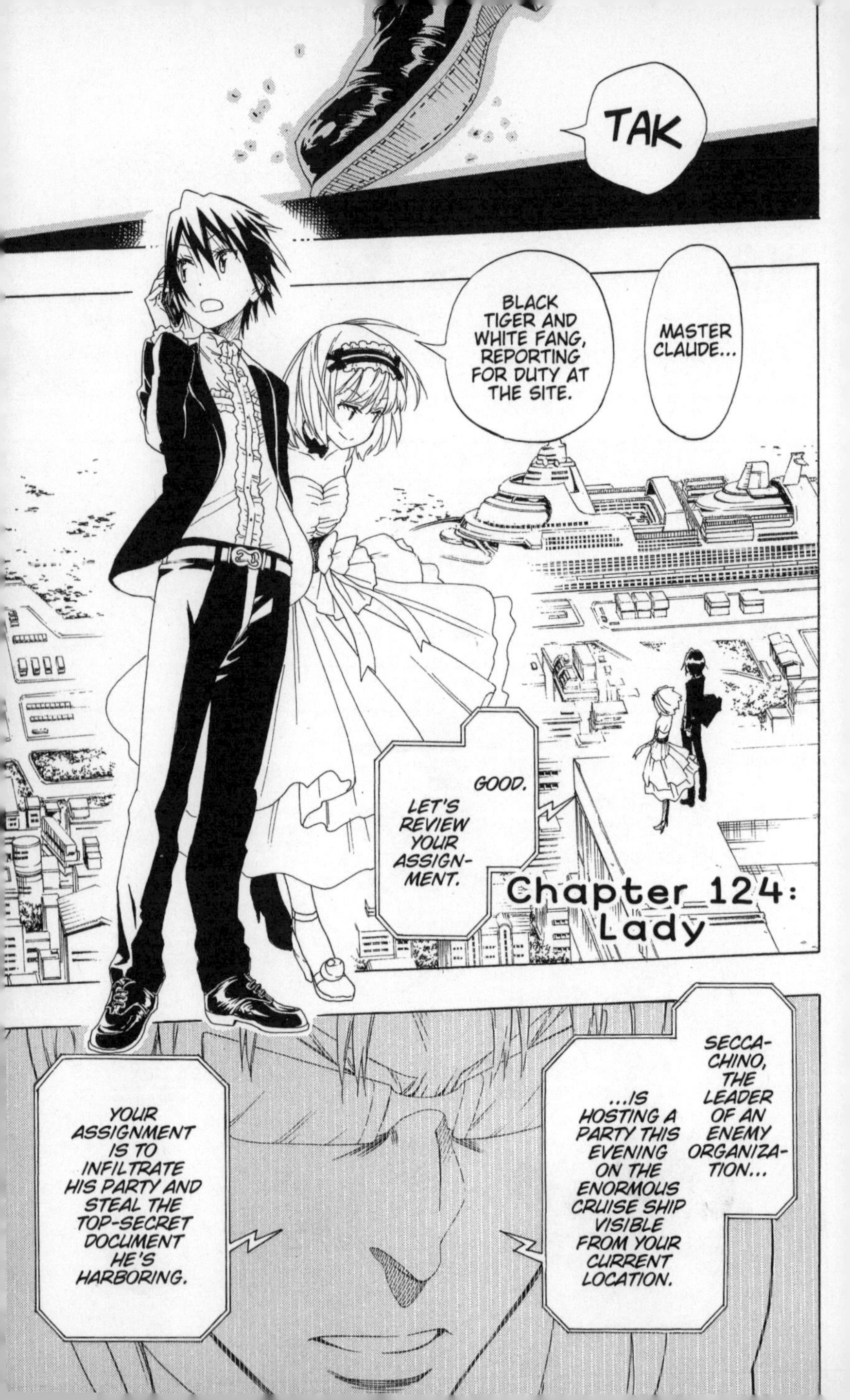
TAK
MASTER CLAUDE...
BLACK TIGER AND WHITE FANG, REPORTING FOR DUTY AT THE SITE.
GOOD. LET'S REVIEW YOUR ASSIGNMENT.
Chapter 124: Lady
SECCA-CHINO, THE LEADER OF AN ENEMY ORGANIZATION...
...IS HOSTING A PARTY THIS EVENING ON THE ENORMOUS CRUISE SHIP VISIBLE FROM YOUR CURRENT LOCATION.
YOUR ASSIGNMENT IS TO INFILTRATE HIS PARTY AND STEAL THE TOP-SECRET DOCUMENT HE'S HARBORING.

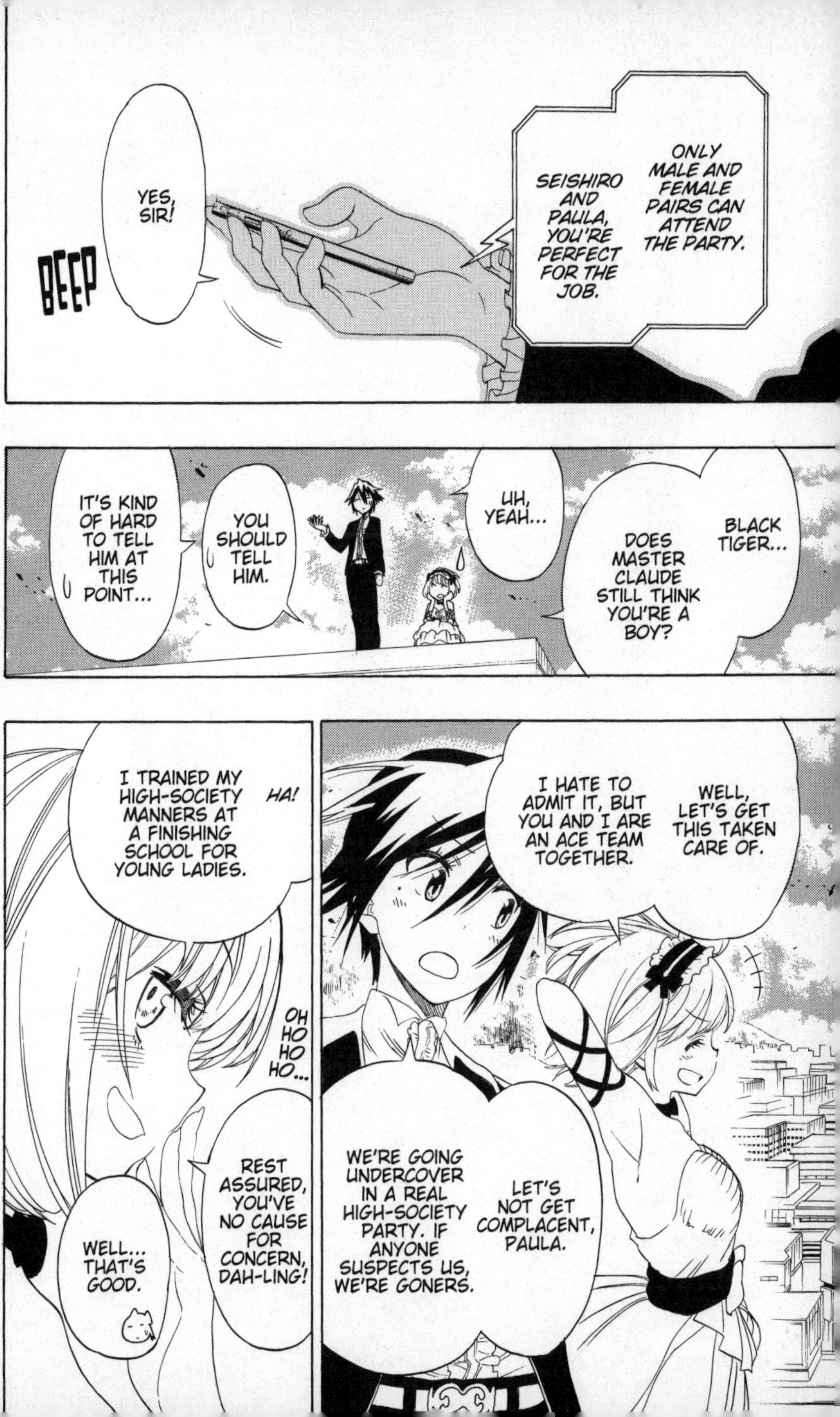
ONLY MALE AND FEMALE PAIRS CAN ATTEND THE PARTY.
SEISHIRO AND PAULA, YOU'RE PERFECT FOR THE JOB.
YES, SIR!
BEEP
BLACK TIGER...
DOES MASTER CLAUDE STILL THINK YOU'RE A BOY?
UH, YEAH...
YOU SHOULD TELL HIM.
IT'S KIND OF HARD TO TELL HIM AT THIS POINT...
WELL, LET'S GET THIS TAKEN CARE OF.
I HATE TO ADMIT IT, BUT YOU AND I ARE AN ACE TEAM TOGETHER.
LET'S NOT GET COMPLACENT, PAULA.
WE'RE GOING UNDERCOVER IN A REAL HIGH-SOCIETY PARTY. IF ANYONE SUSPECTS US, WE'RE GONERS.
HA!
I TRAINED MY HIGH-SOCIETY MANNERS AT A FINISHING SCHOOL FOR YOUNG LADIES.
OH HO HO HO...
REST ASSURED, YOU'VE NO CAUSE FOR CONCERN, DAH-LING!
WELL... THAT'S GOOD.

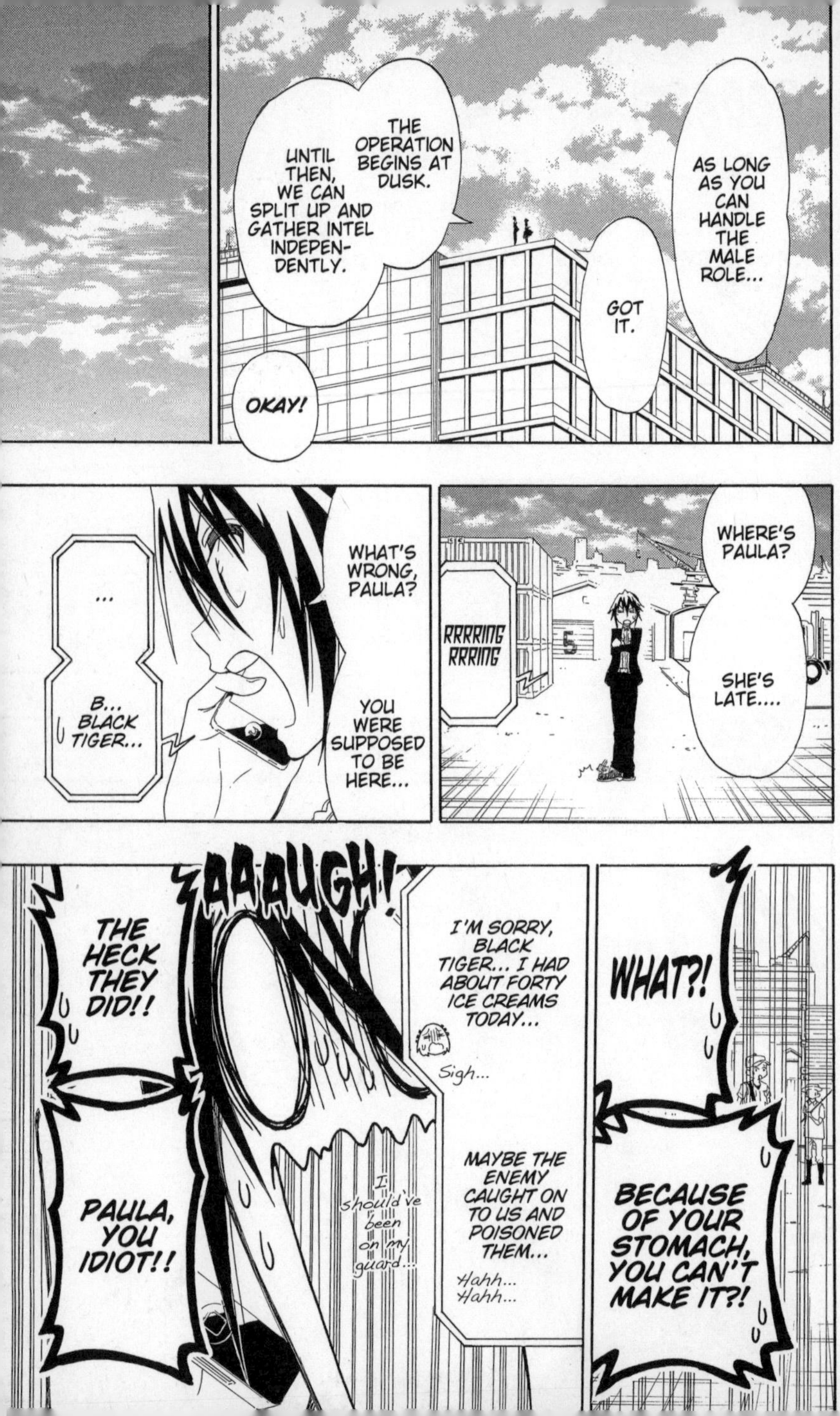
AS LONG AS YOU CAN HANDLE THE MALE ROLE...
GOT IT.
THE OPERATION BEGINS AT DUSK.
UNTIL THEN, WE CAN SPLIT UP AND GATHER INTEL INDEPENDENTLY.
OKAY!
WHERE'S PAULA?
SHE'S LATE....
RRRRING RRRING
WHAT'S WRONG, PAULA?
YOU WERE SUPPOSED TO BE HERE...
...
B... BLACK TIGER...
WHAT?!
BECAUSE OF YOUR STOMACH, YOU CAN'T MAKE IT?!
I'M SORRY, BLACK TIGER... I HAD ABOUT FORTY ICE CREAMS TODAY...
Sigh...
MAYBE THE ENEMY CAUGHT ON TO US AND POISONED THEM...
Hahh... Hahh...
AAAUGH!
THE HECK THEY DID!!
I should've been on my guard...
PAULA, YOU IDIOT!!

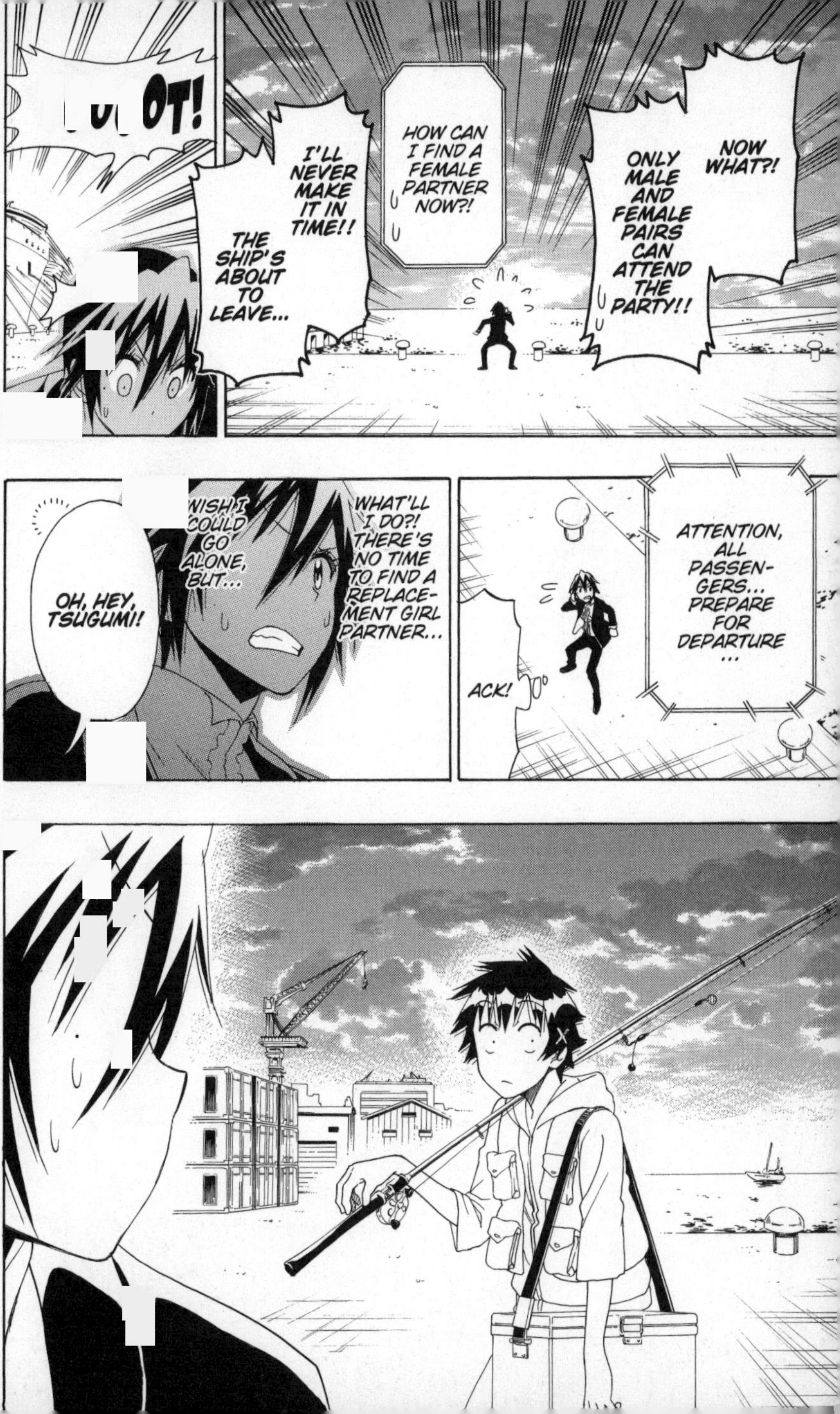
NOW WHAT?!
ONLY MALE AND FEMALE PAIRS CAN ATTEND THE PARTY!!
HOW CAN I FIND A FEMALE PARTNER NOW?!
I'LL NEVER MAKE IT IN TIME!!
THE SHIP'S ABOUT TO LEAVE...
OT!
ATTENTION, ALL PASSEN-GERS... PREPARE FOR DEPARTURE...
ACK!
WHAT'LL I DO?! THERE'S NO TIME TO FIND A REPLACE-MENT GIRL PARTNER...
WISH I COULD GO ALONE, BUT...
OH, HEY, TSUGUMI!

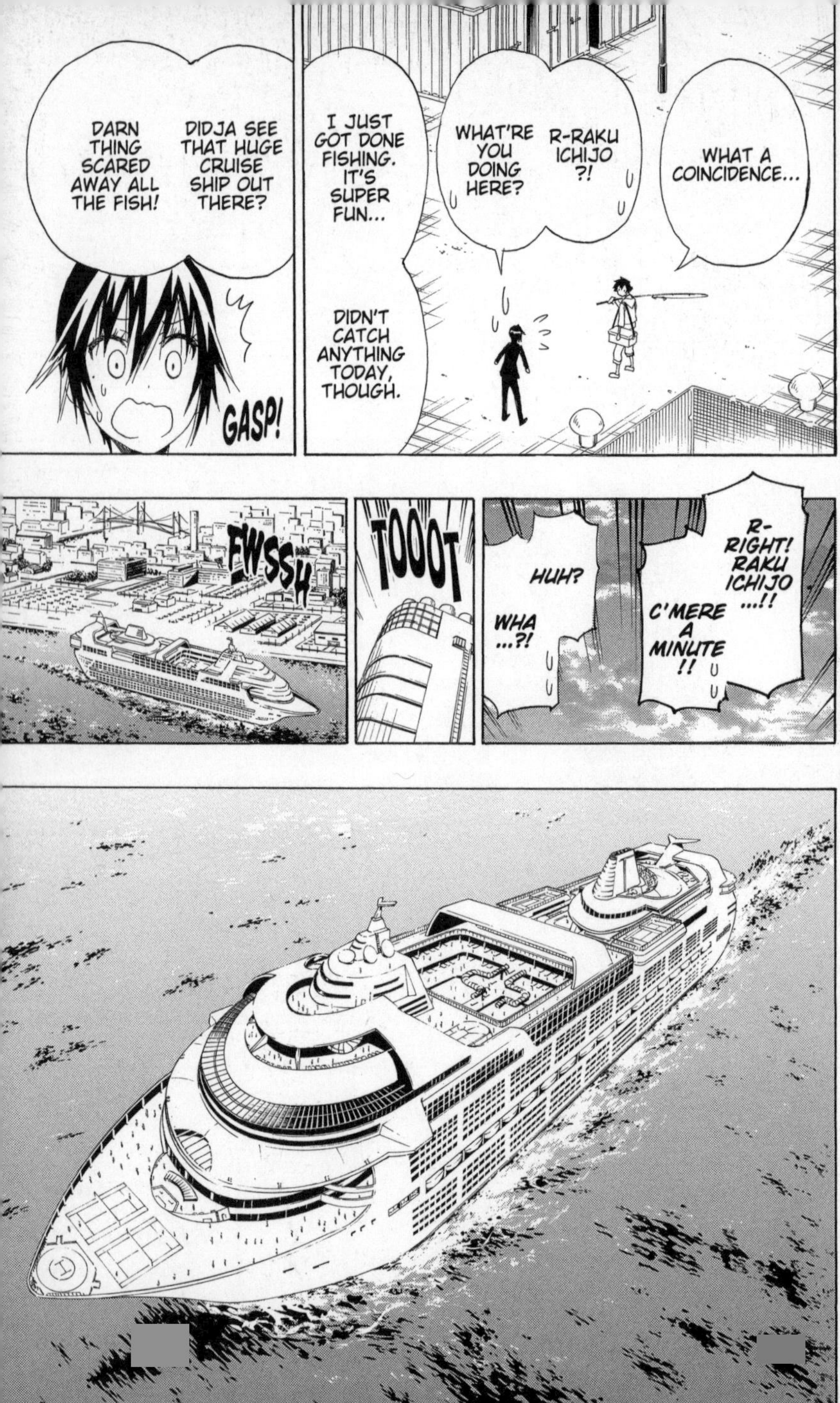
WHAT A COINCIDENCE...
R-RAKU ICHIJO ?!
WHAT'RE YOU DOING HERE?
I JUST GOT DONE FISHING. IT'S SUPER FUN...
DIDN'T CATCH ANYTHING TODAY, THOUGH.
DIDJA SEE THAT HUGE CRUISE SHIP OUT THERE?
DARN THING SCARED AWAY ALL THE FISH!
GASP!
R-RIGHT! RAKU ICHIJO ...!!
C'MERE A MINUTE !!
HUH?
WHA ...?!
TOOOT
FWSSH

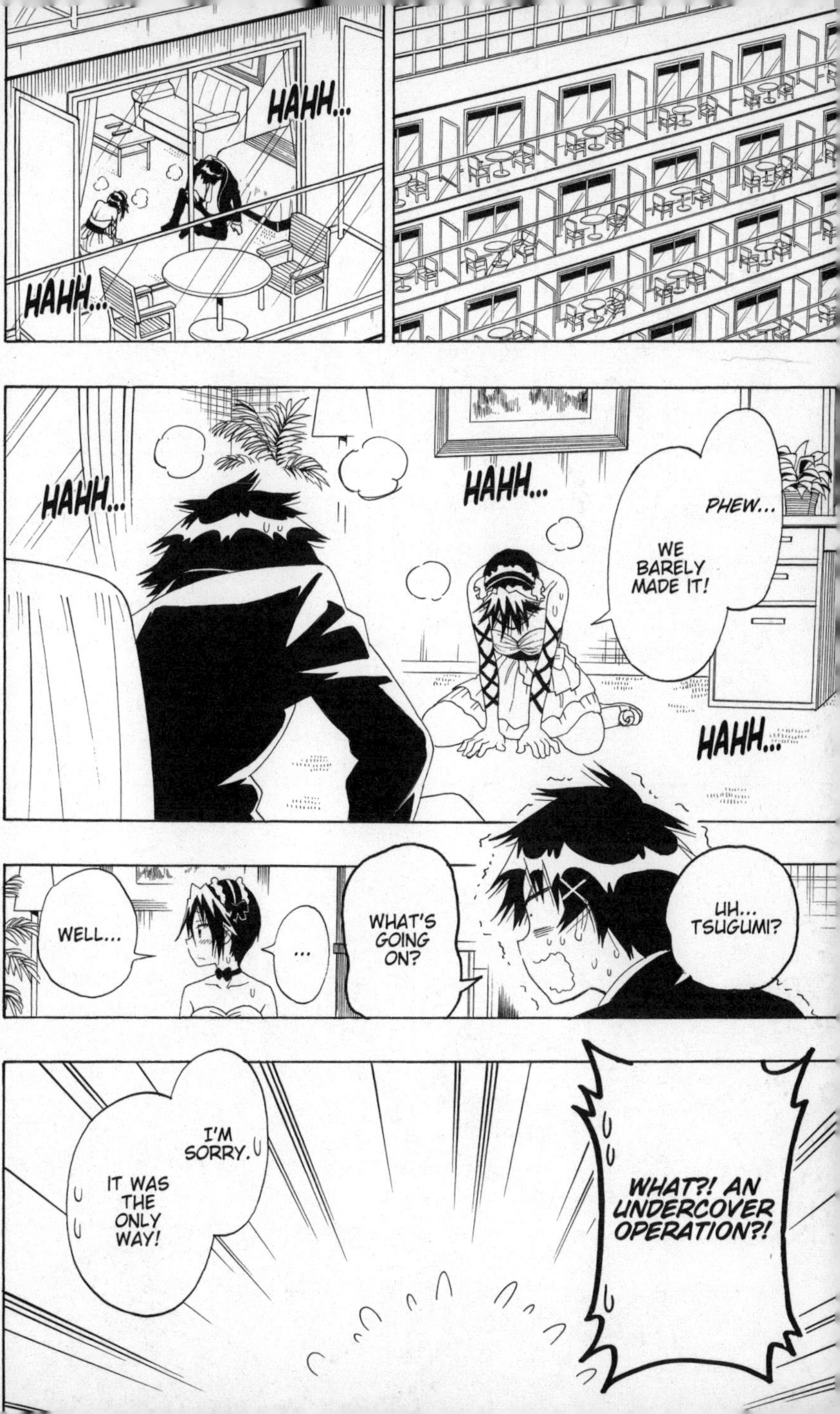
HAHH...
HAHH...
PHEW... WE BARELY MADE IT!
HAHH...
HAHH...
HAHH...
UH... TSUGUMI?
WHAT'S GOING ON?
...
WELL...
WHAT?! AN UNDERCOVER OPERATION?!
I'M SORRY. IT WAS THE ONLY WAY!

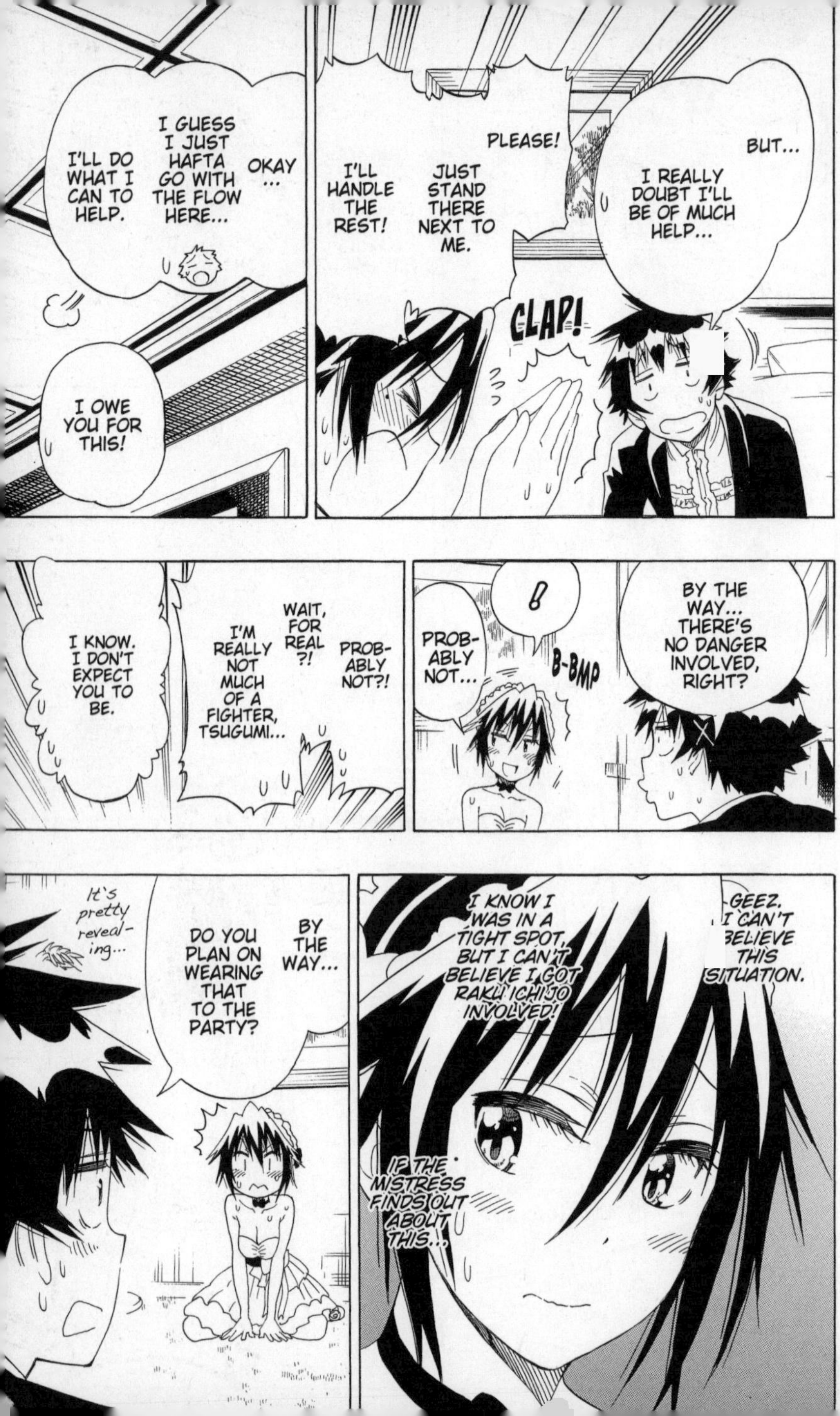
BUT...
I REALLY DOUBT I'LL BE OF MUCH HELP...
PLEASE!
JUST STAND THERE NEXT TO ME.
I'LL HANDLE THE REST!
CLAP!
OKAY...
I GUESS I JUST HAFTA GO WITH THE FLOW HERE...
I'LL DO WHAT I CAN TO HELP.
I OWE YOU FOR THIS!
BY THE WAY... THERE'S NO DANGER INVOLVED, RIGHT?
!
B-BMP
PROBABLY NOT...
PROBABLY NOT?!
WAIT, FOR REAL?!
I'M REALLY NOT MUCH OF A FIGHTER, TSUGUMI...
I KNOW. I DON'T EXPECT YOU TO BE.
GEEZ. I CAN'T BELIEVE THIS SITUATION.
I KNOW I WAS IN A TIGHT SPOT, BUT I CAN'T BELIEVE I GOT RAKU ICHIJO INVOLVED!
IF THE MISTRESS FINDS OUT ABOUT THIS...
BY THE WAY...
DO YOU PLAN ON WEARING THAT TO THE PARTY?
It's pretty revealing...

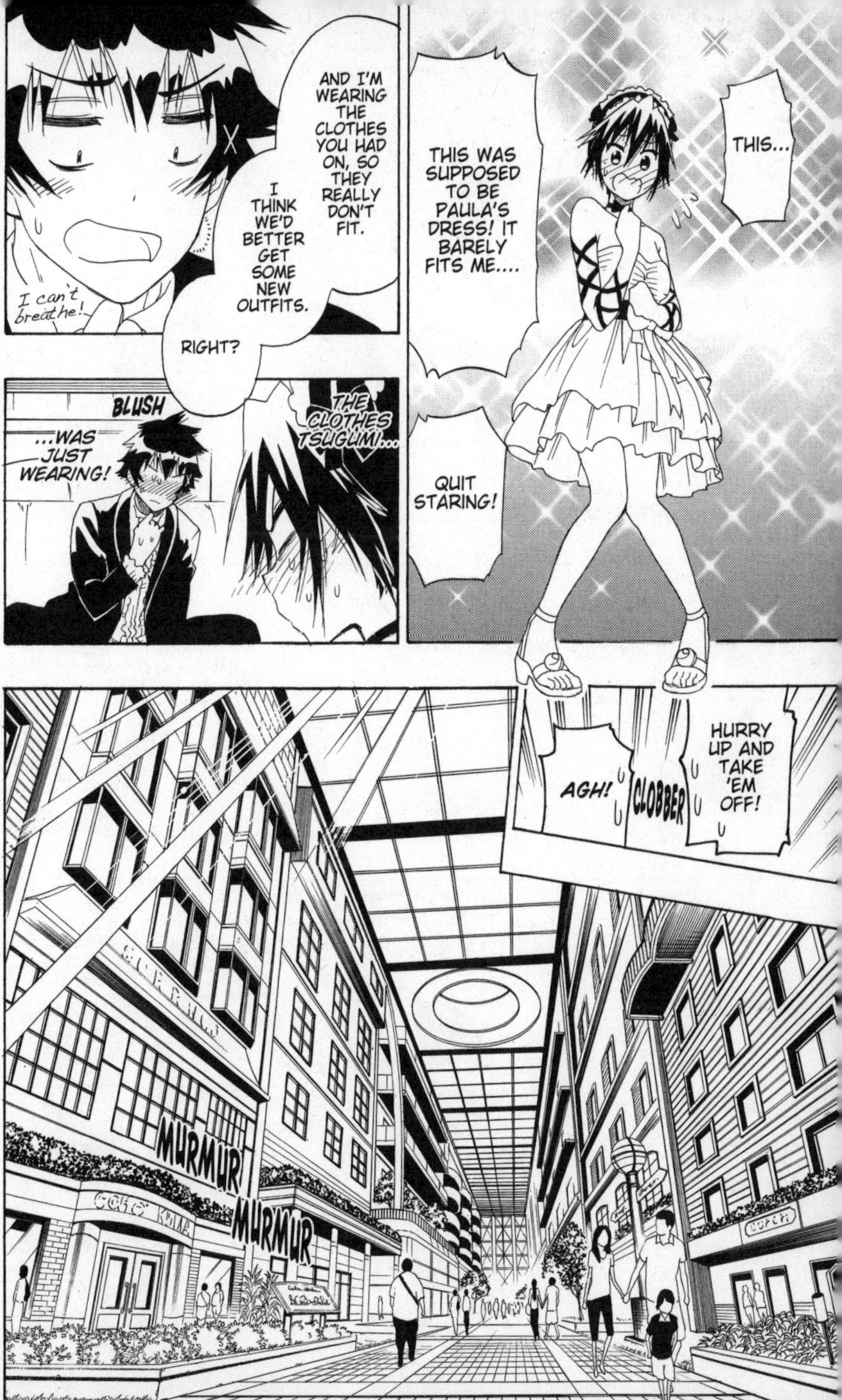
THIS...
THIS WAS SUPPOSED TO BE PAULA'S DRESS! IT BARELY FITS ME....
QUIT STARING!
AND I'M WEARING THE CLOTHES YOU HAD ON, SO THEY REALLY DON'T FIT.
I THINK WE'D BETTER GET SOME NEW OUTFITS.
RIGHT?
I can't breathe!
THE CLOTHES TSUGUMI...
BLUSH
...WAS JUST WEARING!
HURRY UP AND TAKE 'EM OFF!
CLOBBER
AGH!
MURMUR
MURMUR

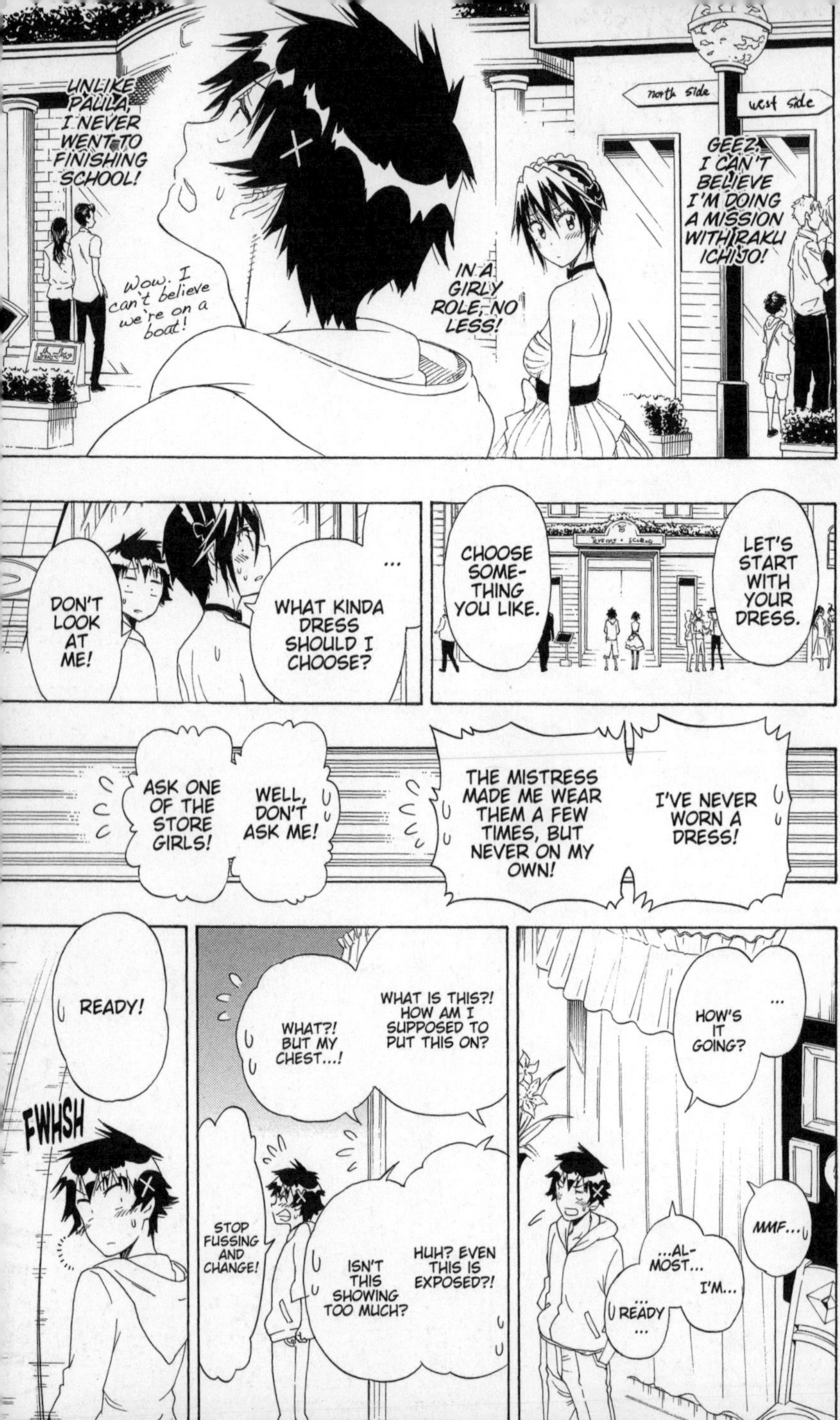
north side
west side
GEEZ, I CAN'T BELIEVE I'M DOING A MISSION WITH RAKU ICHIJO!
IN A GIRLY ROLE, NO LESS!
UNLIKE PAULA, I NEVER WENT TO FINISHING SCHOOL!
Wow. I can't believe we're on a boat!
LET'S START WITH YOUR DRESS.
CHOOSE SOME-THING YOU LIKE.
...
WHAT KINDA DRESS SHOULD I CHOOSE?
DON'T LOOK AT ME!
I'VE NEVER WORN A DRESS!
THE MISTRESS MADE ME WEAR THEM A FEW TIMES, BUT NEVER ON MY OWN!
WELL, DON'T ASK ME!
ASK ONE OF THE STORE GIRLS!
...
HOW'S IT GOING?
MMF...
I'M...
...AL-MOST...
...READY...
WHAT IS THIS?! HOW AM I SUPPOSED TO PUT THIS ON?
WHAT?! BUT MY CHEST...!
HUH? EVEN THIS IS EXPOSED?!
ISN'T THIS SHOWING TOO MUCH?
STOP FUSSING AND CHANGE!
READY!
FWHSH

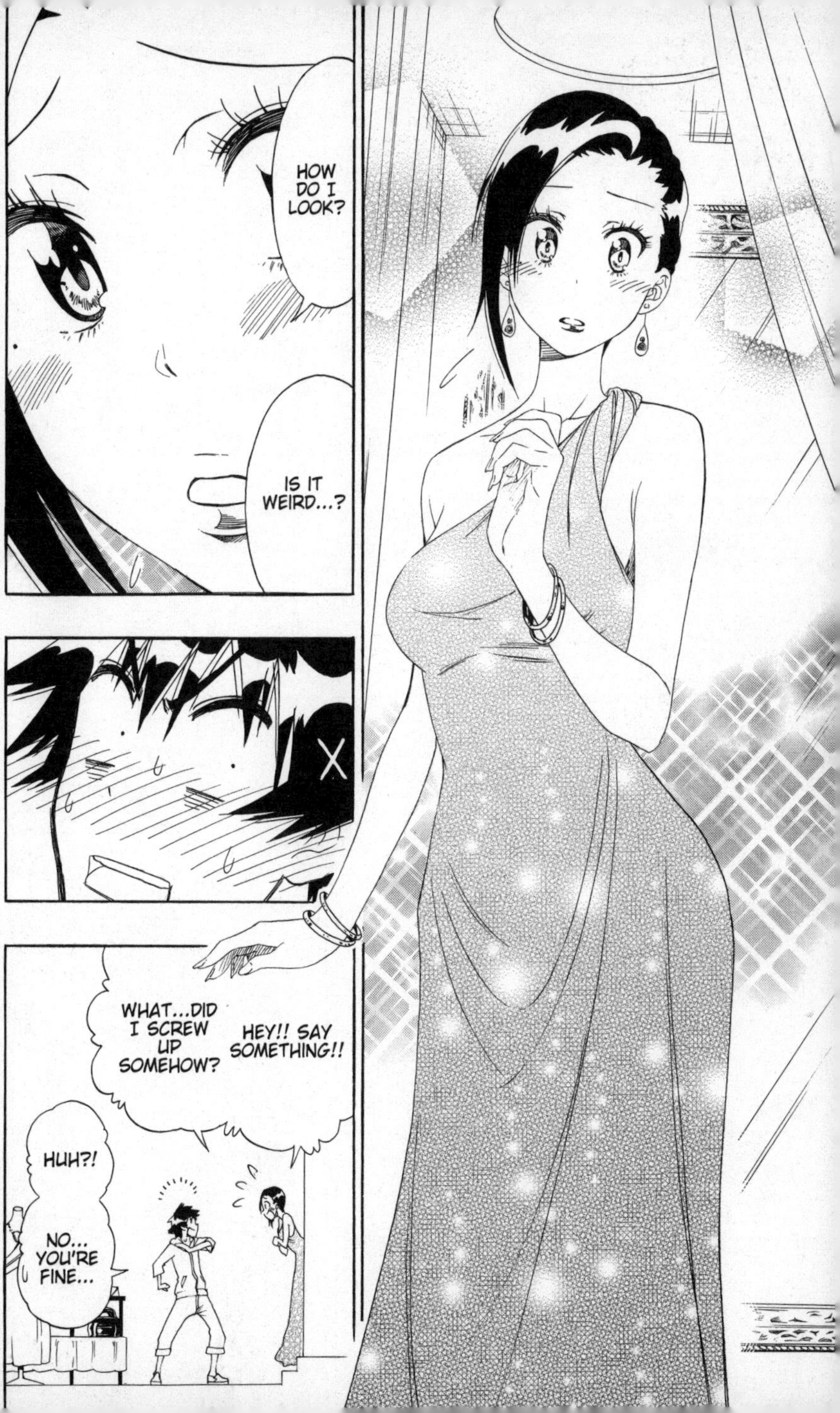
HOW DO I LOOK?
IS IT WEIRD...?
WHAT...DID I SCREW UP SOMEHOW?
HEY!! SAY SOMETHING!!
HUH?!
NO... YOU'RE FINE...

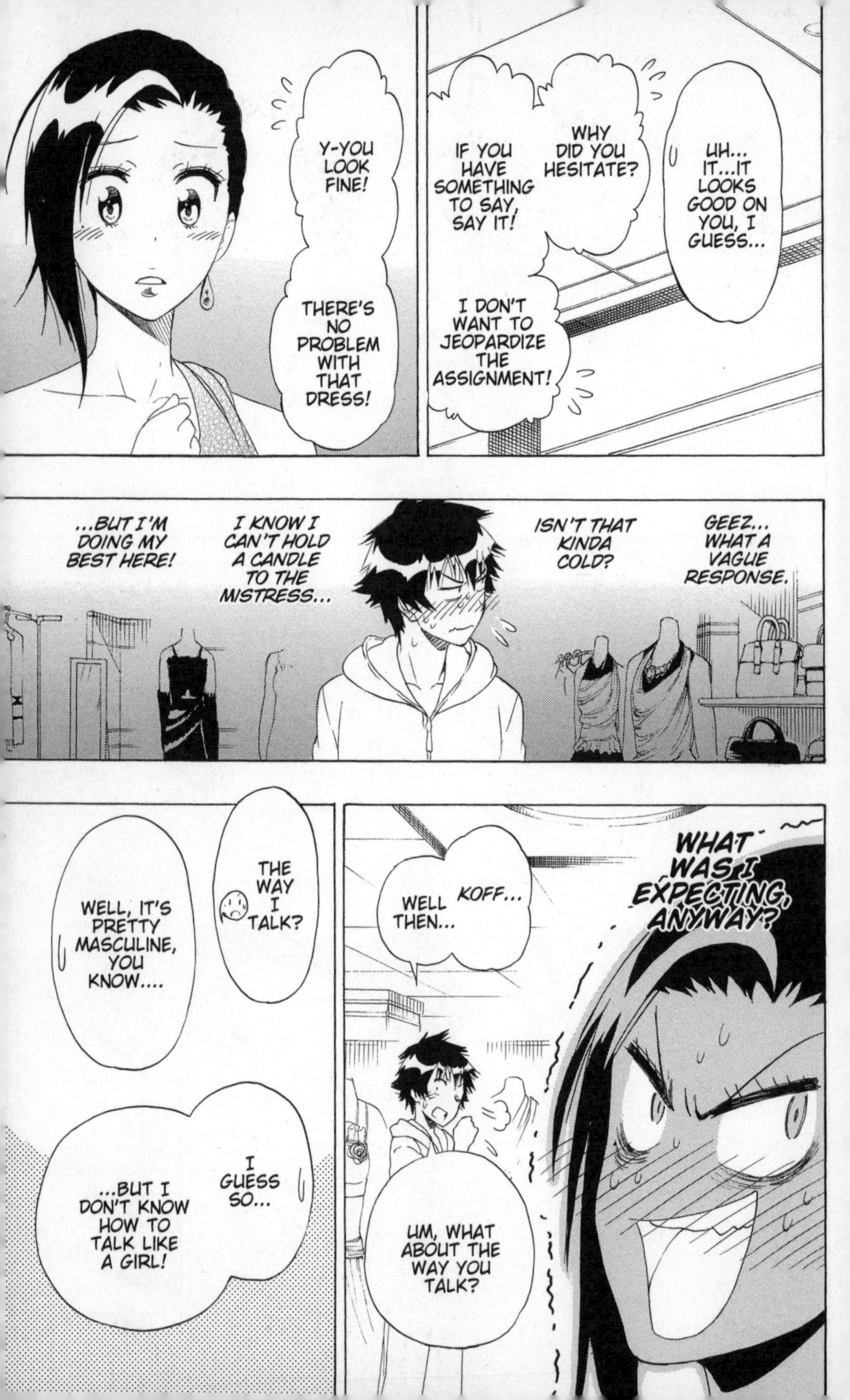
UH... IT...IT LOOKS GOOD ON YOU, I GUESS...
WHY DID YOU HESITATE?
IF YOU HAVE SOMETHING TO SAY, SAY IT!
I DON'T WANT TO JEOPARDIZE THE ASSIGNMENT!
Y-YOU LOOK FINE!
THERE'S NO PROBLEM WITH THAT DRESS!
GEEZ... WHAT A VAGUE RESPONSE.
ISN'T THAT KINDA COLD?
I KNOW I CAN'T HOLD A CANDLE TO THE MISTRESS...
...BUT I'M DOING MY BEST HERE!
WHAT WAS I EXPECTING, ANYWAY?
KOFF...
WELL THEN...
UM, WHAT ABOUT THE WAY YOU TALK?
THE WAY I TALK?
WELL, IT'S PRETTY MASCULINE, YOU KNOW....
I GUESS SO...
...BUT I DON'T KNOW HOW TO TALK LIKE A GIRL!

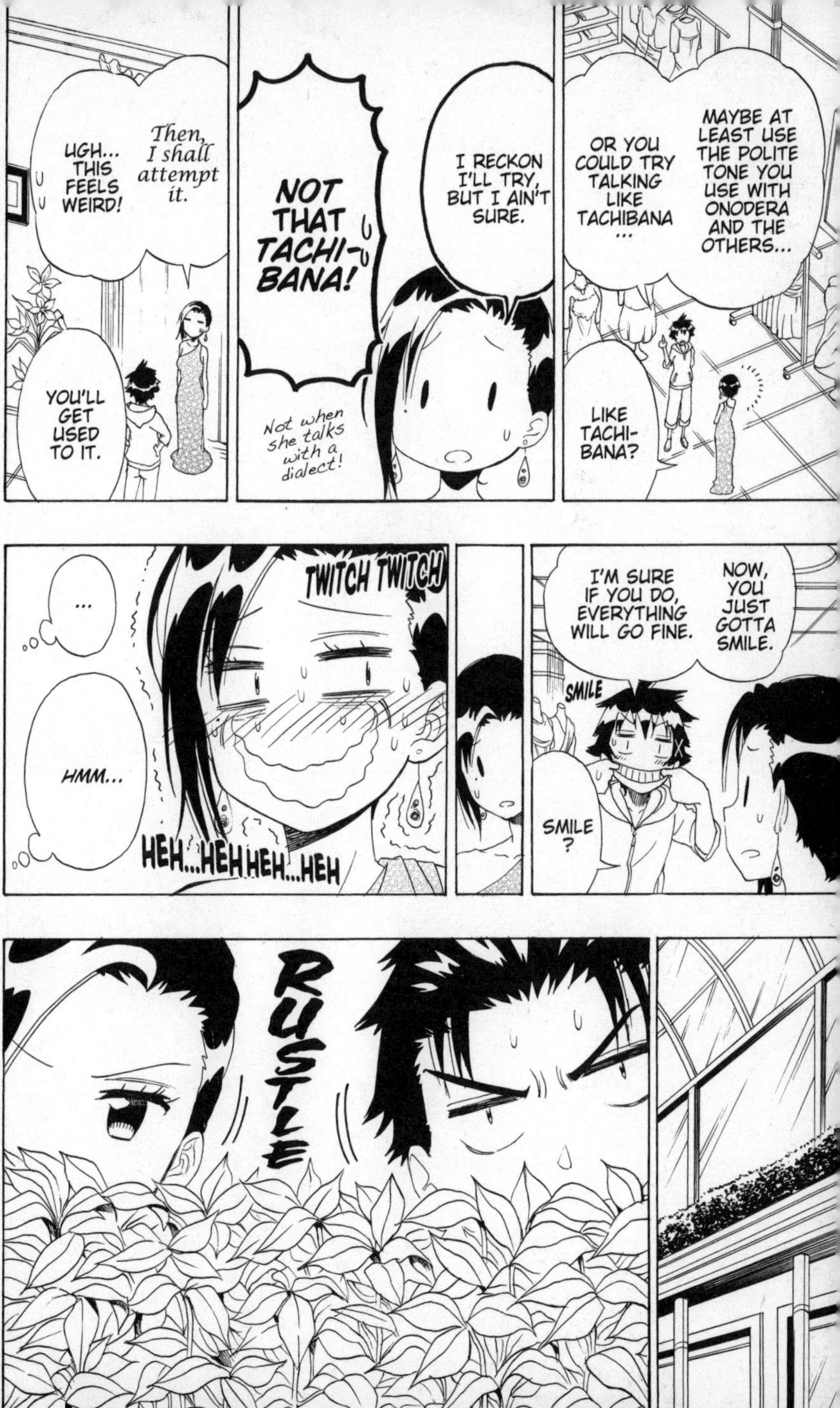
MAYBE AT LEAST USE THE POLITE TONE YOU USE WITH ONODERA AND THE OTHERS...
OR YOU COULD TRY TALKING LIKE TACHIBANA...
LIKE TACHIBANA?
I RECKON I'LL TRY, BUT I AIN'T SURE.
NOT THAT TACHIBANA!
Not when she talks with a dialect!
Then, I shall attempt it.
UGH... THIS FEELS WEIRD!
YOU'LL GET USED TO IT.
NOW, YOU JUST GOTTA SMILE.
I'M SURE IF YOU DO, EVERYTHING WILL GO FINE.
SMILE
SMILE?
TWITCH TWITCH
...
HMM...
HEH...HEH HEH...HEH
RUSTLE

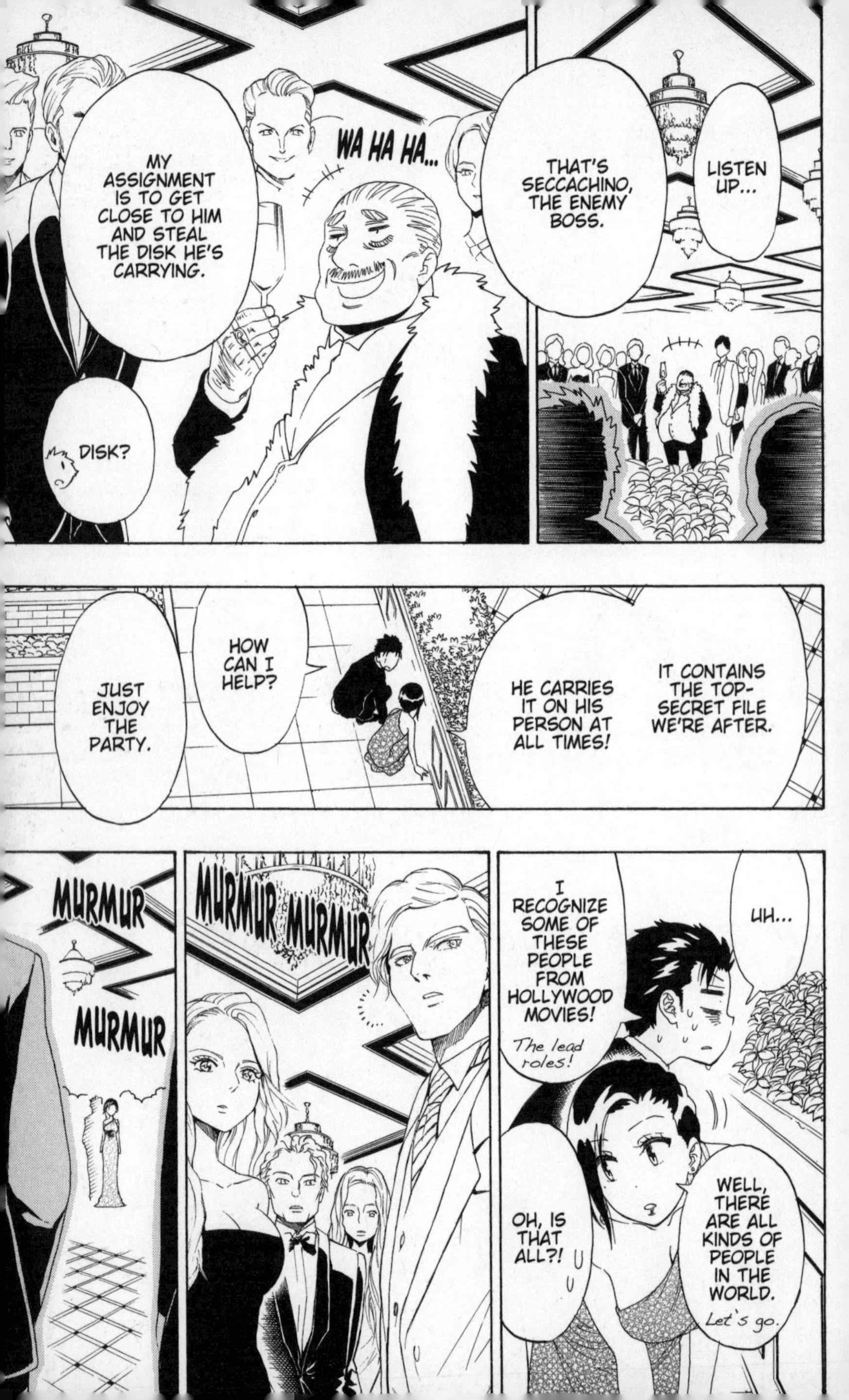

LISTEN UP...
THAT'S SECCACHINO, THE ENEMY BOSS.
WA HA HA...
MY ASSIGNMENT IS TO GET CLOSE TO HIM AND STEAL THE DISK HE'S CARRYING.
DISK?
IT CONTAINS THE TOP-SECRET FILE WE'RE AFTER.
HE CARRIES IT ON HIS PERSON AT ALL TIMES!
HOW CAN I HELP?
JUST ENJOY THE PARTY.
UH...
I RECOGNIZE SOME OF THESE PEOPLE FROM HOLLYWOOD MOVIES!
The lead roles!
WELL, THERE ARE ALL KINDS OF PEOPLE IN THE WORLD.
Let's go.
OH, IS THAT ALL?!
MURMUR MURMUR
MURMUR
MURMUR

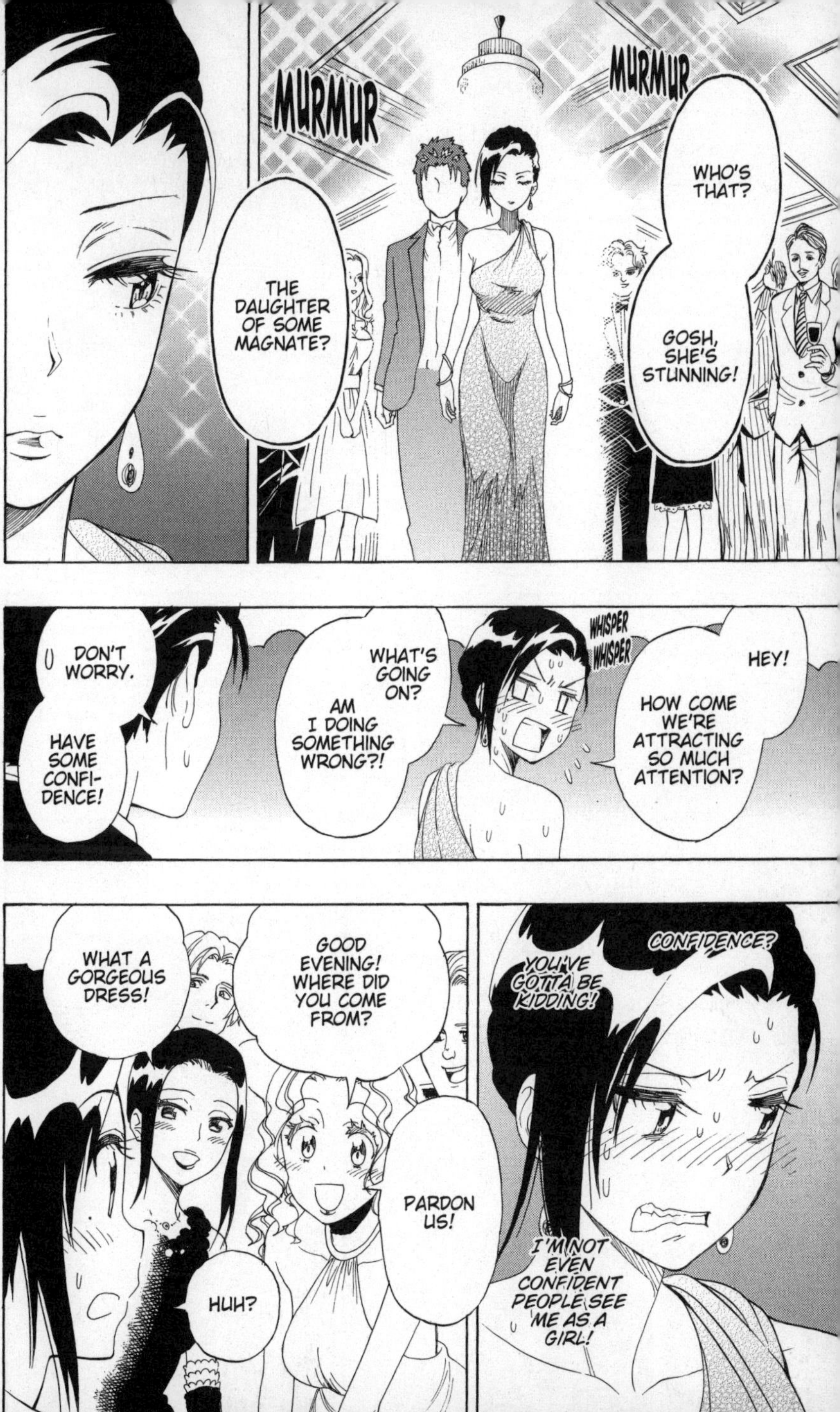
MURMUR
WHO'S THAT?
GOSH, SHE'S STUNNING!
MURMUR
THE DAUGHTER OF SOME MAGNATE?
HEY!
HOW COME WE'RE ATTRACTING SO MUCH ATTENTION?
WHISPER WHISPER
WHAT'S GOING ON?
AM I DOING SOMETHING WRONG?!
DON'T WORRY.
HAVE SOME CONFI-DENCE!
CONFIDENCE?
YOU'VE GOTTA BE KIDDING!
I'M NOT EVEN CONFIDENT PEOPLE SEE ME AS A GIRL!
GOOD EVENING! WHERE DID YOU COME FROM?
WHAT A GORGEOUS DRESS!
PARDON US!
HUH?

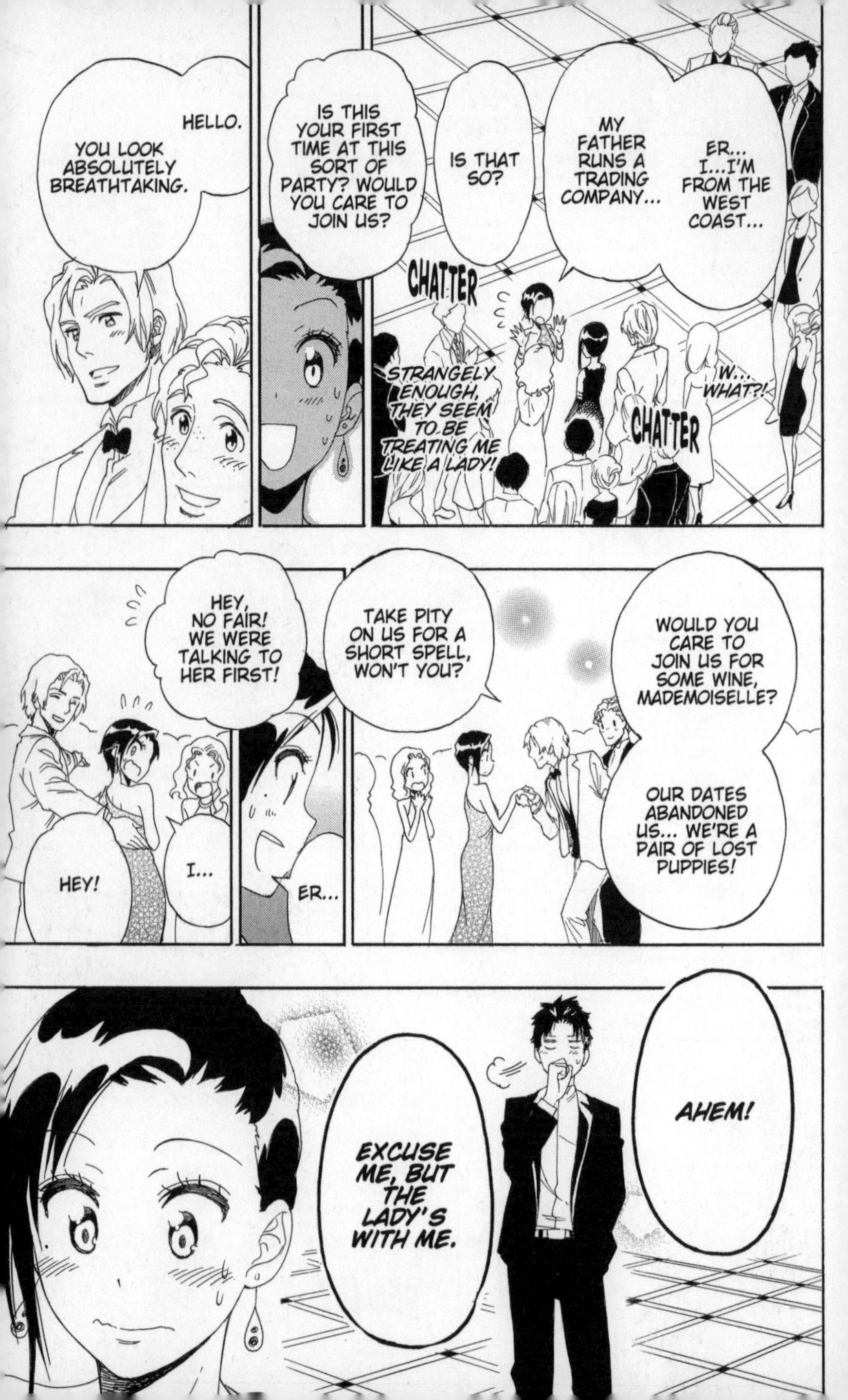
ER... I...I'M FROM THE WEST COAST...
MY FATHER RUNS A TRADING COMPANY...
IS THAT SO?
CHATTER
W... WHAT?!
STRANGELY ENOUGH, THEY SEEM TO BE TREATING ME LIKE A LADY!
CHATTER
IS THIS YOUR FIRST TIME AT THIS SORT OF PARTY? WOULD YOU CARE TO JOIN US?
HELLO.
YOU LOOK ABSOLUTELY BREATHTAKING.
WOULD YOU CARE TO JOIN US FOR SOME WINE, MADEMOISELLE?
OUR DATES ABANDONED US... WE'RE A PAIR OF LOST PUPPIES!
TAKE PITY ON US FOR A SHORT SPELL, WON'T YOU?
ER...
HEY, NO FAIR! WE WERE TALKING TO HER FIRST!
I...
HEY!
AHEM!
EXCUSE ME, BUT THE LADY'S WITH ME.

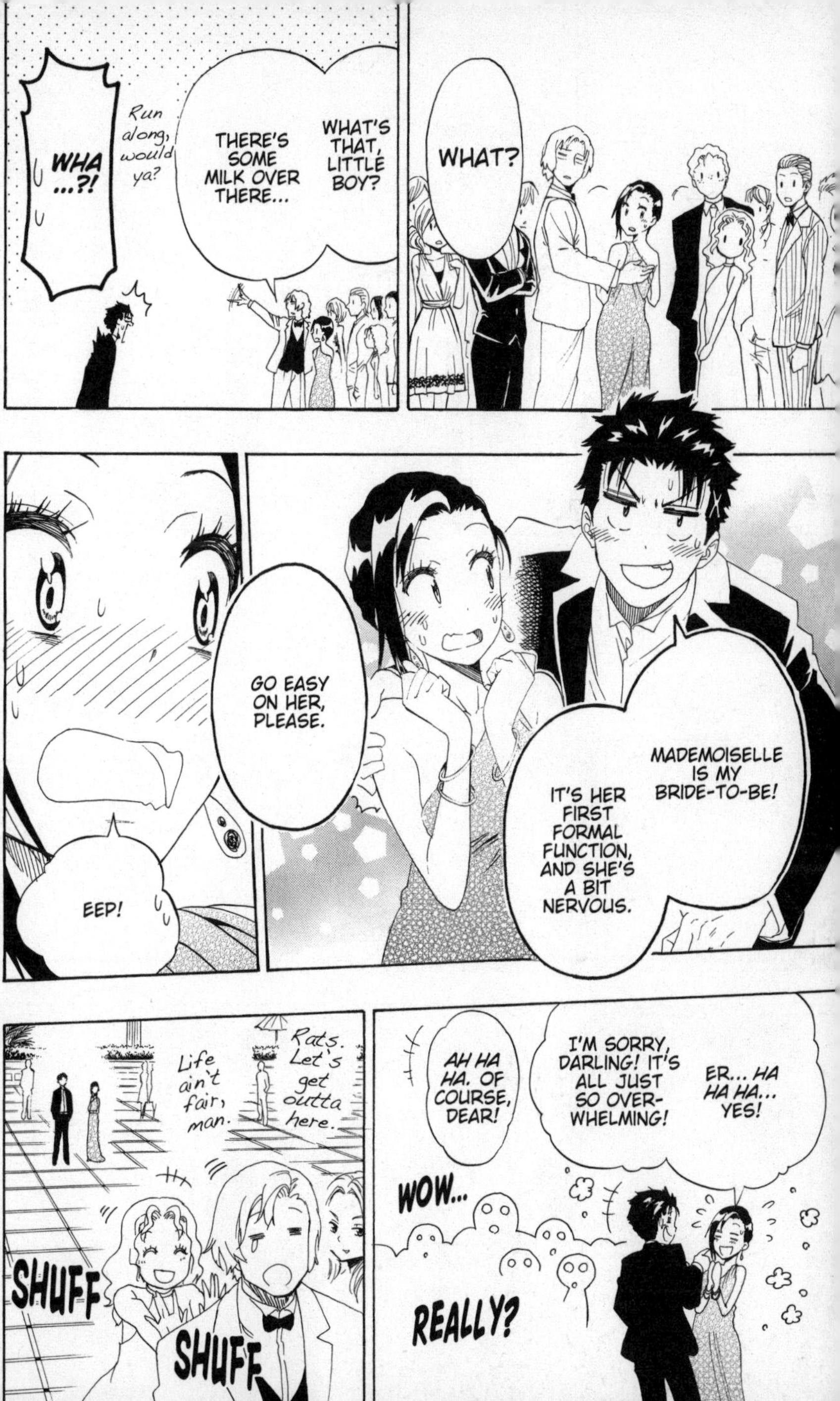
WHAT?
WHAT'S THAT, LITTLE BOY?
THERE'S SOME MILK OVER THERE...
Run along, would ya?
WHA...?!
MADEMOISELLE IS MY BRIDE-TO-BE!
IT'S HER FIRST FORMAL FUNCTION, AND SHE'S A BIT NERVOUS.
GO EASY ON HER, PLEASE.
EEP!
ER... HA HA HA... YES!
I'M SORRY, DARLING! IT'S ALL JUST SO OVER-WHELMING!
AH HA HA. OF COURSE, DEAR!
WOW...
REALLY?
Rats. Let's get outta here.
Life ain't fair, man.
SHUFF
SHUFF

THANKS.
YOU SAVED ME BACK THERE.
DON'T MENTION IT.
GEEZ, I WAS NERVOUS!
IT'S LIKE PLAYING ROMEO AGAIN!
I'm flashing back to the school festival!
I DIDN'T EXPECT SO MUCH ATTENTION...
B-BMP
B-BMP
SIGH
I GUESS MEN WILL HIT ON ANY FEMALE THEY SEE...
HUH?
THAT'S NOT TRUE.
IT'S JUST EVIDENCE OF HOW ATTRACTIVE YOU LOOK.
LIKE I SAID, YOU SHOULD HAVE MORE CONFIDENCE!
It's weird if you don't!
ATTRACTIVE?
Huh?
ME?
Where'd the boss go?

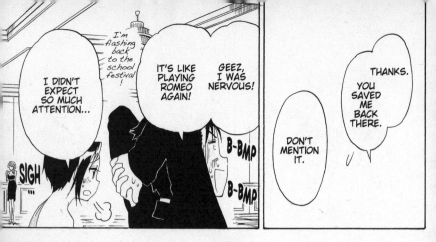

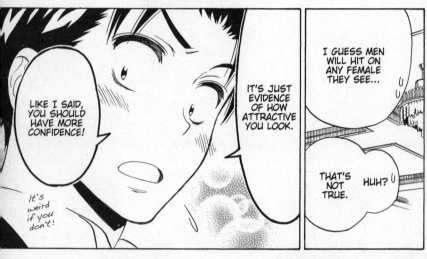

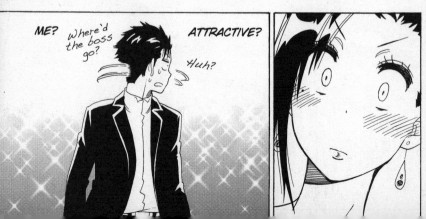

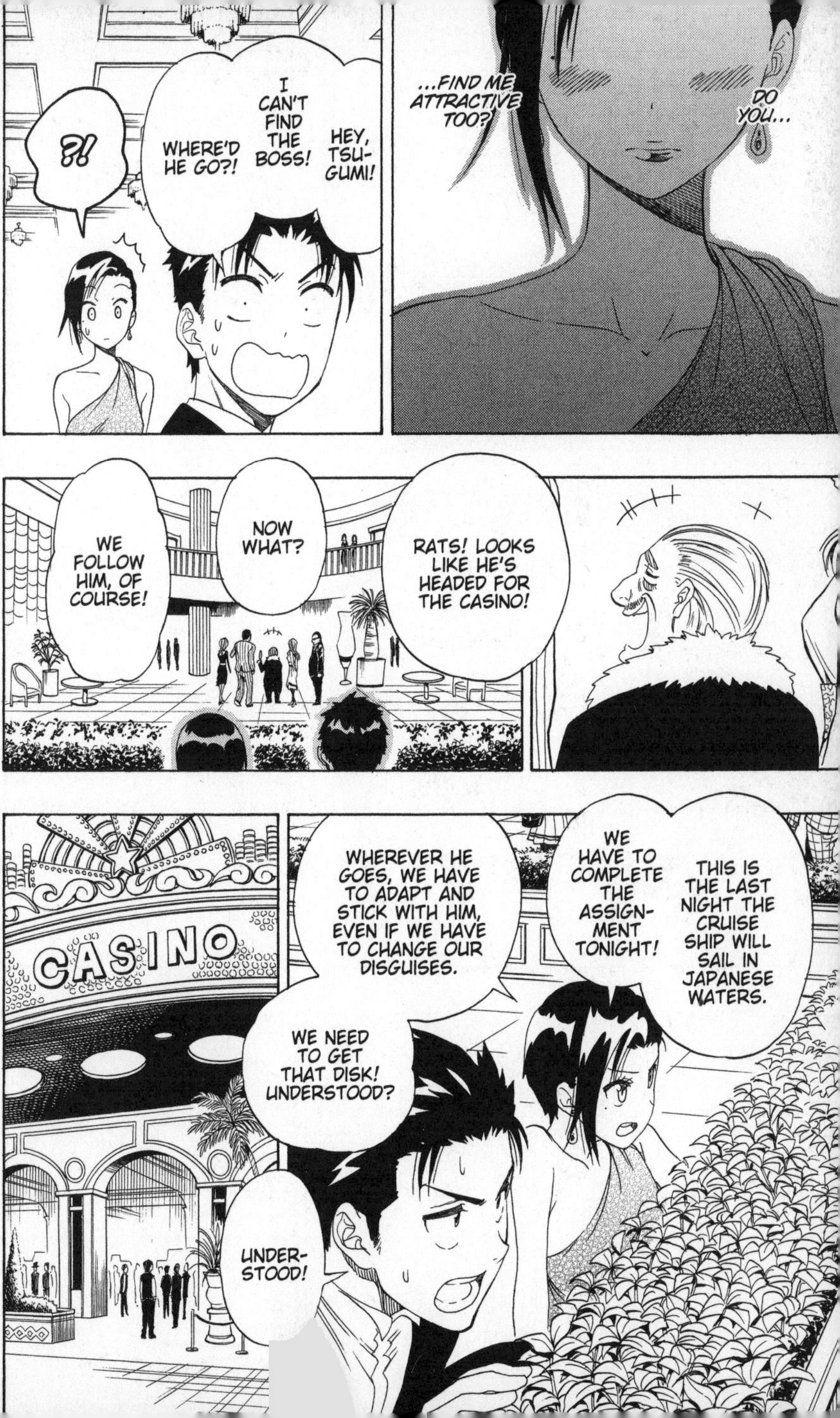
DO YOU...
...FIND ME ATTRACTIVE TOO?
HEY, TSU-GUMI!
I CAN'T FIND THE BOSS!
WHERE'D HE GO?!
?!
RATS! LOOKS LIKE HE'S HEADED FOR THE CASINO!
NOW WHAT?
WE FOLLOW HIM, OF COURSE!
THIS IS THE LAST NIGHT THE CRUISE SHIP WILL SAIL IN JAPANESE WATERS.
WE HAVE TO COMPLETE THE ASSIGN-MENT TONIGHT!
WHEREVER HE GOES, WE HAVE TO ADAPT AND STICK WITH HIM, EVEN IF WE HAVE TO CHANGE OUR DISGUISES.
WE NEED TO GET THAT DISK! UNDERSTOOD?
UNDER-STOOD!
CASINO

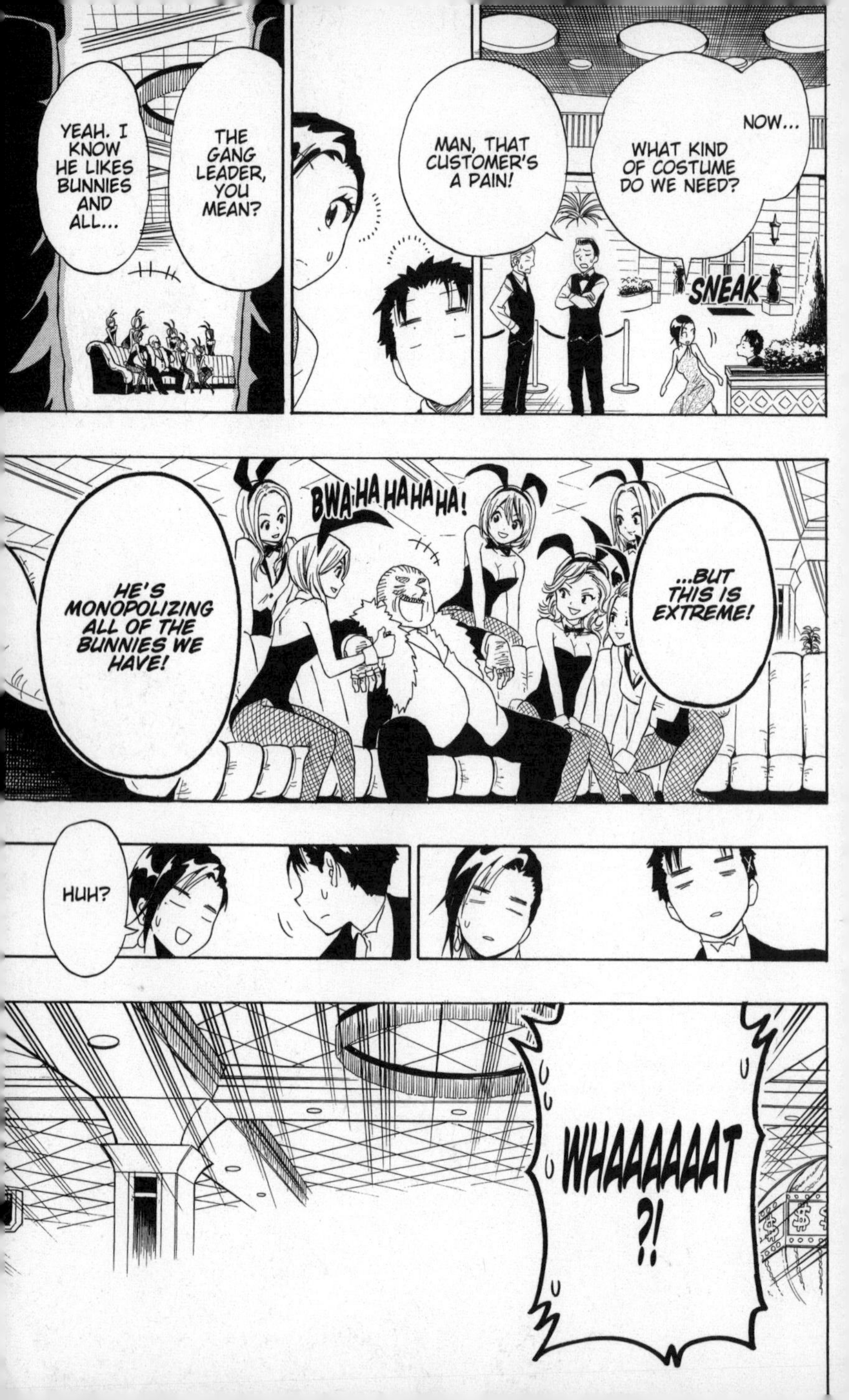
NOW...
WHAT KIND OF COSTUME DO WE NEED?
MAN, THAT CUSTOMER'S A PAIN!
SNEAK
THE GANG LEADER, YOU MEAN?
YEAH. I KNOW HE LIKES BUNNIES AND ALL...
BWAHAHAHAHA!
...BUT THIS IS EXTREME!
HE'S MONOPOLIZING ALL OF THE BUNNIES WE HAVE!
HUH?
WHAAAAAAT ?!

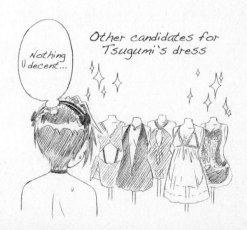

Other candidates for Tsugumi's dress
Nothing decent...

Chapter 125: Girls Are...

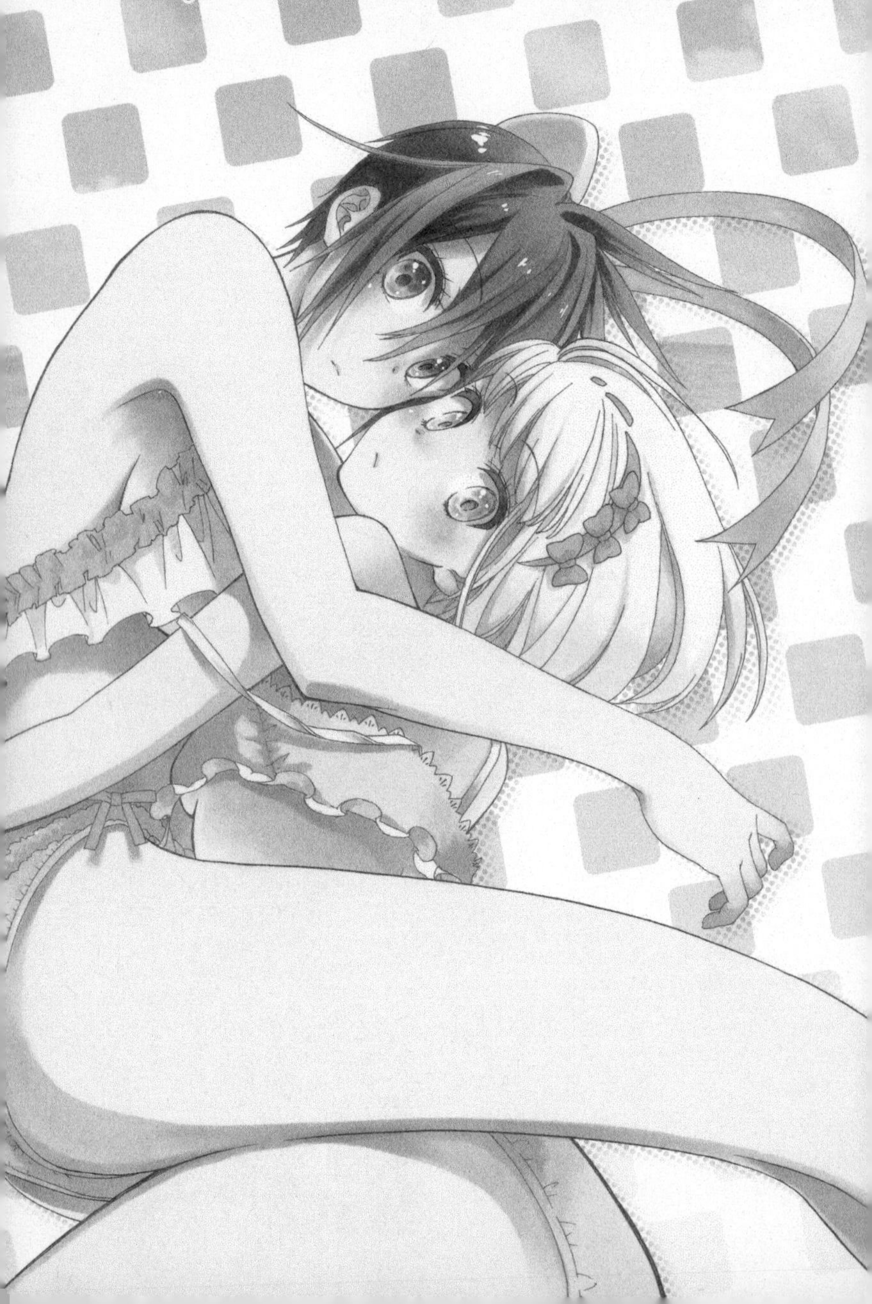

NISEKOI
False Love

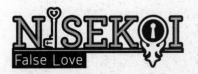

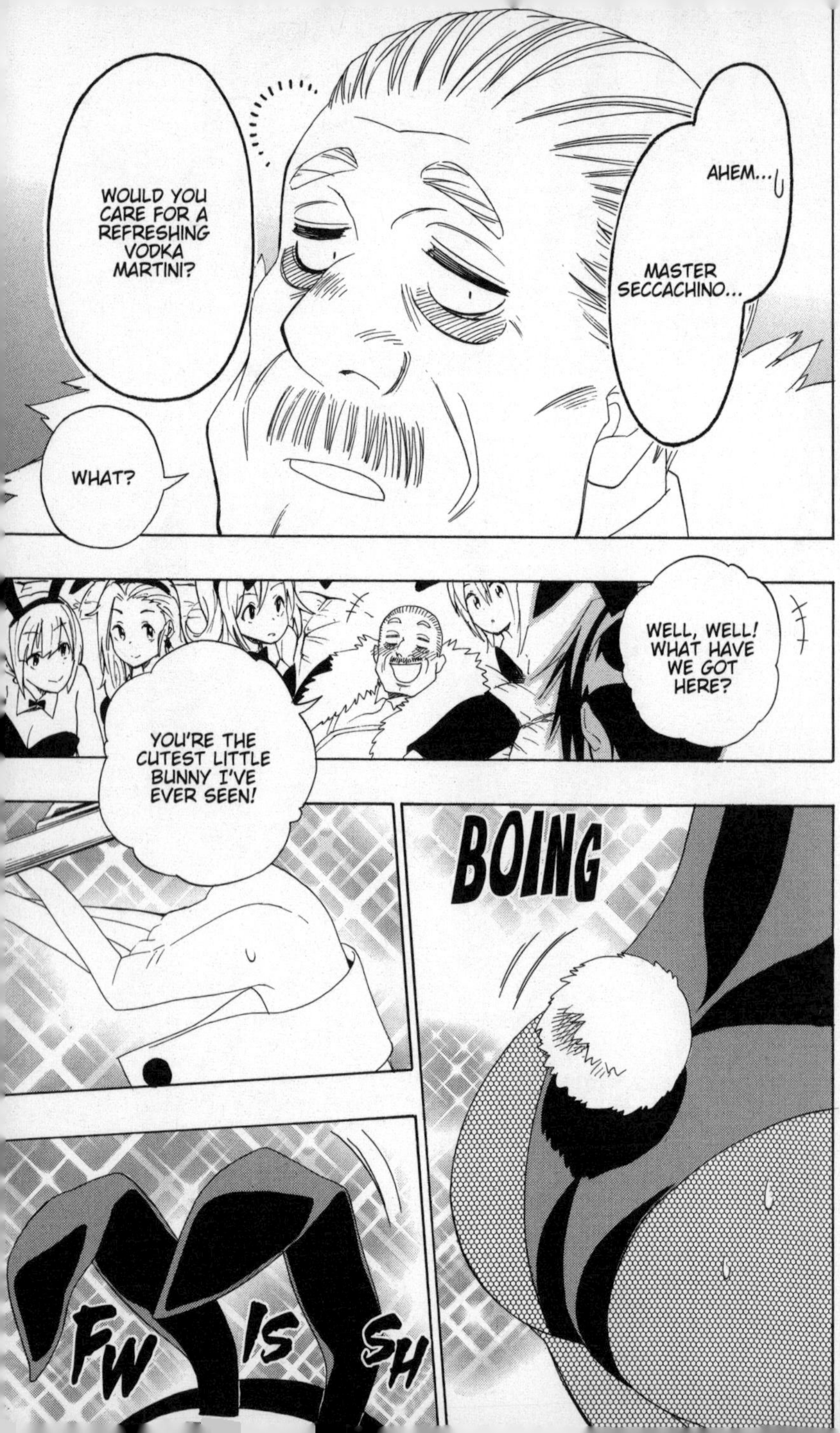
AHEM...
MASTER SECCACHINO...
WOULD YOU CARE FOR A REFRESHING VODKA MARTINI?
WHAT?
WELL, WELL! WHAT HAVE WE GOT HERE?
YOU'RE THE CUTEST LITTLE BUNNY I'VE EVER SEEN!
BOING
FW IS SH

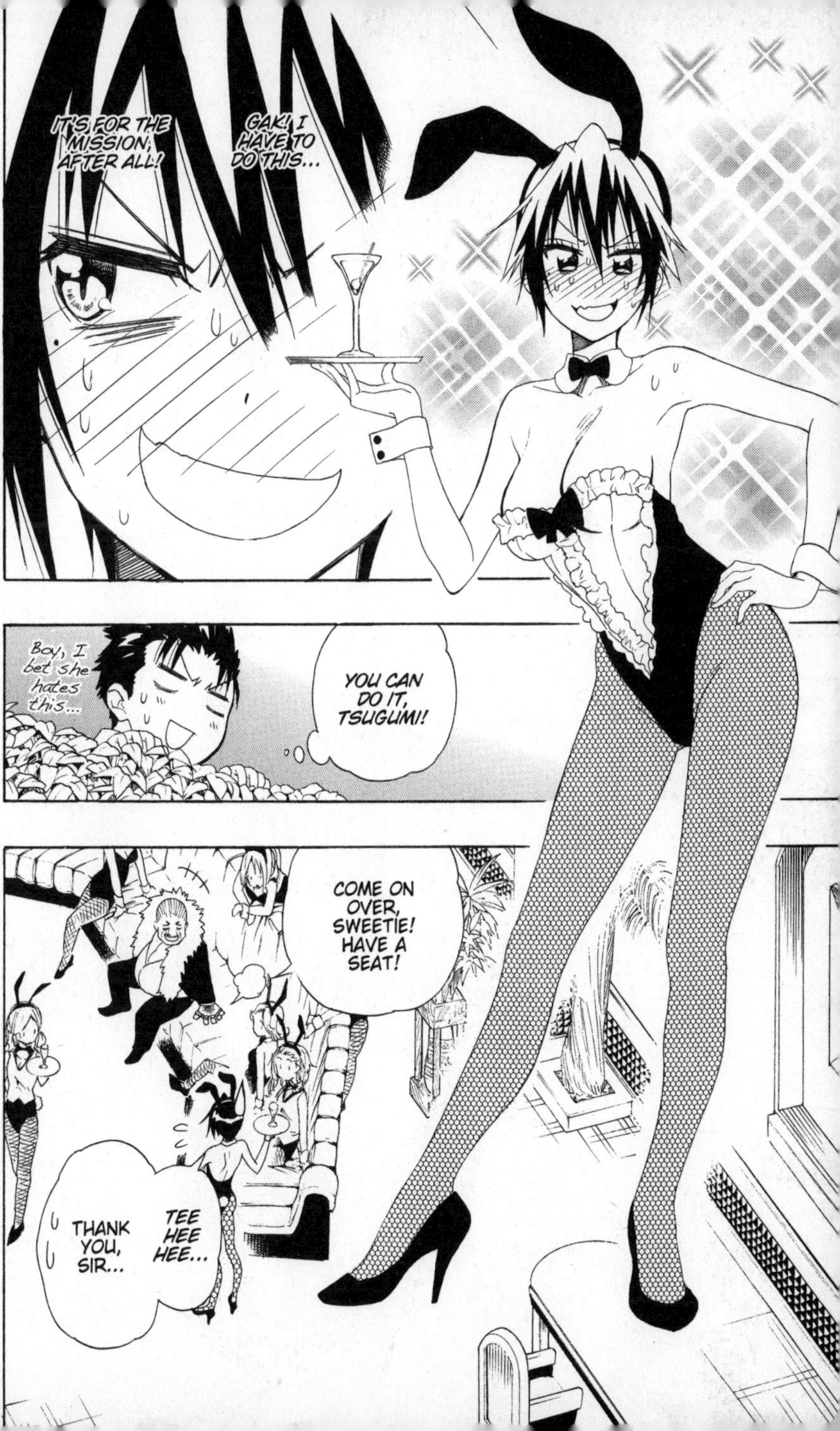
GAK! I HAVE TO DO THIS...
IT'S FOR THE MISSION, AFTER ALL!
YOU CAN DO IT, TSUGUMI!
Boy, I bet she hates this...
COME ON OVER, SWEETIE! HAVE A SEAT!
TEE HEE HEE...
THANK YOU, SIR...

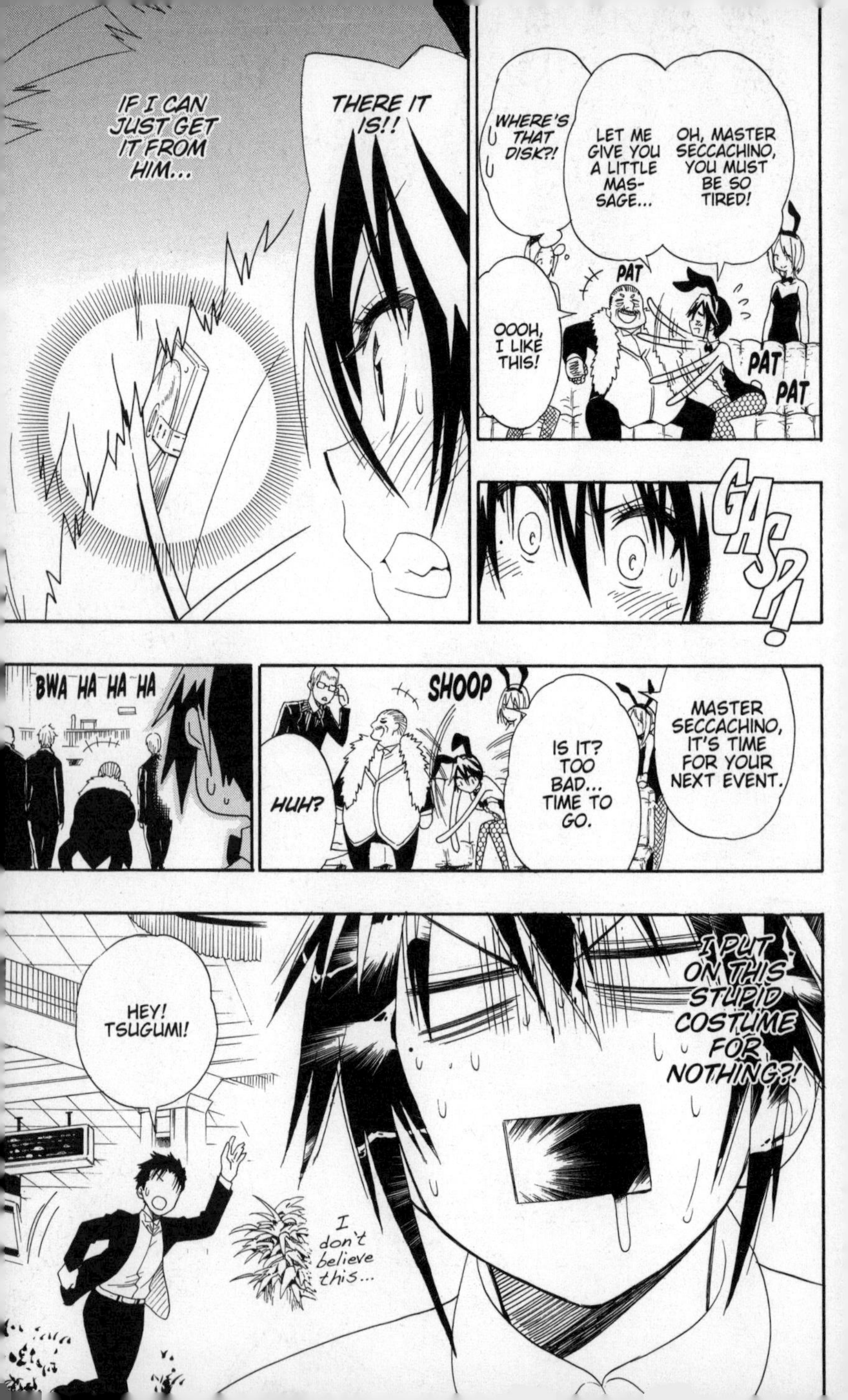
OH, MASTER SECCACHINO, YOU MUST BE SO TIRED!
LET ME GIVE YOU A LITTLE MAS-SAGE...
WHERE'S THAT DISK?!
PAT
OOOH, I LIKE THIS!
PAT PAT
GASP!
THERE IT IS!!
IF I CAN JUST GET IT FROM HIM...
MASTER SECCACHINO, IT'S TIME FOR YOUR NEXT EVENT.
SHOOP
IS IT? TOO BAD... TIME TO GO.
HUH?
BWA HA HA HA
I PUT ON THIS STUPID COSTUME FOR NOTHING?!
HEY! TSUGUMI!
I don't believe this...

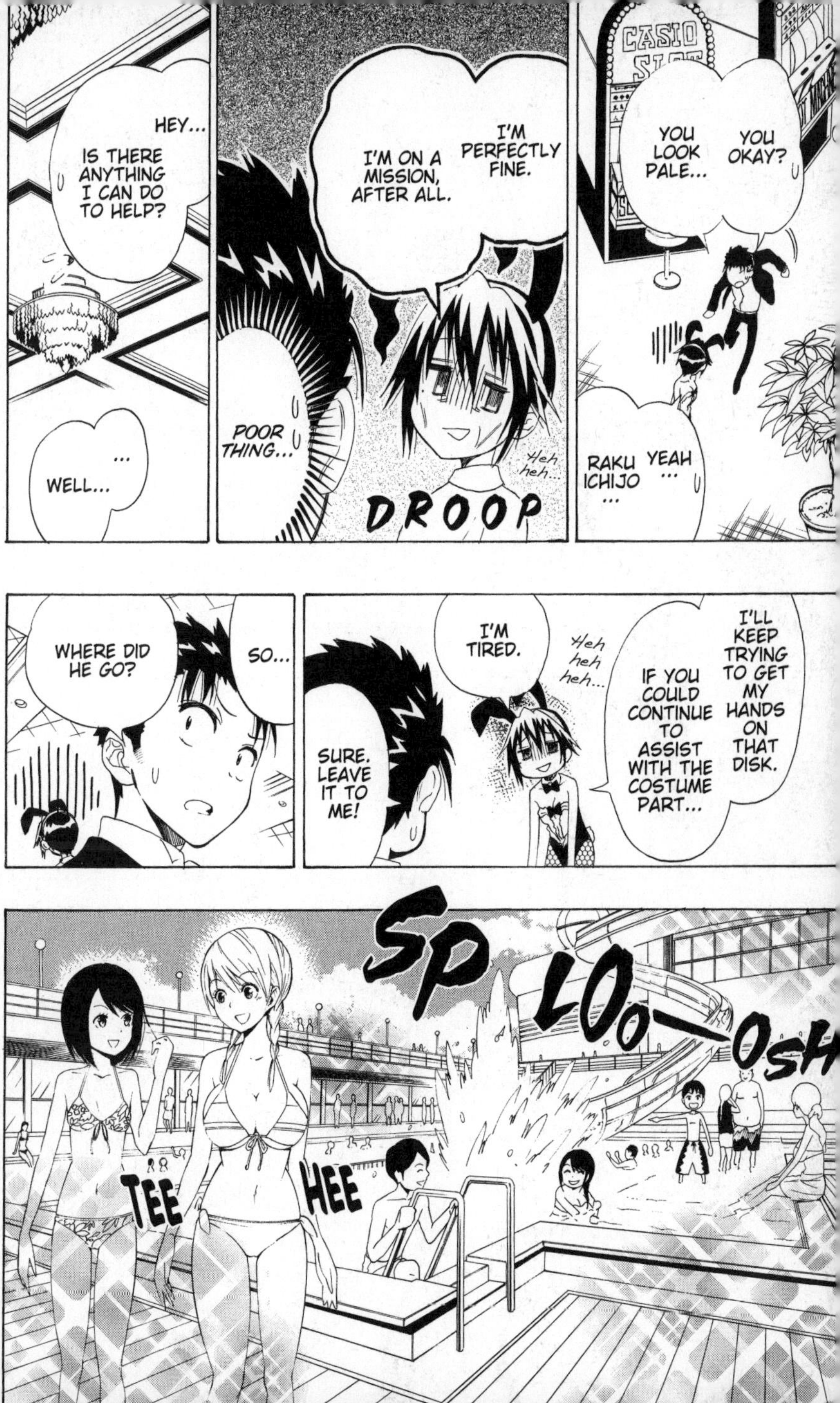
YOU OKAY?
YOU LOOK PALE...
YEAH...
RAKU ICHIJO...
I'M PERFECTLY FINE.
I'M ON A MISSION, AFTER ALL.
Heh heh...
DROOP
POOR THING...
HEY...
IS THERE ANYTHING I CAN DO TO HELP?
... WELL...
I'LL KEEP TRYING TO GET MY HANDS ON THAT DISK.
IF YOU COULD CONTINUE TO ASSIST WITH THE COSTUME PART...
Heh heh heh...
I'M TIRED.
SURE. LEAVE IT TO ME!
SO...
WHERE DID HE GO?
SPLOO—OSH
TEE HEE

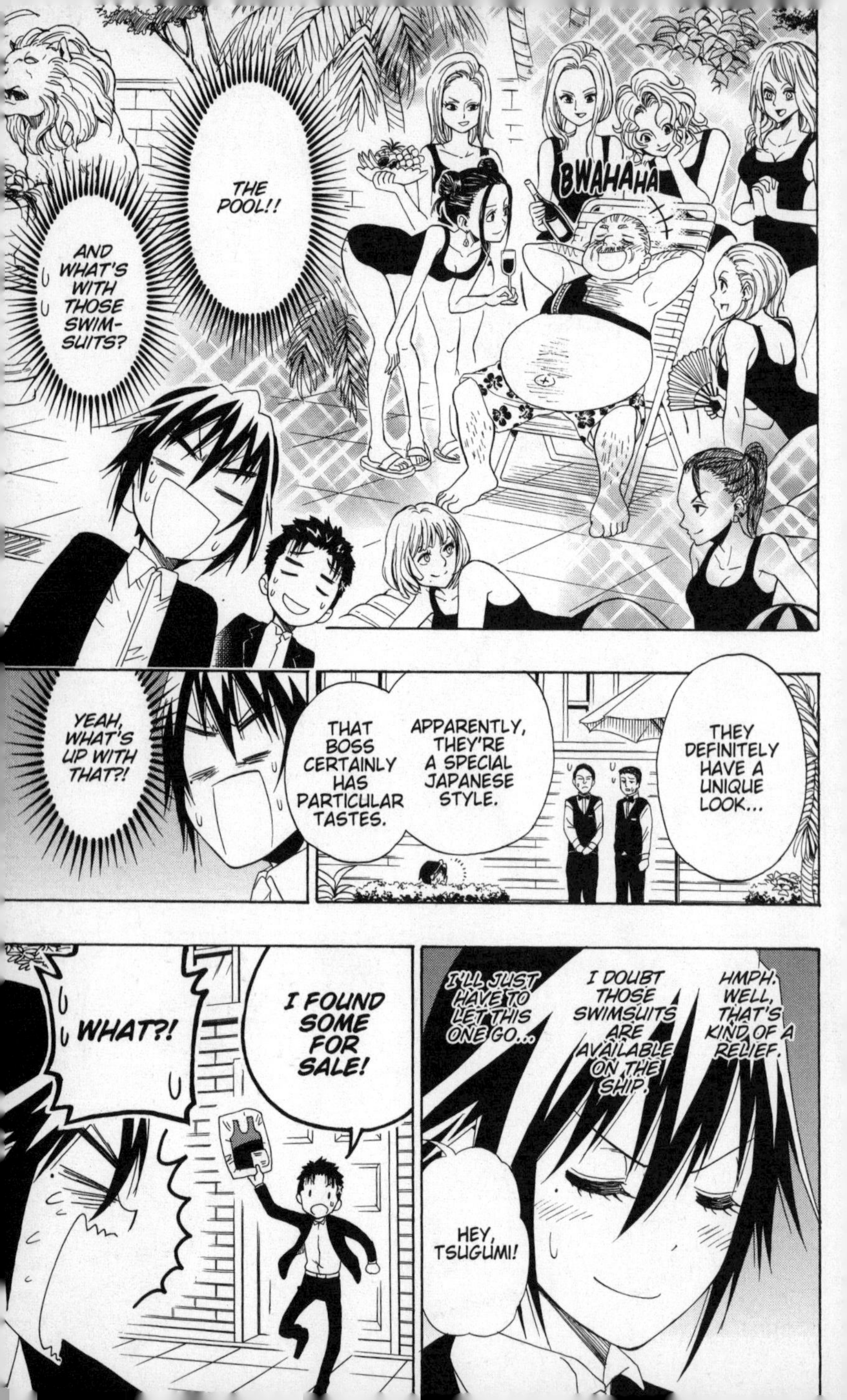
BWAHAHA
THE POOL!!
AND WHAT'S WITH THOSE SWIM-SUITS?
THEY DEFINITELY HAVE A UNIQUE LOOK...
APPARENTLY, THEY'RE A SPECIAL JAPANESE STYLE.
THAT BOSS CERTAINLY HAS PARTICULAR TASTES.
YEAH, WHAT'S UP WITH THAT?!
HMPH. WELL, THAT'S KIND OF A RELIEF.
I DOUBT THOSE SWIMSUITS ARE AVAILABLE ON THE SHIP.
I'LL JUST HAVE TO LET THIS ONE GO...
HEY, TSUGUMI!
I FOUND SOME FOR SALE!
WHAT?!

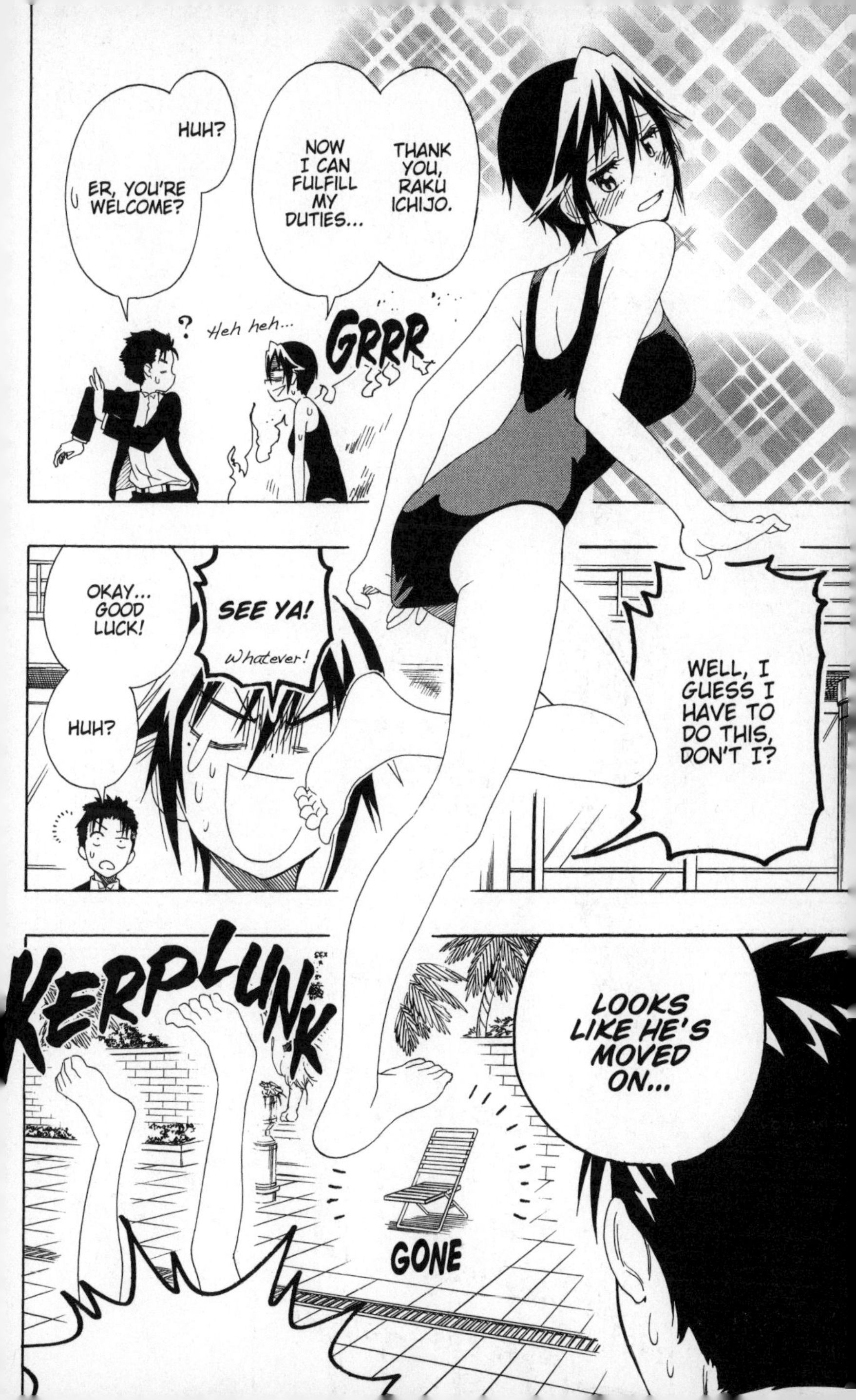
THANK YOU, RAKU ICHIJO.
NOW I CAN FULFILL MY DUTIES...
GRRR
Heh heh...
HUH?
ER, YOU'RE WELCOME?
WELL, I GUESS I HAVE TO DO THIS, DON'T I?
SEE YA!
Whatever!
OKAY... GOOD LUCK!
HUH?
LOOKS LIKE HE'S MOVED ON...
GONE
KERPLUNK

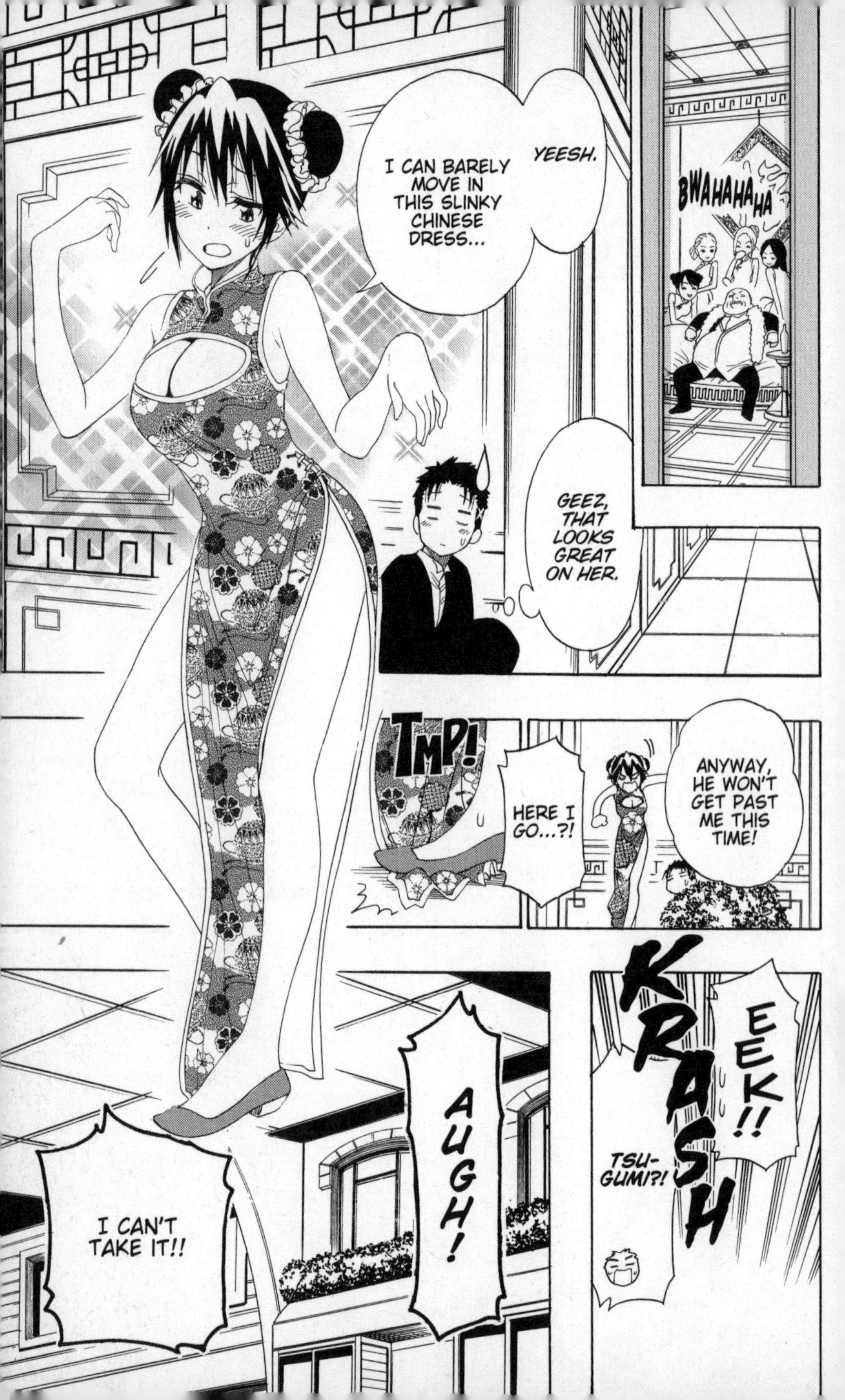
BWAHAHAHA
YEESH.
I CAN BARELY MOVE IN THIS SLINKY CHINESE DRESS...
GEEZ, THAT LOOKS GREAT ON HER.
ANYWAY, HE WON'T GET PAST ME THIS TIME!
HERE I GO...?!
TMP!
KRASH
EEK!!
TSU-GUMI?!
AUGH!
I CAN'T TAKE IT!!

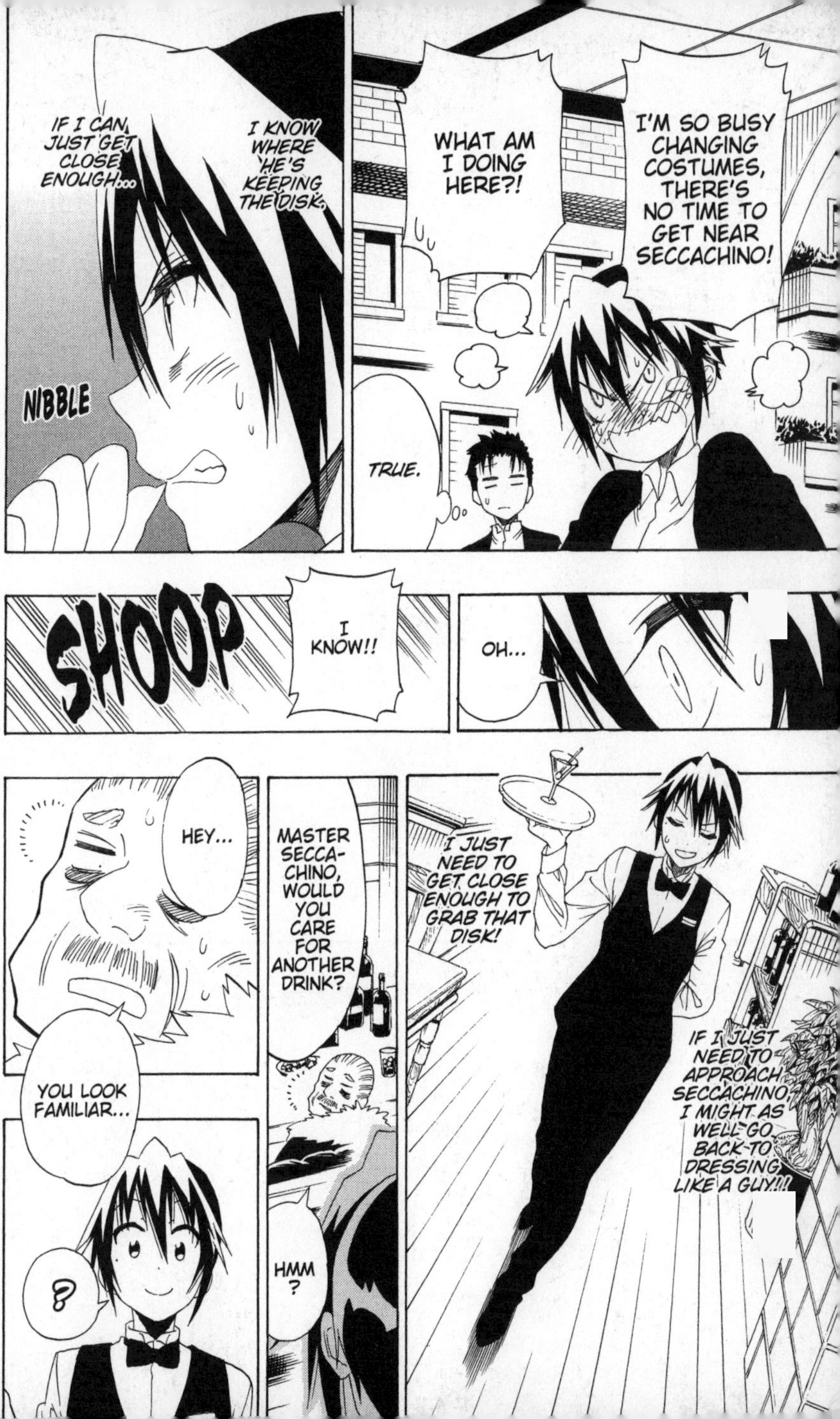

I'M SO BUSY CHANGING COSTUMES, THERE'S NO TIME TO GET NEAR SECCACHINO!
WHAT AM I DOING HERE?!
TRUE.
I KNOW WHERE HE'S KEEPING THE DISK.
IF I CAN JUST GET CLOSE ENOUGH...
NIBBLE
OH...
I KNOW!!
SHOOP
IF I JUST NEED TO APPROACH SECCACHINO, I MIGHT AS WELL GO BACK TO DRESSING LIKE A GUY!!
I JUST NEED TO GET CLOSE ENOUGH TO GRAB THAT DISK!
MASTER SECCACHINO, WOULD YOU CARE FOR ANOTHER DRINK?
HMM?
HEY...
YOU LOOK FAMILIAR...
?

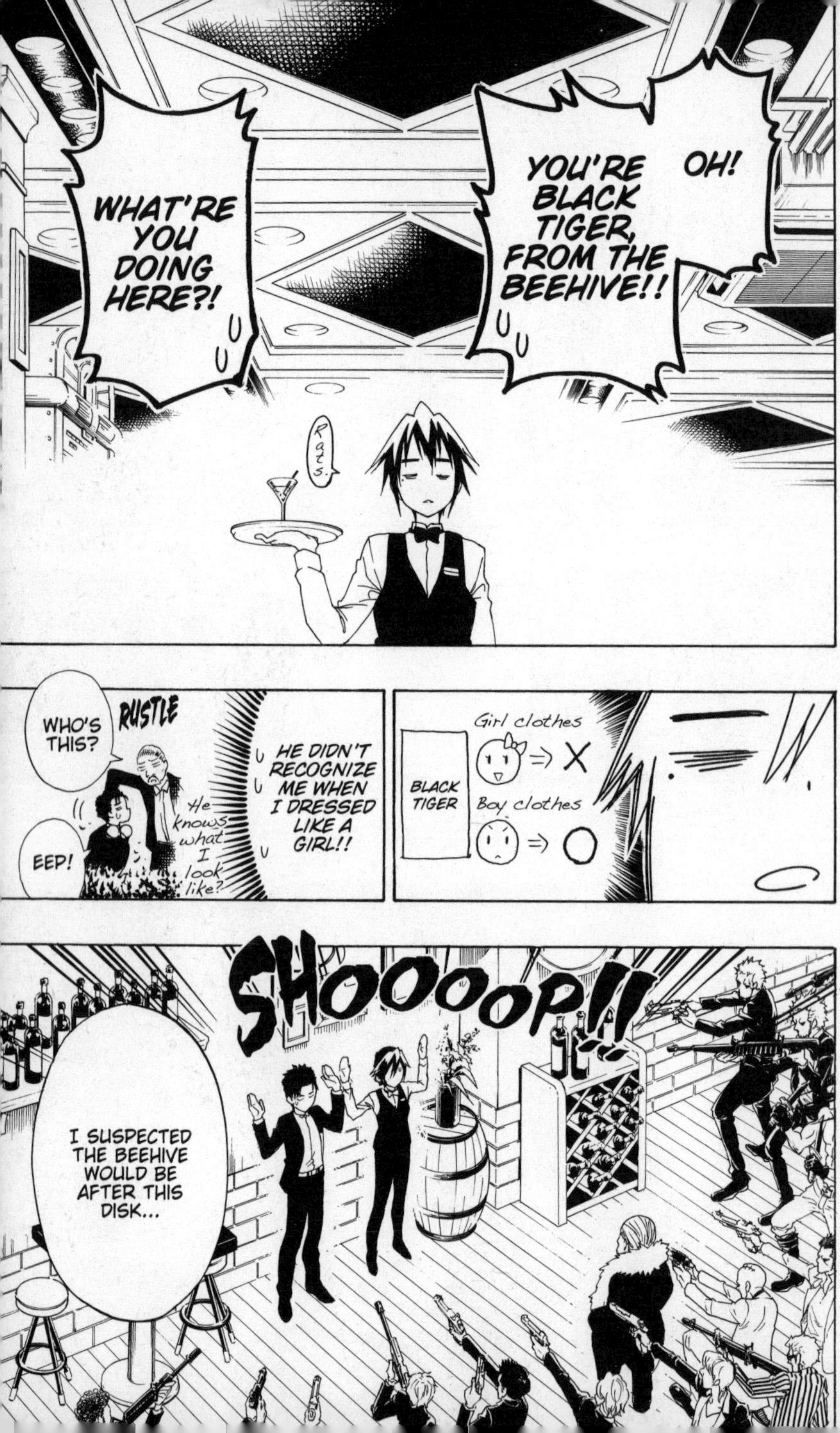
OH!
YOU'RE BLACK TIGER, FROM THE BEEHIVE!!
WHAT'RE YOU DOING HERE?!
Rats.
BLACK TIGER
Girl clothes
Boy clothes
HE DIDN'T RECOGNIZE ME WHEN I DRESSED LIKE A GIRL!!
He knows what I look like?
RUSTLE
WHO'S THIS?
EEP!
SHOOOOP!!
I SUSPECTED THE BEEHIVE WOULD BE AFTER THIS DISK...

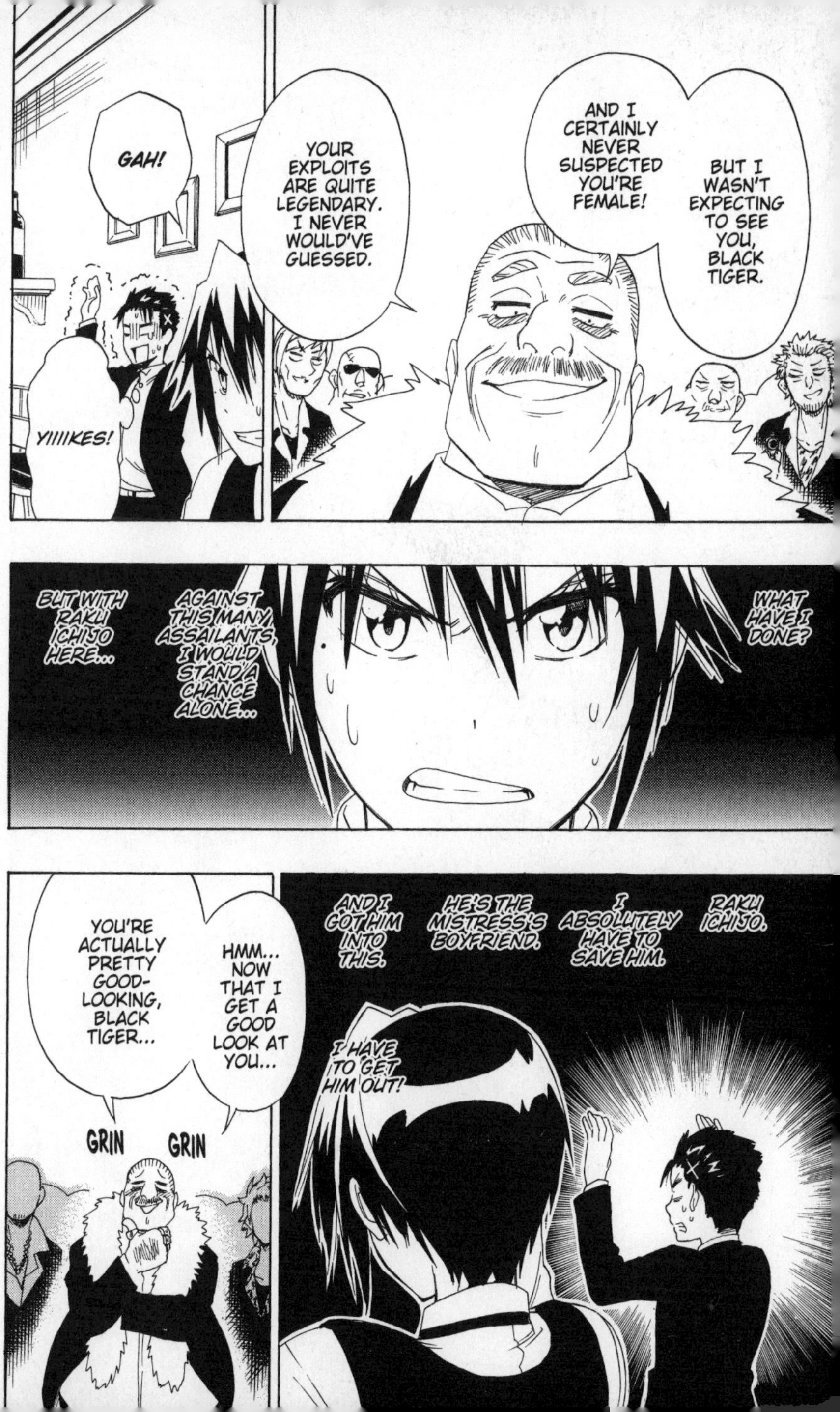

BUT I WASN'T EXPECTING TO SEE YOU, BLACK TIGER.
AND I CERTAINLY NEVER SUSPECTED YOU'RE FEMALE!
YOUR EXPLOITS ARE QUITE LEGENDARY. I NEVER WOULD'VE GUESSED.
GAH!
YIIIIKES!
WHAT HAVE I DONE?
AGAINST THIS MANY ASSAILANTS, I WOULD STAND A CHANCE ALONE...
BUT WITH RAKU ICHIJO HERE...
RAKU ICHIJO.
I ABSOLUTELY HAVE TO SAVE HIM.
HE'S THE MISTRESS'S BOYFRIEND.
AND I GOT HIM INTO THIS.
I HAVE TO GET HIM OUT!
HMM... NOW THAT I GET A GOOD LOOK AT YOU...
YOU'RE ACTUALLY PRETTY GOOD-LOOKING, BLACK TIGER...
GRIN
GRIN

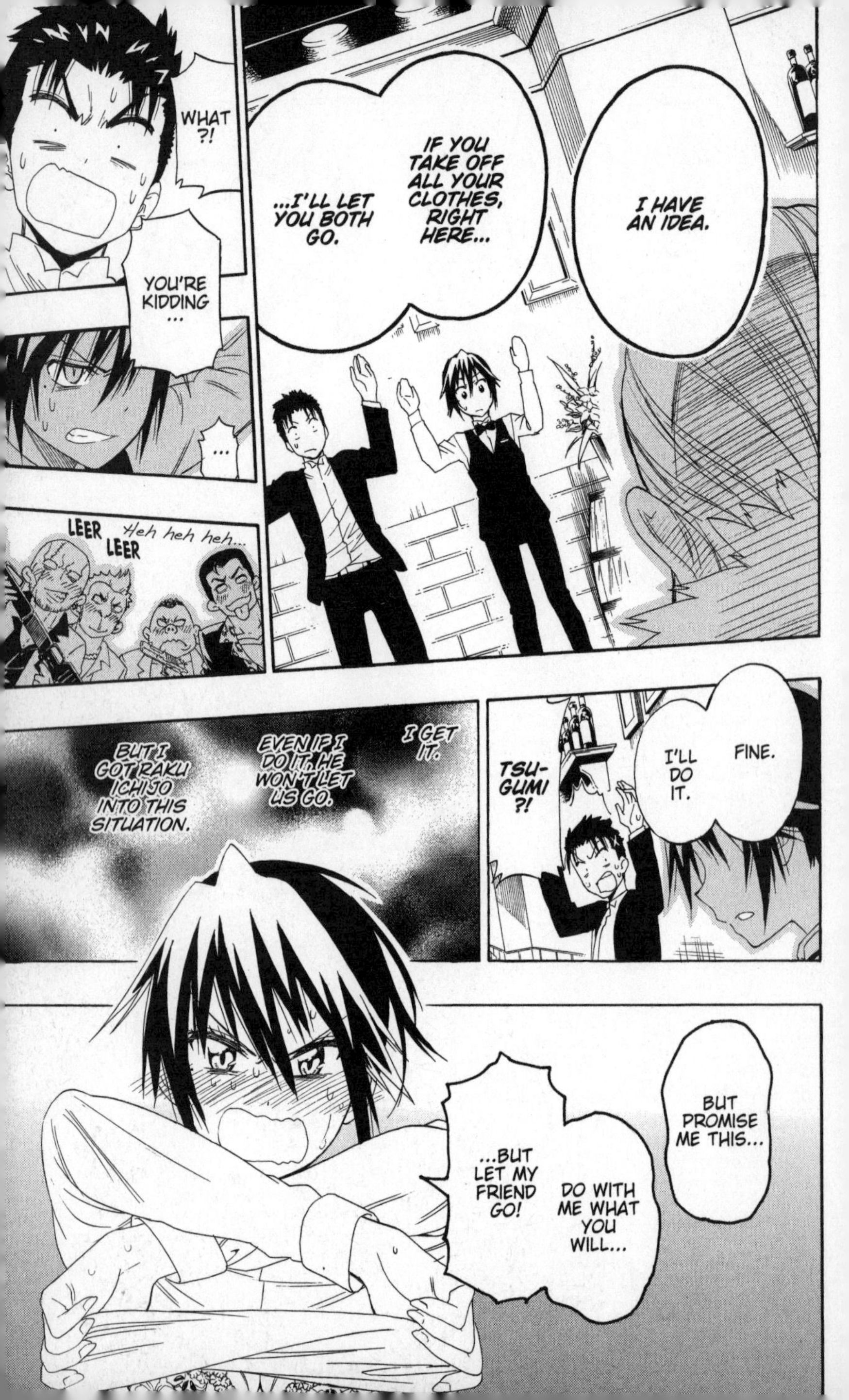
I HAVE AN IDEA.
IF YOU TAKE OFF ALL YOUR CLOTHES, RIGHT HERE...
...I'LL LET YOU BOTH GO.
WHAT?!
YOU'RE KIDDING...
...
LEER
LEER
Heh heh heh...
FINE.
I'LL DO IT.
TSU-GUMI?!
I GET IT.
EVEN IF I DO IT, HE WON'T LET US GO.
BUT I GOT RAKU ICHIJO INTO THIS SITUATION.
BUT PROMISE ME THIS...
DO WITH ME WHAT YOU WILL...
...BUT LET MY FRIEND GO!

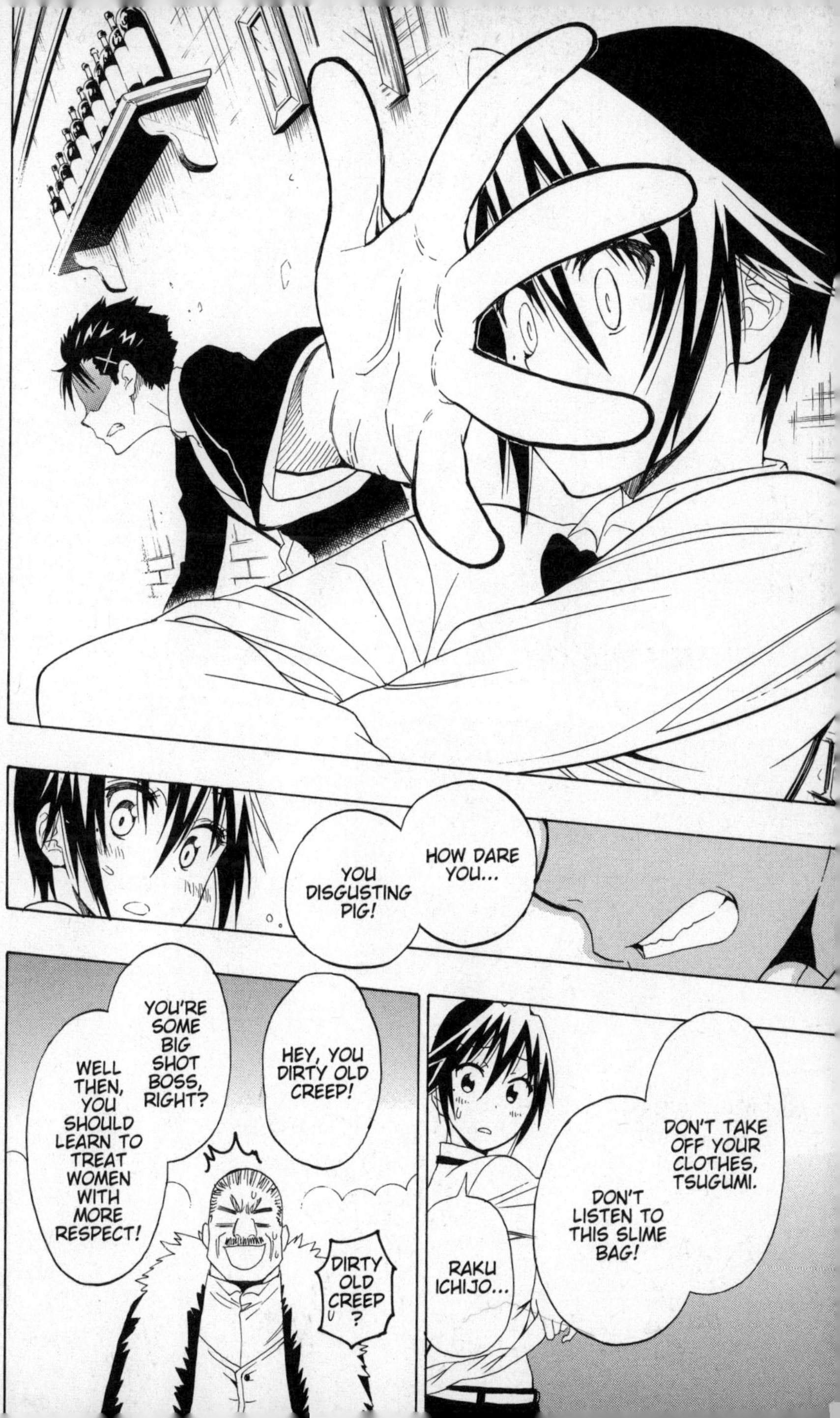
HOW DARE YOU...
YOU DISGUSTING PIG!
DON'T TAKE OFF YOUR CLOTHES, TSUGUMI.
DON'T LISTEN TO THIS SLIME BAG!
RAKU ICHIJO...
HEY, YOU DIRTY OLD CREEP!
YOU'RE SOME BIG SHOT BOSS, RIGHT?
WELL THEN, YOU SHOULD LEARN TO TREAT WOMEN WITH MORE RESPECT!
DIRTY OLD CREEP?

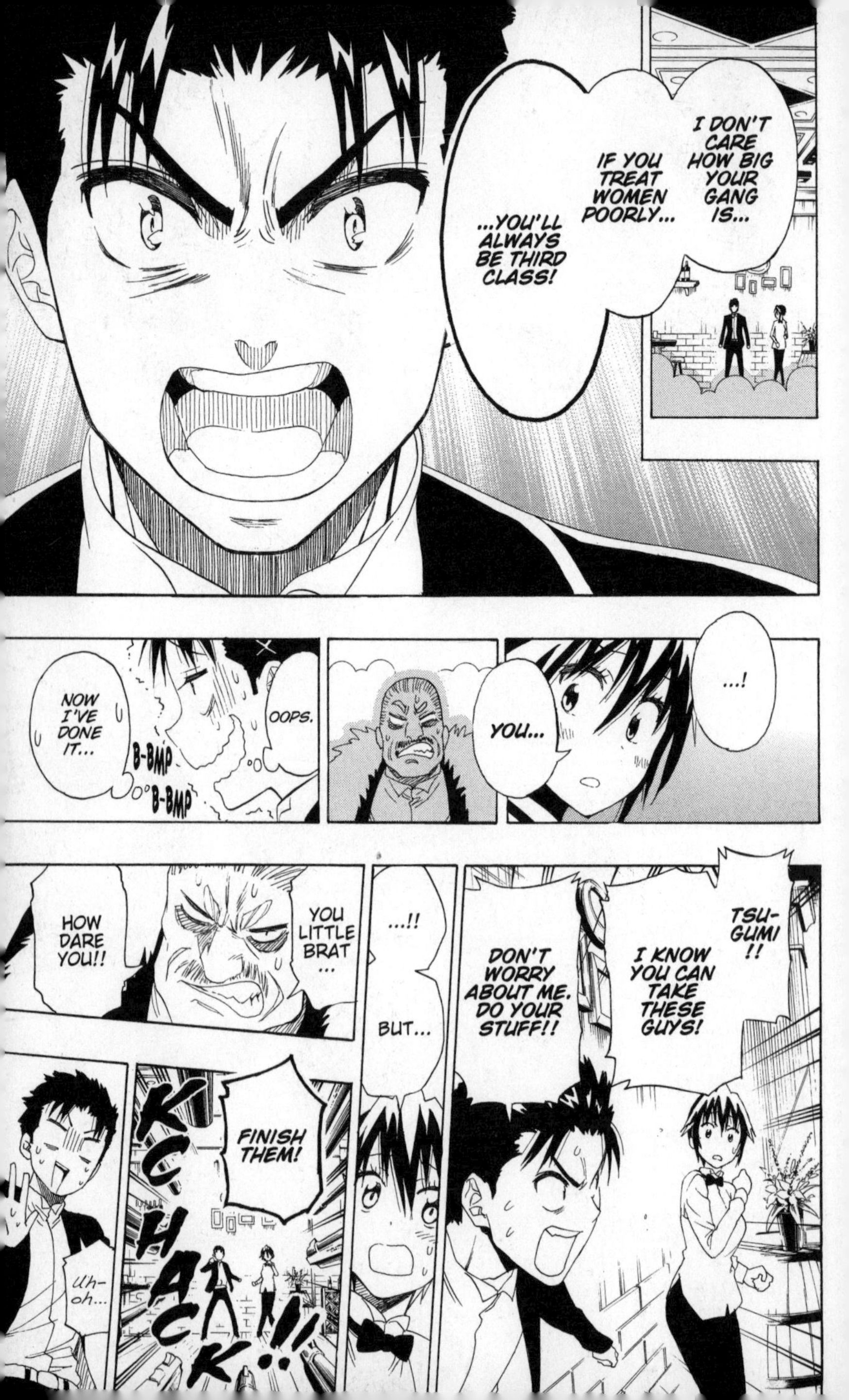

I DON'T CARE HOW BIG YOUR GANG IS...
IF YOU TREAT WOMEN POORLY...
...YOU'LL ALWAYS BE THIRD CLASS!
...!
YOU...
OOPS.
NOW I'VE DONE IT...
B-BMP B-BMP
TSU-GUMI!!
I KNOW YOU CAN TAKE THESE GUYS!
DON'T WORRY ABOUT ME. DO YOUR STUFF!!
...!!
BUT...
YOU LITTLE BRAT...
HOW DARE YOU!!
FINISH THEM!
KCHACK!!
Uh-oh...

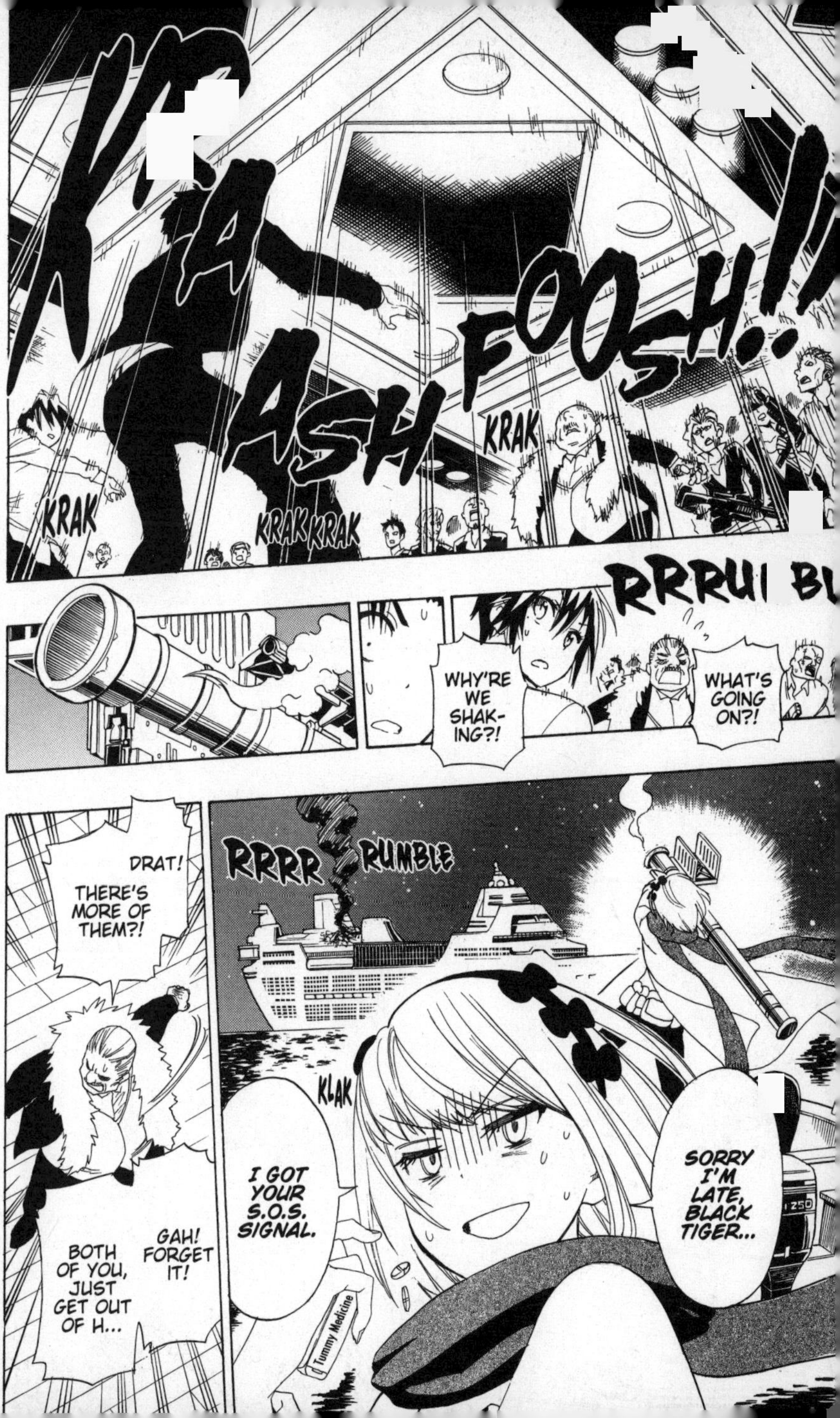
KA
ASH
FOOSH!!
KRAK
KRAK
KRAK KRAK
RRRUI BL
WHAT'S GOING ON?!
WHY'RE WE SHAK-ING?!
RRRR RUMBLE
KLAK
SORRY I'M LATE, BLACK TIGER...
I GOT YOUR S.O.S. SIGNAL.
Tummy Medicine
DRAT! THERE'S MORE OF THEM?!
GAH! FORGET IT!
BOTH OF YOU, JUST GET OUT OF H...

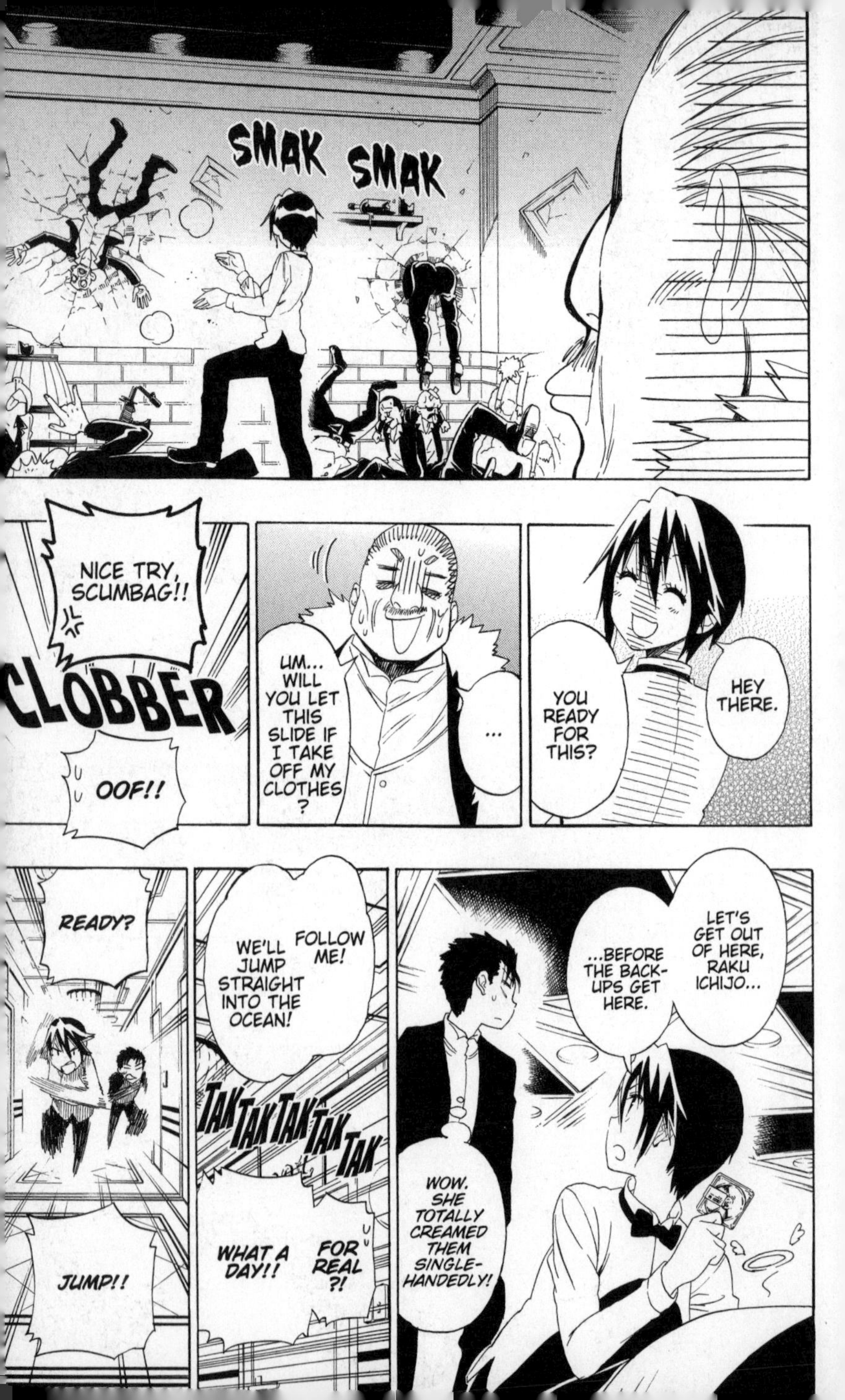
SMAK SMAK
HEY THERE.
YOU READY FOR THIS?
...
UM... WILL YOU LET THIS SLIDE IF I TAKE OFF MY CLOTHES?
NICE TRY, SCUMBAG!!
CLOBBER
OOF!!
LET'S GET OUT OF HERE, RAKU ICHIJO...
...BEFORE THE BACK-UPS GET HERE.
WOW. SHE TOTALLY CREAMED THEM SINGLE-HANDEDLY!
FOLLOW ME!
WE'LL JUMP STRAIGHT INTO THE OCEAN!
TAK TAK TAK TAK TAK
FOR REAL?!
WHAT A DAY!!
READY?
JUMP!!

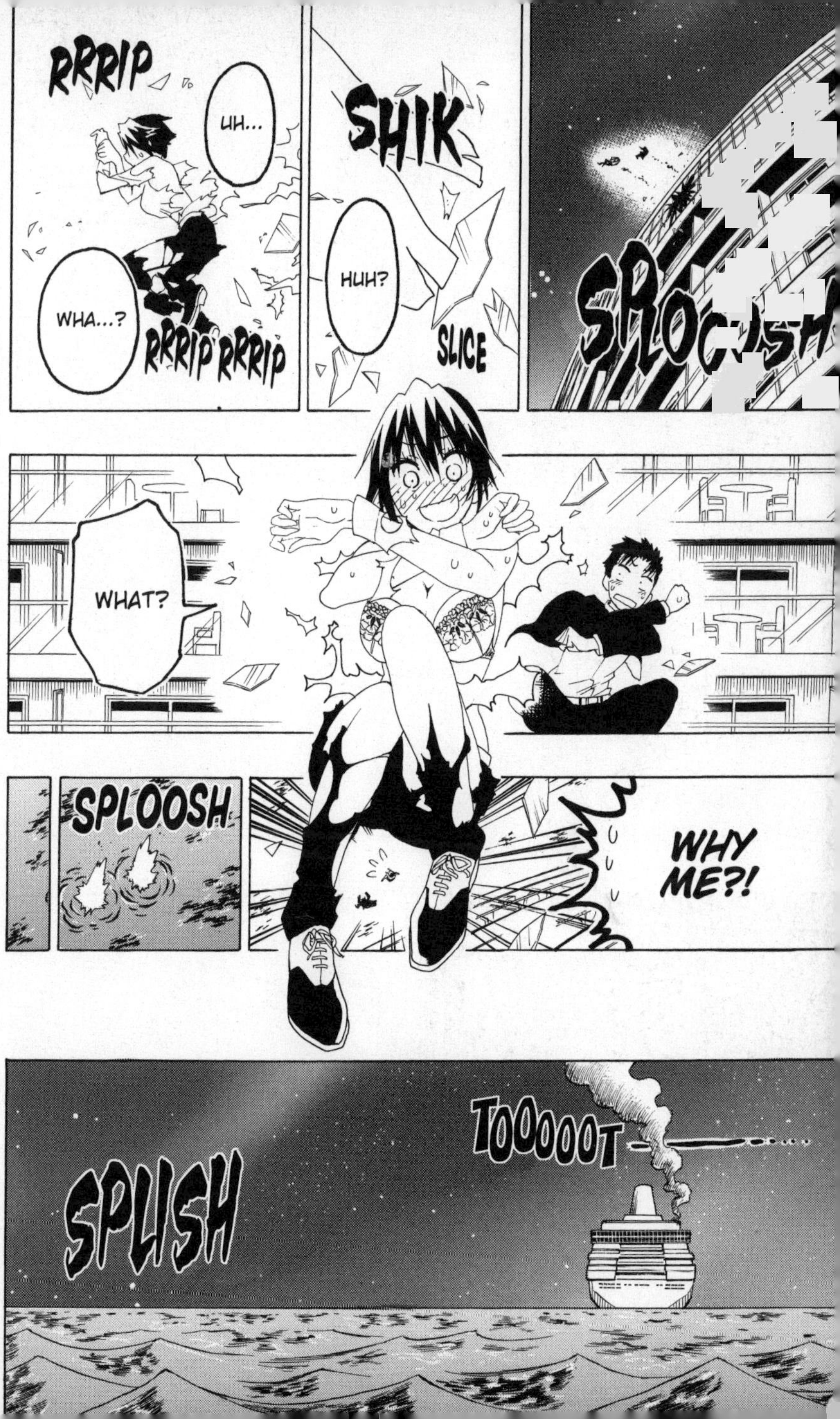
SHIK
HUH?
SLICE
UH...
RRRIP
WHA...?
RRRIP RRRIP
WHAT?
WHY ME?!
SPLOOSH
TOOOOOT
SPLUSH

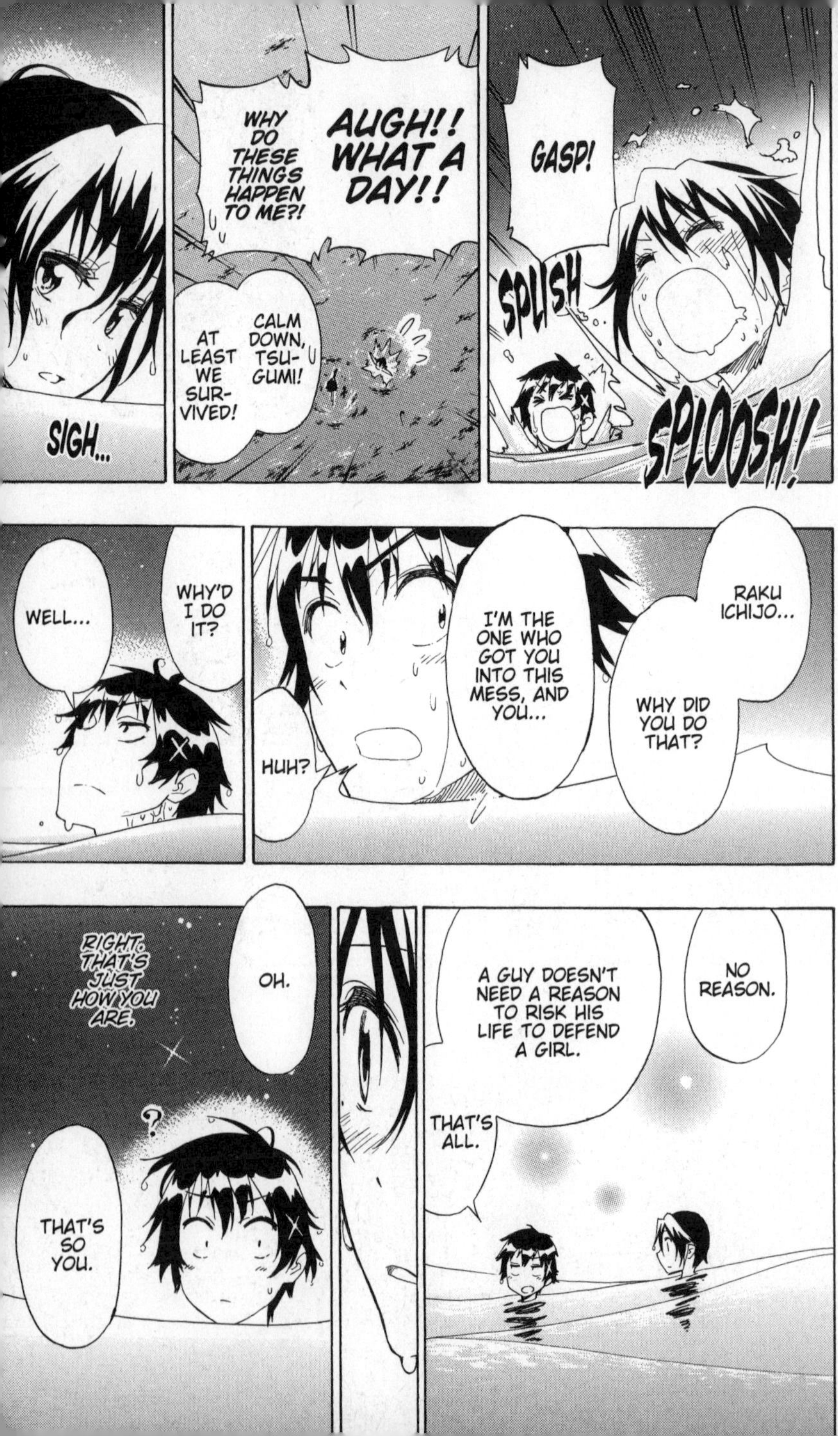
GASP!
SPLISH
SPLOOSH!
AUGH!! WHAT A DAY!!
WHY DO THESE THINGS HAPPEN TO ME?!
CALM DOWN, TSUGUMI!
AT LEAST WE SURVIVED!
SIGH...
RAKU ICHIJO...
WHY DID YOU DO THAT?
I'M THE ONE WHO GOT YOU INTO THIS MESS, AND YOU...
HUH?
WHY'D I DO IT?
WELL...
NO REASON.
A GUY DOESN'T NEED A REASON TO RISK HIS LIFE TO DEFEND A GIRL.
THAT'S ALL.
OH.
RIGHT. THAT'S JUST HOW YOU ARE.
THAT'S SO YOU.

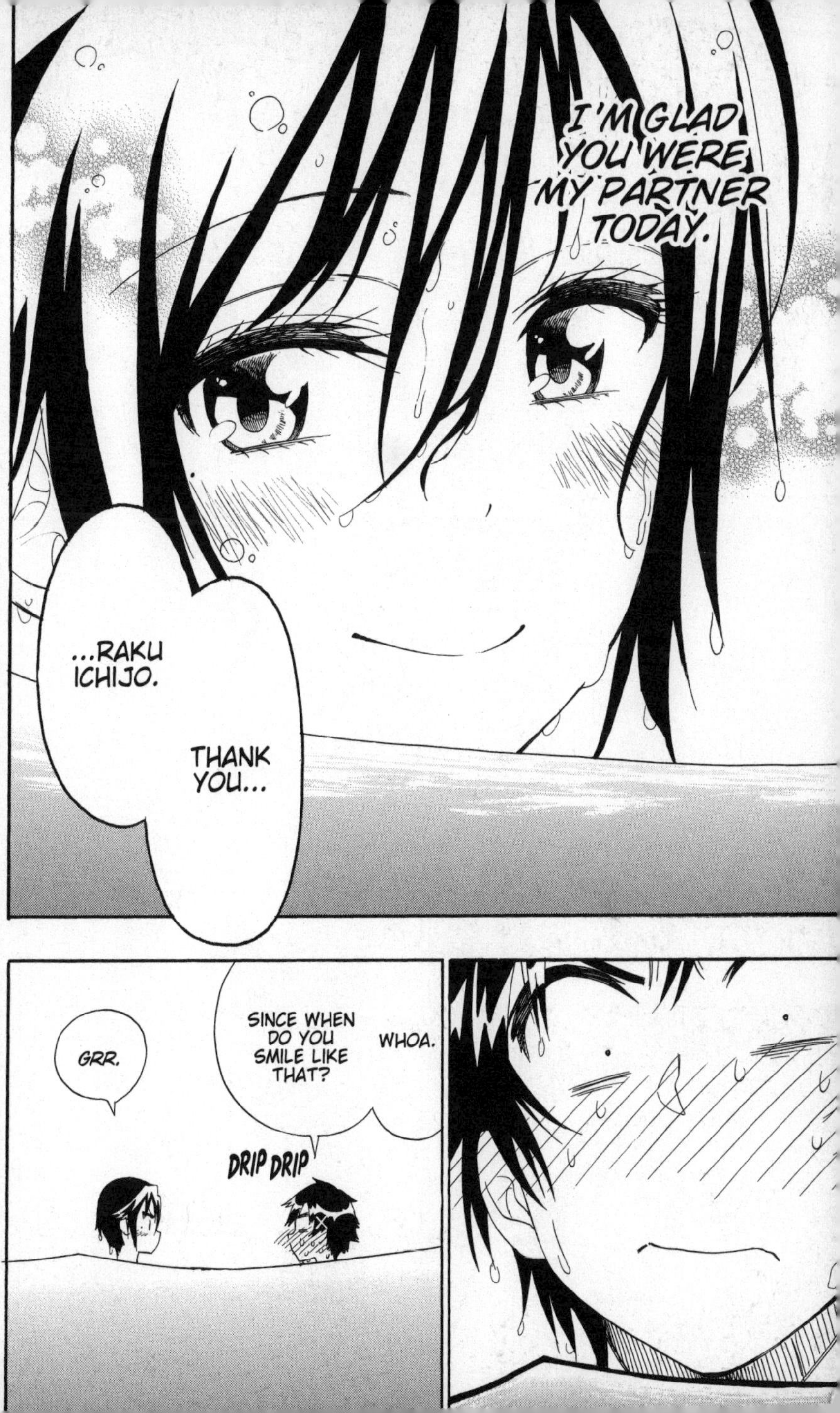
I'M GLAD YOU WERE MY PARTNER TODAY.
...RAKU ICHIJO.
THANK YOU...
WHOA.
SINCE WHEN DO YOU SMILE LIKE THAT?
GRR.
DRIP DRIP

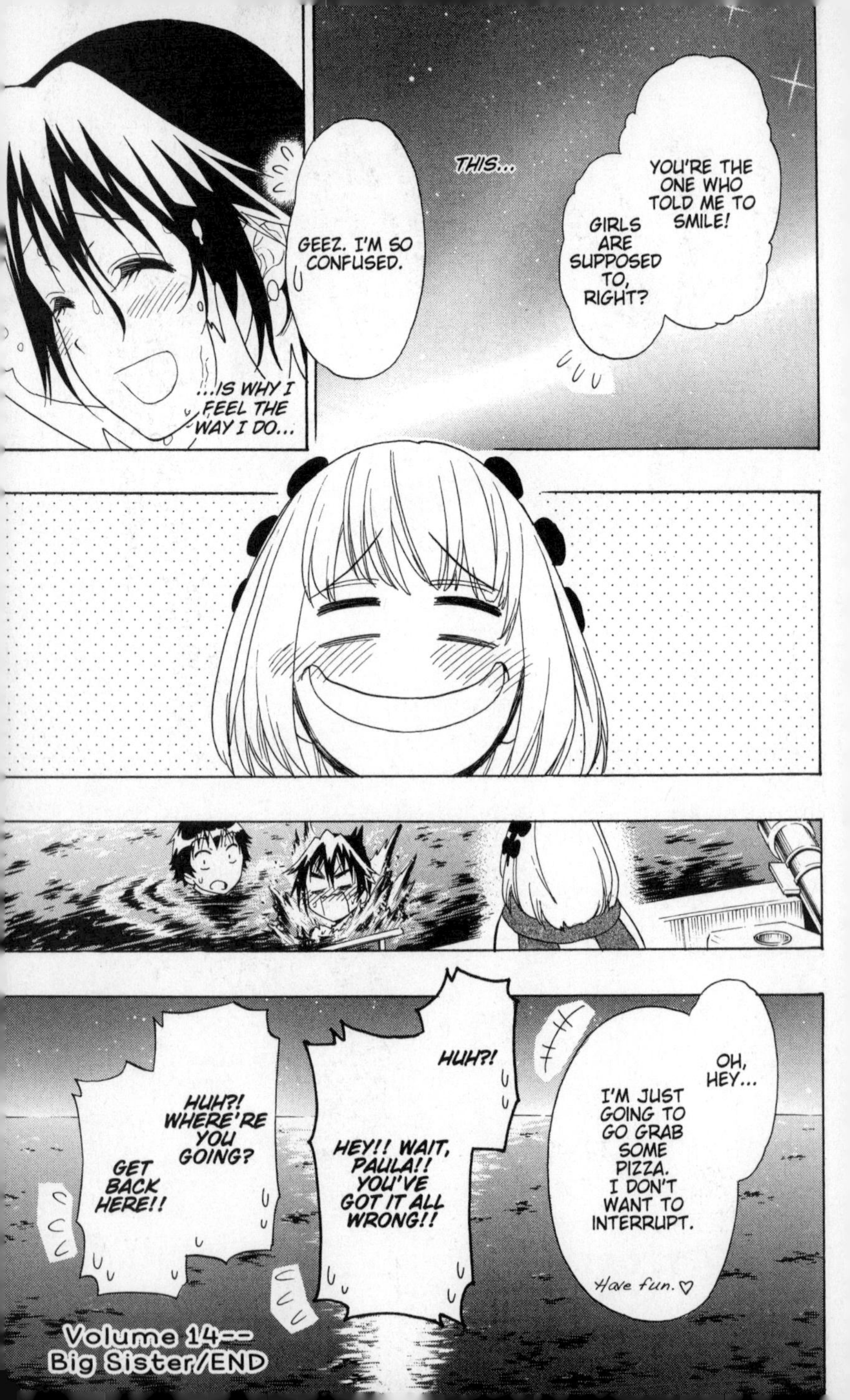

YOU'RE THE ONE WHO TOLD ME TO SMILE!
GIRLS ARE SUPPOSED TO, RIGHT?
THIS...
GEEZ. I'M SO CONFUSED.
...IS WHY I FEEL THE WAY I DO...
OH, HEY...
I'M JUST GOING TO GO GRAB SOME PIZZA. I DON'T WANT TO INTERRUPT.
Have fun. ♡
HUH?!
HEY!! WAIT, PAULA!! YOU'VE GOT IT ALL WRONG!!
HUH?! WHERE'RE YOU GOING?
GET BACK HERE!!
Volume 14-- Big Sister/END

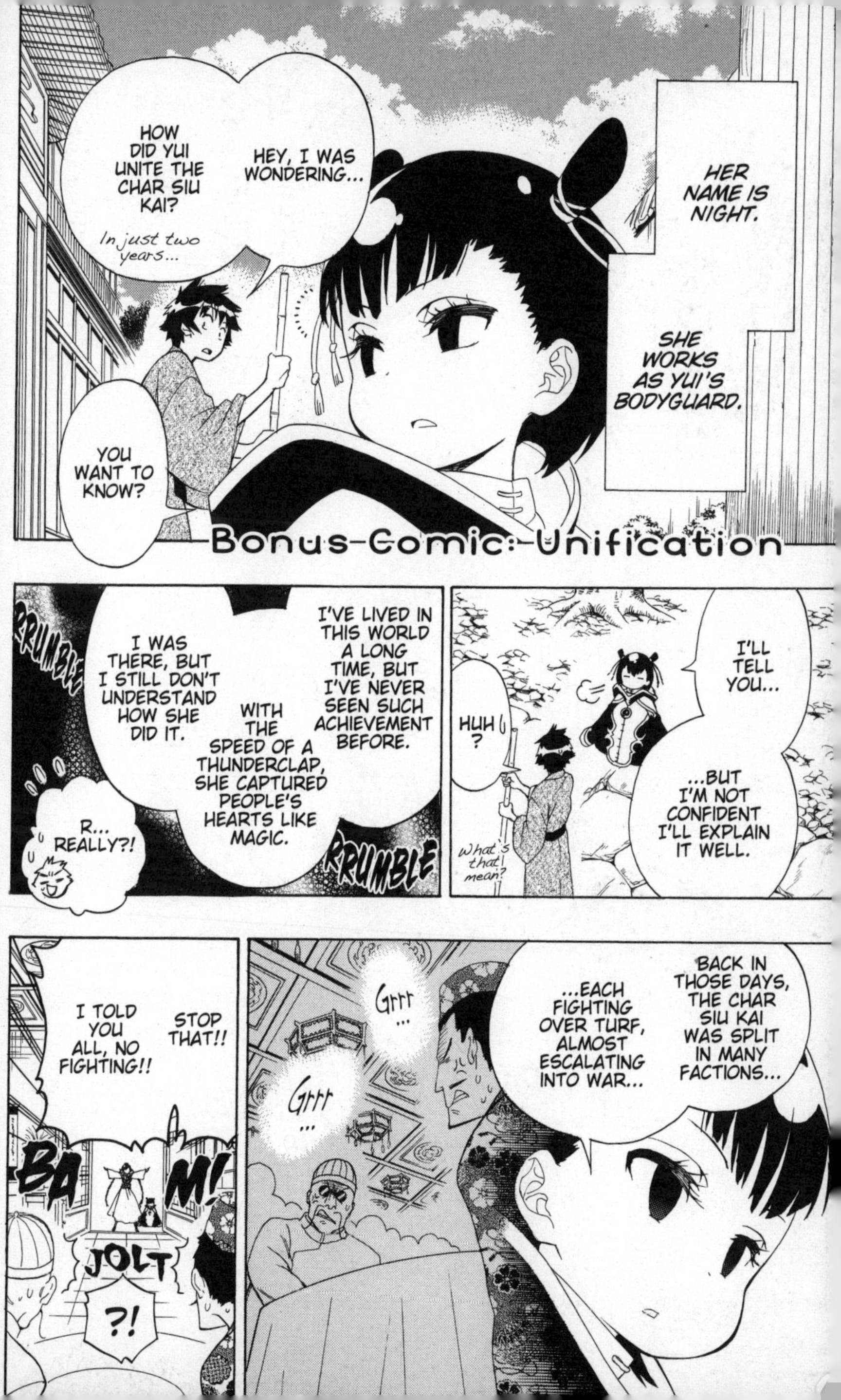
HER NAME IS NIGHT.
SHE WORKS AS YUI'S BODYGUARD.
HEY, I WAS WONDERING...
HOW DID YUI UNITE THE CHAR SIU KAI?
In just two years...
YOU WANT TO KNOW?
Bonus Comic: Unification
I'LL TELL YOU...
HUH?
...BUT I'M NOT CONFIDENT I'LL EXPLAIN IT WELL.
What's that mean?
I'VE LIVED IN THIS WORLD A LONG TIME, BUT I'VE NEVER SEEN SUCH ACHIEVEMENT BEFORE.
I WAS THERE, BUT I STILL DON'T UNDERSTAND HOW SHE DID IT.
WITH THE SPEED OF A THUNDERCLAP, SHE CAPTURED PEOPLE'S HEARTS LIKE MAGIC.
RRUMBLE
RRUMBLE
R... REALLY?!
BACK IN THOSE DAYS, THE CHAR SIU KAI WAS SPLIT IN MANY FACTIONS...
...EACH FIGHTING OVER TURF, ALMOST ESCALATING INTO WAR...
Grrr...
Grrr...
STOP THAT!!
I TOLD YOU ALL, NO FIGHTING!!
BAM!
JOLT
?!

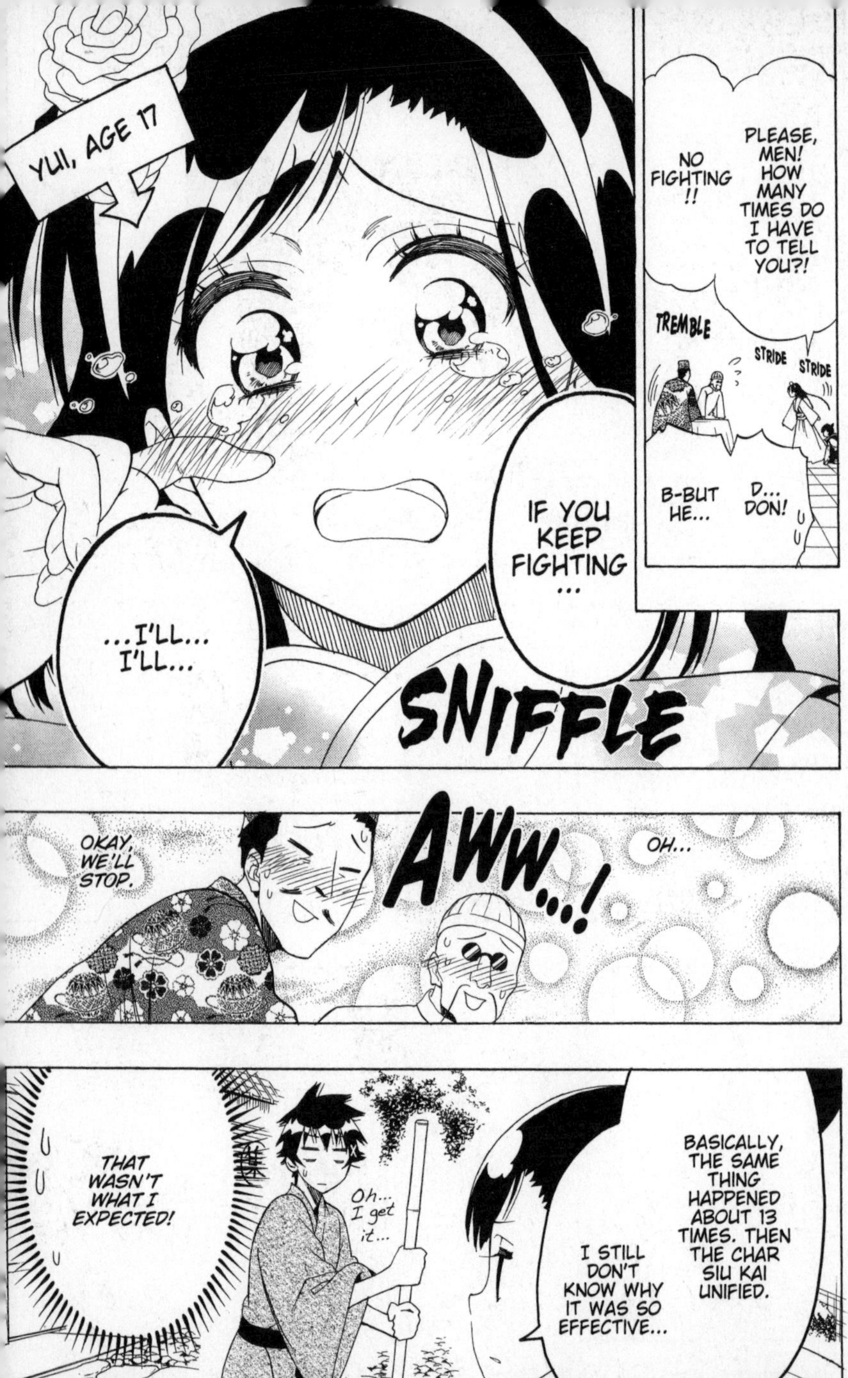
PLEASE, MEN! HOW MANY TIMES DO I HAVE TO TELL YOU?!
NO FIGHTING!!
TREMBLE
STRIDE
STRIDE
D... DON!
B-BUT HE...
YUI, AGE 17
IF YOU KEEP FIGHTING...
...I'LL... I'LL...
SNIFFLE
OH...
AWW...!
OKAY, WE'LL STOP.
BASICALLY, THE SAME THING HAPPENED ABOUT 13 TIMES. THEN THE CHAR SIU KAI UNIFIED.
I STILL DON'T KNOW WHY IT WAS SO EFFECTIVE...
Oh... I get it...
THAT WASN'T WHAT I EXPECTED!

Bonus Comic: Unification (END)

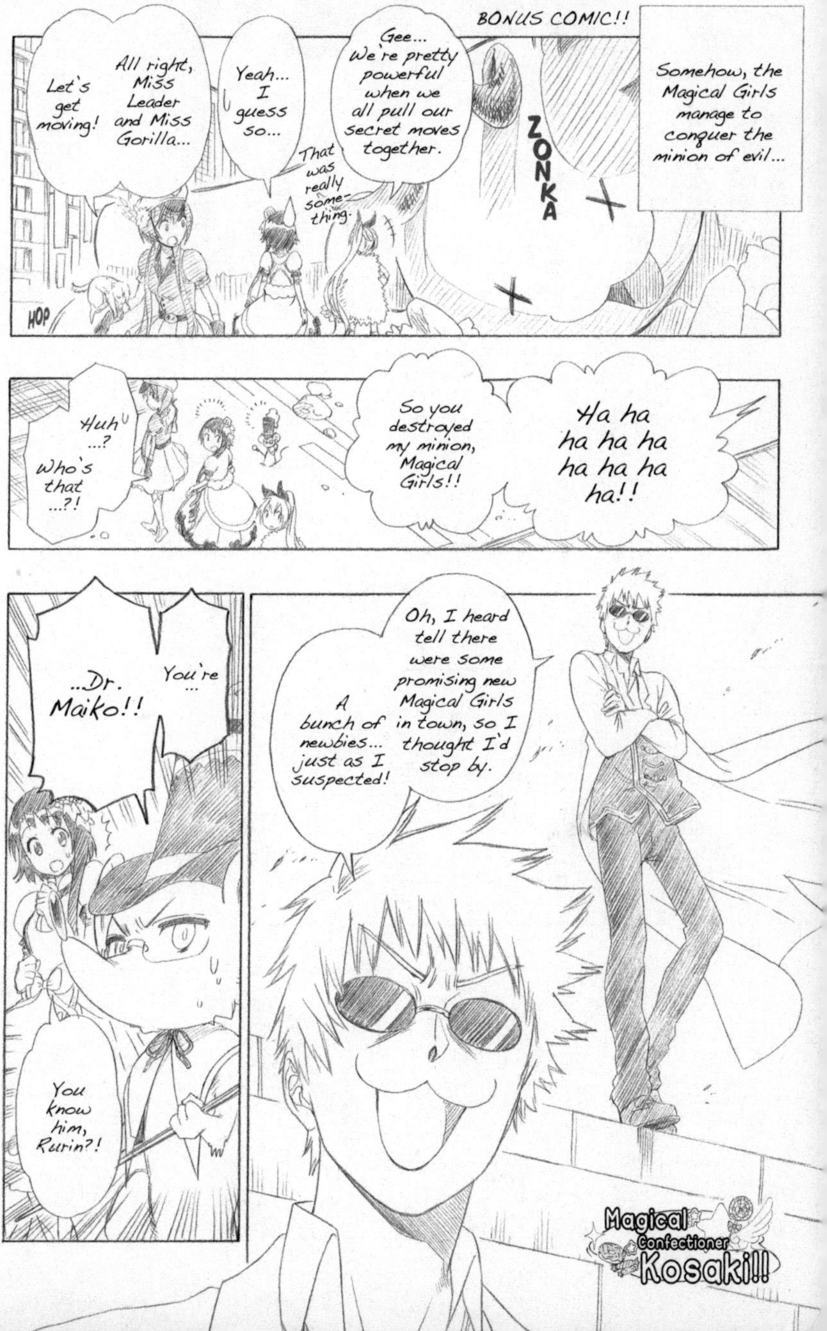
BONUS COMIC!!
Somehow, the Magical Girls manage to conquer the minion of evil...
ZONKA
Gee... We're pretty powerful when we all pull our secret moves together.
That was really some-thing.
Yeah... I guess so...
All right, Miss Leader and Miss Gorilla...
Let's get moving!
HOP
Ha ha ha ha ha ha ha ha ha!!
So you destroyed my minion, Magical Girls!!
Huh ...?
Who's that ...?!
Oh, I heard tell there were some promising new Magical Girls in town, so I thought I'd stop by.
A bunch of newbies... just as I suspected!
You're ...
..Dr. Maiko!!
You know him, Rurin?!
Magical Confectioner Kosaki!!

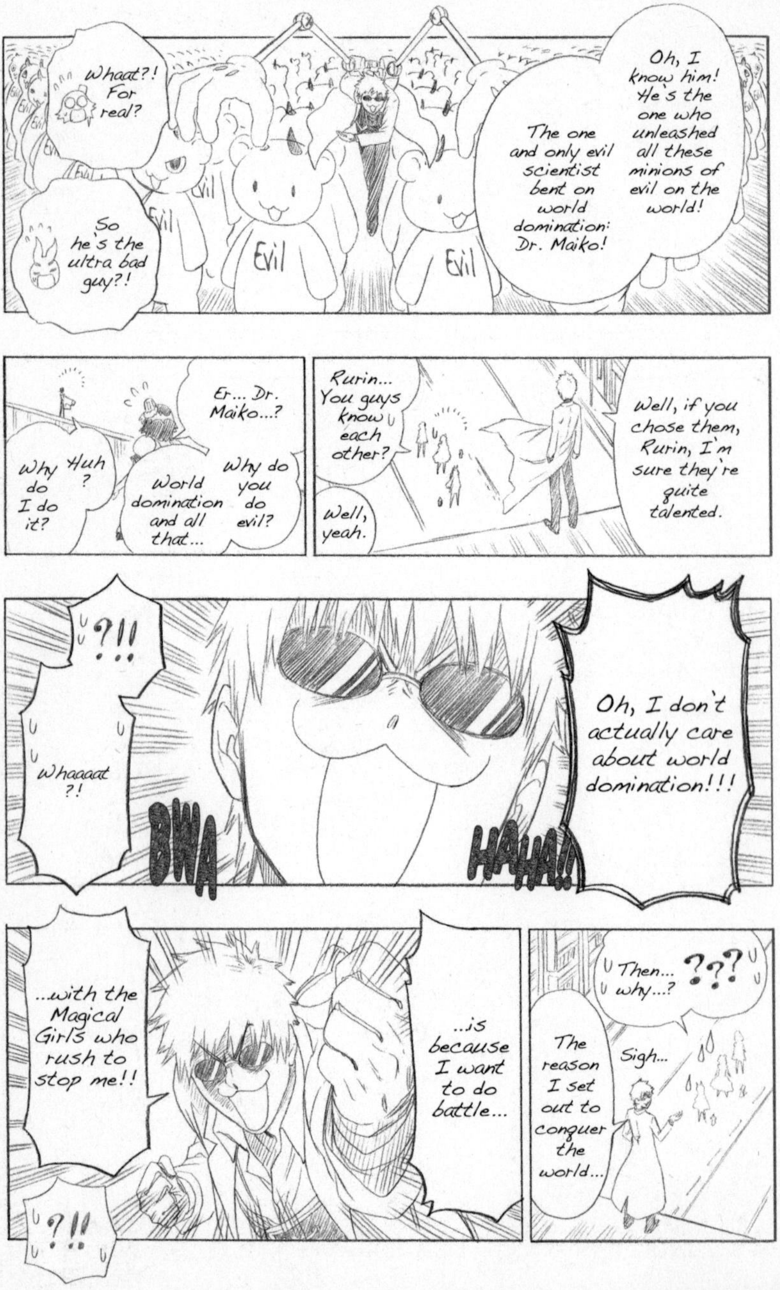
Oh, I know him! He's the one who unleashed all these minions of evil on the world!
The one and only evil scientist bent on world domination: Dr. Maiko!
Whaat?! For real?
So he's the ultra bad guy?!
Well, if you chose them, Rurin, I'm sure they're quite talented.
Rurin... You guys know each other?
Well, yeah.
Er... Dr. Maiko...?
Why do you do evil?
World domination and all that...
Huh?
Why do I do it?
Oh, I don't actually care about world domination!!!
BWA HAHA!!
?!!
Whaaaat?!
Then... why...?
???
Sigh...
The reason I set out to conquer the world...
...is because I want to do battle...
...with the Magical Girls who rush to stop me!!
?!!

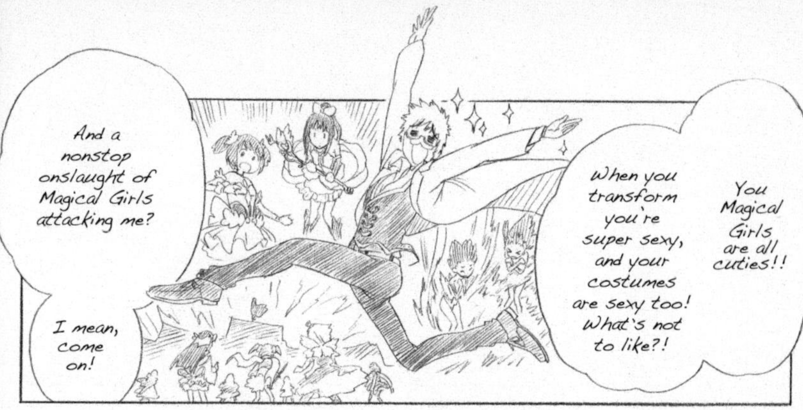
You Magical Girls are all cuties!!
When you transform you're super sexy, and your costumes are sexy too! What's not to like?!
And a nonstop onslaught of Magical Girls attacking me?
I mean, come on!

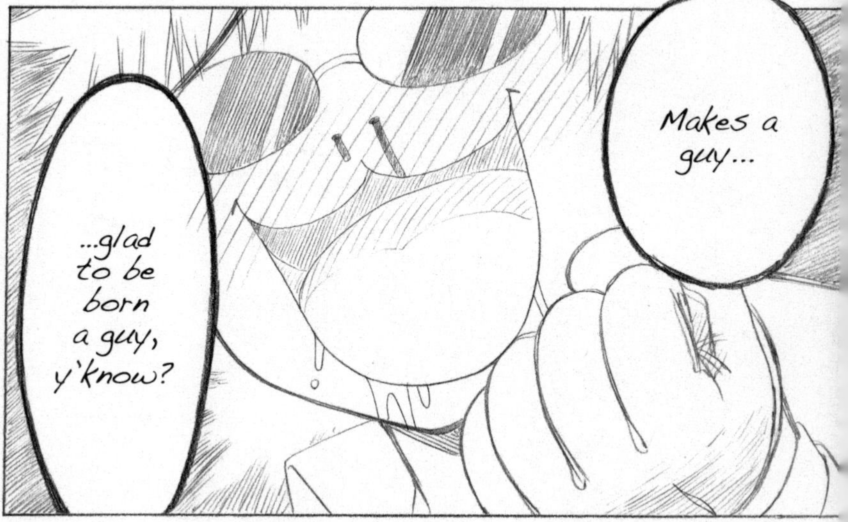
Makes a guy...
...glad to be born a guy, y'know?

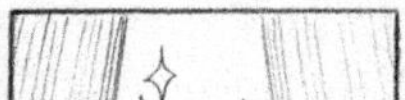

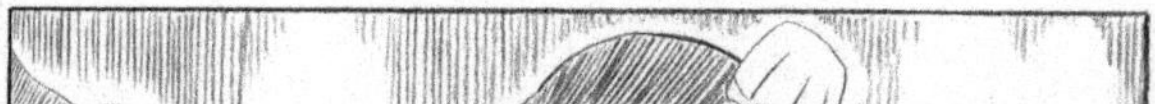
We've got to destroy him.
No matter what.
Right?

To be continued!! ...Probably, given the circumstances.

• There are quite a few of them, actually.

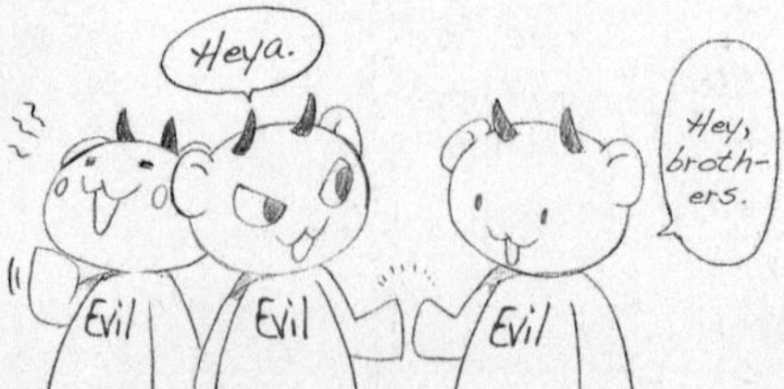
Hey, brothers.
Heya.
Evil
Evil
Evil

You're Reading the
WRONG WAY!

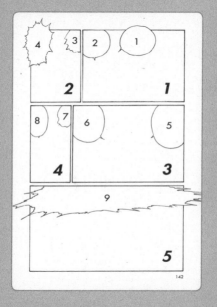

NISEKOI reads from right to left, starting in the upper-right corner. Japanese is read from right to left, meaning that action, sound effects, and word-balloon order are completely reversed from English order.